OF THE FIRST EDITION OF

Fabulous Chicago

TWO HUNDRED FIFTY COPIES,

SPECIALLY BOUND,

HAVE BEEN NUMBERED AND

SIGNED BY THE AUTHOR.

NUMBER 82

Books by Emmett Dedmon

FABULOUS CHICAGO (revised) (1981)
HISTORY OF THE TAVERN CLUB (1978)
CHINA JOURNAL (1973)
HISTORY OF THE CHICAGO CLUB (1960)
GREAT ENTERPRISES (1957)
FABULOUS CHICAGO (1953)
DUTY TO LIVE (1946)

Fabulous Chicago

Emmett Dedmon

"I wish I could go to America if only to see that Chicago."

>Bismarck to General Philip H. Sheridan (1870)

"Good Americans are said to go to Paris when they die; but it appears to depend on whether they have been to Chicago first."

>*Among the Americans,* by George Jacob Holyoake (1881)

"Sir, Chicago is the boss city of the universe."

>An anonymous brakeman on a train coming into the city (1881)

Fabulous Chicago

ENLARGED EDITION

ATHENEUM

NEW YORK

1981

Library of Congress Cataloging in Publication Data

Dedmon, Emmett.
   Fabulous Chicago.

     Includes index.
      1. Chicago (Ill.)—Description—1951–
2. Chicago (Ill.)—Social life and customs.   I. Title.
F548.52.D4 1981   977.3'11   81–66024
ISBN 0–689–11197–5   AACR2

The verses that appear on page 276 are from Chicago Poems by Carl Sandburg. Copyright, 1916, by Henry Holt and Company, Inc. Copyright, 1944, by Carl Sandburg. Used by permission of the publishers.

Verse on dedication of Picasso Statue on page 362 by Gwendolyn Brooks is from her book In The Mecca (Harper & Row). Used by permission of the author.

Copyright, 1953, by Emmett Dedmon
Copyright renewed, 1981, by Emmett Dedmon
Enlarged Edition © 1981 by Emmett Dedmon
All rights reserved
Published simultaneously in Canada by McClelland and Stewart Ltd.
Manufactured by Fairfield Graphics, Fairfield, Pennsylvania
First Edition

FOR *Claire*

MY FABULOUS CHICAGOAN

Acknowledgments

As with the previous edition of this history, it could not have been written without the resources of the Chicago Historical Society. Also without the cheerful cooperation of the society's staff and the research assistance and expertise of my wife Claire, its writing would have required many additional hours.

Those who contributed to the writing of the earlier edition continue to deserve the accolades given them on that occasion. In addition, I would like to acknowledge the assistance given me in gaining an insight into the inner workings of the city under Mayor Daley from his close associate and the city's present mayor, Jane Byrne.

For the pictures that have been added to the present edition, I wish to express my appreciation to Max McCrohon, vice-president, News, of the *Chicago Tribune*, Virginia Butts and Kenneth Towers of the *Chicago Sun-Times*, to John Edwards, to Kee Chang and to the Chicago Historical Society.

Finally, for the preparation of the manuscript and administrative skills in bringing the total project together, I am particularly indebted to my secretary Patricia Wisniewski, and to Shirlene Morris and Iona Smith, who assisted with the typing. My good friend Robert Dilenschneider, executive vice-president of Hill and Knowlton, was most understanding in assuring me the time to accomplish this task.

After a quarter of a century in which the book has established itself as a major source of information about Chicago's past, I remain indebted to the late Paul Angle, director of the Society; to Elizabeth Baughman, who was both helpful and creative in guiding me among the society's source materials; to Grant Dean for checking the manuscript; to H. Maxson Holloway and Walter Krutz for help in obtaining illustrations and to Violett Richardson for help with manuscripts. At Newberry Library, Ben C. Bowman gave important help in securing prints of drawings from the library files.

An uncounted number of books were consulted but there is a special obligation to mention the following which include first-hand material not available elsewhere: *Stormy Years* by Carter Harrison II (Bobbs-Merrill); *Come into My Parlor*, the authorized biography of the Everleigh sisters, by Charles Washburn (Knickerbocker); *My Thirty Years War*, by Margaret Anderson (Covici-Friede); *Always Room at The Top*, by Ganna Walska (Richard R. Smith) and *Mary Garden's Story*, by Mary Garden and Louis Biancolli (Simon & Schuster).

Many Chicagoans participated in the making of this book by giving generously of their time and information. Mr. and Mrs. Cyrus Adams, Mr. and Mrs. Edward McCormick Blair and Jack McPhaul read the entire manuscript and made many helpful suggestions. For help on special sections of the book, I wish to thank Mrs. William McCormick Blair, John Blades, Felix Borowski, Earl Gross, Harry Hansen, Maurene Hudgin, Ogden Ketting, Herman Kogan, Danny Newman, Lucy Nunes, Mrs. Potter Palmer II, Mrs. Higinbotham Patterson, Denton Sparks, Jack Star, Vincent Starrett and Lloyd Wendt. The final responsibility for the choice of material and its treatment is of course my own.

EMMETT DEDMON
June 1981

Contents

PART ONE *The Garden City* 1835-1871

1. Frontier Town — 3
2. The Yankee Out West — 16
3. Long John and His Devils — 26
4. Elegance on a Grand Scale — 37
5. The Little Giant and the Rail Splitter — 49
6. The Civil War and the Chicago Conspiracy — 59
7. Everyone Comes Here: Anything Goes Here — 73
8. The Finer Things of Life — 83
9. The Red Snow — 95

PART TWO *Enter the Ladies* 1871-1890

10. Puritans on Prairie Avenue — 113
11. The Pride of Potter Palmer — 124
12. The Sporting Life — 135
13. The Melting Pot Explodes — 148
14. Chicago Builds Its Parthenon — 163

PART THREE *The Spirit of Democracy* 1890-1910

15. Why Do We Need a Genealogy? — 181
16. The Cultivated Class Is Comparatively Small — 196
17. An Ardent Temperament Rather Than a Weak Will — 210
18. The Glories of the White City — 220
19. From Pullman City to Hull House — 238
20. Life Along the Levee — 250

PART FOUR *The Inheritance* 1910-1930

21. One Ecstasy After Another — 273
22. Nobody's on the Legit — 285
23. Grand Opera—A Libretto for Romance — 301
24. Insull Builds His Empire — 317

PART FIVE *The New Chicago*

25. More than a Century of Progress — 335
26. The Ghost and the Colonel — 342
27. "Chicago Ain't Ready for Reform Yet" — 347
28. "The Most Exciting City in the United States" — 355
29. "I Never Believed this Would Happen Here" — 365
30. "Nobody Is Going to Take Over this City" — 373
31. Life Styles in Nude and Black — 384
32. "I Hate Mediocrity" — 396
33. "The City that Works" — 406
34. "The Ultimate American City" — 415

Index — 425

List of Illustrations

Mark Beaubien's Tavern about 1833   3
(From a diorama at the Chicago Historical Society)

Chicago in 1838, by Francis Castleneau. Earliest known contemporary view of Chicago   5
(Courtesy of the Chicago Historical Society)

Old Barracks of Fort Dearborn and Lake House   7
(From *History of Chicago*, by A. T. Andreas)

Lake Street from Dearborn Street, 1839, by N. Roswell Gilford. The building on the corner is the Tremont House   9
(Courtesy of the Chicago Historical Society)

Chicago in 1845   10
(Courtesy of the Chicago Historical Society)

Entire Block on Lake Street Being Raised to a Height of Four Feet, 1857, by Edward Mendel   13
(Courtesy of the Chicago Historical Society)

Frink & Walker Stage Office, by W. E. S. Trowbridge   14
(Courtesy of the Chicago Historical Society)

Historic Tree on the Site of the Fort Dearborn Massacre   16
(From *History of Chicago*, by A. T. Andreas)

Chamber of Commerce, 1865   19
(Courtesy of the Chicago Historical Society)

Chicago in 1849, as seen from the top of St. Mary's College, looking south on State Street from Chicago Avenue   21
(Courtesy of the Chicago Historical Society)

Rush Street Bridge in 1861, by Edwin Whitefield. McCormick's Works are at the center left   23
(Courtesy of the Chicago Historical Society)

Michigan Terrace (Terrace Row), looking toward the Central Depot, 1863, by Edwin Whitefield   24
(Courtesy of the Chicago Historical Society)

John Wentworth 26
(Courtesy of the Chicago Historical Society)

The "Long John" Fire Engine 28
(From History of Chicago, by A. T. Andreas)

Union Stockyards, 1866 30
(Jevne & Almini print. Courtesy of the Chicago Historical Society)

Hough House, 1866 31
(Jevne & Almini print. Courtesy of the Chicago Historical Society)

Results of Long John Wentworth's Sign Raid, 1857 33
(From History of Chicago, by A. T. Andreas)

Corner of Lake and State Streets, 1866 35
(Jevne & Almini print. Courtesy of the Chicago Historical Society)

Invitation to a Public Ball, 1851 37
(Courtesy of the Chicago Historical Society)

Northwest Corner of LaSalle and Randolph Streets, showing Courthouse Square, 1864 39
(Courtesy of the Chicago Historical Society)

LaSalle Street from Courthouse Square, 1866 41
(Jevne & Almini print. Courtesy of the Chicago Historical Society)

Corner of Clark and Water Streets, 1866 43
(Jevne & Almini print. Courtesy of the Chicago Historical Society)

A New Year's Day Calling Card 44
(Courtesy of the Chicago Historical Society)

John B. Drake, Manager of the Tremont House, about 1864 46
(Courtesy of the Chicago Historical Society)

The New Tremont House, at the corner of Lake and Dearborn Streets, by Edwin Whitefield 47
(Courtesy of the Chicago Historical Society)

Old Market Hall on State Street, 1848 49
(Courtesy of the Chicago Public Library)

Sherman House, looking west on Randolph Street with Courthouse on the left, by Edwin Whitefield 51
(Courtesy of the Chicago Historical Society)

Chicago in 1853 52
(From History of Chicago, by A. T. Andreas)

Church of the Holy Family, 1866 54
(Jevne & Almini print. Courtesy of the Chicago Historical Society)

The Republican Wigwam where Lincoln was Nominated, 1860 56
(Courtesy of the Chicago Historical Society)

U. S. Zouave Cadets (Courtesy of the Chicago Historical Society)	59
Monument to Stephen A. Douglas, 1866 (Jevne & Almini print. Courtesy of the Chicago Historical Society)	60
Grounds of the Chicago Sharpshooters Association (Courtesy of the Chicago Historical Society)	63
Camp Douglas, 1864, by Albert E. Myers (Courtesy of the Chicago Historical Society)	66
Democratic National Amphitheater on Michigan Avenue, 1864. Lithograph by Charles Shober (Courtesy of the Chicago Historical Society)	67
The Great Northwestern Sanitary Fair, 1865 (Courtesy of the Chicago Historical Society)	69
Lincoln Funeral Procession at Chicago, May 1, 1865 (Courtesy of the Chicago Historical Society)	71
Mollie Cosgriff ("Irish Mollie") (Courtesy of the Chicago Historical Society)	73
A Gambling Den on Randolph Street (From Chicago Sporting Life. Courtesy of the Chicago Historical Society)	75
Dexter, the Famous Trotting Horse that Figured in the George Trussell Shooting, 1857 (Currier & Ives print. Courtesy of the Chicago Historical Society)	77
Armory and Gasworks, 1866, showing Police Herding Prostitutes (Jevne & Almini print. Courtesy of the Chicago Historical Society)	78
Michigan Avenue from Park Row, 1866 (Jevne & Almini print. Courtesy of the Chicago Historical Society)	80
Briggs House, 1866 (Jevne & Almini print. Courtesy of the Chicago Historical Society)	82
The Sauganash Hotel, where the First Dramatic Performance in Chicago was Held (From History of Chicago, by A. T. Andreas)	84
Colonel Wood's Museum, 1866 (Jevne & Almini print. Courtesy of the Chicago Historical Society)	86
McVicker's Theater, 1866 (Jevne & Almini print. Courtesy of the Chicago Historical Society)	87
Crosby's Opera House, 1866 (Jevne & Almini print. Courtesy of the Chicago Historical Society)	89
Republican Convention at Crosby's Opera House, nominating General Grant for President, 1868 (Courtesy of the Chicago Historical Society)	93

"Death Shall be Their Fate," a Pinkerton Broadside   95
(Courtesy of the Chicago Historical Society)

The Chicago Water Crib, 1866   97
(Jevne & Almini print. Courtesy of the Chicago Historical Society)

The Chicago Waterworks, 1867   99
(Jevne & Almini print. Courtesy of the Chicago Historical Society)

The Great Fire, by Currier & Ives. (Note that flames are going in the wrong direction.)   101
(Courtesy of the Chicago Historical Society)

Burning of the Crosby Opera House   102
(From Harper's Illustrated Weekly. Courtesy of the Newberry Library)

Refugees in the Street   104
(From Harper's Illustrated Weekly. Courtesy of the Newberry Library)

Business District after the Fire, looking north from Harrison Street   107
(Courtesy of the Chicago Historical Society)

89 Washington Street, by W. P. Burton. The first building erected after the fire   109
(Courtesy of the Chicago Historical Society)

George P. A. Healy, a self-portrait, 1867   113
(Courtesy of the Chicago Historical Society)

Rebuilding Chicago, view at Lake and LaSalle Streets, by Theo. R. Davis   115
(From Harper's Illustrated Weekly. Courtesy of the Newberry Library)

Mrs. Ira Holmes, 1866, by George P. A. Healy. The mother of Burton Holmes   116
(Courtesy of the Chicago Historical Society)

Going to the Races: Carriages on Derby Day, 1893   118–119
(From the Chicago Times. Courtesy of the Newberry Library)

Kinsley's Restaurant, from Kinsley's Catalogue   120
(Courtesy of the Chicago Historical Society)

Racecourse at Washington Park   122
(Courtesy of the Chicago Historical Society)

Mrs. Potter Palmer as a Young Lady, by George P. A. Healy   124
(Courtesy of the Chicago Historical Society)

General Grant in Lincoln Park, with Carter H. Harrison and Thomas Hoyne, 1879   127
(Courtesy of the Chicago Historical Society)

Roof Garden at the Palmer House, 1873   129
(Courtesy of the Chicago Historical Society)

Tally-ho Party Going to the Derby, 1870. Third from left is Carter 132
Harrison. Next and reading to the right are General Philip Sheridan, Potter Palmer, and General John A. Logan
(Courtesy of the Chicago Historical Society)

Mrs. Potter Palmer, 1893, by Anders L. Zorn 134
(Courtesy of the Art Institute of Chicago)

Gardner S. Chapin. A caricature by T. Wust from the Chapin and 135
Gore Restaurant
(Courtesy of the Chicago Historical Society)

A Summer Concert Garden 138
(From *Chicago by Day and Night*, by H. R. Vynne. Courtesy of the Chicago Historical Society)

Charles Comiskey. A caricature by William H. Schmedtgen from 140
the Chapin and Gore Restaurant
(Courtesy of the Chicago Historical Society)

Sporting and Club House Directory 143
(Courtesy of Graham Aldis)

News Items from the Street Gazette, 1877 146
(Courtesy of the Chicago Historical Society)

Board of Trade Building, 1886. Scene of attempted demonstration 148
by Anarchists
(Courtesy of the Chicago Historical Society)

Chicago in 1883, by S. D. Childs 150
(Courtesy of the Chicago Historical Society)

Driving the Rioters from Turner Hall, 1877 153
(From *Harper's Illustrated Weekly*. Courtesy of the Newberry Library)

The Fight at the Halsted Street Viaduct, 1877 156
(From *Harper's Illustrated Weekly*. Courtesy of the Newberry Library)

Trading on the Board, 1891 158
(From *Harper's Illustrated Weekly*. Courtesy of the Newberry Library)

Attack on Police Patrol Wagon near McCormick's Reaper Works, 160
1886
(From *Leslie's Illustrated Weekly*. Courtesy of the Newberry Library)

"Bridged"—a Familiar Chicago Experience, by Charles Graham 163
(From *Harper's Illustrated Weekly*. Courtesy of the Newberry Library)

Interstate Industrial Exposition, 1884 165
(From *Harper's Illustrated Weekly*. Courtesy of the Newberry Library)

Republican National Convention of 1884. A parade on Michigan 168
Avenue
(From *Harper's Illustrated Weekly*. Courtesy of the Newberry Library)

Oscar Wilde. A caricature by E. Jump from the Chapin and Gore　171
   Restaurant
   (Courtesy of the Chicago Historical Society)

Interior of the Auditorium, 1889　174
   (From *Harper's Illustrated Weekly*. Courtesy of the Newberry Library)

Mrs. Edward Tyler Blair, 1883, by George P. A. Healy　181
   (Courtesy of the Chicago Historical Society)

Montgomery Ward & Co. about 1900. Lithograph published un-　184
   der the title "A Busy Beehive"
   (Courtesy of the Chicago Historical Society)

Masonic Temple, 1895　185
   (Courtesy of the Chicago Historical Society)

Natatorium at the Corner of Jackson and Michigan Avenue　188
   (From *Chicago and Its Makers*, by Felix Mendelsohn)

Touring by Bicycle, 1896　190
   (From *Harper's Illustrated Weekly*. Courtesy of the Newberry Library)

"Beauty on a Bike," 1889　191
   (From the Chicago Morning News. Courtesy of the Chicago Daily News)

The Sleigh Ride. Samuel W. Allerton and his son, by Henry H.　193
   Cross, 1879
   (Courtesy of the Chicago Historical Society)

Lake Shore Drive, 1889　195

A Young Student at Bournique's Dancing Academy, 1881. Frankie　196
   May Reece, later Mrs. John Roger Williams, by Edward H. Hart
   (Courtesy of the Chicago Historical Society)

The Water Tank Library, established in an abandoned water tank　198
   in 1871
   (Courtesy of the Chicago Historical Society)

The Pavilion, Jackson Park, 1890, by Charles Graham　200
   (From *Harper's Illustrated Weekly*. Courtesy of the Newberry Library)

Saints' and Sinners' Corner at McClurg's Bookstore　205
   (Courtesy of Denton Sparks & A. C. McClurg & Co.)

The Cliff Dwellers. An Illustration for Henry Blake Fuller's Novel　207
   (Courtesy of the Newberry Library)

Gripman on Cable Car, 1893　210
   (From *Harper's Illustrated Weekly*. Courtesy of the Newberry Library)

Mrs. Leslie Carter in "Zaza"　215
   (Courtesy of the Museum of the City of New York)

Sarah Bernhardt 217
(Courtesy of the Museum of the City of New York)

Carter Harrison. A caricature by William H. Schmedtgen from the 220
Chapin and Gore Restaurant
(Courtesy of the Chicago Historical Society)

Agricultural Building, World's Columbian Exposition, 1893 223
(Courtesy of the Chicago Historical Society)

Grand Court at Night, World's Columbian Exposition, 1893 226
(From Harper's Illustrated Weekly. Courtesy of the Newberry Library)

Mrs. Potter Palmer's Reception for the Spanish Infanta, 1893 230
(From the Chicago Record. Courtesy of Newberry Library)

Midway, World's Columbian Exposition, 1893 233
(From Harper's Illustrated Weekly. Courtesy of the Newberry Library)

Mayor Harrison's Home on the Night of the Assassination, 1893 237
(From Harper's Illustrated Weekly. Courtesy of the Newberry Library)

A Patrol Box Arrest in Chicago, 1893, by T. De Thulstrup 238
(From Harper's Illustrated Weekly. Courtesy of the Newberry Library)

The First Meat Train Leaving the Stockyards under Escort of the 243
United States Cavalry, 1894
(From Harper's Illustrated Weekly. Courtesy of the Newberry Library)

U. S. Troops Encamped in Front of the Post Office, 1894 245
(From Harper's Illustrated Weekly. Courtesy of the Newberry Library)

Lincoln Park, 1887, by Charles Graham 248
(From Harper's Illustrated Weekly. Courtesy of the Newberry Library)

Scene from the First Ward Ball, by John McCutcheon 251
(From Collier's Weekly. Courtesy of the Chicago Historical Society and the artist's family)

The Levee at Night, 1898, by H. G. Maratta 253
(From Harper's Illustrated Weekly. Courtesy of the Newberry Library)

Music Room at the Everleigh Club. (From Minna Everleigh's Brochure) 255
(Courtesy of the Chicago Historical Society)

Bathhouse John, by John McCutcheon 261
(From Collier's Weekly. Courtesy of the Chicago Historical Society and the artist's family)

Hinky Dink, by John McCutcheon 264
(From Collier's Weekly. Courtesy of the Chicago Hisotrical Society and the artist's family)

The First Ward Ball, 1909, by John McCutcheon. "Led by Bathhouse John, Ten Thousand Joyless Reveling Pickpockets, Bartenders, Prostitutes and Police Captains Celebrate the Reign of Graft, while Grief-Stricken Hinky Dink Sways in the Corner." (From Collier's Weekly. Courtesy of the Chicago Historical Society and the artist's family) — 267

Carl Sandburg as a Young Man — 273
(Courtesy of Harcourt, Brace & Co.)

Margaret Anderson's Camp at Braeside — 277
(Courtesy of the Chicago Daily News)

Lunch at Schlogl's, 1925. Seated, left to right: Philip Davis, Alfred MacArthur, Ashton Stevens, William F. McGee, Charles Collins, Harry Hansen, Leroy T. Goble, John Gunther, Peter Hecht, Dr. Morris Fishbein, J. U. Nicholson, Lloyd Lewis. Standing: Richard Schneider, Dwight Haven, Keith Preston, Pascal Covici, Ben Hecht, Vincent Starrett, Henry Justin Smith — 282

Al Capone — 285
(Courtesy of the Associated Press)

Big Bill Thompson — 286
(Courtesy of the Chicago Sun-Times)

The Elevated at Night, by Aaron Bohrod — 293
(Courtesy of the artist)

The Funeral of Antonio Lombardo — 297
(Courtesy of the Chicago Daily News)

Mary Garden, 1935 — 301
(Courtesy of the Chicago Tribune)

Mrs. Harold McCormick (Edith Rockefeller). From a painting by Frederic August Von Kaulbach — 306
(Courtesy of the Chicago Tribune)

Ganna Walska and Harold McCormick, 1929 — 312
(Courtesy of the Chicago Sun-Times)

Samuel Insull as he appeared when he arrived in Chicago — 317
(Courtesy of the Chicago Historical Society)

Mrs. Samuel Insull in "The School for Scandal" — 324
(Courtesy of the Chicago Daily News)

Grand Foyer at the Civic Opera House — 327
(Courtesy of the Chicago Public Library)

Samuel Insull at the Height of His Power — 330
(Courtesy of the Associated Press)

Sally Rand and her Fans at the Century of Progress 335
(Chicago Tribune. Used by permission)

Colonel Robert R. McCormick 342
(Courtesy of Chicago Historical Society)

Field Museum of Natural History 344
(Kee Chang. Chicago Association of Commerce and Industry)

The Original McCormick Place 346
(Torkel Korling. Courtesy of Chicago Historical Society)

Jacob M. Arvey, Adlai Stevenson, and John S. Boyle 347
(Courtesy of Chicago Historical Society)

Paddy Bauler and Alderman Weber Celebrate 353
(Courtesy of Chicago Historical Society)

After a Bookie Raid 354
(Chicago Tribune. Used by permission)

Downtown Skyline 355
(Kee Chang. Chicago Association of Commerce and Industry)

Sears Tower 358
(Kee Chang. Chicago Association of Commerce and Industry)

First National Bank Plaza 360
(Courtesy of First National Bank of Chicago)

Picasso Statue at the Civic Center 361
(Kee Chang. Chicago Association of Commerce and Industry)

Alexander Calder's "Universe" in Sears Lobby 363
(Courtesy of Sears, Roebuck and Company)

Mahalia Jackson, Dr. Martin Luther King, Jr., and Mayor Daley 365
(Chicago Tribune. Used by permission)

Dr. King Leads March Protesting School Segregation 368
(Chicago Tribune. Used by permission)

The City Burns 371
(Chicago Tribune. Used by permission)

Demonstrators Attack Police Car 372
(Chicago Tribune. Used by permission)

U.S. Troops on Michigan Avenue 373
(Courtesy of Chicago Historical Society)

Demonstrators Outside Hilton Hotel, 1968 377
(Dave Nystrom. Courtesy of Chicago Historical Society)

War Protesters Rally at Statue of General Logan 381
(Ed Wenger. Courtesy of Chicago Historical Society)

Chicago-Style Television 384
(Courtesy of Chicago Historical Society)

LIST OF ILLUSTRATIONS xxi

A Second City Cast   386
(Arthur Siegel. Courtesy of Chicago Historical Society)

Inside the Playboy Mansion   388
(Don Bierman. *Chicago Sun-Times*. Used by permission)

World Heavyweight Champion Muhammad Ali   389
(*Chicago Tribune*. Used by permission)

Coach Halas and Quarterback Luckman   390
(Courtesy of Chicago Bears and George Halas)

Mike Royko and Bill Veeck   395
(*Chicago Sun-Times*. Used by permission)

Sir Georg Solti Conducts   396
(Courtesy of The Chicago Symphony Orchestral Organization)

"Not So Prim a Donna"   400
(© Field Enterprises, 1955)

Carol Fox with Princess Margaret of Britain   401
(Courtesy of Lyric Opera)

Saul Bellow and Milton Friedman Receive the Nobel Prize   404
(*Chicago Tribune*. Used by permission)

Mayor Richard J. Daley   406

Queen Elizabeth and Mayor Daley   407
(*Chicago Tribune*. Used by permission)

Mayor Daley Leads the St. Patrick's Day Parade   408
(*Chicago Tribune*. Used by permission)

Chicago Welcomes the Astronauts   409
(Betty Hulett. Courtesy of Chicago Historical Society)

The Snows Came, 1978–1979   415
(*Chicago Tribune*. Used by permission)

Mayor Byrne and Former Mayor Bilandic   417

O'Hare Airport   419
(Kee Chang. Chicago Association of Commerce and Industry)

The Lakefront at Night   421
(Kee Chang. Chicago Association of Commerce and Industry)

Looking North along the Lakefront   422
(Kee Chang. Chicago Association of Commerce and Industry)

PART ONE *The Garden City*

1835=1871

MARK BEAUBIEN'S TAVERN
ABOUT 1833

Frontier Town

"INTERESTING women are in demand here," a correspondent wrote from Chicago to the New York Star in 1837. "I understand that when the steamboats arrive from Buffalo and Detroit that nearly all business is suspended; and crowds of desolate, rich young bachelors flock to the pier and stand ready to catch the girls as they land." The description was hardly an exaggeration. In the winter of 1834 there had been only two girls of marriageable age in the small village of Chicago. The town's first fashionable wedding, which had such touches of style as printed wedding invitations, was that of an Indian chief's daughter, Josette LaFramboise, and Thomas Watkins, the post-office clerk who handed every Chicagoan his mail. The Reverend Isaac W. Hallam of St. James Episcopal Church performed the wedding ceremony in the chief's house while outside a group of Indian braves with tomahawks, clubs and even human scalps at their belts punctuated the sentences of the Episcopal Book of Common Prayer with the whoops and shrieks of tribal dances. The noise of the Indian dances brought echoes of terror to the white guests at the wedding. Only a few years before they had lived in fear of an Indian attack after Blackhawk and his warriors paddled across the Mississippi to reclaim lands taken from them by treaty. Runners brought word almost daily of massacres on outlying farms. Refugees from western Illinois streamed in to the protection of Fort Dearborn, reactivated because of the Indian menace after having been abandoned several years earlier. When Blackhawk won an initial skirmish against a band of untrained troops the panic increased and did not subside until the brave but foolhardy chief was put to flight after a battle in Wisconsin.

Until 1835 Chicago had been essentially an Indian town. Pelts, furs, guns, blankets, kettles, knives, hatchets, vermilion and whiskey were the principal commodities of commerce and Indians the chief customers. Blackhawk's escapade led to a renewal of demands that this large Indian population be moved west of the Mississippi. This was made possible in September of 1833 when the government called a grand council at Chicago of seventy-seven chiefs of the Chippewa, Ottawa and Pottawatomie tribes. On the 26th of the month a treaty was signed to which seventy-six Indian chiefs affixed their marks and one—Sau-Ko-Noek—his name. Under the treaty the Indians were dispossessed of lands later to be valued at hundreds of millions of dollars; in return they were given an annuity that for the first two years was to be paid at Chicago. By 1835 they were to be west of the Mississippi.

In 1834, when the first of the annuity payments was made, four to five thousand Indians, far outnumbering the population of Chicago, camped outside the town. The village traders were looking forward to the event greedily, but the majority of the townfolk thought nervously of the Blackhawk uprisings and hoped for the best. The distribution of the payments was primitive and haphazard. The whole quantity of goods to be given the Indians was piled in a heap on the west side of the river near the modern corner of Randolph and Canal Streets. The Indians were made to sit down in a circle around the pile with their squaws behind them. A group of halfbreeds and traders who had been appointed to pass out the merchandise grabbed it up by the armful and started tossing it to the Indians. There was no system or fairness about this method and the Indians soon made a rush for the pile, snatching at the goods in a disorderly turmoil until the final piece had disappeared. When the merchandise was gone, the Indians headed for the traders to swap blankets and clothing for whiskey. The one unsatisfactory note for almost everyone but Chicago's pioneer preacher, the Reverend Jeremiah Porter, was that several ships bearing cargoes of whiskey were not able to land for sixteen days because of high winds.

The performance of the Indians at the final annuity payment in 1835 was more awesome. Aware that this was their final stand before leaving the country of the Illinois forever, the Indians were brightly decorated with scarlet, yellow and blue paint. For several weeks after receiving their goods and money they lingered around town, encouraged in their reluctance to leave by traders who had been amply foreprovisioned against any such ill winds as had marred profits the previous year. On the final day set by the government for their departure, a thousand warriors assembled at the government council house on the north bank of the river. All were covered with vivid daubings of paint and naked except for a breechclout. Their faces were covered with curved stripes of red or vermilion and edged with black points to give the impression of a ferocious grin. Their long black hair was tightly gathered in scalplocks that bore decorations of hawk and eagle feathers, some of them strung together until they touched the ground. All were armed with tomahawks and clubs. Soon a band of music makers striking sticks and clubs together and beating on Indian drums took up positions for a war dance. The long column of the shrieking, dancing Indians started moving toward the center of the town. The column paused at every house and log cabin, while Indian warriors rushed up to the door or gate brandishing their primitive weapons. The morning was hot and the muscles of the perspiring Indians glistened like cast bronze as they moved in a torrent of motion down the narrow streets.

John Dean Caton, later to be a Chief Justice of the Illinois Supreme Court, watched the spectacle from behind closed curtains at the Sauganash Hotel. To him it seemed that "all the worst passions which can find a place in the breast of a savage—fierce anger, terrible hate, dire revenge, remorseless cruelty—" were to be seen in the demonstration of the Indians. Finally the passion of the warriors was spent and they filed away to the west and to an oblivion which the United States Government had arranged for them. To Caton it had been a scene "to try the nerve of the stoutest." The question of what might have happened if the Indians, "in their maddened frenzy," had turned the sham warfare into a real attack forced itself even on those who had seen the Indians most. It would have been easy, Caton thought, for the Indians to have massacred the entire town and left "not a living soul to tell the story." That there was no massacre was in part the difference of a generation between these Indians and those who had ravaged Fort Dearborn in 1812. Another factor was the leadership of the Indian Sauganash, known also to Chicagoans as Archibald "Billy" Caldwell.

Sauganash was born in Detroit in 1780, the son of an Irish colonel and a Pottawatomie maiden. As a boy he had attended the Jesuit school in Detroit

CHICAGO IN 1838, by Francis Castleneau. Earliest known contemporary view of Chicago

and learned to write English and French. His fine, slim figure led the Indians to call him "Tall Tree" but he was more often known as Sauganash, which meant Englishman. Sauganash was a loyal follower of Tecumseh who had served on Tecumseh's staff until the chief's death and who had come to the region around Chicago for the first time as a messenger to the Pottawatomies shortly before the Fort Dearborn massacre. It had been through the efforts of Sauganash that the family of John Kinzie had been saved. In 1820 he settled near Chicago and in 1827 was credited with preventing the Winnebagoes and Pottawatomies from staging an uprising which might have repeated the tragedy of 1812. When the Indians were forced to move west, Sauganash volunteered to go with his people and direct migration, though the government had specified he was free to remain. It was a gesture which gave meaning to Mark Beaubien's explanation, when he was adding the frame addition to his Eagle Exchange, the first building in Chicago not a log cabin, that he would name his new hotel "after a great man: Sauganash."

Beaubien himself contributed much to early Chicago, including an imposing total of twenty-three children (borne by three wives). He had arrived when an Indian trail was the only route into the city and had hired an Indian guide to show him the way. In addition to running a hotel, he was charged with the operation of the free ferry across the river, though the records show that on several occasions he was fined because he was off racing his horses against the ponies of young Indian sports rather than at his post of duty. In the evenings Mark was more easily located. He would play his fiddle for any who cared to dance. In his own words, "I play the fiddle like the devil and keep hotel like hell." When his hotel was crowded, Mark gave a traveler a blanket to cover himself on the floor, warning him to be careful that the Indians did not steal it. Then when the guest was asleep, Mark carefully removed the blanket and held it for the next arrival. In this way, he said, "I always had beds for all who wanted them."

Chicago's social life had its origins in the public balls held at Mark Beaubien's hotel. These were dances arranged by a board of managers from among the town's leading citizens. Everyone of respectability was invited. Servant girls danced in the same sets with their mistresses. (Many of the servants were daughters of new families "working out" in order to help the family get extra money to invest in Chicago real estate.) It was already a tenet of the town that there was "no place for drones or luxurious idlers in Chicago." Industry and frugality were alone respectable. Families came to the balls in wagons or oxcarts sufficiently sturdy to cope with Chicago's mud. The men walked alongside in heavy boots which they exchanged at the door of the hotel for dancing slippers. The carts were usually filled with hay and buffalo robes. An early visitor reported that while one lady was

OLD BARRACKS OF FORT DEARBORN AND LAKE HOUSE

sufficiently wealthy to wear a five-hundred-dollar gown, she arrived like all the rest—"in a cart, sitting upon the straw."

"At these Chicago cotillions," wrote Charles Fenno Hoffman, in an account of a journey to the West, "you might see a veteran officer in full uniform balancing a tradesman's daughter still in her short frock and trousers, while there the golden aiguillette of a handsome surgeon flapped in unison with the glass beads upon a scrawny neck of fifty. In one quarter, the high placed buttons of a linsey woolsey coat would be *dos-à-dos* to the elegantly turned shoulders of a delicate southern girl; and in another, a pair of Cinderella-like slippers would chassez cross with a brace of thick soled broughans, in the making which, one of the lost feet of the Colossus of Rhodes may have served for a last. Those raven locks, dressed à la Madonne, over eyes of jet, and touching a cheek where blood of deeper hue mingles with the less glowing current from European veins, tells of a lineage drawn from the original owners of the soil; while these golden tresses, floating away from eyes of heaven's own color over a neck of alabaster, recall the Gothic ancestry of some of England's born. How piquantly do these trim and beaded leggins peep from under that simple dress of black as its tall nut-brown wearer moves, as if unconsciously, through the graceful mazes of the dance."

Reminders that Chicago was a frontier town were everywhere. Yet there were already those who were predicting that one day Chicago would be a great city. They pointed to the fact that more than half the continent lay to the west, still undeveloped. The timber for the houses on the western prairies would have to pour through the funnel of Chicago from the wide forests of Wisconsin and Michigan. The manufactured goods from the East would have to be channeled through the young port at the end of the lake waterway. Nor were the prospects for trade one-sided. Already from the West were coming wagonloads of grain and livestock to be shipped to eastern markets. Wagon trains entering the city from the south after bending their way around the tip of Lake Michigan carried other vital cargo. By this route came families and whole communities which hoped to find their promised land in the West. Chicago was not always their stopping point. In 1849, when the gold-rush fever fired adventurous imaginations, many of those who had first chosen Chicago yielded to the greater lure of gold. The makers of covered wagons worked overtime and the price of guns for defense against the Indians rose as much as 50 per cent.

A vacant field south of Fort Dearborn had been set aside as a camping ground for the wagon trains and every evening it was filled with new arrivals. At twilight, the air above the river to the north was marked by a red glow from the reflections of the multiplying campfires. Chicagoans often stopped to watch and listen as the subdued excitement of a hundred conversations rose like a murmuring zephyr from the crowded prairie. Chicago's town crier, carrying a lamp and a bell to aid his quest for lost children, was frequently to be seen peering dutifully at the faces of the children in the throng around the camp ground. Every morning camp was broken early and the wagons started moving slowly down the town's main streets toward one of the roads leading over the prairie and swamp to the west. On the sides of the sturdy, big-ribbed wagons were the familiar slogans of "We'll Get Thar," "Reach It or Die," the ambitious "Pike's Peak or Bust" and, by one scribbler more ambitious than most, a line from a popular tune—"Plenty of Gold in the World I'm Told—On the Banks of the Sacramento."

The more prosperous among the arrivals preferred to come on a lake ship rather than put up with being bounced over "2,000 miles of connecting routes" of the Frink and Walker stagecoaches. The lake traffic was of such importance that most hotels were equipped with cupolas on the roof from which observers watched for incoming vessels and dispatched the hotel omnibus to the dock to pick up incoming guests.

Chicago's first hotel of any elegance was the Lake House, constructed of brick (then a rarity) at the corner of Rush and North Water Streets. It brought for the first time the novelties of napkins, toothpicks, printed menus and a French chef. Such touches of style were not without dangers. In 1838, the hotel manager announced a party for "the whole set of 200 North Side aristocrats." There was Bordeaux claret, champagne and oranges and grapes it required weeks to get from the East. (One early restaurateur made a buggy trip to Cleveland and waited two weeks to get a supply of fresh oysters.) The last dish which the Lake House manager put before his guests was new to most of them—it consisted of a piece of lemon peel floating in a tumbler of water and was served with a small glass bowl. Most of the guests thought it was an effete form of lemonade and drank it. To their consternation, they saw Mrs. John Kinzie, literally the first woman of Chicago, dip her fingers in the glass and let the water trickle over her hands in the bowl. Such incidents had not been eliminated by the 1850's. A visiting magazine correspondent, dining at the Briggs House where young Philip Henrici was introducing the city to fancy pastries, found that he might have as his "confectionery" or dessert a dish described by the printer as "Glass E. Jenny Lind." Pointing out that the same dish existed elsewhere as "Glace Jenny Lind," the writer nonetheless conceded the Chicago version was more "phonographic, Websterian and independent."

During the 1850's, the Lake House was replaced in popular favor by the Sherman House at the corner of Randolph and Clark and the Tremont House that seemed reasonably secure at Lake and Dearborn after having been burned down twice in the preceding ten years. Among the guests who stopped at the Sherman House was Ralph Waldo Emerson, who found it fit for a philosopher. He wrote his friend Thomas Carlyle that "it shows no signs of the rough and uncouth." On a later visit he added that the people who came to the hotel were "very earnest and active." He found many of them "quite intelligent," a fact he explained by their "being brought up in the East." Emerson also reported to Carlyle that the rooms at the Sherman House were lighted with gas, "and so, unlike English taverns, there is no charge for candles. I am told there is a bathroom on every floor and the hotel is four stories high. These bathrooms are at the disposal of the guests, a nominal charge being made for towels and soap; but if you supply your own soap and towels, there is no charge for the use of the water."

When elevators, or vertical railways as they were then called, were first

LAKE STREET FROM DEARBORN STREET, 1839, by N. Roswell Gilford. The building on the corner is the Tremont House

CHICAGO IN 1845

introduced, they were restricted to the use of the guests; luggage was not permitted. Trunks and suitcases still had to be carried by porters up and down five or six flights of stairs. To summon the elevator, guests had the choice of shouting down the shaft or banging on the wire cage with their room key. In less elegant hostelries, there was no central heating and an overnight guest was required to pay a special fee for a fire as well as for his soap and towel. Often he would have to retire by the light of a kerosene lamp. In such hotels, if warm water were desired, it was necessary to tip the chambermaid who would then fetch a pitcher from the kitchen. The frontier quality of life in Chicago was dramatized for one fair visitor when she found on the table in the "ladies' parlor" of her modest hotel "two rifles, a pistol and a powder flask." In her room, a buffalo skin took the place of the customary blanket.

The portrait artist, G. P. A. Healy, who arrived in 1850, found all the city "in a somewhat rough stage." Healy penned a Lincolnesque portrait of Chicago as "an overgrown youth whose legs and arms are too long for his clothes and who scarcely knows how to dispose of his lank awkward body. The city stretched along the lake shore and out on the prairie, unfinished, ragged and somewhat uncouth as yet." He found "The streets were abominably paved; the sidewalks, raised high above the level of the streets, were composed of rough planks, often out of repair so that one had to pick one's way carefully for fear of accidents. Big nails seemed placed there on purpose to catch in the women's dresses; and as the hideous fashion of crinolines or hoops as they were called, had just reached the Far West, many were the falls occasioned by these nails. The mud was so deep in bad weather that from side to side rickety boards served as unsafe bridges and the unfortunate hordes waded laboriously along as best they could."

The mud was probably the most famous topic of conversation in early Chicago. It was also a barrier to the development of a genteel society. The wheels of carriages could not always cope with the persistent muck. When the ladies went calling, it was frequently necessary for them to gather up their finery and huddle in the back of a sturdy wagon or a potato cart whose wheels would not break in the mud. On arrival, the cart or wagon would be backed up to the doorstep so that the visitor could step directly into the house. One frustrated young lady, confined to her house by the mud, composed her own soliloquy that compensates in graphic detail for what it lacks in poetic virtues.

March 7, 1868

Dearest Cousin

I should have written long before
But trouble entered at my door
And with it I am quite bowed o'er,
          The mud.

I strove to visit you last week
But went no farther than the street
Ere I was buried up complete
          The mud

All whom I met wore faces new
Bespattered all and sad to view
With skirts most heavy laden too
          The mud.

As home from school the children came
I durst not call them one by name
To tell my own I tried in vain
          The mud.

Indoors all things with blackness spread
E'en to our butter and our bread
And out doors nigh up to your head
          The mud.

I looked within the glass today
But frightened, hasted fast away
My beautous face was inky clay
          The mud.

Afflictions not from ground arise
If that is so, I have no eyes
You'll not see me until it dries,
          The mud.

With the exception of the high ground around Fort Dearborn, most of Chicago was located on a drained marsh. In earlier years, when the lowest sections were covered with flood waters, Indians paddled canoes from the Desplaines River to the South Branch of the Chicago River and down that sluggish stream to Lake Michigan. In the winter, it was still possible to skate for miles over the frozen prairies and swamps to the west. The entire city was cut by gullies and inlets leading to the river. In some seasons enough water stood in the gully at State Street for guests at the Tremont House to sit on the front steps and shoot the ducks that swooped down on the water.

With the rapid growth of the city, various plans were advanced to defeat the mud. None was successful until a decision was reached to build an entirely new surface. The South Division, as the South Side was known, was about ten feet higher than the downtown area and provided much of the dirt for elevating the business streets. Fort Dearborn, the only high spot in the central district, was torn down so that the land on which it stood could be carted to Randolph Street and bring that thoroughfare up to the new level. Some streets were raised as much as ten feet in a process that required twenty years to complete and left Chicago with a legacy of uneven sidewalks for another generation.

But as the streets went up, the buildings appeared to go down. The effect on the two-story courthouse was so depressing that a new third story and cupola were added so that it would rise far enough above the new surface to achieve a suitable height and dignity. Such expensive alterations were not practicable for most buildings and many viewed the raising of the streets as a calamity. A young man who saw it as an opportunity was a Yankee cabinet-maker, George M. Pullman. He had heard of the problem while he was helping to move buildings to allow for the widening of the Erie Canal. Shortly after coming to Chicago, Pullman undertook (with two other contractors) to raise an entire block of buildings on Lake Street at the same time. Pullman and his collaborators placed six thousand jackscrews under the buildings in the block and hired a small army of six hundred men to turn the screws. At a signal, each man gave the eight or more screws of which he was in charge a half-turn, raising the buildings a fraction of an inch. As the block rose slowly into the air, it was shored up by timbers. In this way the block, with its sidewalk, was raised four feet into the air in a period of four days without interrupting the business of any of the stores in the block. When the new foundations were ready, the buildings were lowered by the same gentle method. Acting alone, Pullman later engaged five hundred men and raised the Tremont House by the same means.

Others were also employing these same methods. All over the city buildings rose out of the holes into which the new street grades had plunged them. Not all the buildings were lifted up. Some were shifted to new locations and the sight of a building rolling down the street was a normal part of the day's street traffic. A visitor counted nine houses in one day being shifted out of the business district. One of the peripatetic dwellings was partially occupied by a cigar store whose proprietor stood in the entryway puffing a

ENTIRE BLOCK ON LAKE STREET BEING RAISED TO A HEIGHT OF FOUR FEET, 1857, by *Edward Mendel*

cigar and ready to serve his customers while the move was under way. Uncertainty about how high the street grades might go led many builders to erect foundations that rose high above either the new or the old level. A result of this practice was the development of the "Chicago cottage" with the front porch and main entrance at the second-floor level. Long after there was any possibility that the street grades might catch up to these elevated houses, the style continued to be a popular one in Chicago.

Uncertainty over the height of the streets led to a notorious capriciousness among Chicago sidewalks. Builders with varying ideas about the height of the new grade constructed their walks at different levels. Frequently it was necessary to walk from one sidewalk level to another several times in a single block, a hazard not without problems for the hoopskirted women. It was with justification that periodic signs warned the pedestrian to "Use Your Intellect." In a small visitor's guide, aptly titled "Tricks and Traps of Chicago," feminine tourists were cautioned about "sidewalk oglers" who loitered near these sidewalk stairs hoping to catch the sight of a lady's limb. The author gave a hint of some keen scrutiny on his own part by saying that "it was the remark of observant travelers that in no American city do the ladies present more divine charms of limb than those of Chicago." He attributed this on the basis of "strictly scientific principles" to the fact that Chicago ladies had so much exercise in going up and down the steps in the sidewalks. The space under the sidewalks was used for a number of purposes, though in popular conversation this area was chiefly noted as the abode of gargantuan rats. On the lake front, where the waters touched Michigan Avenue, the area under the walk was used as a mooring and shelter for rowboats. On the North Side, one ambitious citizen was found by a revenue officer to have dislodged the rats and installed an illicit distillery under the walk.

FRINK & WALKER STAGE OFFICE, by W. E. S. Trowbridge

The streets were always crowded with a motley and colorful traffic. Carriages drawn by handsome horses passed side by side with creaking wagons drawn by stolid oxen. On almost every street were to be seen the horse-drawn omnibuses of Franklin Parmelee. Parmelee, who a few years before had been a clerk on a lake steamer, first introduced his coaches on Wabash Avenue. Successful in this enterprise, he formed another company which provided baggage vans to pick up luggage for the hotels. Soon he was a wealthy man. Conscious of his new eminence, he ordered the portraits of the members of his family painted on the panels of his coaches. They were soon dubbed "Parmelee's family coaches"; when all of them were drawn up before the Sherman House, Chicagoans pointed out Mr. Parmelee and all the little Parmelees, one of them a young girl whose luxuriant tresses covered half the side of the bus.

Riders on horseback were a common sight, among them hunters who rode powerful and spirited horses held in check by large metal bits and a tight rein. Most of these frontier men had pistols in their holsters; they rode in high-peaked saddles with short stirrups and long Spanish spurs shining against highly polished saddles and boots. Frequently knives were stuck in their belts and light rifles slung over their shoulders. The hunter and his game bag were as common as the truck farmer and his produce wagon. Wild fowl hung in the doorways of the meat commission houses on South Water Street in profusion—teal, partridge, jacksnipe, quail, prairie chicken and grouse—all of it to be bought for at most $2 a dozen while on the walls nearby hung the carcasses of deer and bear.

The buildings which lined the streets could not be identified by any dominating style of architecture. A correspondent of the London *Times* described them as "an extraordinary melange of the Broadway of New York and little shanties—of Parisian buildings mixed with backwoods life." Most of the store fronts were covered with signs distinguished more for their boldness and noticeability than style. Frequently only the first floor of the building was used for business purposes. The upper floors were converted into dormitories for the young men who were crowding into the young city with the hopes of making a fortune. That the streets were not completely bleak was attributable to the trees, of which there was an abundance even in the business district.

Looking down upon the city from the new Courthouse tower the visitor saw frequent patches of green among the buildings. Houses and churches alike were set in the midst of wide lawns or under the sheltering shade of elm, cottonwood, ash and linden trees. The land at the edge of town burst forth each summer with a profusion of prairie flowers. To Sarah Margaret Fuller these brilliant flowers, "which gemmed and gilt the grass . . . between the low oakwood and the narrow beach near the blue lake, stimulated a sort of fairyland exultation." Frederika Bremer, another early tourist, told of seeing the prairies splendid with sunflowers "four yards high" and asters which "grew above my head." Each month the prairies were covered with a different class of flowers—"in spring white, then blue and (in summer) mostly of a golden yellow."

The pastoral quality of the surrounding prairies was in direct contrast to the hustling commerce of the rapidly growing town. With the accumulation of greater wealth there were changes in the social life as well. "There is a good deal of style here," a newly arrived young lady reported to her cousin back East, "and considerable rivalry among the leaders of the town—the two most prominent don't speak." A hint of other improvements is also given in the letter. "Things are not so bad now," the correspondent cheerfully concluded. "The walking is pretty fair and ladies do not apprehend, in stepping out of doors, the loss of a shoe." For Chicago, it was a step in the right direction.

HISTORIC TREE ON THE SITE OF THE FORT DEARBORN MASSACRE

The Yankee Out West

IN 1847, Chicago was ready for its first great convention. The leaders who sent out the call for the meeting called it The River and Harbor Convention, but its purpose was much wider than that of attempting to persuade President James K. Polk to develop the rivers and harbors of the Northwest. On the opening day three thousand delegates from eighteen of the twenty-nine states in the Union assembled in a huge tent erected on the courthouse square to consider "whatever matters pertain to the prosperity of the West." The resolutions the delegates passed had little effect on President Polk who thought it unconstitutional to use Federal money to develop the country's internal resources. But in the dispatches which the editors at the convention sent back to their papers was the first recognition of the importance of the port at the foot of Lake Michigan.

Thurlow Weed, a big man in New York politics and journalism, wrote to his Albany *Journal* that the Chicago meeting was the "largest deliberative body ever assembled" and predicted that "in ten years Chicago will be as big as Albany," a boast which was no more than an understatement. Equally enthusiastic was another New York editor, Horace Greeley, who was most impressed by Chicago's hospitality and particularly by the grand parade. He wrote the New York *Tribune* that "though the route traversed was short

THE GARDEN CITY 16

in deference to the heat of the weather, the spectacle was truly magnificent. The citizens of Chicago furnished the most imposing part of it—the Music, the Military, the Ships on Wheels, ornamented Fire Engines, etc. I never witnessed anything so superb as the appearance of some of the Fire Companies with their Engines drawn by led horses, tastefully caparisoned. Our New York firemen must try again; they have certainly been outdone." Among those whose presence was particularly noted by Greeley at the convention was Abraham Lincoln, "a tall specimen of an Illinoisan, just elected to Congress from the only Whig district in the state."

The stories of Chicago's progress were confirmed by the conversation of travelers returning to the East through the Erie Canal. It had been the opening of the Erie Canal in 1825 which had actually started the great migration to Chicago. The canal was the principal link in a new water route for commerce that was obvious to the eye on any map. It led from the Erie Canal through the Great Lakes to the Chicago River and then by the Illinois and Michigan Canal to the Illinois River and down the Mississippi to the great ports of St. Louis and New Orleans. Chicago, the gateway to the canal, lay at the natural junction of the two great inland waterways of the United States. The stories of the fortunes that were to be made in the rapidly growing city stirred the imagination of such ambitious New Englanders as George M. Pullman. Throughout New York State and New England other young men were heading west. Not all set their goal for Chicago but most planned at least to take a look at it. The greater part of those in this migration traveled light. Their assets were a small sack of savings, a letter of recommendation and a yen for adventure, preferably profitable. More than a few were resolute, tight lipped and tighter fisted, bent on making a killing in the city where millionaires could be made overnight. Quill pens at registry desks in the second- and third-floor dormitories of the business district scratched the names of the eastern seaboard's first families among those of more humble origin. So great was the influx that the newly-elected county commissioners established ceiling prices for the protection of travelers. Tavern keepers were ordered to charge no more than 25 cents for a half-pint of wine, rum or brandy; 12½ cents was the top price for a half a pint of whiskey or a night's lodging and 25 cents the limit for breakfast or supper. It was the city's first melting pot and into it went all sorts of men, including horse thieves, land speculators, and, as one chronicler put it, "other birds of passage—mostly vultures." Most of the new arrivals from New England were not "birds of passage" but eager young men whose leaving led one Yankee editor to protest the loss of the "most vital elements of progress and our future good condition."

Throughout the 1850's, this Yankee Exodus, as Stewart Holbrook was to call it, continued. Many a New England village was to see the prospects of its own future sacrificed to the greater promises of the West. The character of Chicago early reflected the objectives of these New England emigrants. The "Anglo-Saxo-Yankees," as they were called by the Chicago newspapers, ranged in viewpoint from stern moralists indoctrinated with the precepts of Puritanism to sharp speculators whose ethical antecedents were traceable to the Yankee horse trader. These men more than any others were the leaders of Chicago. When a visitor talked of meeting a Chicagoan, he usually meant he was talking to a transplanted Yankee. Of the first thirty-two mayors, twenty were from New England.

A Yankee who came early to Chicago was William Butler Ogden. He came west in 1835 as a representative of his brother-in-law Charles Butler, who had invested $100,000 in Chicago property he had never seen. Ogden found the land ankle deep in water and wrote that the purchase had been one of the "grossest folly." Determined to salvage what he could, he made a methodical survey of the land; by the time the summer sun baked the area dry, he was ready to auction it off. The sale caused him to revise his original opinion of the investment; one-third of the property sold for more than the original cost. Ogden decided to abandon an incipient political career that had already won him a term in the New York legislature and to cast his lot with a city where even swampland could be made to produce a fortune.

Two years later Ogden was elected Chicago's first mayor and throughout most of his life he was to remain its foremost citizen. Self-reliant, he was not willing to wait for the city to act when improvements were needed. He designed and built the first swinging drawbridge over the Chicago River. To enhance the value of the real estate he owned, he and his clients constructed nearly a hundred miles of streets on the North and West Sides and put in bridges where they were needed, including two over the Chicago River. He was preparing to dig a tunnel under the river at Washington Street when the city agreed to do it. Chicago's growth could be measured by his investments: in 1844 he bought a tract of land for $8,000; eight years later he sold it for three million. When work on the Illinois and Michigan Canal was stopped for lack of funds, he saw that the necessary bonds were issued and the money raised. Then, in the same year the canal was opened, he was ready with another project that within a generation was to render the canal obsolete: he built Chicago's first railroad.

The year 1848 had been an important one for the city. For the first time it had been linked with the East by telegraph. Then, after twelve years of intermittent construction, had come the opening of the Illinois and Michigan Canal and the realization of Louis Joliet's dream of a continuous waterway to the Mississippi. Finally, in the fall, had come the first railroad; a second-hand locomotive and two cars made a run of five miles to the west over the tracks of Ogden's Galena and Chicago Union Railroad. Ogden had

CHAMBER OF COMMERCE, 1865

not waited for the railroads to reach Chicago from the East but had shipped in his locomotive by water so that he could start his trains running toward the West in the future of which he so confidently believed.

Another of the Anglo-Saxo-Yankees was Potter Palmer, who made his fortune in a dry-goods store before he was forty and sold out to another new arrival from Pittsfield, Massachusetts, named Marshall Field. Not content to be idle, Palmer invested in real estate along State Street and by his leadership made it the main thoroughfare of Chicago. From Blandsford, Massachusetts (by way of Michigan City, Indiana), came three Blair brothers; Chauncey, Lyman and William. Washington P. Brink, a Yankee from Vermont, set himself up in the business of delivering parcels of any value. A newcomer from Maine was William Wallace Kimball, who thought there was a need in the young town for another dealer in pianos and organs. A Yankee packer, Philip D. Armour, found Milwaukee too small for him after the Civil War and moved to Chicago. He made a trip East in 1865 to sell pork for future delivery at $40 a barrel to eastern speculators who thought the war was nowhere near an end and that pork was due to rise to $60. After Appomattox, Armour delivered the pork and collected his $40 a barrel on meat he was buying for $18. In a single stroke of business, he had become a multimillionaire and lent credence to the legend that the smart Yankees had gone West.

Many of the migrant Yankees were first settlers in Chicago. The first lawyer, Russell E. Heacock, came from Litchfield, Connecticut. The first city prosecutor was John Dean Caton, who had come West via boat and wagon from New York, only to have the town's first law violator jump bail bond and disappear so that the city's first law case could never be prosecuted. The first druggist was Philo Carpenter, who came from the Hoosac Mountains of Massachusetts and brought with him a conviction that alcohol should be taken only for medicinal purposes; he also became one of the town's earliest temperance crusaders. One of the early meat packers as well as the first ship owner, the first lumber dealer and the first insurance salesman was Gurdon Saltonstall Hubbard of Middletown, Connecticut, who passed through Fort Dearborn initially in 1818 when he was on his way to the Mississippi as a sixteen-year-old fur buyer for John Jacob Astor and the American Fur Company. The New England lawyers could scarcely be counted, though outstanding among them was Jonathan Young Scammon from Lincoln County, Maine, whom history credits with introducing the boutonniere as an acceptable article of masculine wearing apparel in Chicago.

The newspapers and magazines, many of them Yankee owned or edited, were fond of speculating on the causes of this dominance of Chicago by a relatively small group of men. *The Chicago Magazine* said it thought "The Yankee out West is an enlarged and improved edition of a specimen of the species man. . . . Had there first been no East, rigid, stern, homes strict and puritanical, a land where industry is made a prime virtue and accumulation like unto it there could have been no West, fertile, expansive, liberal . . ." It was the magazine's opinion that when the Yankee "departed the home of his maturity he carried with him his outfit of religion, morality, perseverance, cuteness and tact; and when transferred to the area of favorable circumstances it is enlarged to the attitude of the best specimen of man." The definition of a "real genuine Yankee" by the Chicago *Times* was less respectful. The editor found the Chicago Yankees "full of animation, checked by moderation, guided by determination and supported by education." A Yankee, "just caught," he said, "will not be deficient in the following qualities:

He is self-denying, self-relying, always trying and into everything prying.
He is a lover of piety, propriety, notoriety and temperance society.
He is a dragging, gagging, bragging, striving, thriving, swiping, jostling, bustling, wrestling, musical, quizzical, astronomical, philosophical and comical sort of character, whose manifest destiny is to spread civilization to the remotest corners of the earth, with an eye always on the lookout for the main chance.

It was this interest in the "main chance" that characterized the early

Chicagoan in all that he did. Joseph T. Ryerson, son of a pioneer steelmaker, was to recall later that "each one seemed to have but one object in life and that was to strive for the main chance, the means to live and get along, so that in this respect all were very much on a level." Frugality and hard work were the only virtues recognized. Very little was spent on outward show. A man's character was of more importance than the size of his bank account or his business. Banks that refused to extend credit to the city of Chicago or the Galena and Chicago Union Railroad handed over money readily in return for no more than William B. Ogden's personal note.

The life and philosophy of Ogden were in many respects typical. In a terse autobiography he recorded that he had been "born close to a sawmill, was early left an orphan, graduated from a log schoolhouse and at fourteen fancied I could do anything I turned my hand to and that nothing was impossible." There was very little in his later life to dispute this early appraisal of his potentialities. When Ogden had been refused capital for his first railroad by both the bankers of Boston and the merchants of Chicago, he drove up and down the Fox River valley with his Yankee friend, Jonathan Young Scammon, persuading the farmers to buy stock in the railroad that would be serving them.

A southern exception to the Yankee rule among the early builders of Chicago was Cyrus H. McCormick, who was born on a farm in Rutland County, Virginia. Even McCormick had his debt to the Yankees, for when he brought his reaper plant to Chicago it was William B. Ogden who advanced $25,000 to get the factory started. And the woman the reaper king

CHICAGO IN 1849 as seen from the top of St. Mary's College

eventually married was Nettie Fowler, whom he brought West from Jefferson County, New York.

Because of the few women in the community and the much smaller number who had matrimonial qualifications, "going East for a bride" was a regular occurrence. When Dr. William Mason, the Boston pianist, visited Chicago in the 1850's, he was surprised to be greeted at a reception by a crowd of predominantly young girls. "Where are your married women?" he asked. His youthful reception committee told him they represented the married women; they had been girls in New England, but were all married now to "our fellows." The arrival of a new bride was an event of special significance for the local dressmakers, who were frequently among her first callers. Having examined the bride's trousseau, a seamstress would then go from door to door, like a census taker or tax collector, soliciting orders based on the latest fashions from the East.

Though these early Yankees believed in "everything at high pressure" in their business lives, they tried to create in their home surroundings some of the atmosphere of the New England communities they had left. There was a large colony of Anglo-Saxo-Yankees on the North Side, living in large frame houses situated amid spacious yards and lawns. The residents prided themselves on their gardens and shade trees and spoke with proprietary pride of the motto in the city's seal, "*Urbs in Horto.*" This, they explained to the Latinless or curious, might be translated freely as "The Garden City."

The house of William B. Ogden dominated this area much as its owner dominated the business community. The house was the only one in the block; from its place in the center of the square it looked south over another block-square area of trees and grass known, not surprisingly, as Ogden's Grove. A broad piazza extended across the south front of the house and on the north was a conservatory always bright with flowers. Near the large stables was a fruit house in which Ogden raised exotic grapes, peaches, apricots and figs in a perpetually maintained artificial climate. Around the house, maple, oak, cherry, elm, birch and hickory trees were festooned with climbing vines. The entire grounds were handsomely landscaped with ornamental shrubs, climbing roses and other flowers. Ogden's home was a stopping place for many of the celebrities who passed through the city— Daniel Webster, William Cullen Bryant, Margaret Fuller, Ralph Waldo Emerson and others were entertained there. The artist G. P. A. Healy, whom Ogden had persuaded to leave the court of France for the crude conveniences of early Chicago, ranked Ogden as a conversationalist with the three best Healy had ever known—Louis Philippe of France, John Quincy Adams and Dr. Orestes A. Brownson, the New England religious polemicist and iconoclast.

Adding to the pastoral quality of the neighborhood was the custom of

RUSH STREET BRIDGE IN 1861, by *Edwin Whitefield*. McCormick's works are at the center left

keeping a cow for the family milk supply. Each day the cows would be led to and from free pasturage at the edge of town. The city's wealthiest citizens had their own herd of bovine commuters—though the herdsman of this Yankee flock had more the aspect of a Cossack than a cowherd. His coat and cap were in the Cossack style and a generous beard plus an untrimmed crop of long black hair gave him the appearance of wearing a beard both fore and aft. With his trousers tucked in his rough boots he rode north on Rush Street each morning blowing a brass horn as a signal for his patrons to let their cows into the streets. As the herd was driven home in the evening, each cow turned from habit into her own dooryard. Almost every family of any affluence had its own cow. The penchant for milk extended to the boarding houses where an early guest found that "any man who calls for milk at breakfast or supper is generally called 'a cussed Yank.'"

Soon after Cyrus McCormick had successfully established his reaper factory, he sent for his brother Leander to help him in the business. Leander and his wife were also to provide a home for Cyrus, who had not yet found his own bride. Mrs. Leander McCormick was not long in recording her impression of Chicago. "A great many Yankees here," she wrote. "Mrs. Hamilton [a Kentuckian], does not like them much. She says that we must have a Southern society and let the Yankees, Germans, Irish, French all alone." Even though the McCormicks were among the wealthiest of Chicagoans, their home was furnished on utilitarian principles rather than for ostentation. Mrs. McCormick wrote proudly to Virginia that there was "a beautiful flowered red and green carpet in the chamber and parlor, and when the folding doors are open the stove in the chamber will heat both rooms . . . I would like to have a sofa and a pretty lamp in the parlor and think likely we will get them before long. The stairs are carpeted and the passage floor

MICHIGAN TERRACE (Terrace Row), looking toward the Central Depot, 1863, by Edwin Whitefield

has oilcloth on it. The dining room is not furnished except with nice chairs and tables; my dishes and eatables are kept in the pantry. There are three rooms upstairs, one finely furnished for Cyrus, the others will not be furnished till we get our boxes of beds and bedclothes."

The most elaborately landscaped of the North Side residences was that of S. H. Kerfoot, a real-estate dealer, whose carriage drives were said to be more solidly constructed than the city's streets. The grounds around his house were ornamented with artificial ponds, rustic bridges, fine greenhouses and all the other accouterments of new wealth. Another of the elegant homes was that of Julian Rumsey, an early mayor, who moved to the Near North Side shortly after his marriage in 1848 in the face of the strenuous objections of his father-in-law, who felt the location at 40 East Huron was "too far out in the woods."

A hazard to be faced by all who lived on the North Side was the crossing of the Chicago River on bridges manned by notoriously unreliable bridge tenders. The river skyline was thick with masts of vessels. The frequent passage of these ships in and out of the river made the bridge tender a functionary with considerable power. He was the most unruly member of the city's staff and until 1868 the city had no control over him. In that year an ordinance was passed limiting the amount of time a bridge could be open to ten minutes, but the boats still ruled as tyrants of the river. An intoxicated skipper who, according to the official report, "was coming up the river with full sheet besides his own three sheets in the wind" had sailed directly over a low float bridge. Another time James Dole was driving across the Rush Street Bridge at the same time a herd of cattle was passing in the opposite direction. The bridge tender swung open the bridge in response to the whistle of a tugboat and stampeded the frightened cattle toward one end of the bridge. Their combined weight tipped the bridge, dumping Dole, his fine buggy and span of horses and the cattle all in the water. Dole was rescued, but the bridge was ruined. In a lawsuit against the city a plaintiff complained that another bridge tender had delayed so long in opening a bridge that a damaged vessel being towed up the river had sunk for a second time.

Rivaling the North Side as a fashionable residential area was Michigan Avenue. From Dearborn Park at Randolph and Washington, south to Park Row at Twelfth Street, the avenue was a succession of imposing residences. A large number were constructed of Athens marble, a deceptively named limestone that had been discovered during excavations for the Illinois and Michigan Canal. The most exclusive area on the avenue was Terrace Row, a group of three-story buildings largely occupied by pioneer families. The showplaces of the street were the large new home of William Blair and the "Bishop's Palace," the home of the Reverend Dr. O'Regan. Chicagoans claimed that "in architectural proportions" the latter was not "surpassed by any residence in the West."

Probably the most unusual residence of any of these early Anglo-Saxo-Yankees was that of "Long John" Wentworth, who made his home on a five-thousand-acre stock farm near Summit and tried to pattern his way of life after that of Mount Vernon and Monticello. Before he retired to his life of statesmanlike detachment, however, he was to stride in giant steps through an important part of the Chicago story.

JOHN WENTWORTH

Long John and His Devils

LONG JOHN WENTWORTH was for twenty-five years editor of the Chicago *Democrat*, twelve years a member of Congress from the Chicago district and twice mayor of the city. The Yankee virtues and shortcomings were not concentrated in Long John but rather expanded. He was a giant of a man, six feet six inches in height. He had been too impatient to wait for a wagon to carry him into Chicago in 1836. He preferred to stride barefoot into Chicago carrying giant shoes fourteen inches long and six inches wide and clinging to a jug of whiskey "with which to bathe my blistered feet."

On his first day in the city, Long John observed everything that a Yankee might be interested in, from morality to economics. "Land is worth $40 per square foot," he reported to his sister. "The young men are mostly those who have made a fortune out of nothing and are consequently quite dissipated. Such a place for smoking I never saw. Out of 150 boarding at this house, not ten refuse to smoke. Here, as also at Detroit, ardent spirit is always put upon the table for dinner and most all take their drink."

In the history of Chicago there was never another man cut to so individual a pattern as John Wentworth. He said bluntly he refused to be "one of your bell livers." He said he "never had and never will live on time. Got no use for call bells, dinner bells or alarm clocks. My doctrine is this: eat when you're hungry, drink when you're thirsty, sleep when you're sleepy and get up when you're ready." It could be said of Long John that he was thirsty fairly often; his favorite beverage was brandy and he drank from a pint to a quart of "ardent spirit" every day of his long life. He spent more time in Chicago hotels than he did in his Summit home and the best table in the hotel dining room was always reserved for him alone. He planned his meals in his room, placing a mark on the menu before each dish he wanted. When he was ready to eat, he went down to the dining room expecting to find every dish he ordered—sometimes there were as many as thirty or forty—on the table ready for him. That the soup was cold or the ice cream melting did not bother him; most important was the fact no time had been spent in waiting, which he regarded as an intolerable waste.

When Long John was a member of Congress during the controversy over the Oregon question, there was some fear that in a war with England the British might take Fort Mackinac, use it as a base and attack the Lake Michigan towns. As Long John proudly and publicly traced his ancestry back to Thomas Wentworth, Earl of Stafford (who through the weakness of Charles I had been beheaded on Tower Hill), his political enemies began to make an issue of this English connection. Long John, who said he was "desiring to show my constituents that I was fully alive to their interests," made a speech in Congress so vigorously opposing the English view that the New York *Herald* printed a caricature showing the British lion being chased by Long John Wentworth. It was the first show of hostility between Chicago and the British Empire.

Although Wentworth was elected to Congress for six terms as a Democrat, his greatest exploits occurred during the two terms he was in the mayor's chair as a Republican. He was completely independent and honest, though his yearning for prompt action on every issue sometimes led him to ignore the normal forms of the democratic process. He was the city's first "strong-man" mayor; if he did not change Chicago's heart, at least he made a considerable difference in its face. His predecessor as mayor had been Thomas Dyer, whose inaugural parade had included a group of "female convivials" in open carriages, escorted by what the newspapers reported as "a miscellaneous crowd of men." The scandalized city, wishing to correct the situation but not wanting to be distracted from the more important business of making a dollar, voted Wentworth into office with a confidence that he would take care of the matter personally.

The new mayor immediately enunciated a tougher policy for criminals. He said that prostitutes posing as the mothers of large families had in many cases secured pardons for known criminals and warned that no such tricks would get his sympathy. He did not think criminals merited the luxury of idleness in jail and put them to work upon the city's streets, wearing a ball and chain and supervised by an armed overseer. The city had not wanted to go quite this far in setting an example for criminals and public protests forced him to abandon the practice. His political opponents were never to let him forget it.

The mayor's spear of righteousness was dulled but not broken. He next declared war on The Sands, a collection of tumble-down shanties along the lake shore on the North Side. The area housed a collection of the worst kinds of cheap lodging houses, saloons, gambling dens and bordellos. The pride of the community included such characters as Mike O'Brien, alternately a burglar and prize fighter; his son, Mike, Jr., a pickpocket and pander for his four sisters; John Hill and his wife, Mary, who are credited with being the first couple in Chicago to work the badger game on a gullible male. At Freddy Webster's, one of the worst of the houses, there was an inmate who, it was said, had been neither sober nor out of the house for five years and who had not had her clothes on for three. She died on March 8, 1857, from what the coroner called "intemperance."

Because the property in the area was involved in several lawsuits, none of the owners was willing to risk an eviction. Timidity gave way to boldness when the rights of one of the owners were purchased by the ever at hand William B. Ogden. He promptly told the occupants in his buildings to get

THE "LONG JOHN" FIRE ENGINE

out or he would tear their places down. At the same time, he offered to buy any of the other buildings in the area whose owners were willing to sell. The occupants turned down Ogden's bid, giving Mayor Wentworth a new opportunity to enter the jousting field as the representative of civic virtue.

Ignoring the legal procedures with which Ogden had been concerned, Long John told the residents to get out by April 20, 1857, or their houses would be burned down. The threat to set fire to the houses was a shrewd strategy that enabled the mayor to bring to the scene as his allies the members of the city's volunteer fire department.

A few of the fire companies were manned by scions of the first families and membership was as exclusive as in any private club. Others were made up of rough and ready volunteers who "ran wid de masheen" and worked the brakes, or the pumps. For their services this group enjoyed the privilege of chopping up the shanties of the poor or a discreet amount of looting in the property of better endowed citizens who needed their assistance. Occasionally the companies would fight over the honor of being first to the fire, stopping to carry on the battle for honors with little concern for the consequences to the flaming buildings of which they were the theoretical protectors. At a fire on Lake Street, which caused a million dollars in damage, the fire fighters were hampered because two engines had been so badly damaged in a battle for a prized silver trumpet that they were unable to be used.

Company No. 6 had its headquarters in the Silver Fountain saloon of its captain, Pat Casey. Casey dispensed a brand of whiskey known as "Casey's No. 6" which was warranted to get the imbiber drunker and incite him to more reckless deeds of daring than any other brand on the market. The company never went to a fire without a supply of its own "Casey's No. 6." Wentworth beamed with pride on all factions; when the city's first steam engine was acquired it was christened "Long John." The next two were named—in accordance with the principles of his political beliefs—"Liberty" and "Economy."

On the morning of April 20th, the mayor, with his fire department in support and flanked by a deputy sheriff and a semi-official posse, marched down to The Sands to carry out his threat. A few of the entrepreneurs had moved their businesses elsewhere but most of the inhabitants knew of no place else they could go. When the mayor arrived, many of the tougher members of the community were absent. They had been lured away by the greater attraction of a dogfight for a $500 purse at the Brighton race track between the dog of Dutch Frank, a Sands brothel owner, and the hound of William Galligher. According to the *Journal* the fight was witnessed by "a large crowd of pimps and bullies."

In the absence of masculine protectors, the girls in the area offered little resistance. They were given a short time to move their furniture into the

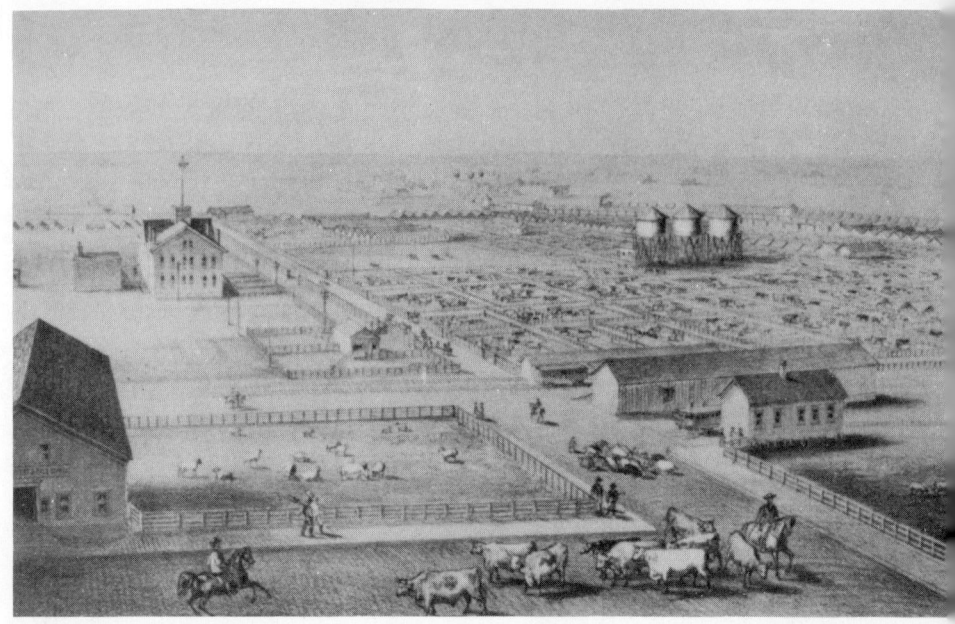

UNION STOCKYARDS, 1866

street. Their flimsy buildings were then hooked up to a strong chain and pulled down by a team of horses. A short time later, fire broke out in several of the remaining buildings. The newspapers reported it as an act of spite against the new owner of the property. Chicagoans thought it more plausible the fires had been set by members of the fire department anxious for a little sport before they went home. The spectacular nature of the raid, the notoriety of the area and the method used to tear down the buildings made the raid a subject of conversation all over the West. Local residents did not take such pride in it; they knew the evicted tenants were in business again in another part of the city.

The Sands was not the only vice area. Individuals of sufficient means could patronize Lou Harper's place at 219 Monroe. It was the finest brothel in Chicago, charged the highest prices and was invariably referred to by Madame Harper as The Mansion. Lou Harper's was not for the workingman but for the business and professional class and the rich young man about town. The proprietress attempted to give her business a show of style by attiring her girls in evening gowns rather than the customary chemise. She insisted that all should be introduced by name and did away with the practice of herding the girls into the living room and lining them up for the customer to make his selection.

The most flagrant of the town's "free and easies" was Roger Plant's Under the Willow at the southeast corner of Wells and Monroe Streets. This establishment expanded during the 1860's until it covered half a square block and was dubbed by the police "Roger's Barracks." Roger was a small

Englishman from Yorkshire. His wife, who had borne him twenty children, including several sets of twins, was a huge woman who had grown up on the waterfront in Liverpool and was the actual boss of the place. It was Roger, however, who had chosen the name Under the Willow as an expression of his sentimental side and it was Roger who had painted on every flaring blue shade in the entire series of buildings the large gilt question, "Why not?" a phrase that was repeated frequently on the streets every evening. The police seldom bothered Roger's place. He paid his toll "with extreme regularity" and there was also the practical consideration, as the police expressed it, that trying to raid the barracks would have been "like pulling in an elephant." During the Civil War, Roger made a small fortune. At its close he decided to become a landowner and farmer, explaining that "a country life was best for the children." He also became a patron of the most fashionable race tracks and otherwise "blossomed into respectability." To this Frederic Francis Cook, one of the city's ablest reporters, was to add as a postscript, "Well, why not?"

Still another collection of brothels was to be found on Wells Street. Long John Wentworth, attempting to stamp them out, thundered that "inefficient city officers allowed gamblers to settle and with them came the disciples of Potiphar's wife and that crowd of moral and social outcasts which gamblers instinctively draw around themselves wherever they go." The street was in

HOUGH HOUSE, 1866

such ill repute that the property holders away from the street's vice area sought to obliterate the disgrace to themselves and to Captain William Wells, a hero of the Fort Dearborn Massacre. They petitioned the City Council to change the name to Fifth Avenue, assuming that an affront to New York's most fashionable street was less to be censured than despoiling the name of a Chicago hero.

Another section of the city that Long John wanted to tear down was Conley's Patch, a collection of hundreds of the "dirtiest, vilest, most rickety, one-sided, leaning forward, propped up, tumbled-down, sinking fast, low-roofed and most miserable shanties." It was the worst of several "patches" which came to life during the winter months when the close of navigation on the Great Lakes added thousands of idle sailors to the town's population. Chicago was the foremost grain and lumber market in the country and much of this commerce was carried by water. During the 1860's more than thirteen thousand vessels a year docked at the port. Some of the sailors took winter work in the forests of Wisconsin and Michigan but a larger proportion found temporary quarters in such patches as that of Mother Conley, whom the Chicago *Times* felt it was in no danger of libeling when it said she was "one of those unfortunate individuals in whom love of liquor is the ruling passion."

Mother Conley was an aging virago who gave the patch its name but its ruler was a powerful procuress known only as the Bengal Tigress. In addition to her other pleasures, the Bengal Tigress loved to fight. When she was in a boisterous mood the men in the patch barred their doors and windows and stayed out of sight. She was reputed to have torn down, single-handed, several of the shanties in one of her rages. The police avoided her as much as possible and when it was necessary to lock her up a sizable squad was sent for the purpose. Fortunately, the police station was nearby in the old Armory at Adams and Franklin so the officers had only a short distance to transport their obstreperous prisoner. Patrol wagons were scarce and police had to bring their victims in as best they could. An officer in the Bridgeport district, faced with the problem of getting Jimmy Kilfoil, an Archer Avenue character, into a cell, loaded the inebriated Jimmy into a wheelbarrow and pushed him the two miles to the Armory.

Police raided the patches and brothels at intervals but with little effect. After one raid, the *Tribune* reported "police authorities invited a score or two of the demi-monde in the South Division, on Saturday night, to be locked up at the Armory till Sunday morning. The raids were not successful, as usual, many of the girls being absent in places of amusement." The concentration of brothels is indicated by a police report that in one night's raid they had broken up "fourteen dens of infamy and vice" in a two-block area on Clark Street. Gamblers were also targets of the mayor. A short time after the raid on The Sands, Long John led a raid on Burrough's Place, one of the local gambling dens. Two officers were sent around to gain entrance by a back door. When the surprised gamblers fled to the street they found the huge mayor and a squad of police waiting for them. Long John left nothing to chance. He personally supervised the booking of the prisoners. When the gamblers' attorney tried to speak to his clients through the bars of an open window, the mayor seized the lawyer and personally threw him into another cell.

Long John's war on the vice districts did not cause him to neglect what he considered the abuses of the more respectable elements of the city. First to catch his eye were the awnings and signs which the merchants had erected over the downtown sidewalk. It is not known if some of these were hung too low to permit the passage of the six feet six inches of Long John Wentworth, but more diminutive Chicagoans were in agreement that the signs were a menace and an eyesore. Businessmen had also added to the clutter with boxes and display cases on the sidewalks. The mayor decided to put an end to such practices. As his experience with reform had taught him to expect little in the way of co-operation, he undertook to correct the situation himself.

On the night of June 18, 1857, he summoned the police force and gave orders that every overhanging sign, awning, and all posts or other obstruc-

RESULTS OF LONG JOHN WENTWORTH'S SIGN RAID, 1857

tions in the downtown streets were to be removed immediately. As the police started down the street to carry out his command a series of express wagons he had hired to stand by for further orders began to appear out of nearby alleys and livery stables. All the loose signs, awnings and display cases were ripped off and loaded into the wagons. The mayor ordered all of the debris taken to the municipal market building in the center of Randolph Street north of State where the signs were piled up until such time as their owners could retrieve them. The next morning Chicago found the downtown streets free of every obstruction that had been blocking the sidewalks. The merchants complained about the violation of their rights but Long John sensed the public was on his side and refused to let them put the signs or awnings back up. One dentist lost a repulsive set of mechanical false teeth under a glass bell which were capable of "masticating the air for twenty-five days at a time." He refused to claim his property but took the opportunity to advertise that "Long John or one of his imps, or someone else, stole my sign away, but not my official instruments. I remain at 77 Lake Street, Tremont Block." The mayor was also charged with preparing the force for the raid by a generous distribution of bourbon. He admitted that whiskey had been given to the force but denied anyone had been given too much drink on the grounds that he had poured every man's drink personally!

The police who executed this raid were known as the leather-badge force. Their name was derived from the leather insignia that Long John had designed and required them to wear on the plain uniforms made to his specifications. The police were distinguishable only by the heavy canes which they carried during the day and the heavy batons they wielded at night. Instead of whistles, the police were provided with "creakers," such as had been used by the watchmen of London for three centuries.

When John C. Haines succeeded Wentworth as mayor in 1858, the police were given uniforms with a short blue frock coat, a navy blue cap with a gold band and a brass star. When Wentworth returned to the mayor's chair he stripped the force of its finery and restored his plain garb and leather badges. In the name of economy, he reduced the size of the force to a captain, six lieutenants and fifty patrolmen; they were to police a city of more than one hundred thousand. As a result of his refusal to reconsider his action and expand the police force, a law was put through the legislature setting up an independent police board and taking the control of the force out of the mayor's hands.

On the night the new board held its first meeting, Long John called the entire police force to City Hall. At about 2 o'clock in the morning, after the new board had adjourned, the mayor had the force called to attention and made a speech lauding the men as America's finest police. Then he had

CORNER OF LAKE AND STATE STREETS, 1866

a surprise for them. Having learned, he said, that the new board was going to fire them all, he wanted to spare them that humiliation by discharging them himself. The firings were to take place immediately. The mayor's action, which at a minimum was capricious, left the city without police protection until the following morning. The papers, in reporting the episode, charged that the city had been turned over to "burglars, robbers and incendiaries." However, as the lawless elements had no way of anticipating their good fortune, the night passed with only two robberies. The newspapers took consolation in the fact that one of the thefts had occurred at State and Van Buren, "one of the most frequented thoroughfares" in the city.

Early the next morning the police board was hastily called into a special session. A new superintendent of police was appointed and about two dozen patrolmen rehired. Requirements for members of the new force were published soon afterwards. All were required to be more than five feet six inches tall, were forbidden mustaches and required to wear their whiskers "à la militaire." The leather badges vanished forever and the police were given new uniforms, necessary, as the announcement explained, "to distinguish a policeman from a drayman or a baggage wagon driver."

There was never a full explanation from the mayor of why he had fired the force. The *Tribune* charged that it was a sly bit of sabotage to discredit the Republican Party before the impending election. As the police board was predominantly Republican, the paper charged Wentworth was trying to force it to act immediately on the fifteen hundred applications for police jobs. As "19 out of every 20" would have to be disappointed, the majority of the men would tend to side with the Democrats on election day. The *Tribune* concluded an editorial on the episode with the indignant comment that "the offense deserves punishment in the penitentiary, but unfortunately it has not been provided against by statute, for the reason it was not deemed possible that such an act would ever be committed on the same principle that the Spartans had no rule for the punishment of patricide."

In 1861, Long John retired temporarily to his farm at Summit, returning at intervals to serve on public commissions or give the city a bit of advice. He sold his newspaper when he retired from politics. If he wanted an audience he had only to rent a hall and advertise that he was to give a lecture. He always drew a full house. Chicago thought he was a big man, even if he had not been quite the size to change the operations of either the laws or the lawless.

Allan Pinkerton, who had been hired as Chicago's first detective nearly a decade before, also found the task of dealing with the formidable underworld too large. Within a year he said he was "impressed with the importance of establishing a detective agency which would be independent of political influence and by whose efforts the criminal could be punished without fear or personal favor." The city hall was not a favorable climate for such an agency, so he formed a private detective force. Within a short time, most of the buildings in the business district were guarded by a corps of watchmen under his direction. To Chicago's businessmen it was more practicable to buy honesty as they bought everything else than to try to improve the quality of law enforcement through the unpredictable channels of municipal reform.

Attempts at reform were small and sporadic. In 1863 the Chicago Erring Women's Refuge for Reform opened its doors. A few years later a special department of the Washingtonian Home was opened for "female inebriates" in what was formerly the large house of C. J. Hull at Halsted and Polk. By 1870, a need for more constructive measures was felt and a Society for the Promotion of Social Purity was formed to "help the fallen" and study the causes of prostitution. Despite these gestures, however, Chicago remained a place that an editorialist described in the St. Louis *Democrat* as a town of "fast horses, faster men, falling houses and fallen women."

INVITATION TO A PUBLIC BALL, 1851

Elegance on a Grand Scale

SOCIETY as it existed in the older communities of the East was unknown in Chicago until after the Civil War. Visitors frequently commented on the absence of any women on the streets. One traveler confessed that "as to the ladies, I did not see them in the West and have not a word to say respecting their beauty." An author in the *Atlantic Monthly* found the streets "very peculiar in not having a lady walking on them—by this I mean that I did not meet a woman who seemed to claim that title or any title much above that of an ordinary domestic."

The only social affairs with any pretensions to elegance were the Bachelors' Assembly Balls at the Tremont House. These were planned and sponsored by the town's young men to repay the families in whose homes they had been entertained (and who might have eligible daughters). The single girls were so few that it was impossible to make up a sizable party with them alone. As a consequence, a bachelor's invitation traditionally included all the feminine members of the family, including the mother.

If there were any divisions among Chicago society during the fifties, they were formed principally by the choice of a church. A few congregations were recognized as aristocratic. Membership or attendance in these was a valid passport to social recognition. On the North Side, fashionable worshippers attended either St. James Episcopal Church, where William B. Ogden was a regular occupant of a pew, or the North Presbyterian Church around the corner. North Presbyterian was known as McCormick's Church because it was so thoroughly dominated by the theology and philanthropy of Cyrus H. McCormick. The most select congregation in the South Division was that of the Second Presbyterian Church at Wabash and Washington. Among its members were such political adversaries as Long John Wentworth and William "Deacon" Bross, one of the owners of the *Tribune*. The church building was erected of tar rock, a blue bituminous limestone that exuded black pitch and resulted in a mottled appearance that caused it to be dubbed the church of the spotted saints.

Many members of the Second Presbyterian found the easy morality of Chicago alien to the principles of their New England upbringing. They were willing to concede the city was the place to make a fortune, but they were not reconciled to what they considered the horrors of living among so much wickedness. After talking the situation over with their minister, the Reverend Dr. Robert Patterson, they embarked on a trip north from Chicago in search of a location for a community where Presbyterian standards of morality would be less threatened. Finally, after following a deer path through heavy groves of trees, the group came to a site near the edge of Lake Michigan where nothing was visible but lake and forest. As the spot seemed to be satisfactorily isolated, it was chosen as the spot for the new village, to be called Lake Forest. Jed Hotchkiss, a landscape architect, was engaged to lay out the town as a model community; the new settlers counted on their own ideas to make it a model of moral rectitude.

The Methodists were also restive about the moral influences of the young city, particularly about the absence of a suitable school in which to train their children. In 1850, a group of young men, all under forty years of age, met in the offices of lawyer Grant Goodrich and outlined plans for a midwest university around which might spring "a community of desirable citizens." There were practical reasons for their hopes of success. Dr. John Evans, who with Orrington Lunt and Goodrich was a leader in developing plans for the university, estimated it would cost a thousand dollars less to educate a son near Chicago than at Yale or Harvard. Lunt thought he had found the ideal site for the university near a grove of oak trees on the lake shore north of the city. The trustees agreed with his choice and on January 28, 1851, the state granted the trustees a charter for the establishment of Northwestern University. It was not until 1855 that the first students were

NORTHWEST CORNER OF LaSALLE AND RANDOLPH STREETS, showing Courthouse Square, 1864

enrolled—only ten in number. The students wore a uniform cap while their two professors appeared in Prince Albert coats and tall silk hats.

It remained to establish a community of desirable citizens. This was also accomplished by the trustees; they purchased nearly three hundred acres lying west of the University, laid it out in lots and gave it the name of Evanston after Dr. John Evans. The original plan had been to name the new suburb after Lunt, but he refused to leave his house in Chicago where the waves of Lake Michigan washed almost up to his door. The early commuters from Evanston had little in the way of streets or sidewalks to aid them. Those who worked in the city carried lanterns to and from the Evanston station each day. When they boarded the Chicago and Milwaukee train, pulled by a wood-burning locomotive, they left a row of lanterns standing on the platform for their return in the evening. The Methodists, strict believers in temperance, forbade the sale of liquor in the new community. The saloon keepers' association sued to set aside the ban on liquor, but finally lost its case in the Supreme Court. The Methodists were inclined to accept the final court hearing as an indication of intervention by Divine Providence. The lawyer for the distillers and saloon keepers was too intoxicated to speak; Harvey Hurd, the attorney for Evanston, was required to present both sides to the court. It would have been rather a severe setback if he had lost his own case.

In Chicago, the outstanding date on the social calendar was New Year's Day, when the girls received gentlemen callers in a day-long ritual that began at 10 o'clock in the morning. Lists were kept of the number of carefully groomed visitors in white gloves and swallowtails and these records were minutely compared during the next twenty-four hours to see who had triumphed and who had failed. Every house had its own refreshments. This custom added to the arduousness of the day; the callers could eat only so much chicken salad or scalloped oysters, no matter by how lovely a hand it was prepared. Serving of wine was considered "fast," except in the West Division, where the large southern colony often augmented its mahogany sideboard with a decanter of madeira or a bowl of eggnog, a fact that had as much to do with the traffic in that direction as the charm of the southern girls.

Almost all entertaining was done at home. Every party of any size required such an expenditure of energy and planning that few were eager to play the role of hostess. Invitations had to be written in the hostess' own hand and delivered personally. Sending invitations by mail was considered to be the worst of form because of the danger of their getting lost. For many years, Chicagoans refused to trust a message of such importance as a party invitation to a paid messenger. The only concession was to permit the hostess to send the invitation up to the house by her coachman or footman while she sat in the carriage. On the day of the party all the food had to be prepared at home; caterers were not yet considered stylish. In the summer, the girls might wear corsages of prairie flowers but during the winter months flowers could be had only from the single florist who kept a shop and greenhouse south of the city near Cleaverville at Thirty-fifth Street.

Visitors were likely to describe Chicago society as a mushroom aristocracy. Because of the newness of local society, there were many opportunities for sophisticated witnesses to subject it to ridicule. One supercilious visitor from Albany, New York, complained that at a reception given by one of the most prominent men of Chicago, he met "out of a company of thirty-six men, ten pork packers, three butchers, four railroad men, two bankers, one lawyer, eight doctors and a number of clerks." He noted a "prominent fiddler" had come "dressed in swallowtails, a checked vest, green necktie and red gloves." At another party the same fastidious reporter was offended by the sight of "a young man whose parents do a large business in the retail boot and shoe trade who danced with one of the prettiest girls in the room, whilst his cheek was swollen with an enormous quid of tobacco."

There were evidences, however, that Chicago was trying to catch up to the times in both society and style. The German Cotillion, which Empress Eugénie had designed to take the place of schottisches, redowas and polkas for proper French young ladies and their escorts, found its way to Chicago

LaSALLE STREET FROM COURTHOUSE SQUARE, 1866

during the same season it was introduced in New York at the Schermerhorn costume ball. The intricate, formal dance was immediately popular and remained a favorite until the end of the century.

Simplicity was the theme of most of the local styles. Not many years before a good number of Chicago women were riding to church on horseback behind their husbands. They continued to be cautious in adopting fancier ways, particularly as their husbands' reputations in the business community might be damaged if people thought the family's money was going for fancy clothes and other luxuries rather than investments in land. When the *Chicago Magazine of Fashion, Music and Home Reading* was founded to bring culture to Chicago homes, the editors reminded readers its purpose was "to give home fashions; styles that do not involve a great outlay of money and which can be utilized by Western women in their homes." They added with provincial pride that "we omit mentioning many rose-colored or violet-tinted silks or point-lace sets; because the majority of our readers do not wear such articles and we do not want them to look upon such things as necessary either to their comfort or happiness. We would rather be the useful friends of the American representative woman in her family than the protégé of the greatest lady foreign soil ever produced."

The advice of the *Chicago Magazine* was usually of this practical nature. One report was written with special reference to the Chicago weather. "The uncertainty and inclemency of the spring weather interferes sadly with the permanency of a new toilet, since, if one day is warm enough for a parasol, the next demands a resume of cloak and furs." The fashion arbiter continued with a suggestion that a "warm underwaist" be worn with spring suits and warned against "entirely tight outside garments hardly suitable for the street [which] display the form too liberally for the promenade, especially upon ladies of middle age." If some ladies were too bold, others were perhaps not quite honest. The magazine suggested that the Greek bodice be worn by "flat-chested persons who desire a fuller outline of figure" and gave instructions for forming its shape with folds of velvet or muslin or silk.

Most of the town's fashionable gowns were styled by seamstresses from patterns in Godey's Lady's Book, the Report of Fashions or the Dressmakers' and Milliners' Guide. So complete was the reign of the dressmaker that the Chicago Magazine found it necessary to advance a series of arguments in favor of ready-to-wear clothing; the women were assured they could now go out in such a dress in a Chicago gale and not be afraid of unraveling "yards of ruffling and bolts of lace."

The informal nature of most social life was reflected in the popularity of skating and sleighing. It was around these activities rather than around formal balls and parties that most of the social events were centered. "Picknicking" was a favorite pastime; after collecting the members of their set, young couples clambered into a low, racy-looking sleigh piled high with hay and buffalo robes and drove north to a friend's house or an inn for a supper and a dance to music most frequently furnished by a German band. Skating was as popular as sleighing. Skaters patronized one of five rinks where the younger members of society were to be found curvetting, wheeling and freezing through the forward roll, the Dutch roll, the figure three, the double roll, the figure eight and all the other maneuvers so important in their vocabulary.

The severe Chicago winters did not catch the editors of the Chicago Magazine unaware. "Not less interesting," its fashion expert reported, "now that winter has shown its true colors and the cold breath of the lake visits us, is the study of the articles of comfort and underwear which combine no little elegance with their increasing utility. Colored trousers for street wear (under the dress) are a necessity in western cities, where soft coal leaves its tinges on everything that dares to be white. Ladies make up very loose Turkish drawers of opera flannel in pearl gray or ash color with embroidery of crimson or scarlet to draw on before walking out. The comfort of these garments cannot be estimated by those who have not worn them."

Less practical matters were in the minds of Chicagoans in 1860, when it was learned that Mayor Long John Wentworth had left for Montreal with an invitation for Albert Edward, Prince of Wales (later Edward VII), who was then on a tour of Canada, to visit Chicago. The city's numerous foreign

CORNER OF CLARK AND WATER STREETS, 1866

societies began polishing up their regalia and practicing special drills for the parade they were certain would be part of the celebration. Ladies who had hopes of being invited to the elaborate formal ball planned for the prince sent hastily to the East for special gowns. Disappointment was widespread when word was received that the prince had accepted the offer only if he could come incognito as Baron Renfrew. He stipulated there were to be no honors or attention other than those "any English gentleman might be given."

Some placed the blame on the mayor for such an arrangement, reasoning that he thought he would be able to dominate a civic reception much easier than a formal ball. On his side, the mayor used the editorial columns of his Chicago *Democrat* to justify accepting the prince's terms, explaining that the prince's wishes were really those of most Chicagoans, who did not like "kow-towing to royalty."

The morning before the prince was to arrive, Mayor Wentworth and a committee of citizens took the Michigan Central train for Detroit to meet the prince and his party. There were no ceremonies, according to the reporters who were present, not even the customary introductions all around. Finally, everyone climbed aboard the prince's special train—but with the British and Americans traveling in separate cars. Every precaution had been taken for the prince's safety and a special pilot engine preceded his train by about ten minutes to be sure that no accident should mar his visit.

43 ELEGANCE ON A GRAND SCALE

Chicago's enthusiasm for his appearance could not be entirely restrained. The railroad station was brilliantly illuminated for his arrival and a crowd of about five thousand was pressing about for a view of the royal tourist. Many wore special medallions which had been prepared in honor of the visit. The satisfaction of the group at the station was slight. The prince was taken quickly to a carriage and driven to the Richmond House, where the entire second floor had been redecorated and refurnished before his arrival. The following morning the prince stayed behind the closed shutters of his apartments while crowds milled around the hotel in the hopes of catching a glimpse of him.

During the morning, a committee of Mayor Wentworth, William B. Ogden, William Bross and E. W. McComas called on Lord Lyons, the British minister accompanying the prince. They presented the nobleman with an address of welcome for the prince that was equally a document of surrender for Chicago's hopes of carrying out its elaborate plans. "Learning that his lordship's fatigue arising from the exciting scenes through which he so recently passed would render such attention undesirable to him, we have forborne from every demonstration calculated to disturb his privacy and repose," the committee promised. If this forbearance excluded a grand ball, it was not taken to rule out a parade. The prince, who had agreed to a tour of the city, could hardly escape when his route took him down Wabash Avenue and back up Michigan while a crowd of fifty thousand—then about half the population of the city—lined the sidewalks to watch. Nor was he able to protest effectively when the city's fire department fell into line behind him with its new engines decked out in flowers and followed by the usual floats representing the town's industries.

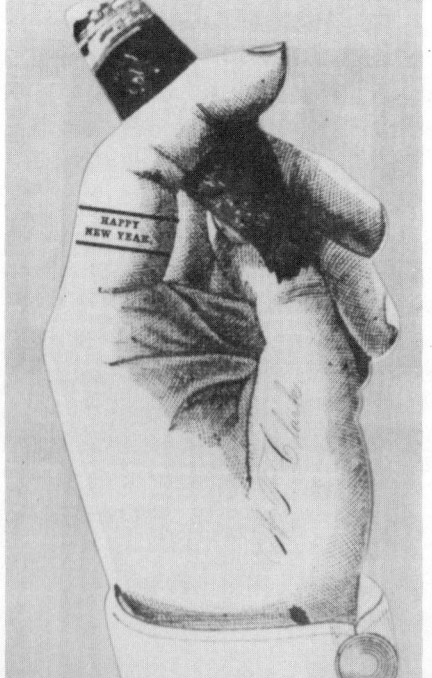

A NEW YEAR'S DAY CALLING CARD

After the parade the prince was taken to see the Courthouse, the pumping works which kept the water flowing in the Illinois and Michigan Canal, the Chicago Historical Society and other points of civic pride. He expressed some disappointment that he had not been allowed to visit one of Chicago's towering grain elevators, so an additional excursion to one of these was undertaken with Fernando Jones, the city's unofficial host to distinguished guests, acting as guide. In the evening, the prince left on his special train for Dwight, where he was to do some shooting, leaving a nervous and divided Chicago to appraise the success of his visit.

The uneasiness with which the young city had anticipated its first experience with royalty, especially English, was reflected in the editorial columns of the *Tribune*. It was able to record "with great thankfulness that the visit of Baron Renfrew and his party did not bring out, in this city, the exhibition of vulgar curiosity and a more vulgar flunkeyism which many feared. On the whole, the people behaved very well. There was, as Princes are rare in this country, a general desire to get a glimpse of royalty, but we have not heard that anyone forced himself upon the distinguished strangers nor that any outrageous breach of propriety was committed."

In this respect, Chicago counted itself ahead of New York, where the young ladies pressed about the prince at a grand ball in a manner which the Duke of Newcastle observed was "not in strict accordance with good breeding." When Long John Wentworth was asked how it felt to sit next to the future King of England, he replied: "I was not sitting beside the prince. He sat beside me."

Eight years were to pass after Chicago's disappointing experience with royalty before the city staged its first society function of any magnificence. The occasion, actually the birth of Chicago society, was a Charity Ball at Crosby's Opera House, suggested to Chicagoans by P. G. Gilmore, the Boston band leader who was never happier than when dealing with the colossal. Society columnist Peregrine Pickle stated the subject of the grand ball in a style that was at least succinct:

> Let them [in the East] learn that Chicago can do enough business in hogs and horn cattle on Saturday to make them dizzy, hear better sermons Sunday and pay more for them, array herself in a manner on Monday that would make the lilies sick, not to speak of Solomon, and drive a fiddler *in articulo mortis* either of himself or the last strand of his catgut Chicago now proposes to show them the finest men, the handsomest women, the most elegant toilets, the largest ball floor, the handsomest ball room, the best music and the best supper ever known in this country. . . . The reputation of Chicago should henceforth rank as high for balls as for wheat.

The arrangements for so important an affair were not entrusted to the

JOHN B. DRAKE, MANAGER OF THE TREMONT HOUSE, ABOUT 1864

ladies but were taken over by such men as Joseph Medill, George M. Pullman, Isaac Arnold, Mahlon D. Ogden and Jonathan Young Scammon, the same group which directed the other phases of Chicago life. The price of tickets was set at $20 but the Yankee influence was so strong in this city of new millionaires that loud cries of protest went up over this extravagance. The committee, who were mostly Yankees themselves, were aware that not to attend was to be out of society, and saw no reason for lowering the price. The preparations were so elaborate that the affair had to be postponed in order to allow time for the decorations at the opera house to be completed. As the time for the ball approached, Chicagoans forgot the importance of being practical. The tickets, which had sold slowly at first, were suddenly not to be had at any price. Gowns were chosen without respect to cost and "tearful were the faces of many" whom economy or lack of funds reduced to the Flora McFlimsey dilemma of "Nothing to Wear." At the milliners and mantua-makers there was "mounting in hot haste." Many dresses were ordered from London, Paris and New York while Chicago dressmakers found themselves floundering in mazes of gores and flounces. The hairdressers sent emergency appeals to the East for more hair to build up the elegant "waterfalls" with which every fashionable lady hoped to top her coiffure.

The ball was scheduled to begin at ten o'clock. As "there was no distinction in being late," the opera house was crowded early in the evening. Many Chicagoans arrived in carriages but those who lived near the opera house strolled over from their Michigan and Wabash Avenue homes as though they were attending a neighborhood party. There were some who walked because the livery operators had raised their prices for the evening and it was not considered good business to pay more than the market price. The stage of the opera house was decorated with flags from the world's nations, standing in front of a stage-high backdrop that had been painted for the occasion. Over the center of the stage hung a chandelier forty-five feet in circumference and holding ninety-five lights festooned with flowers and leaves. An artificial platform from the stage extended out into the auditorium to form the dance floor. Overhead a chandelier seventy-five feet in diameter hung beneath a double canopy of fresh flowers, extending in festoons to the far corners of the auditorium and populated by an inanimate flock of stuffed doves.

As elegant as the decorations was the supper arranged by caterer John Wright, whose restaurant under the opera house was the city's most fashionable eating place. In the music hall next to the opera house, a table was spread with delicacies and ornamented with such architectural-gastronomic features as "a Swiss chateau in color, a church, *Charlotte russe de la Reine*, pyramids *d'Espagnol*, pagoda temple, four illuminated ice baskets in colors, two nougat temples and ornamental prairie chicken patties, boned turkey, boneless hams, a boar's head, patties of quail" and other luxuries. The bewilderment with which the guests must have viewed the skyline of their supper table extended to the grand march. Gilmore neglected to tell the committee that the "grand old march" would precede the "grand march" and the leaders had to be called back for consultation with the band leader. Two orchestras furnished the music, Gilmore's Boston Band playing for the dances while a reed orchestra provided the accompaniment for the promenades.

Generally, Chicagoans preferred more robust entertainment than Gilmore's Charity Ball. The most popular event of the year was one which excluded the ladies entirely—the annual Thanksgiving Day game dinner given at the Tremont House (and later at the Grand Pacific) by hotel man John B. Drake. The menus for these affairs suggested the continuing identification of Chicago with the frontier. The number of dishes dwarfed the traditional Thanksgiving Day feast. To be invited to one of these dinners was a sign that a young man had been accepted by the business community— which in Chicago was identical with being accepted socially.

A menu from one of the dinners is a measure of the host's liberality:

THE NEW TREMONT HOUSE, corner Lake and Dearborn Streets

SOUP

Venison, Hunter Style   Game Broth

FISH

Boiled Trout with Shrimp Sauce
Baked Black Bass with Claret Sauce

BOILED

Leg of Mountain Sheep. Ham of Bear. Venison Tongue. Buffalo Tongue.

ROAST

Loin of Buffalo. Wild Goose. Quail. Mountain Sheep. Red Head Duck. Jack Rabbit. Blacktail Deer. Coon. Canvasback Duck. Prairie Chicken. English Hare. Bluewing Teal. Partridge. Widgeon. Saddle of Venison. Pheasant. Mallard Duck. Wild Turkey. Spotted Grouse. Black Bear. Opossum. Leg of Elk. Wood Duck. Sandhill Crane. Ruffled Grouse. Cinnamon Bear.

BROILED

Bluewing Teal. Jacksnipe. Blackbirds. Reedbirds. Partridge. Pheasant. Quail. Butterball Ducks. English Snipe. Ricebirds. Redwing. Starling. Marsh Birds. Plover. Gray Squirrel. Buffalo Steak. Rabbits. Venison Steak.

ENTREES

Antelope Steak with Mushroom Sauce. Rabbit, Braised with Cream Sauce. Fillet of Grouse with Truffles. Venison Cutlet with Jelly Sauce. Ragout of Bear, Hunter Style. Oyster Pie.

SALADS

Shrimp.   Prairie Chicken.   Celery.

ORNAMENTAL DISHES

Pyramid of Game en Bellevue. Boned Duck au naturel. Pyramid of Wild Goose Liver in Jelly. The Coon at Night. Boned Quail in Plumage. Redwing Starling on Tree. Partridge in Nest. Prairie Chicken en Socie.

As the menu makes plain, the standards of Chicago were those of the gourmand rather than the gourmet. From charity balls to game dinners, everything had to be on the grand scale.

OLD MARKET HALL ON STATE STREET, 1848

The Little Giant and the Rail Splitter

IF MAKING money was Chicago's vocation, politics was its hobby and pursued with equal dedication. The language of political argument was either eulogistic or vituperative; the reaction to such incendiary oratory was violent nearly as often as it was reasonable. Among the political issues of the day none caused greater indignation than the dominance of the South in national politics. One measure after another for the improvement of the Northwest had been defeated by southern votes in Congress. Throughout the Midwest there was a growing determination to break up the power of this southern bloc.

In the vocabulary of the transplanted Puritans who were the leaders of Chicago, rightness and righteousness were the same. Motivated by a practical desire to achieve political recognition, the midwesterners found inspiration for their crusade in an abhorrence to the institution of slavery maintained by the southern states. Joseph Medill, the editor of the *Tribune*, began to talk of a new Republican Party that would break the power of the South and East by forming a new coalition of North and West. The new party was not to be formed on political and economic principles primarily but on the moral issue of slavery. As the new party took form, Chicago became the testing ground for ideas that were to divide the country in civil war but ultimately to form the framework for reunion on a basis better suited to a free nation.

Anti-slavery sentiments were popular in Chicago. It had been an early stop on the Underground Railroad that transported fugitive slaves to Canada and freedom. Only perfunctory efforts were made to enforce the Fugitive Slave Law and it was not uncommon for runaway slaves to be loaded aboard Canadian-bound lake ships in large groups of twenty or thirty. One of the managers of the Underground Railroad was Allan Pinkerton. His house on West Adams Street often was surrounded by groups of petitioning Negroes seeking help for a trembling relative or fugitive friend.

Another leader of the anti-slavery movement was Dr. C. V. Dyer, a physician who was credited with helping the first slave to come to Chicago make his escape. He was always ready to aid the fugitives. On one occasion he heard a commotion outside his office and saw that an owner had just captured a runaway slave and was dragging him down the street. A crowd had gathered but was afraid to interfere because of the penalties of the Fugitive Slave Law. Dr. Dyer rushed down from his office, slipped through the crowd until he was behind the southerner and then cracked the slave owner over the head with a heavy cane. As the owner fell to the ground stunned, his slave escaped down the street. Dr. Dyer made no effort to flee but shouted "Make way here! There's a man hurt!" The southerner, slowly regaining his wits after the hard jolt to his head, willingly accepted the fortuitous offer of first aid from the sympathetic doctor.

Dr. Dyer's cane was itself the memento of another exploit. A plantation owner who had tracked down his slave and lodged the Negro in the city jail for safekeeping registered at a downtown hotel to spend the night. The doctor, hearing of the incident, assembled some friends and together they called on the southerner at his hotel. What they wanted, they said, was to offer him protection from the mob that was gathering to run him out of town. The victim of the hoax, unwilling to test the veracity of a story that might easily have been true, left Chicago that night without attempting to collect his property from the jail. For his part in the hoax, Dr. Dyer was given an inscribed cane by his friends. In a similar episode, a Missourian with the miserly name of Uriah Hinch was reported in the papers to have left town without his slave when city authorities "refused him protection."

The founding of the Republican Party presented a confusing issue to the unsophisticated voter, who was as firmly Democratic in politics as he was anti-slavery in his morals. The choice was made more difficult when the great spokesman for the Democratic Party in its efforts to preserve its own unity and that of the nation became Stephen A. Douglas. "The Little Giant," as he was known, was popular in Chicago and an infallible hero to the Irish, who made up about 20 per cent of the population. During the ten years before the Civil War, when public opinion swayed first toward Democratic compromise and then firmly away from it toward Republicanism and abolition, Douglas was to experience the gamut of political fortune.

He came into his greatest disfavor immediately following the passage of the Kansas-Nebraska Act, which allowed the settlers in the new territories to make their own decision about slavery. Traveling westward after his support had resulted in passage of the bill in Congress, he said he was able to go from Boston to Chicago by the light of his burning effigies. He refused to evade the problem, and on his return announced he would speak the evening of September 1st from the steps of Market Hall. On the afternoon of the day scheduled for his speech, the flags on the ships in the harbor and river were lowered to half mast. For half an hour in the evening the bells of many churches tolled mournfully as a sign of their displeasure at the compromise with slavery embodied in the law. Because of this hostility, a rumor circulated that Douglas would appear with a bodyguard of five hundred Irish.

That evening an uneasy crowd of about ten thousand filled the streets, windows and rooftops of buildings near Market Hall. When Douglas stepped to the front of the platform, his voice was smothered by a wave of hisses and groans and an answering volley of shouts and cheers. William "Deacon" Bross, sitting by the platform as a reporter for the *Tribune*, hurled what the crowd considered a taunting question at Douglas. According to another reporter, "it was a firebrand in the midst of the combustibles." The audience became a mob and for nearly four hours drowned every attempt of Douglas to speak. Added to the hoots and jeers were rotten apples and other fruit thrown at the platform where he stood. Convinced at last that no speech was possible, Douglas hurled his final words at the crowd: "Abolitionists

SHERMAN HOUSE looking west on Randolph Street with Courthouse on the left, by *Edwin Whitefield*

CHICAGO IN 1853

of Chicago! It is now Sunday morning. I'll go to church and you may go to Hell."

Another source of hostility toward Douglas was the Know-Nothing or Native American Party that resented his alliance with the Irish. In the year following the Market Hall riot, the Know-Nothings, who feasted on a chauvinistic hatred of all foreigners, were able to elect their candidate, Dr. Levi D. Boone, mayor of Chicago. It was not a wise choice for a city in which almost 50 per cent of the population was of foreign origin. Boone's first administrative act was to decree that all policemen must be native-born Americans, a blow which more than decimated the force and was a particular insult to the city's Irish. Not satisfied, Boone next turned on the Germans, who made up about 25 per cent of the population. The issue over which he picked a quarrel was beer.

Before the rapid growth of the German community, beer was almost unknown in Chicago, which showed a marked preference for whiskey. But when the Germans arrived, they brought their own customs with them and tended to preserve their traditional way of life in a series of somewhat segregated communities within the city. They patronized their own German theater (probably the best in any language in the city), German churches, German trade unions and even showed a liking for patent medicine bearing German labels. They also established their own beer gardens, though at least one of these—across from St. James Episcopal Church—was Americanized in name to a tea garden. Initially, all of the beer was imported from Milwaukee, as engineers thought it impossible to construct the subterranean

THE GARDEN CITY 52

vaults needed for brewing in the swampy soil of Chicago. Adolph Mueller thought it could be done, however, and soon was brewing Chicago's first locally produced beer.

Mayor Boone, who regarded beer drinking as a foreign and un-American custom, set out to stop it. His first action was to raise the liquor license fee by 600 per cent and to recommend that no license be issued for more than three months. Both these proposals would have put most of the small saloon keepers in the German neighborhoods out of business. As the next step Boone ordered the enforcement of a half-forgotten law closing the saloons on Sunday. The Sunday closing, which the mayor made plain applied only to beer emporiums and not saloons that sold only whiskey, caused an uproar on the North Side which was so predominantly German it was known as the "Nord Seite." The first Sunday about two hundred Germans were arrested for violation of the ordinance and their trial set before Squire Henry L. Rucker, a justice of the peace whose office was opposite the Courthouse.

The case was called the morning of April 21, 1855. At the hour for the hearing, a tumult was created as the saloon keepers with about three hundred of their friends marched into the Courthouse Square accompanied by the music of a fife and drum. After threatening and defying the judge, the column retreated to Randolph and Clark and took possession of the intersection in front of the Sherman House. The police arrived and forced the mob north across the river where it disbanded. By afternoon, another crowd larger than the first had gathered and was supported by a group of Irish volunteers. It was armed with shotguns, rifles, pistols, clubs, knives and shillelaghs. Rumors of an intended raid reached City Hall and about 150 special deputies were sworn in to fight the Germans.

At 3 o'clock the mob made its way down Clark Street but was disrupted temporarily when the mayor ordered the bridge tender to swing the bridge open after half the crowd was across. Using the added time to place his forces in strategic spots, the mayor confidently ordered the bridge closed. The crowd surged forward and was soon battling the police and deputies in an effort to force its way to City Hall. One member of the mob blew off the arm of a policeman with a shotgun blast and was shot down and killed. Firing broke out on both sides until the defeated rioters retreated across the bridge carrying their wounded with them. That evening cannon were placed at the approaches to the Courthouse but the worst of the disturbances were over. The effect of these "lager beer riots" was to lessen the mayor's zeal for closing the German saloons and prohibiting beer drinking. Though he did not pursue his quarrel with the Germans, the violence during the riots discredited his party and the Know-Nothings were never again a factor in Chicago politics.

CHURCH OF THE HOLY FAMILY, 1866

Political turmoil of a different kind continued to surge through the city as the young Republican Party boldly stated its credo of no compromise with slavery. In 1858, the Republicans nominated Abraham Lincoln as their candidate for the United States Senate. His opponent was Stephen A. Douglas, who had regained a considerable part of his earlier popularity. The candidates began their campaigns with speeches from the balcony of the Tremont House on succeeding nights. Later they were to meet on the same platform in a series of debates whose significance was fully appreciated by those who heard and read the arguments of the two speakers.

Lincoln was nearly as well known as Douglas and each man had the physical vigor, political background and power of expression to state his case forcibly and well. Douglas had the greater experience of the two. For years in the House of Representatives and the Senate he had debated with the country's ablest orators. It was said that no matter how many speakers were arrayed against him, he had never been discomfited. He was bold, aggressive and when necessary, defiant. He had tremendous moral courage and with it a confidence in himself as well as his cause. Lincoln, though his experience had been more limited than that of Douglas, was also a thoroughly trained speaker. Because of the greater reputation of Douglas, Lincoln welcomed the chance to meet him in debate; he knew it was as rigorous a test as he would ever face. When the two met, each put forth his utmost strength.

Both men were conscious that Illinois was no more than an arena for their contest; their real audience was the nation. Isaac Arnold, Lincoln's friend and biographer, described it as "not a single combat" but a competition that "extended through the whole campaign [as] the American people paused to watch its progress and hung, with intense interest, upon every movement of the champions." As is always the case with those who bear the burden of compromise, Douglas had the poorer cause; he argued it with an eloquence which made the impossible seem necessary. Because of the large Democratic vote in Chicago his party won control of the state legislature (which still elected United States Senators) and he was sent to Washington. More important to the backers of Douglas was the fact he was in a good position to win the party's presidential nomination in 1860. Lincoln's friends were of a similar mind; the debates had established the ability of their candidate to deal with national issues. They said it was of small importance the Republican Party had been unable to win a place in the Senate; Lincoln would have the presidency instead.

Joseph Medill, the editor of the *Tribune*, who had shrewdly foreseen and encouraged the alignment of forces out of which came the Republican Party, was convinced that it could win in 1860 only by nominating a westerner. Lincoln did not seem an ideal candidate to Medill but because of the debates with Douglas was the logical choice to oppose the "Little Giant" whose nomination by the Democrats was taken for granted. The favorite for the Republican nomination was William H. Seward of New York. As the Republican National Committee met to select a convention site the contest appeared to be Seward against the field. This expectation enabled Illinois committeeman Norman B. Judd to persuade the committee to hold the convention in Illinois as neutral ground. Once the decision to hold the convention in Chicago was reached, the spring of the trap was set. Medill then declared for Lincoln and the *Tribune* began a sustained campaign to win the nomination for him. As a basis for Republican Party policies, Medill took the ideas outlined by Lincoln in the debates with Douglas.

To house the convention, the Republicans of Chicago erected a rectangular wooden building at the southeast corner of Lake and Market (Wacker) and named it the Wigwam. Its acoustics were so remarkable that speakers could be heard in any part of the building with little difficulty. As the opening day of the convention drew near, straw votes on the trains coming into Chicago gave Seward a tremendous lead over the other candidates. The ardent Seward supporters called themselves the Irrepressibles. After their arrival they paraded the streets behind brass bands and passed out champagne and cigars in the hotel lobbies. Medill, Judd and Arnold, who had set up headquarters in the Tremont House, ignored

THE REPUBLICAN WIGWAM WHERE LINCOLN WAS NOMINATED, 1860

the noisy demonstrations; with other members of the Illinois delegation they employed their trading abilities in dickering for votes. Lincoln had given orders there were to be no deals but he was safely out of the way in Springfield. At the political huckster shop in the Tremont there was lively bargaining. In the columns of the *Tribune*, Medill doubled his barrage of arguments in support of nominating "The Westerner," Abraham Lincoln.

The meeting at the Wigwam was Chicago's first national political convention, but there was nothing amateur about the arrangements. Medill and Judd, who were in charge of seating the delegates, put New York at one end of the hall and surrounded it with other states that were conceded to be for Seward. Pennsylvania, an important state in the doubtful column, was placed at the opposite end of the hall where it would be nearly inaccessible to New York representatives. In between as a buffer were placed the Lincoln delegations from Illinois, Indiana and New Jersey. With these arrangements perfected, the Lincoln supporters outlined a plan to assure their control of the galleries. Judd arranged with the Chicagoans who controlled the railroads to bring in Lincoln men free of charge. On the night preceding the day for the nominations the committee distributed hundreds of tickets to Lincoln boosters. All were instructed to report early to the Wigwam and jam it to the doors before the Seward supporters, who had scheduled a grand parade, could arrive to claim their seats. The next morning while the Sewardites were marching from their headquarters at the Richmond House behind an elegantly uniformed band, the Lincoln "shouters" were pouring through the three doors of the Wigwam to pack the galleries. The "shouters" did their work so effectively that reporter Murat Halstead

THE GARDEN CITY 56

wrote in the Cincinnati *Commercial* the nomination of Lincoln was followed by a sound "like all the hogs ever slaughtered in Cincinnati giving their death squeals together and a score of big steam whistles going." Adding to the pandemonium was a "stamping that made every plank and pillar in the building quiver."

The first two roll calls after the nominating and seconding speeches were concluded did not give any candidate a majority, but Lincoln's strength continued to grow. On the third ballot he lacked only a vote and a half of the total needed for nomination. Then a delegate from Ohio, a group so badly split it was considered to be without influence, asked to be recognized. He was David Kellogg Cartter, who spoke hesitatingly because of a speech impediment while a taut convention listened. "I rise (eh), Mr. Chairman (eh)," he said—the impatient delegates bent forward in their chairs—"to announce the change of four votes of Ohio from Mr. Chase to Abraham Lincoln." Halstead wrote his paper in Ohio that after a moment's silence, "there was the noise in the Wigwam like the rush of a great wind in the van of a storm—and in another breath, the storm was there. There were thousands cheering with the energy of insanity." On the roof of the Wigwam the sly and confident Lincoln men had mounted a cannon. An observer who had been shouting the results of the balloting to those outside gave the signal that Lincoln was nominated and the cannon boomed forth in a salute that spread the news to all Chicago.

The nomination of Douglas, the city's native son, by a divided Democratic convention in Baltimore came as an anticlimax to all but the city's Irish. The split among the Democrats assured the Republican Party of its first President. Jubilant Chicagoans joined the Republican Wide Awake marching clubs and, protected by oilcloth caps and capes, carried dripping oil torches through the streets. In November Lincoln was elected President and a new era of American politics and a somber chapter of American history had begun.

The Lincoln triumph had its bitter taste for his Chicago backers. Norman B. Judd who maneuvered to bring the convention to Chicago and nominated Lincoln, was passed over for the cabinet post he expected. He was later given a consolation prize in the form of a ministerial post to Prussia. Medill fared better. He wanted the postmastership for John L. Scripps, one of the partners in the *Tribune*. Charles Ray, another of the partners, said it was not wanted "wholly for the money there is in it, but as a means of extending and insuring our business and extending the influence of the *Tribune*." The argument consisted of the same combination of public interest and private gain that Chicagoans considered infallible. Medill reasoned that if Scripps received the appointment, the country postmasters of the Northwest would work to extend the newspaper's circulation; since it was a Republican newspaper, this in turn would "benefit the party," which in turn was best for the country. Scripps received the appointment and one of the foundation stones of an American newspaper empire was set into place.

Patronage, however, was overshadowed by the great question of secession. Medill counseled his readers to accept a "bloodless separation" but his candidate was not of any such mind. When the Confederate forces fired on Fort Sumter, Lincoln stood steadfast by the principles of "no compromise" that had led to the founding of the Republican Party. The first call for troops to preserve the Union was issued and Chicago prepared to take up arms.

ZOUAVE CADETS

6

The Civil War and the Chicago Conspiracy

THE PRIDE of Chicago's military forces in the years before the war had been the Zouave cadets of Colonel Elmer Ellsworth. Impressed by the valor of the French Zouaves in the Crimean War, Ellsworth had organized his own company of cadets in Chicago, modeling the uniforms after those of the French troops. Ellsworth was a fanatic about discipline. To qualify for membership in his corps, the cadets were required to sign a pledge of monastic severity. A cadet could be expelled from the group for "entering a drinking saloon at any hour day or night"; entering "a house of ill fame under any circumstances or pretext whatever"; entering a gambling saloon or gambling for any sum of money or even for playing billiards in a public hall or saloon. The latter, the pledge explained, was "interdicted not because of any objection to the game but because it is a step toward the other offenses named, and the excitement and associations of the billiard saloon naturally lead to drinking."

The cadets were famous for their precision drill. In 1860, challenging any similar organization to match their skill, they made a tour of the East for a series of contests. After appearances at West Point, New York and other eastern cities, the Chicago Zouaves returned undefeated, marching from the railroad station with their uniforms adorned with ladies' gloves, lace

MONUMENT TO STEPHEN A. DOUGLAS, 1866

handkerchiefs and dried and faded flowers as well as epaulets, swords, pistols, plumes, badges and medals. Shortly afterward, Colonel Ellsworth left the cadets to study law in the office of Abraham Lincoln in Springfield. When Lincoln was elected President, Ellsworth followed him to Washington. After the firing on Sumter, Ellsworth took a commission with the New York Fire Zouaves. Serving with them, he became the first Union officer to fall in the Civil War.

Without Ellsworth, Chicago's Zouaves disbanded for lack of leadership. The outbreak of war found the city with almost no well-trained troops. When Governor Richard Yates sent word that Chicago should raise as strong a force as possible and have it armed and equipped to march immediately, the city was in a state of alarm. There were already fears that the southern part of Illinois might try to secede to the Confederacy; the public interpreted the call for troops as a sign that Rebel forces were preparing to invade the state. A stock-taking of the city's arsenal reassured no one. The four hundred members of the militia who had been mustered into service were without arms. To meet the crisis, the city borrowed fifty muskets from a Milwaukee company. The remainder of the troops were a pawnshop army equipped with squirrel rifles, shotguns, single-barreled pistols or any other weapon that could be obtained from a gun store or pawnshop.

Only eight days after the beginning of hostilities at Sumter, the troops were ordered aboard a special train at the Illinois Central station—"destination unknown." The commander alone knew that the troops had been assigned to Cairo, in "Egypt" to guard the confluence of the Ohio and Mississippi Rivers. With only four cannon and assorted small arms, the poorly organized companies were expected to prevent supplies from being shipped to the Confederacy over the river route and to guard against an invasion of Illinois. Extensive security precautions were made necessary because of pro-slavery sentiment in the southern part of the state and the possibility that armed groups sympathetic to the South might already be secretly formed. Through skillful planning by the officials of the railroad, the troop train ran the length of the state without advance notice of its coming. The regular trains preceding it had left on schedule and been sidetracked by prearrangement. After leaving a small force to guard the wooden trestle over the Big Muddy River a short distance to the North, the expedition arrived in Cairo "to the astonishment of all and the rage of many."

Back in Chicago, Bryan Hall on the east side of the Courthouse Square was crowded for a loyalty meeting. Resolutions were adopted supporting the Union and the inevitable committee of business leaders that was part of any Chicago activity appointed. Most Chicagoans, who considered the war a crusade to stamp out the evils of slavery (and destroy the political and economic power of the South), gave it unqualified support. The Irish community, because of its sympathies for the South through the common bond of the Democratic Party, was the only area of the city where the war was unpopular. In the Irish areas of Archer Road and Bridgeport, Rebel victories were more likely to be celebrated than those of the northern armies. The possibilities of any active resistance from the Irish died away, however, when their great hero, Stephen A. Douglas, appeared before a crowd of ten thousand to pledge his support to Lincoln and ask his audience "never to permit the government to be destroyed."

Though the Irish felt themselves stubbornly bound to disapprove of the war, individually they enlisted as rapidly as any other group. And it was the Irish troops of Colonel James Mulligan's Brigade who were Chicago's first heroes of the war. On the day after Douglas spoke to his Irish followers, an announcement appeared in the papers of a rally of patriotic Irish to form a regiment of volunteers. The regiment was immediately filled. As more companies had been formed than the government could equip, the regiment was not mustered into service until June. Once accepted, it was sent to Lexington, Missouri. There the army neglected to reinforce or supply it and allowed the men to be cut off by Confederate forces. After a long and hopeless stand, the troops surrendered. Colonel Mulligan refused to give his parole that he would not fight again and was kept a prisoner for several months until exchanged for a Confederate officer prisoner. Upon returning to Chicago, Mulligan formed a new brigade to replace the one captured in Missouri. He fought at its head throughout the war until July 24, 1864, when he fell fatally wounded near Winchester, Virginia. Then, seeing that his aids' concern over his condition was increasing the danger that the colors of his troops might be captured a second time, he gave his final command: "Lay me down and save the flag."

Colonel Mulligan's dying phrase, sent home to Chicago in a hundred letters, was the inspiration for the city's patriotic song writer, George F. Root, to write a war ballad taking its title from the gallant colonel's command. Root's war songs, among them "The Battle Cry of Freedom," known as the "Northern Marseillaise" and "Tramp, Tramp, Tramp" were known by every Union soldier. The composition of a new song was an important event for Chicagoans. A crowd would gather in front of the courthouse steps to hear it sung for the first time by the city's favorite singers, Frank and Jules Lumbard. The Lumbard brothers would sing it over and over until the crowd knew the words by heart. In this way the song was widely circulated before it was printed. The tunes could not be called folk music, but their popularity was born in much the same manner as that of folk songs. Another Chicagoan who kept the Yankees singing was Henry C. Work, who wrote "Marching Through Georgia," as well as the famous temperance ballad, "Father, Dear Father, Come Home with Me Now."

Patriotic fervor was high in Chicago. Early in the war vigilance committees had been formed to watch for traitors and guard against attempts to blow up the city's powder magazines. The courthouse square was filled with tents of organizations recruiting soldiers for volunteer companies. Theater owner J. H. McVicker offered a silk flag for the first company raised in Chicago and gave it to Fred Harding's company at the Tremont House on the day the group started for Cairo. On it were the words "Retaliation! No mercy to traitors." The Board of Trade put as its first order of business the enlistment of new troops. One ardent supporter of the war, Solomon Sturges, equipped an entire regiment, The Sturges Rifles, out of his personal fortune. Letters were mailed in patriotic envelopes with pro-Union slogans emblazoned on red, white and blue borders.

The Germans' thrifty patriotism took the form of scraping large quantities of grease from under the ice on the Chicago River, which they cooked with lye to make soap. Everyone in the city boasted of McCormick's reaper factory; the newspapers promised that these new reapers, by freeing young men from the farm for the battlefield, would eventually give the North its coveted victory.

The first major break in Chicago's patriotic ranks came after the Emancipation Proclamation. Democrats who had supported the war as necessary to preserve the Union now felt its purpose had been subverted by the

Abolitionists. The leader in speaking out against the continuation of the war for such a purpose was a six-foot, forty-five-year-old editor, with "the grace of an Apollo" and snowy-white beard and hair. He was Wilbur F. Storey, editor of the Chicago Times. Storey had purchased the Times from Cyrus McCormick in 1861, intending to use it to support the conciliatory views of Stephen A. Douglas. The start of the war and the death of Douglas shortly afterward left Storey with no political champion. As the city soon learned, however, Storey could speak for himself.

The newspaper philosophy of Storey was "to print the news and raise hell." He followed it to the letter. It was Storey's newspaper which announced the execution of four murderers with American journalism's most famous headline, "Jerked to Jesus." Subheads immediately beneath this alliterative summary explained that "Two of Them, in Louisiana, Died with the Sweet Confidence of Pious People," and continued "While Yet Two Others, in Mississippi, Expired Exhorting the Public to Beware of Sisters-in-Law." During the war Storey spent money lavishly for news from the front. His instructions to his correspondents were simple: "Telegraph fully all the news you can get and when there is no news, send rumors."

It was not surprising that when Storey chose to oppose the war, he did it in the most vehement fashion possible. As his newspaper was the semi-official spokesman for the Democratic Party which controlled the City

GROUNDS OF THE CHICAGO SHARPSHOOTERS ASSOCIATION

Council and had recently elected a mayor, his views carried added authority. His diatribes against Lincoln and the war plus the relationship of his paper to the party in control of the city's administration ultimately were brought to the attention of General Ambrose E. Burnside, then in command of the military district which included Chicago. Burnside, "famous for his sideburns, his inventions in firearms, his nobility of character and his military mistakes," made one of his more illustrious errors by ordering General J. B. Sweet at Chicago to suppress the *Times*. Simultaneously, he ordered the anti-war New York *World* excluded from the mails within his military jurisdiction.

The order from Burnside against the *Times* was based on its "repeated expression of disloyal and incendiary sentiments" such as the paper's charge "the war, as waged by military satraps of the administration, is a subversion of the Constitution and the people's rights under the law." Storey, who knew another man's mistake when he saw it, accepted the news of the proposed suppression calmly. He dispatched a rider to Sweet's headquarters with instructions to report back when the troops left for the *Times* building. Meanwhile, he succeeded in getting most of the day's publication off the press and into a safe place for later distribution before the troops arrived.

When the news was circulated that the *Times* had been suppressed a crowd gathered in front of the paper on Randolph Street to protest this arbitrary military intrusion into Chicago's political differences. Shouts for Storey failed to bring the editor to the window. He sat in his office unperturbed, confident that the order would not be upheld and satisfied that meanwhile it would create a schism among the Abolitionists. The crowd continued to grow until it had reached twenty thousand—which meant it was the equal of all the Chicagoans who had voted in the previous election. The Democratic sympathizers were in a majority and the threat was frequently heard that "If the *Times* is not allowed to publish, there will be no *Tribune*."

To calm the crowd a series of Democratic speakers made talks urging patience until Burnside's order could be countermanded. Wirt Dexter, a prominent Republican lawyer, appeared to promise that his own party was urging the President to nullify the edict. Away from the scene of the demonstration a group of Republican and Democratic leaders sat down together in a tense meeting called by Judge Van H. Higgins, a large stockholder in the *Tribune*. The Republican delegation was headed by Senator Lyman Trumbull and Representative Isaac Arnold. The leader of the Democrats was the omnipresent William B. Ogden. Being practical men, the conferees did not argue about principle or the justice of the cause. Rather they adopted a cleverly worded resolution asking President Lincoln to lift the ban against the *Times* "upon the ground of expediency alone."

That night the correspondent of the New York *Herald* closed his dispatch from Chicago with the words, "At this hour the *Tribune* still stands." The streets during the night were full or rumors about the measures the *Tribune* had taken for its own defense. One of these was that Colonel Charles Jennison, a lieutenant of John Brown during the Bloody Kansas days, had enlisted a corps of gunmen and smuggled them into the lofts of various buildings about the *Tribune*. Jennison was something of a poseur who dressed cowboy fashion and was usually to be found swaggering down the street with a retinue of admirers. The crowd had no doubts that if he were about the premises of the *Tribune*, there would be no hesitancy about shooting anyone who attacked.

The tension remained high until shortly after midnight when Judge Henry Drummond of the United States District Court issued an order directing the military authorities to take no further steps in carrying out the Burnside order. "I desire to give every aid and assistance in my power to the Government and to the administration in restoring the Union," he said. "But I have always wished to treat the Government as a Government of law and a Government of the Constitution and not as Government of mere physical force. I personally have contended and shall always contend for the right of free discussion and the right of commenting under the law and under the Constitution upon the acts of officers of the Government."

The next day it was the radical Republicans who crowded around the courthouse. They were angered by the judge's ruling and by the action of their party leaders in appealing to the President to rescind the Burnside edict. Senator Trumbull tried to speak but was interrupted with cries of "Traitor" and "We want Jennison." The meeting broke up after demands for the resignation of Senator Trumbull and Representative Arnold. The next day President Lincoln revoked Burnside's order against both the *Times* and the New York *World*. Wilbur F. Storey went back to editing the *Times* as calmly as was possible for an individual of his temperament; his enemies had given his newspaper a new fame and started it on the path to prosperity.

More southern sentiment came to the surface when the government converted Camp Douglas, an induction center at Thirty-third Street and Cottage Grove, into a prisoner of war camp for Rebel troops captured at Fort Donelson. When the prisoners arrived, hopes of an early victory were raised by the sight of the southerners marching through the streets. They carried ragged old bed quilts and pieces of carpet for blankets and were clothed in homespun pants colored simon's blue or "oilnut bark." To others the sight of the bedraggled Confederate soldiers was a cause for sympathetic concern. Later a free hospital known as St. Luke's was founded where the sick of both Confederate and Union forces might be cared for by qualified nurses and physicians. Some of the captives had visited in Chicago before the war; others had relatives in the city and about 10 per cent of the prisoners were Irish. Many of the women whose homes were originally in the South formed committees to distribute food and clothing to the prisoners. On Sundays a visit to Camp Douglas became a regular part of the schedule for an afternoon drive. The situation soon became too much for the ardently patriotic Board of Trade. It passed a resolution stating that it "frowns upon and condemns any attempt to make lions and distinguished visitors of any of the prisoners now among us. We recommend to the citizens of Chicago to abstain from offering those polite and marked attentions that make [the prisoners] heroes to the manifest degradation of ourselves."

As the war progressed, the population of the camp increased to about seven thousand and the uneasiness of Chicago grew correspondingly. So few soldiers were available for guarding the camp that a special force of volunteers was enlisted to help keep watch at nights. One mass break from the camp was tried but an informer revealed the plot to the camp officials. When the prisoners rushed the wooden fence and knocked it down they found a regiment of Pennsylvania troops waiting for them. A volley from the soldiers drove most of the prisoners back to their barracks and the few who did escape were soon recaptured.

A more serious threat to the city was the "Chicago Conspiracy" in which the prisoners at Camp Douglas were to play an important role. In the spring of 1864, Jacob Thompson, a member of the Confederacy who had been

CAMP DOUGLAS, 1864, by Albert E. Myers

DEMOCRATIC NATIONAL AMPHITHEATER ON MICHIGAN AVENUE, 1864
Lithograph by Charles Shober

Secretary of the Interior under President Buchanan, went to Canada with $250,000 in sterling exchange for the purpose of organizing an expedition to release prisoners of war at camps in the Northwest. The plot had two purposes. One was to strike at the enemy far behind the front lines. The other was to increase the sentiment in support of the Democratic Party and defeat Lincoln for re-election in the fall.

Arms were to be supplied to the prisoners through the Sons of Liberty and Knights of the Golden Circle, two secret organizations sympathetic to the South. Both were heterogeneous collections of Copperheads, riffraff and solid citizens who resented the super-patriots of the Republican Party and their "petty tyrannies." The plan was to stage a mass break during the excitement and confusion of the Democratic national convention, to be held in Chicago late in July. The released troops were to do as much damage as possible by burning and pillaging. Chicago was still a city of wooden buildings and there was reason to believe that properly located incendiary fires could destroy an important part of the business district. As another part of the plot, armed men were to be introduced into the city under the guise of convention delegates. These men would join with the escaped prisoners for a drive on Camp Morton in Indianapolis and free the southern captives there.

As the convention opened, men characterized by "bad whiskey and seedy homespun" clothes hung about the street corners. They announced in loud voices they had come to nominate a "peace President" but brandished ominous bowie knives and guns. For the second time an informer prevented a serious conflict by relating the plot to the commandant at Camp Douglas who wired for reinforcements. Within a day a thousand additional troops arrived to guard against the uprising. The leaders of the conspiracy, realizing they had lost the secrecy which was an essential part of their plan, passed the word during the third day of the convention that the project had been temporarily abandoned. Though it is probable the more grandiose parts of the plot would have been impossible to achieve, the insurrection could have caused great damage in the city and would have created wide demoralization throughout the North if even a part of it had been realized.

In November, information was allegedly obtained that the conspiracy was under way again. The purpose of the new plot, according to a report issued by the United States Judge Advocate General on the eve of the presidential election between General George C. McClellan and Lincoln, was "a general uprising in Missouri" and similar uprisings in Indiana, Ohio, Illinois and Kentucky. The plan in Chicago was for a thousand men to attack Camp Douglas, liberate the prisoners there and march to the Courthouse Square where they would be joined by five thousand Sons of the Illinois, another organization supporting the southern cause. This much of the plot might have been credible, but the report continued with an allegation there is reason to believe was based more on political inventions and motivations than on fact.

The government claimed confessions had been obtained from southern officers of a plan "to attack Camp Douglas, release the prisoners there, with them to seize the polls, allowing none but the Copperhead ticket to be voted and stuff the boxes sufficiently to secure the city and state for General McClellan; then to utterly sack the city, burning and destroying every description of property, except what they could appropriate for their own use and that of their southern brethren." The idea of creating a revolutionary force to stuff the ballot boxes and then burn up the ballots along with the rest of the city was farcical. But there was hardly time to point out the absurdity of the charge before the election; the army quickly took action on the basis of the judge advocate's report before any doubts could be raised about its accuracy.

In a series of arrests, soldiers brought in a group charged with the conspiracy, including Colonel G. St. Leger Grenfell and J. T. Shanks, two of the actual leaders of the earlier conspiracy. Chicagoans Charles Walsh, a Brigadier General of the Sons of Liberty, and Judge Buckner S. Morris, the second mayor of Chicago and treasurer of the Sons of Liberty, were also arrested. The arrest of Judge Morris was the worst injustice of the fiasco. Although a stout Democrat and opposed to the war, he was completely innocent of treason, as even his persecutors later were anxious to concede. His fault had been not one of the law but of matrimony. He was married to a Kentucky woman who was in charge of distributing clothing and goods to prisoners and frequently sheltered escaped prisoners in her house. Morris

THE GREAT NORTHWESTERN SANITARY FAIR, 1865

was acquitted at his trial but his reputation was never restored. As a pathetic epilogue, his wife, whose actions had involved him in the repercussions of the plot, left him and went to live with her family in Kentucky. Walsh and two others were convicted on charges of conspiring to release the prisoners and destroy the city of Chicago. All the others picked up in the pre-election raids were found not guilty. The case of the Chicago Conspiracy was over but it left the city puzzling over one question: Had it ever existed?

More on the creditable side among Chicago's war activities was the Soldier's Fair of 1863 to raise money for the Sanitary Commission. The Commission was a deceptively titled organization which did relief work among the soldiers. One feature of the fair was the sale at auction of the original Emancipation Proclamation for $3,000. But the center of most attention was Old Abe, the eagle mascot of the Eighth Wisconsin Regiment and a veteran of "twenty battles and sixty skirmishes." Both the eagle and the regimental "eagle bearer" were granted special leave for the fair and all Chicago paid them honor. In a city of about one hundred and fifty thousand more than one hundred thousand photographs of the bird were sold. The traffic was nearly as heavy for the sale of feathers, real and false, which were supposed to have been shot from his tail in battle. A purchaser of one of the genuine feathers was Joseph Medill. He had it made into a quill pen and kept it above his desk over the legend, "The pen is mightier than the sword."

The fair of 1863 had been little more than a grandiose bazaar and a much bigger exposition was planned for 1865. It was to have its own buildings and exhibit halls in Dearborn Park, east of Wabash between Washington and Randolph Streets. The war was over before the doors of the fair were open, but the plans were carried out to raise funds for returning veterans. Both

General Grant and General Sherman visited the fair. They were not, however, as loquacious as Old Abe, who at the first fair would respond to any resounding cheer or even a political speech with a loud screech. General Grant had been exptected to speak, but when he was introduced he declined. General Sherman was then asked to talk but demurred with the explanation, "I have always been willing to do anything the Lieutenant General asked me to do, but he has never asked me to make a speech." To this Grant replied, "I have never asked a soldier to do anything I couldn't do myself." Both of the generals were tremendously popular in Chicago, Grant because he had lived in Galena and Sherman because many Chicagoans had been among the force of "yellow-haired Germans and dark-haired, blue-eyed Irish, Scotch and English" that had marched with him to the sea.

The end of the war found Chicago counting with pride the number of volunteers it had provided for the Union forces. But in 1864 this same arithmetic had produced resentment against Lincoln when the President issued an extra call for the drafting of more troops. Chicagoans felt that because of the number of volunteers the city had provided its draft quota should not be so high. A mass meeting was held and a committee headed by Joseph Medill deputized to go to Washington to get a change in the quota. In Washington, the committee was turned down first by Secretary of War Stanton and then by Lincoln himself. The President did consent to go along for a second meeting with Stanton and listen to the arguments of both sides. After the discussion had gone on for some time, Lincoln suddenly lifted his head and turned on the committee a "black and frowning face."

"Gentlemen," he said in a voice full of bitterness, "after Boston, Chicago has been the chief instrument in bringing this war on the country. The Northwest has opposed the South as New England has opposed the South. It is you who are largely responsible for making blood flow as it has. You called for war until we had it. You called for Emancipation and I have given it to you. Whatever you have asked for you have had. Now you come here begging to be let off from the call for men which I have made to carry out the war you have demanded. You ought to be ashamed of yourselves. I have a right to expect better things of you. Go home and raise your six thousand extra men. And you, Medill, you are acting like a coward. You and your *Tribune* have had more influence than any paper in the Northwest in making this war. You can influence great masses, and yet you cry to be spared at a moment when our cause is suffering. Go home and send us those men."

Medill later told Ida Tarbell, "We all got up and when the door closed one of my colleagues said, 'Well, gentlemen, the old man is right. We ought to be ashamed of ourselves. Let us never say anything about this but go home and raise the men.'" Medill recalled that the six thousand additional men made a total of 28,000 at war from a city of 156,000. "There might have been crepe on every door almost in Chicago," he said, "for every family had lost a son or a husband. I lost two brothers. It was hard for the mothers."

The grief over the loss of sons, husbands and brothers at the front was submerged in a mourning that gripped the entire city when news was flashed of the assassination of Lincoln. The funeral train was to pass through Chicago on its way to Springfield and the city began making preparations for the reception of the body of the President. One of those who was able to offer a suggestion was George M. Pullman, who with the financial help of Marshall Field had completed the first of his new palace cars. Would it not, he asked, be appropriate for the funeral train to carry the most elegant railroad car in the country? Those in authority agreed, even though it meant that bridges along the route had to be altered to accomodate the wider Pullman car. Indirectly, the Lincoln funeral train became the showcase for America's first Pullman car.

In Chicago no group was more indignant about the assassination than the actors who felt the crime had disgraced their profession. In a special meeting at the Sherman House, the companies then at Wood's Museum and at McVicker's, where assassin John Wilkes Booth had been a local sensation several years before, voted to express "their detestation and abhorrence at him who has spread the somber pall of sorrow over our land." As a further

LINCOLN FUNERAL PROCESSION AT CHICAGO, MAY 1, 1865

mark of respect they agreed to close the theaters until after the funeral services.

The funeral train arrived in Chicago on May 1st, the last stop before its final destination at Springfield. Both the engine of the train and the pilot engine which preceded it were adorned with portraits of Lincoln. Black blankets trimmed with silver stars were draped over the boilers in simulation of the mourning gear worn by the horses that pulled the funeral hearse. The train came to a stop on the pilings of the Illinois Central tracks at the lake's edge and, as the *Tribune* reported the next morning, "The waters of Lake Michigan, long ruffled by the storm, suddenly calmed from their angry roar into solemn silence as if they too felt that silence was an imperative necessity of the mournful occasion." From the train the casket was carried slowly to the Courthouse while three dozen high-school girls scattered flowers along the way. For a day and a night Lincoln lay in state in the Courthouse where every window and doorway had been draped in black. A crowd that had been pouring into the city for two days stood shoulder to shoulder with Chicagoans until nearly 125,000 people had passed through the double line into the Courthouse.

The tribute to Lincoln in death was to be followed within a year by a tribute to his chief adversary in the great debates, Stephen A. Douglas. The Little Giant had died in 1861, shortly after pledging his life and support to Lincoln and the Union cause. With the pressures of the war gone, Chicago remembered Douglas again. Funds raised through thousands of pledges were used to post a tall monument on the lake shore near Thirty-fifth Street. The statue was on land that Douglas had once owned; he had purchased it as he had the land much farther to the south on the shore of Lake Calumet, because he had confidence it would one day be part of a great city. The dedication ceremonies for the monument were attended by President Andrew Johnson, General Grant and Admiral David G. Farragut. Before them spread a crowd of one hundred thousand who by lifting their eyes toward the sky could see the figure of Douglas on his towering pedestal. At the base of the pedestal on the sarcophagus were his final words to his sons: "Obey the laws and uphold the Constitution." It was the platform which had lifted the debates of two sons of Illinois to greatness.

MOLLIE COSGRIFF ("Irish Mollie")

Everyone Comes Here: Anything Goes Here

VIOLENT CRIME was rare in early Chicago, if the scarcity of judicial executions may be taken as an index. The first official hanging took place in 1840 in a prairie south of the city, now Twenty-ninth and South Parkway. The second execution, which did not occur until after a lapse of seventeen years, was staged at the corner of Jackson and Ashland Boulevards. The new location was for the greater convenience of the public, which was permitted to attend in the absence of more delicate forms of amusement. By 1865 the atmosphere of the growing city had changed; it was sophisticated enough for a double hanging (conducted in private).

There were several explanations for the rarity of crime during the first period of Chicago's growth. One of these was that anyone with the initiative to commit armed robbery could with less risk make a fortune speculating in land. A writer for *Leslie's Illustrated Weekly*, after commenting on the city's "broken down adventurers, real estate sharks, fast men [and] fast nags," described Chicago's capital as city lots and its currency as bonds and mortgages. "Every man owes five times the amount he can pay," he reported, "and is considered a 'poor cuss' if his collateral don't foot up to a hundred thousand."

In such an atmosphere, where everyone "from your bootblack to your hack driver . . . put on real estate airs," the highest stakes were to be found in the gamble over land. Professional bettors found only a limited market. There was no reason to risk a stake at cards when anyone who enjoyed "skinning a sucker" could wander down to the comparatively unregulated Board of Trade where he would find any number of similarly minded individuals willing to match wits with him. The extent of the hazards for the unwary was illustrated in the case of one speculator who bought two hundred barrels of pork. Later, the speculator from whom he had purchased it refused to buy it back on the grounds that it had been short in weight. At least one visitor to the city had the impression that "the secret actions of some of the most prominent men, who under the praise of performing what was considered a smart transaction, were literally conniving at open fraud and robbery" explained Chicago's increasingly indulgent attitude toward official corruption and even crime. David MacRae, an English tourist, was surprised to find that "in the case of a downright swindle, the criminal, in public estimation, seems to be the man who has allowed himself to be swindled." Though the swindler might be called a rogue, it was MacRae's observation that the so-called rogue usually would be recommended when there was "a keen stroke of business to be done."

It was the Civil War, accentuating a number of forces which had been building up since the opening of the Illinois and Michigan Canal, that finally brought the professional gambler to Chicago. He was strictly an imported product. The Illinois and Michigan Canal had always been an important part of the city's history. The first streets of Chicago had been laid out and named by a surveyor of the canal commission. The continuous waterway which the canal provided from the Great Lakes to the Mississippi and the port of New Orleans had contributed much to Chicago's burgeoning prosperity. Silent cargoes of wheat and cotton moved north and south along this waterway and with them went loquacious sailors and travelers to tell of the tremendous fortunes being made in the young city by the lake. With the outbreak of the Civil War, the South could no longer afford the luxury of gentlemen gamblers or of the afternoons of idleness that brought customers to their tables. It was time for a smart man to be on the move— and what was more natural than to come to Chicago where big fortunes were certain to grow larger during the fat war years? It was at least worth a single pass of the dice.

The gamblers—affluent, picturesque and bold—added color and gaiety to somber streets ordinarily dominated by the stern faces of the hustling Yankees. Some of the gamblers affected the mannerisms and toggery of their favorite victim, the loquacious and elegantly attired plantation owner. Others sought to surround themselves with a romantic air by dressing as plainsmen. Still others were obviously the end result of social devolution—degenerate

A GAMBLING DEN ON RANDOLPH STREET

scions of old families who prided themselves on distinguished ancestry, real or imagined. They came from every port of call along the Mississippi and almost all of them prospered. The Chicago *Times* had cause to complain that "our country cousins need to be more than ordinarily on the lookout, as in these times that try men's souls, there are a greater number than usual of those who try the depths of men's pockets." Any hope there might have been of dislodging the newcomers rapidly faded as they established a proprietary claim to their own special area of the city.

On Randolph Street, where most of the gambling dens were located, the new arrivals were the kings of the street. The subjects who paid them the allegiance of admiration and imitation were the single men living over stores in barrack dormitories, soldiers on leave, bounty-jumpers in a hurry to spend their bounty money before the law put them back in the army, veterans celebrating the end of their enlistment or sailors whose vessels had just tied up in the harbor. Day and night this transient population crowded the wooden sidewalks of Randolph Street to try its luck. The hero of every man around a card or dice table was the "sport" with the Mississippi River antecedents. His sayings and doings were the most widely quoted topics of conversation on the street. His feuds, which erupted in so many shootings that the block between State and Dearborn was known as Hairtrigger Block, evoked violent partisanship and demonstrations of loyalty among his followers.

Late afternoon was a good time to see most of the gamblers, who appeared regularly to do a bit of sidewalk strutting. At about the same hour, the gaudy hats and brightly colored gowns of the *nymphes du pave* and girls from the more prosperous bordellos would join the promenade, either singly or in the company of a "gentleman friend," as the phrase went in any introduction. The wealthier gamblers could be seen riding down the street in open carriages, often accompanied by bejeweled and brilliantly dressed consorts who advertised the gambler's prosperity and, in some cases, good taste. The consort of a successful gambler was usually the mistress of a brothel; if she were not already in such a position of business eminence, the gambler customarily provided the capital so that she could have her own "establishment." Like most aspects of Chicago life, this arrangement was directed toward practical ends; the reputation of one partner in each of these highly specialized fields added luster to the name of the other.

The most famous of such romances was that of George Trussell and Mollie Cosgriff, proprietress of a parlor house with pretensions to gentility. Mollie, who was equally well known as "Irish Mollie," was a handsome woman who chose her clothes with care and wore them with chic. Trussell, according to a contemporary reporter, was "tall, straight as an arrow and might have stood as a model for one of Remington's Indian-fighting cavalry officers. As a gamester he was 'top sawyer' among the highest rollers with the record of many broken banks to his credit."

After the Civil War, when Trussell was in a mood for expansion, he bought the famous trotting horse, Dexter. The horse held several track records and was of sufficient distinction to merit a portrait by Currier and Ives. With the acquisition of Dexter, Trussell spent an increasing amount of time at the stables and track preparing the horse for the opening day's races at the Chicago Driving Park. Mollie, whose experience with racing had been limited and who did not have a high opinion of the fascinating qualities of the equine species, grew increasingly suspicious of her lover's frequent absences. She appeared to bear her new loneliness in good spirit, however, and even acquiesced to George's request that she plan a champagne dinner to celebrate his approaching debut as a racing manager. To her chagrin and

DEXTER, the famous trotting horse that figured in the George Trussell shooting, 1857

embarrassment in front of her guests from the "select" sporting houses, the guest of honor did not appear for the dinner. After her guests were gone, Mollie was left alone with her humiliation and champagne. A brief soliloquy convinced her that George needed a lesson in the practices of domesticity. Still wearing the white moire gown she had put on for dinner, Mollie equipped herself with what the next day's paper described as the means of "enforcing the new household ordinance about stay-out-lates." She found George in Seneca Wright's saloon on Randolph Street, adjoining Price's livery stables where Dexter was quartered. George was standing at the bar listening with approval to a rendition of the "Limerick Races" by a singer from North's Circus. Mollie, relieved to find him at such an innocent pastime, rushed into the saloon and threw her arms around his neck. Then, for reasons never fully explained but possibly having something to do with her charms being less than those of a four-footed beast, she shot him dead.

The shooting occurred in Hairtrigger Block and at first caused little excitement outside the saloon. In the offices of the Chicago *Times* across the street, the city editor who presided proudly over a staff of "two ex-convicts, ten divorced husbands and not a man living with his own wife," didn't bother to send out a reporter. A moment later the shrieks and cries of the bereaved Mollie gave notice that the shooting was more than an exchange between two gamblers. The *Times* reporter rushed across the street to find Mollie bending over her lover and crying "George! Have I killed you? Have I killed you?" George didn't say; but the coroner, who did, called it murder. A jury set Mollie free after the gun inexplicably disappeared and her counsel pleaded "temporary emotional insanity," an excuse which a few nervous males thought might set an unhealthy precedent. Meanwhile, the court listed the estate of George Trussell as containing, among other items, "five gold watches, two diamond pins, one revolver, one single barrel pistol, five hats and twelve pairs of cassimere pantaloons."

ARMORY AND GASWORKS showing police herding prostitutes, 1866

The Chicago Driving Park continued to be under a jinx after the death of Trussell. It was closed by a second and equally sensational scandal only a month later. A race for a $5,000 purse for the best three out of five heats was scheduled between the trotters General Butler and Cooley. Although Cooley was the underdog, he won the first two heats with his trainer, Bill Riley, driving. Then William McKeever, the owner of General Butler, took the reins of his horse away from the trainer and pushed to victory in two heats to deadlock the contests. By the end of the fourth race it was dark and Riley wanted to quit. He charged that McKeever had broken the rules by running Butler instead of trotting him on the far side of the track out of sight of the judge's stand. So much money had been bet that the judges insisted the fifth race be run; to satisfy Riley they sent watchers to the far side of the track. The fifth race started with the horses even but as they thundered out of the darkness into the home stretch, the judges saw McKeever was missing from the racing sulky behind General Butler. After a brief search, McKeever was found lying on the backstretch, his head crushed by a piece of fence rail. The coroner's hearings in the case dragged on for days, with all of the testimony reported word for word in the newspapers. No flaw could be found in any man's account of the accident which might point to a possible murderer. Finally, the jury called it the work of "persons unknown." The killer, whoever he was, gained nothing. There was justice among gamblers if not under the law—all bets were off.

After the death of Trussell, the slain gambler's foremost rival, "Cap" Hyman, emerged as boss of Randolph Street. When both men were alive, an exchange of shots was commonplace when they met. Trussell when sober was quiet and usually managed to avoid Hyman. But when Trussell was loaded with whiskey, his own temperament was a good match for that of his more excitable adversary. As far as police records show, both men consistently missed their target. It was not for lack of practice, for it was Hyman who caused the *Tribune* to issue its famous editorial complaint that "the practice of shooting people upon the most trifling provocation is becoming altogether too prevalent in this city." Occasionally public indignation forced the police to clamp down on Cap's rampages. At such times, Hyman would vanish from the streets for a month or two and wait patiently until the public's mood had returned to its customary indifference.

During one of Hyman's obstreperous moments, he paid an afternoon visit to the Tremont House. To amuse himself he drew a pistol and held everyone in the hotel prisoner. Walking back and forth at the top of the high steps at the Dearborn Street entrance, he refused to allow anyone to leave or enter the hotel. The street was soon deserted. The officer on the beat and the house detectives were all afraid of trying to shoot it out with Hyman and an appeal for help was sent to Captain Jack Nelson at the detective bureau. Nelson strode into the deserted street and abruptly ordered Hyman to put up his gun. Hyman, without any show of defiance, complied and surrendered. When he was asked why he had not threatened Nelson as he had the others, Hyman had a practical reply that was possibly a clue to his longevity. "Jack can shoot too quick for me," he explained.

With this combination of bravado and discretion, Hyman was destined to prosper. He acquired as his mistress Annie Stafford, reputedly the fattest madame in town and for reasons somewhat obscure referred to as "Gentle Annie." Like Mollie Cosgriff, Annie was given to worrying about her lover's fidelity. Frequently she suggested that a matrimonial alliance would have the desired effect of letting others know Cap was marked property. The prospective groom evaded all suggestions until after the shooting of George Trussell. Annie, inspired by the effectiveness of Mollie's direct action methods, armed herself with a rawhide whip which she was confident would be effective without being lethal. Storming into Hyman's gambling house, she found her lover asleep on the sofa. Waking him up with a crack of the whip, she chased him into the street. No record can be found of the end of this curious pursuit but its effectiveness cannot be doubted. It was announced soon afterward that Cap and Gentle Annie were to become husband and wife.

MICHIGAN AVENUE FROM PARK ROW, 1866

The newspapers called the wedding of Cap and Gentle Annie the "swellest show" Chicago had seen. It was attended by members of the sporting set from as far away as St. Louis, Cincinnati, Louisville and New Orleans. The wedding was not the only cause for celebration. The same day the newlyweds opened a roadhouse in Lake View for which they had chosen the radiant name of Sunnyside. The advent of Sunnyside had been well advertised and the opening-night party was the most important social event of the year for the gambling fraternity. The guest of honor was to be the same Captain Jack Nelson who had subdued Cap Hyman at the Tremont House and who had since been elevated to deputy superintendent of police. This curious role for a member of the law-enforcement detail was explained on the grounds he was to be present "by no means in his capacity as a keeper of the peace." Other city officials had also promised (unofficially) to be present and there were even a few businessmen with "a tincture of sport in their blood" who had invitations.

There was a heavy snowfall on the day that Gentle Annie succeeded in her ambition of becoming Mrs. Cap Hyman. The snow only added to the evening's prospects. The town was well supplied with sleighs and that evening the fanciest among them were to be found speeding northward to the merry jingle of the bells on the horses' harness. In the city most of the gaming dens were dark as their owners headed toward Sunnyside with a "most particular feminine friend" snuggling beside them in their sleighs.

THE GARDEN CITY 80

The bolder men from the Board of Trade who acknowledged they had invitations gathered for a preliminary celebration at the Matteson House. Shortly after eight o'clock, amid a fanfare of horns and the shouting of a sizable crowd, the group made its start in a gondola-shaped sleigh pulled by four horses and filled from prow to stern with boisterous celebrants.

Cap Hyman, who reputedly had a college education and a better-than-average social background, planned the details of his party with meticulous care. He invited the members of the press to act as moral censors and gave them a suitable briefing beforehand. "I would like you gentlemen of the press to understand that the affair will be straight to the wink of an eyelash," he said. "All the ladies are here on their honor and Mrs. Hyman will see to it that nothing unseemly will take place. We want the best people in town to patronize Sunnyside and will make them welcome."

As the guests arrived, Hyman presided with the air of Ward McAllister. Gentlemen were ceremoniously introduced to the ladies, engagement cards were consulted, and all the rest of the formalities which are characteristic of similar functions in a more sedate society were observed. A few of the feminine guests gave evidence of earlier social training, a reminder that there were then no gradations to the glamorless substrata of prostitution; one false step and the victim was precipitated straight to "the depths." For this reason many of the "boarders" of the more sumptuous establishments often played a leading role in the romantic dramas of the period. Most of the guests at Sunnyside's premiere, however, had been culled by Gentle Annie with an eye for their abundant physical charms (too often marred by an excess of cosmetics). For these the role of intellectual companion was awkward, even when quoting carefully memorized sentences about Lord Byron. Efforts to "do the lady business" resulted in embarrassing breaks. Several of the hostesses made it plain they were getting impatient for the moment when "this honor business" would be over. There was an intermission for supper, or rather a banquet, at which Jack Nelson took his seat of honor. Each male guest was assigned a female companion to "take in"—clearly a reversal of the role to which most of the feminine guests were accustomed. As the banquet started, everything seemed to be agreeable, so much so that the *Tribune* reporter found it "portentous." What it portended was recorded in his story the following day:

> About midnight a group, consisting of several ladies(?) and gentlemen(?) [the question marks are the reporter's], became quite animated in conversation. Something was said which was construed by the person addressed to be a reflection upon her character as a lorette. The person addressed replied she was as good as the rest, she thought, and clinched the observation with a very strong epithet. These researches into character naturally shocked those whose sensibilities were most tender and

BRIGGS HOUSE, 1866

it was but a few moments before some of the more ingenious in the use of language, uttered expressions provocative of blows. One of the young women, Eileen McMasters, residing on West Madison Street, was constrained to wear her eyes in mourning for the remainder of the evening. Another, whose name was not ascertained, is represented to have her face left in the condition of dissolving views, the red, white and blue each striving to be the predominant color, a third is reported to have had her nose changed from a pug to a Roman. How much hair bestrewed the floor, what became of the waterfalls and hoop skirts in the conflict, will never be known.

A footnote indicating that the social impact of the party was not confined to a single night was provided by Frederic Francis Cook. "For many days after the event, police justices were worked overtime issuing warrants of arrest for assault and battery," he wrote in Bygone Days In Chicago. "On successive mornings the old Armory Court exhibited such varied facial disfigurement that the reporter's psychologic interest was completely lost in the shock to artistic sensibilities, when one recalled how these animated canvases, now so streaked and splotched, but a few nights before had dazzled the beholder with their deftly composed color schemes."

Happily for the peace of the city not all gamblers had the social ambitions of Cap Hyman. A gaming proprietor who stayed close by his tables was Frank Connelly, proprietor of the Senate gambling den. The Senate was

THE GARDEN CITY 82

known as a "high-toned game" and no small-money players were allowed. The dealer was George Holt, known as the "gentleman par excellence" of Chicago gamblers. The place was raided periodically but the guests were never taken to the station in police wagons. They were driven in carriages at Connelly's expense. After he paid the fines of the entire party, Connelly would have the carriages return the players to the Senate and resume the game.

Chicago became a completely wide-open town with the introduction of Keno. It was argued that the game was not gambling but only another name for an innocent German game called lotto. At first, the police couldn't come to any conclusion in the matter—presumably, said a reporter at the time, because of the regularity of the pay-off. But Keno also had the effect of moving gambling further into the open. Faro had been played at least one flight up and with some pretense of closed doors. Keno transformed the stores of Randolph into a gambling midway. Buildings were renting at exorbitant prices and still the gamblers could not accommodate all who wanted to play. On Saturday nights the crowds pushed out into the street from every Keno game and above the din of those outside could be heard the voice of the proprietor calling out the lucky numbers as they were drawn. An order from police headquarters would have been sufficient to close the games but the police authorities avoided such direct action in order to stage a massive raid. (Knowledgeable Chicagoans pointed out that the raid would produce a record volume of bail-bond business, with the professional bond operators cutting the captains and sergeants in on the night's profits.)

A major part of the police force was mobilized for the raid. Because the Keno players far outnumbered the raiders, the police first blocked the outlets of the various buildings and kept the players prisoner until enough transportation could be found to haul them all to jail. The raid began shortly after 10 o'clock but it was not until two hours later that the last of the players had been taken away. The three-story Armory Court and jail were soon packed with victims and part of the overflow jammed into a large barn at the rear. When the barn would hold no more, a temporary camp was set up in front of the armory and the prisoners surrounded by a corral of blue-coated policemen. The process of setting bond and getting bail was started immediately and went on through the night and all day Sunday. When the supply of bail blanks was gone, the sergeants ordered the patrolmen to write out the necessary wording on blank sheets of paper. As a move to close down Keno, the raid was effective. But its only effect on the gamblers was to cause them to move back upstairs.

THE SAUGANASH HOTEL, where the first dramatic performance in Chicago was held

The Finer Things of Life

THE BEGINNINGS of the theater in Chicago were not auspicious. The first permanent theater was established in 1837, in the converted dining room of the Sauganash Hotel. In the following year the managers planned to move to a building nearer the center of the business district but ran into opposition based on a combination of New England conscience and Yankee thrift. A group of the town's businessmen presented a petition to the City Council asking that no license for a theater in such a location be permitted. They argued that "Theaters are subject to take fire and are believed to be dangerous on that account to property in their vicinity ... insurance cannot be obtained on property in their vicinity except at greatly advanced premiums." They were alarmed, they said, over the danger to "the property and lives of your petitioners," giving their property a significant precedence over their lives in their concern. Grant Goodrich, a member of the council committee which considered the petition, felt that the danger to the moral welfare from the establishment of a permanent theater was even more to be abjured. In a minority report, filed after the majority of the committee had voted to grant the license, Goodrich called the tendencies of the performance of "modern theaters" to be "grossly demoralizing, destructive of principle" and "nurseries of crime."

The theater which produced this contention was no more than a makeshift auditorium that had formerly been an auction hall. Among the players at the first performance were Mr. and Mrs. Joseph Jefferson. A special attraction of every evening's show was a curtain song by their son, Master Joseph Jefferson, whose favorite appears to have been a number called "Lord Lovel and Lady Nancy." Master Joseph saw the theater during these many curtain appearances as one of "stuffed seats in the dress circle and planed boards in the pit." In his autobiography he recalled that the new drop curtain contained "a medallion of Shakespeare suffering from a severe pain in his stomach over the center." The dome of the theater was pale blue, with pink and white clouds surmounted by four awkward ballet girls representing the seasons and presumably strewing flowers, snow and grapes over the unsuspecting audience. At the heads of the seasons were four fat cherubs, which Jefferson found to be in "various stages of spinal curvature."

The theatrical season was unorthodox by modern practices. It began in the spring and continued only through the summer months. This eliminated both the problem of heating a building susceptible to fire and the hazard to the audience furnished by Chicago's muddy streets. The theaters drew a large proportion of their audiences from visitors. The most regular patrons were prosperous speculators attracted to the city by the opportunities in real estate (which always rose in value during the summer when the sun had dried up most evidences of its swamplike character). The local press was divided about the theater. One editorialist argued that it was no more proper to allow young people to sample the pleasures of the theater than any other form of vice. Others, under the guise of helpfulness, offered ideas to improve the respectability of the plays and therefore make them more palatable. The Chicago American suggested that managers bring to an end "the habit of throwing out extemporaneously obscene witticisms, which, while they catch the laugh of some, are very offensive to ladies and gentlemen in attendance." It then offered its own rather puzzling formula for wit, which it said should be "chaste and salty enough to preserve its purity," a remarkable use of salt as a preservative. The same arbiter of moral propriety, more than anxious to be of service, advised the ladies that if they were waiting for "fashionable precedents" he could tell them that, at Springfield, the theater was attended generally by the "beauty and fashion of the fair sex and by all the gentlemen of the town, from Supreme Court judges down."

Various means were used to "bend the devil round the stump" in circumventing transplanted Yankee prejudice against frivolous entertainment. One of these was to establish a theater as part of a museum. The museums had, in addition to a series of exhibits labeled educational, an adjoining lecture room for both plays and speakers. Chicago's leading museum was that of Colonel Joseph H. Wood. The Wood's Museum, according to its proprietor, contained "150,000 curiosities of every kind," including a ninety-six-foot fossil caled Zeuglodon, a sea lion, a lighted panorama of the city of London and a hall of paintings. The quality of the art exhibited was not high and the Tribune critic complained that "the drawing and anatomy of some of the Indians was at fault." He did, however, find something to approve in "the marble and moonlight beauty of the slaughtered maidens." An adjoin-

COLONEL WOOD'S MUSEUM, 1866

ing lecture room was large enough to accommodate fifteen hundred people and during the season a stock company offered plays there.

The first theater to be patronized in large numbers by respectable Chicagoans was that built in 1847 by John B. Rice, a theatrical manager from Buffalo. Rice erected a new building on the south side of Randolph, following the plan of the old Coliseum for his seating arrangement. For the first time Chicago saw boxes elegantly fitted up with carpets and comfortable furniture. A competent company of actors and sedate surroundings enabled Rice to overcome much of the resistance to theatrical performances. It was not long before the Chicago Journal was reporting that "a large number of ladies—the beauty and fashion of the city—are in nightly attendance." Respectability was also maintained by a line in the advertisements to the effect no females would be admitted unless "accompanied by gentlemen." This precaution was considered necessary to exclude foot-weary prostitutes who might consider the admission fee a suitable price for finding a more comfortable situation in which to interview their prospects.

It was at Rice's theater that opera was first presented in Chicago in a season notable for its brevity. The bill was Vincenzo Bellini's *La Sonnambula*

(*The Sleepwalker*). A visiting company of singers took the leading roles, assisted by a "home chorus" and supported by a local orchestra. Before the hero, Elvino, could discover what force had taken his somnambulant Almina to another man's bed, the performance was interrupted by cries of "fire" outside the theater. Rice, who was his own manager, stepped to the front of the stage and shouted "Sit Down! Sit Down! Do you think I would permit a fire to occur in my theater?" Such was the confidence of the members of the audience in Rice, who was twice to be mayor of the city, that they took their seats. A voice—appropriately from the prompter's box—startled the manager with the information that the theater was in fact on fire from flames that had originated in a livery stable across the alley. The theater was cleared and Chicgo's first opera season brought abruptly to an end; but only after an inebriated opera lover, who sat applauding the holocaust on the stage as the best imitation of a fire he had ever seen, had been dragged to safety. Rice was undaunted and constructed another theater in which he offered Chicago its first full season of Italian opera in 1853.

Concert music was provided for the most part by touring singers and musicians. In 1850, Julius Dyhrenfurth conducted an aggregation of twenty-two musicians in a symphony concert to dedicate the music hall at the Tremont House but did not attempt anything as ambitious as a symphony. Three years later, during a visit of the Germania Orchestra, the young city heard a performance of Beethoven's Second Symphony—which by that circumstance became Chicago's first.

McVICKER'S THEATER, 1866

It was in the music hall at the Tremont House in 1853 that Chicagoans became acquainted with Adelina Patti, who as a "somewhat delicate, pale-faced, dark-browed child with thick glossy hair hanging in two long braids down her back, dressed in rose-colored silk, pink stockings and pantalettes," was singing bravura airs at the age of twelve. Patti was always to be a favorite of listeners who might also remember it was at her debut that such evidences of sophistication as numbered tickets and ushers appeared for the first time. When Patti returned in 1855, she was in the company of Ole Bull, the famous Norwegian violinist. The concert was billed as the "farewell to America" concert of Ole Bull. However, on June 29, 1857, he was back for "one farewell concert" and the following evening was up to giving a "positive farewell." It would have seemed to him poor form to describe his subsequent visits in 1868, 1869, 1872 and 1877 as anything but "farewell concerts," an invention in which he appears to have anticipated Buffalo Bill.

Ten years passed after the erection of Rice's Theater before the opening of another playhouse of comparable importance. Then James H. McVicker, who had been among the most popular of Rice's performers, established McVicker's Theater on Madison Street west of State. It was the most costly and impressive theater in the West and McVicker made it a hospitable place for distinguished drama. On the McVicker stage Chicagoans saw E. A. Sothern, Edmund Keane, Edwin Forrest, Jane Coombs, Mrs. John Drew, Ada Rehan and Joseph Jefferson, no longer singing his curtain song, but now starring in *Rip Van Winkle*. It was at McVicker's that the touring company of America's first musical comedy, *The Black Crook*, attained a run of fifty-six nights, considered extraordinary for the time.

John Wilkes Booth, whose murder of Lincoln evoked a terrible denunciation from his fellow actors, had achieved a personal triumph in Shakespeare's *Richard III* when he played at McVicker's in 1862. During the run of the play he had attended a charity party and was asked for his autograph to sell. He demurred on the grounds that his signature was worthless, but a young girl convinced him that she could sell all he would provide at 25 cents each. When Booth's murder of Lincoln assured the actor of a prominent if villainous role in American history, many Chicago families spent hours trying to salvage these autographs from attic trunks and cluttered bureau drawers.

Edwin Booth, the assassin's brother, also acted at McVicker's. Playing Juliet to Booth's Romeo was Mary McVicker, the daughter of the theater's proprietor. The romance was carried over from the stage to life and Mary later became Mrs. Edwin Booth. In one of Booth's performances at McVicker's, the actor was shot at by an insane clerk named Mark Gray. The bullet missed Booth and lodged in the framework of the scenery. The imperturbable Booth later had it removed and encased in a gold cartridge

CROSBY'S OPERA HOUSE, 1866

which he wore on his watch chain. On it was engraved "From Mark Gray to Edwin Booth."

All the theaters which Chicago had seen up to the end of the Civil War were eclipsed by the splendors of Crosby's Opera House. Uranus H. Crosby was a young Cape Cod distiller shrewd enough to anticipate the wartime tax on liquors. By building up his supplies before its imposition he had become rich. He was determined to use his money to erect a magnificent building for grand opera that would be a "temple of the arts." He selected a location on Washington Street west of State and at a cost of $700,000 erected a combination opera house, art gallery, and office building. The first floor was rented by W. W. Kimball's piano store, John Wright's restaurant that later became H. M. Kinsley's "celebrated and elegant confectionery, ice cream and dining establishment," and George F. Root's music-publishing firm. The second and third floors overlooking the street were occupied by offices. On the fourth floor was an art gallery and ten artists' studios, including that of G. P. A. Healy. The opera house auditorium was in the rear of the building. It had a seating capacity of three thousand, including a dress circle of fifty-six private boxes. A special wing, with an entrance on State Street, was occupied by a music hall for smaller concerts.

The fortunes of Crosby's tremendous showplace were erratic. The grand opening, scheduled for April 17, 1865, had to be postponed because of the mourning for Lincoln. At the end of a year, Crosby realized that he had falsely calculated the demand for grand opera as well as the cost of producing it. For the first time he was aware that the symbolic statues of Painting, Sculpture, Music and Commerce which stood above the entryway to the opera house were not comfortable neighbors. However, if Crosby was not on intimate terms with the first three arts, he was with the fourth. He soon had conceived an audacious plan to retrieve his fortune: he would give away the $700,000 opera house and the most valuable of its art treasures in a lottery.

The emphasis in his plan, as it had been in the construction of the opera house, was cultural. He did not sell the chances directly as a lottery, but formed the Crosby Art Association, which offered buyers a lottery ticket along with the purchase of one of a series of engravings of popular paintings. Art catalogues took the place of lottery books and even those who were opposed to gambling could with good conscience participate in the lottery on the ground that they had acquired a valuable engraving. The drawing was first announced for October 11, 1866, but not enough of the 210,000 chances had been sold by that date; the drawing was postponed to January 21, 1867. During the intervening months, thousands of people who expected their five-dollar ticket would make them the owners of the imposing edifice strolled through the corridors of the opera house with a proprietary air. Between acts of the opera they were to be found gazing condescendingly at the paintings which less fortunate ticket holders might hope for as a consolation prize. Sales boomed. On the day set for the drawing, all the tickets had been sold except 25,593 which Crosby retained as his own.

For several days before the drawing the trains were bringing in ticket holders who had come to claim their prize. The hotels were filled and temporary barracks were set up in the saloons. The night before, ticket holders too excited to sleep roamed the streets, stopping only long enough to take a little sustenance from an ubiquitous carpetbag. Early in the morning a long line had formed in front of the doors to the opera house. The city slowed almost to a halt. The rooms of the Board of Trade were deserted. Not a single spectator was in the only courtroom that opened for business. At 11 o'clock, the doors of the opera house were thrown open and the crowd surged in, kept under control by an extra force of police. The excitement was so great that a few women dared convention to fight their way to places in the gallery. For the most part the audience was made up of men, some of them on the "fancy order" as one newspaper observed.

On the stage of the opera house were two wheel-shaped cages. The larger contained the numbers of the 210,000 lottery tickets. In the smaller was a list of 302 prizes, ranging in value from the opera house itself to worthless paintings from the art gallery's storage bin. A committee that included representatives from Detroit, St. Louis, New York, Boston and Philadelphia, had been appointed to take charge of the drawing. A total of 112 prizes had been drawn from the prize wheel when the ticket of the opera house was drawn. From the other wheel a judge drew ticket number 58,600. As the numerals were read out the hushed audience waited for the owner to rise and identify himself. When no one rose there were shouts for the committee to read the name of the winning ticket holder. These demands were ignored and the drawing continued, only a few noting in the continuing furor that Crosby himself had drawn two of the best paintings with a combined value of $26,000 as well as Volk's bust of Lincoln.

The drawing was finished with the name of the winning ticket holder a mystery. In a midnight bulletin attached to the end of its story, the *Tribune* began to suspect all was not as it should be. "It is asserted in the best informed circles that Crosby holds the tickets for the three chief prizes next after the first, and it is not certain that he has not that also. It also turns out that the opera house to be deeded is not the whole building as represented but only the audience room in the inaccessible center of the block. If this proves the biggest swindle of the season, no one will pity the victims." In later editions, the *Tribune* added the information that the winner was A. H. Lee of Prairie du Rocher, Randolph County, Illinois.

There were some who doubted if either A. H. Lee or Prairie du Rocher existed. As if to forestall such skeptics, a letter written to Lee's brother-in-law in St. Louis was reprinted with a suspicious alacrity in a St. Louis newspaper. The letter contained in great detail a picture of the scene when Lee was notified he was the winner after he "had undressed and was sitting in my long-tailed nightshirt." He then went on to the purpose of the letter: "I just say this to you; it is for sale. I suppose that somebody wants to buy it and I have to ask you to sell it for me. It is impossible for me to leave my wife in her present condition or I would go up to you at once." By the 25th of January, Mrs. Lee was sufficiently recovered for her husband to get to Chicago if not to his brother-in-law in St. Louis. Chicago was not to know of his arrival until after his departure. Then it was informed only through a letter to the editor in the Chicago *Republican*, a form of communication for which Lee showed continuing preference. In the letter to the editor he explained "it was my wish and request that I might come here and transact my business with Mr. Crosby without becoming the object of unpleasant notoriety and without having my name heralded in the newspapers; and I feel deeply indebted to him for the considerate manner in which the request has been observed, especially as it has cost him some embarrassment as well as occasioned invidious comment. Feeling that the opera house should properly be owned by Mr. Crosby, I made him the offer to sell it to him for $200,000 and the offer was accepted in a spirit which was most gratifying and the money promptly paid me."

The letter did not convince Chicagoans. They had only to figure out that Crosby had sold more than $900,000 worth of chances on a $700,000 investment. Apart from his expenses and even after the payment of $200,000 (which there was reason to doubt had been made) he still retained the total amount of his first investment, plus the opera house. The statue of Commerce must have been smiling broadly as Uranus Crosby passed through the portals of his "temple of the arts."

The question of whether Crosby had swindled the public was not quickly dropped. The promoter found it expedient to retire to a New England village and leave the management of the opera house in the hands of his uncle, Albert Crosby. Under the uncle's management, the opera house continued to be a showplace, though not always for grand opera. In 1867, the *Tribune* exclaimed belligerently that "the public will receive with feelings akin to indignation, the announcement that Mr. Maretzek of New York after his flourish of trumpets, has canceled his arrangements and decided not to give a season of opera here, offering the excuse for this breach of promise, that the season subscriptions are too small to warrant him in bringing an expensive troupe here. We need hardly say the excuse is a very flimsy one. We have only to chronicle the fact and inform Mr. Maretzek of New York that if he can do without Chicago, Chicago can do without him and that in all probability when Mr. Maretzek of New York demises, opera will still exist and be heard in Chicago as heretofore." On Thanksgiving Day of the same year, the opera house was used for a public reception for Edward Payson Weston, the great "walkist," who had walked from Portland, Maine, to Chicago at an average rate of fifty-two miles a day and in some days had traveled more than ninety miles. In 1868, music gave way to politics as the Republicans took over the opera house for their national convention and nominated General Grant for the presidency.

In November of 1869, the attraction at the opera house was not one Uranus H. Crosby had envisioned for his dwelling place of the arts. It was Lydia Thompson and her British Blondes, the large-limbed beefy specimens who introduced burlesque to America. The display of "personal charms" was rated far greater than that of the sensational *Black Crook* and denunciations of the show from the city's pulpits were followed by a rushing business at the box office. The hit of the show was a number called "Sinbad the Sailor," with Lydia, who specialized in boy parts, playing Sinbad. The company played a return engagement the following year and during its second stay incurred the ire of Wilbur F. Storey, the hot-tempered owner

REPUBLICAN CONVENTION AT CROSBY'S OPERA HOUSE, nominating General Grant for President, 1868

of the *Times*. Storey thought the company immoral and was angry at its success because he was in the middle of a feud with Crosby.

Storey published a daily attack upon the morality of the show. When this had no effect he printed comments on the chastity, or rather lack of it, of members of the company. The climax came in a one-line editorial: "Bawds at the Opera House! Where's the Police?" Lydia vowed revenge for this insult. That afternoon she, Pauline Markham, her featured dancer, Archie Gordon, a press agent, and Mr. Henderson, her company manager, waited near Peck Court on Wabash Avenue for Storey to come by on his customary afternoon walk. When Storey came into sight, Henderson saw that Mrs. Storey was with the editor and suggested the attack be postponed. "Not at all," said Lydia. "So much the better. She will get an idea of what it means to attack one of her sex."

As the Storeys approached, Lydia drew a riding whip from under her wrap. Calling Storey a "dirty old scoundrel," she tried to beat him. He caught the blow on his left arm and with his right hand seized Lydia by the throat. Gordon sprang on Storey's back while Henderson pulled Lydia out of Storey's grasp. During the affray the belligerence of Mrs. Storey for once exceeded that of her husband. "Wilbur," she shouted, "draw your pistol." A policeman arrived in time to help a group of passers-by disentangle the combatants and the next day the four appeared before Justice Augustus Banyon, a paunchy, swollen-nosed, red-faced celebrity of the day. He found Lydia and her companions guilty of charges brought by Storey, fined them $100 and then suspended the fine.

Plans were under way in the summer of 1871 for events of a more dignified character. Throughout the summer, the opera house had been redecorated and modernized at a cost of more than $100,000. Crosby announced he would inaugurate a new season on October 9th with a series of "ten grand symphony and popular concerts" by Theodore Thomas and his orchestra. Every effort had been made to make the new opening as resplendent as the manager's nephew had hoped the first opening would be six years before. But the fate which had pursued the opera house since it was built had one final irony to reveal. Theodore Thomas and his musicians were turned back in a scorching hot train at Twenty-second Street. The stage—that October 9th of 1871—had been set for far greater drama.

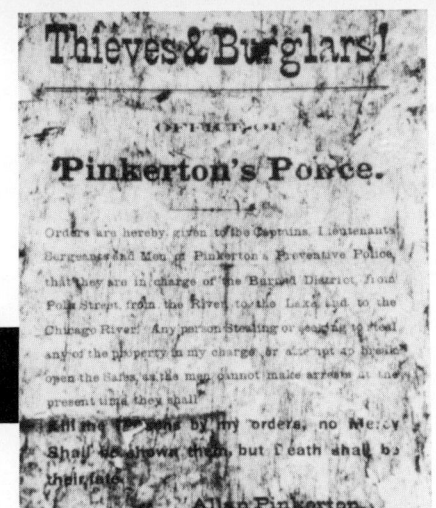

"DEATH SHALL BE THEIR FATE."
A Pinkerton broadside

The Red Snow

To CHICAGO it appeared that Crosby's Opera House had a kinship with catastrophe. The first opening had been delayed by the assassination of Lincoln. Then, on October 8, 1871, less than twenty-four hours before the grand reopening, the city's eyes were turned anxiously toward the West Side as the Sunday papers headlined stories of "The Great Conflagration." For seventeen hours a fire stormed out of control over four blocks west of the river before Chicago's weary firemen could master it. The damage amounted to nearly a million dollars; if it had not been for the generosity of saloon keeper Daniel W. Quirk, the sum might have been ten times greater and the entire West Division destroyed.

Quirk owned a saloon on the southeast corner of Adams and Canal Streets, several blocks north of where "The Great Conflagration" had started. Throughout Saturday night and Sunday morning the fire moved steadily in a path pointing toward Quirk's saloon. Seeing that his business was doomed, Quirk announced to the crowd watching the fire that anyone who wished could help himself to a supply of liquor and cigars. After a sampling of Quirk's hospitality, the men in the saloon reassured their generous host that they would do all they could to save his buildings. Buckets of water were carried from the river to soak the walls and roof. The portable fire extinguishers that were to be found among the crowd at every Chicago fire were brought into use and sparks from the blaze were extinguished before they could do any damage. The fire, that had been pacing steadily northward, came to a halt before the stout defense of Quirk's volunteer fire brigade.

Spectacular fires were not an uncommon occurrence in Chicago. In 1868, a fire on Lake Street had done more than two million dollars' damage and hastened the exodus of stores to the new business district developing on State Street. By 1871, Chicago was paying more for fire insurance than was collected for state, county and municipal taxes. The city had sixty thousand buildings of which forty thousand were wholly of wood and only a handful of the remainder were fireproof. Roofs were made of felt and tar or of wooden shingles. Year by year the loss from fire was increasing. The *Tribune*, housed in a new fireproof building, was uneasy about the contrast between its own structure and most of the others around it. In an editorial in the summer of 1871, it warned that the city's marble fronts were only a "thin veneer" and the "dispensation of sheet iron and pine planks" had made of Chicago's buildings a "cheat, a snare and a lie." It also told of buildings with walls a hundred feet or more in height that were not more than "a single brick's thickness" and deplored the menace to pedestrians from cornices that "come rattling down to the street in a high wind." The fact was, as the editorialist noted, that the city had been debauched by its own prosperity. Its population had risen from slightly more than four thousand in 1840 to nearly three hundred thousand in 1870. In the haste to grow and prosper it was content to keep roofs over the heads of the newcomers; corrective measures could be taken later.

The summer of 1871 increased the hazards of flimsy construction. The weather was the dryest in the city's history. From the fourth of July to the first of October, a period when there normally was a total of eight to nine inches of rain, less than an inch and a half had fallen; this was distributed over six different days. The city, its factories, its frame houses, wooden pavement and plank sidewalks were dry as tinder. Prematurely withered leaves from the trees of "The Garden City" covered the ground.

These omens were largely ignored, principally because of the city's pride in the new waterworks on the North Side. The opening of the waterworks in 1867 gave many Chicagoans the feeling that all the water in Lake Michigan was available on a moment's notice. Watching clear water pour from their faucets, they remembered the years when small fish squeezed through the city's filters and newspapers reported a "four-inch fish made its appearance through an office hydrant," or that "thousands of minnows have been found in Chicago water pipes this winter." The water tower, standing nearly one hundred feet high, was an assuring symbol of the city's readiness.

Only the scorched and weary members of the fire department, returning to their station houses after winning their desperate battle with the West Side fire, realized how inadequate a symbol it was.

At the station of the Little Giant fire company most of the men were near exhaustion when the equipment was finally put away about dusk Sunday afternoon. There was still a need to keep watch, however, and the fireman assigned to the station watch tower during the night hours took his post as usual. About 9:15 P.M. he saw flames leaping toward the sky about six blocks north of the station house. He sounded the alarm and the engine company was on its way toward the blaze as rapidly as the tired crews could harness the horses. As the company rolled out of the station, the fire alarm telegraph box began sounding an alarm. It was the signal of a fire nearly a mile south of where the watchman had seen the flames. The firemen ignored it.

The Little Giant company followed the beacon of fire to De Koven Street, about a half-mile south of the fire of Saturday night. Three barns, a paint shop and a shed were on fire and burning fiercely. Members of the crowd told the firemen the blaze had been going in the area of closely built wooden cottages and shanties for nearly an hour. Across the street in a vacant lot, his hair singed by flames and his face blackened by smoke, stood Peg Leg Sullivan. He was leaning on the neck of a badly frightened calf

THE CHICAGO WATER CRIB, 1866

he had rescued from the barn. Seeing the flames, he had gone into the barn to drag the calf out by the halter. In the struggle, his peg leg had plunged through a rotten board in the floor, catching the top of it so that he could not move. As quickly as possible he unfastened the straps, abandoned his peg and hobbled out with his arms around the neck of the calf. The rescued animal was not Sullivan's but one of the small herd of five kept by Mrs. Patrick O'Leary. She was explaining that a cow had kicked over a lamp when she had gone to the house to get some salt for an ailing animal.

The Little Giant company hooked up its hose and turned a stream of water on the fire, puzzled by the failure of any other company to arrive. Bruno Goll, a druggist who had turned in a fire alarm shortly after nine in the box outside his store and repeated it ten minutes later, watched anxiously for fire companies to be sent in response to his signal. The key to the puzzle lay in the Courthouse tower, where the city's fire watcher had sent out the alarm that rang at the Little Giant's station house. The watcher there had seen the flames but had misjudged their location by more than a mile. Then, as the blaze from the O'Leary barn increased, he realized his error and asked the operator to change the signal. The alarm operator refused to change it, compounding his stubbornness by repeating the wrong alarm a second time. As nearly as could be ascertained later, the alarm from Bruno Goll failed to register on the central board. By the time this accumulation of errors and mechanical failures could be overcome, the fire was moving swiftly northward toward the scene of Saturday night's blaze, urged along by a brisk southwest breeze.

About 10 o'clock a mass of burning material from one of the burning cottages or barns whirled four blocks through the air to the steeple of St. Paul's Roman Catholic Church. The flames that started in the steeple soon enveloped the church and burned over an adjoining factory into Bateham's lumber mill on the bank of the river. There the fire feasted on a thousand cords of kindling for Chicago stoves, half a million feet of furniture lumber and three-quarters of a million wooden shingles. Bateham, an early fire marshal, enlisted volunteers to fight the flames with pumps from the river, but was forced to abandon the attempt despite a fear that burning brands from the yard might ignite the entire South Division. By this time all the fire-fighting equipment of the city was mobilized against three separate fires that had gone out of control. Two separate columns of flame were moving northward from the O'Leary fire and it appeared that nothing could prevent their junction with the inferno in Bateham's mill. But before this consolidation could take place, the capricious fire struck unexpectedly east of the river.

The Parmelee Omnibus and Stage Company had just completed a new stable at Jackson and Franklin on the southwest edge of the business dis-

THE CHICAGO WATERWORKS, 1867

trict. The stalls were new and the lofts freshly filled with hay for the horses which were to be moved in two days later. It was on this target that a mass of blazing timber descended after hurtling nearly a quarter of a mile from the holocaust on the west bank of the river. The hay and newly painted lumber blazed up instantly. A short time later the gas works nearby were on fire. The heroism of a watchman who transferred the gas to tanks on the North Side prevented an explosion but simultaneously put out every light on the South Side of the city. The situation was suddenly desperate. The fire was in the heart of the city, while west of the river an inferno of flames three-quarters of a mile long and one hundred fifty acres in extent defied the best efforts of the firemen against it.

The new fire in the business district forced the fire companies to divide their efforts. Some of the engines, giving up the West Side as lost, rushed over to the South Division. There the fire, like a shrewdly commanded army, moved forward in a pair of flanking movements around the business area. One column moved north from the tinderbox shanties of crime and vice in Conley's Patch to the proud buildings of LaSalle Street. Another arm stretched eastward and south toward the lake. Wild flames hurled brands of fire high in the sky. The watchman in the wooden crib at the end of the lake tunnel—two miles from shore and three miles east of the fire—found the sky filled with a rain of sparks. With the help of his wife he began soaking the roof of the crib to keep it from burning down to the waterline.

At midnight Mayor Roswell B. Mason wired as far as New York City in an appeal for extra fire-fighting equipment. In Milwaukee, St. Louis and Cincinnati, fire engines were loaded on railroad cars to be rushed to Chicago. Meanwhile, as the moon rose dully through a thin pall of smoke, the fact became increasingly clear that a firebreak of some kind would be needed to stop the progress of the flames. James H. Hildreth, a former alderman, asked for authority to blow up buildings in the path of the fire and was granted it. His zeal was greater than his skill and his first effort in the Union National Bank did no more than blow out all the windows. About the same time, General Philip Sheridan, commander of the Army of the Missouri with headquarters in Chicago, also had the idea of blowing up buildings. Hildreth, however, had the powder and used his civilian prerogatives by refusing to share it with the general.

While Hildreth experimented with explosives, the fire continued its unpredictable leaps over the city. Shortly after one o'clock in the morning, a flaming beam landed in the cupola of the Courthouse and the fire soon spread to the lower floors. In the jail on the ground level the prisoners screamed for their freedom as the Courthouse bell pealed monotonously over their heads and the crackling of flames signaled the spreading of the fire. Finally most of the prisoners were freed, the exceptions being accused murderers who were led handcuffed to the lake shore. In the deserted building an automatic mechanism continued clanging the bell until the tower itself fell, to be quickly followed by the crash of the building.

The pace of the fire increased. At Jackson and LaSalle, the new Grand Pacific Hotel—six stories of olive-tinted Ohio sandstone, with a carriage court roofed over by a glass dome, five hundred rooms each equipped with an "electric annunciator" and "a vertical railway to connect all floors"—crashed to the earth before a single guest had scratched his name on its register. At Dearborn and Adams, the equally new Bigelow Hotel with its red carpeting, carved walnut furniture and art galleries disappeared in the flames before it could open its doors for a single moment of elegant existence. The Tremont House went up in flames for the fourth time in its history. Its intrepid manager, John B. Drake, was able to save only the money from the safe and a few pillowcases full of silver. Hurrying along the streets with his salvage, Drake heard men prophesying Chicago would never recover. He did not believe them. On his way to his home he paused in front of the Michigan Avenue Hotel at Congress Street. He saw that it was directly in the path of the flames but still untouched. He turned and strode into the lobby where he confronted the startled manager with an offer to buy the hotel's lease and furniture. The distraught proprietor, besieged by pleas for help from guests dragging their belongings into the street, could not believe the offer

THE GREAT FIRE, by *Currier & Ives*. Note that flames are going in the wrong direction

was a serious one. Drake handed him a thousand dollars in cash from the Tremont moneybox as an advance payment. Even a thousand dollars was a good price for a hotel that appeared destined to burn and the offer was accepted. Copies of an agreement to buy if the hotel survived were hastily drawn up and witnessed by guests at the hotel. With his copy in his pocket, Drake picked up his pillowcase of silver, and hurried down Michigan Avenue toward his home hoping for the best.

The flames by this time had lighted the sky almost to the brilliancy of daylight. From a distance the whole city appeared to take on the appearance of a lurid, yellowish red. The fire burned so intensely there was only a minimum of smoke. Everywhere in and around the burning areas there raged a blizzard of hot cinders, falling in a steady downpour that stung the skin like needles. In many places the red flakes and hot black ashes filled the air until it was impossible to see the distance of a block ahead. Adding to the terror was the danger from maddened animals, dashing through the streets in a torture of pain from the red snow that blistered even the toughest hide. In the heart of the fire, the heat was as intense as that of a welding torch. Iron columns two feet in thickness were burned into dust. Car wheels from the streetcars stood in the tracks half burned away while the tracks turned upward in grotesque patterns from the twisting force of the flames. Jets of fire consumed fireproof safes and bored holes of fire

BURNING OF THE CROSBY OPERA HOUSE

through fireproof walls. The noise was tremendous as the roar of the flames and the crash of falling walls formed a deep-throated chorus to the staccato explosion of barrels of oil and paint.

There were no passive spectators of the fire. The crowds were fleeing for their lives, trying desperately to save something which would provide the basis for a new start if they should survive. The streets between the buildings were narrow gorges of pushing, struggling mobs. People crowded upon such points of vantage as high sidewalks and fences only to have them collapse beneath the weight of harried refugees. Fifth Avenue (Wells Street) and Conley's Patch had already emptied their population into the streets. Debauched, pinched with misery, the flotsam of the city's slum floated along with the crowd. Some smashed windows with their bare hands and snatched what they could, ignoring bleeding hands that sometimes spoiled the fine clothes and silks before they could be taken from the displays. In front of Shay's dry-goods store a man loaded one of the company's trucks with silks and drove away, defying a store guard's command to halt with a curt, "Fire and be damned." A ragamuffin with white kid gloves on his hands and gold-plated jewelry in his back pocket was less fortunate; a falling marble slab from a burning building crushed him to earth.

Daniel Quirk's Saturday-night hospitality would have been wasted on Sunday's mob. At Chapin and Gore's restaurant and liquor store, men were hired to roll a hundred barrels of whiskey down to the comparative safety of the lake shore before the liquor could be seized by the looters who operated just ahead of the flames. Elsewhere beer and whiskey were to be had for the taking and the unruliness of the crowd in at least one instance forced the firemen to turn the hoses from the flames to the mob. The crowd only laughed and in a combination of hysteria and drunkenness taunted the firemen to do it again. The madness was increased by the desire of Chicago to save not only its life but its property. Express wagons, dirt carts and even coaches were used to haul goods to places of safety. One driver asked—and was given—a thousand dollars to haul a half million dollars of a bank's currency to a safe place on the far West Side. A frantic bride rushed along carrying her half-wrapped wedding presents. A round-faced man had seized a woman's turban to protect his hair from the cinders and pushed his way uncertainly down the street while a feather on the turban waved weirdly in the gusts of wind. Women, shrieking with hysterical laughter, dragged large Saratoga trunks slowly down the sidewalks. A red-faced German pushed a wheelbarrow full of clothing that did not obscure the keg of beer over which it was draped. A radical, who stood on top of an abandoned piano to declare that the fire was the friend of the poor and urge the crowd to help itself to what it wanted, was suddenly quieted by a well-aimed whiskey bottle. A woman kneeled in the street with a crucifix held up before her and the skirt of her dress burning while she prayed. Along the river, burning ghost vessels drifted with their masts aflame. Bridges that had caught fire teetered wildly on their centerposts like grotesque fireworks.

About an hour after the Courthouse crashed to the ground the flames leaped the river again, carrying the fire into the North Division where a group of railroad cars containing kerosene on the Chicago and North Western Railway tracks caught fire. From the railway the flames jumped to Wright's livery stables to form another column of fire. The fire rolled north on a wild revel through the neighborhood of frame houses and stately homes of Chicago's first settlers. A short time later a burning brand about ten feet long landed on the slate covering over the wooden roof of the waterworks. The entire building was soon on fire and the pumps destroyed. When the last reserve of water from the tower had been used there was no more water for the city's fire lines except where it could be pumped from the river.

Five separate fires were then eating at the heart of the city. Early Monday the fire on the North Side reached from LaSalle Street and the river to

Oak Street and the lake. The original fire on the West Side had stopped its spread at the firebreak formed by the burned-out area of Saturday's fire but the entire district was a smoldering ruin. In the business section, the flames continued to advance voraciously. During the morning the fire started to backtrack and those buildings that had been saved during the night were caught up and destroyed. At 9 o'clock the Palmer House burned and a short time afterwards McVicker's Theater and the "fireproof" *Tribune* building toppled to the ground. East of the business area, on Wabash and Michigan Avenues, the yards and sidewalks were heaped high with household goods, trunks and stocks of supplies from the stores along State and Lake Streets. At the lake front baseball park, at the foot of Washington and Randolph Streets, refugees from the fire sat despondently on piles of mattresses and clothing. As the circle of flames to the west was drawn more tightly around these temporary islands of safety the weary refugees had to move again. At the ballpark there were hurried attempts to bury silver and other heavy but valuable belongings while a lone policeman shouted purposeless threats about defacing the ball grounds.

On the North Side, where the extremes of wealth and squalor had been separated only by the commonplace barrier of Clark Street, the disparate classes huddled together without distinction on the lake shore. The once-notorious Sands were covered for a distance of about a mile with men, women and children in a variety of undress. Many of the women were in nightgowns

REFUGEES IN THE STREET

with a wrapper pulled tightly around them and the men had tucked their nightgowns hastily and inadequately in the tops of their trousers. Each family sat on an island of personal property—silver, boxes of valuable papers, chairs and even disjointed bedsteads. There was a mixture of the ludicrous and pathetic. Great plate-glass mirrors flashed back the illumination of the fire and elegant carpets served as temporary shelters. Mattresses and carpets continually caught fire from falling sparks and there was a constant procession to the edge of the lake for buckets of water to extinguish the smoldering flames.

Early Monday morning, when the great lumber mills along the river caught fire, the heat was so intense that those on the beach were forced into the lake to avoid being suffocated. A. T. Willett ordered his horses and wagons driven as far out as possible and many of the refugees clambered into these high-wheeled vehicles to wait out the fire. Others spent hours sitting on the backs of chairs, their feet resting on the seats in the water. Judge Lambert Tree and his wife stood knee-deep in water for fourteen hours. Others on the North Side sought protection in Lincoln Park, still in the process of being evacuated as a cemetery. For hours they sat gloomily among the open graves and upended tombstones keeping a death watch on the city. Later the shower of sparks was so thick that the park had to be abandoned. Even those who had been able to get to an artificial island in the middle of the park lagoon had to pour water over their clothes to keep from burning alive.

Meanwhile, the fire was moving among the frame houses and yards of dry leaves on the North Side with the force of a hurricane, lifting up whole buildings and throwing them on top of others. The terrific draft created by the heating of the air sent the fire hurtling along the tops of the buildings, skipping from one block to another. In front of the actual line of fire moved a zone of intensely heated air that cracked windows and sent black smoke pouring from walls and furniture until whole houses burst into flames almost as quickly as the flaring of a match. During the night the servants in the bigger houses had been burying such property as they could in the spacious yards, hoping that the fire would pass over it. Most remarkable was the number of pianos which were recorded as being buried, an indication of the social importance attached to these instruments as well as of the prodigal labors which were inspired by fear of the fire. Not all of those who buried valuables were able to save them. Mary Arnold Scudder, newly married daughter of Lincoln's friend, Isaac Arnold, buried her wedding presents only to have them fused and destroyed from the heat.

At the Chicago Club, whose membership was restricted to the wealthiest businessmen, the members toasted their defiance of the destruction of their businesses with a champagne breakfast. Before they could finish, the fire roared into their exclusive club. Hastily filling their pockets with cigars and taking along all the liquor they could carry, they picked up the red satin sofas from the lobby and took them to the lake shore where they sat down and finished their meal. The fire which destroyed the Chicago Club was on the south fringe of the flames and not burning as fiercely because of the prevailing southwesterly wind. At 11 o'clock Monday the final row of buildings to be destroyed in the South Division caught fire. It was Terrace Row, the fashionable collection of row houses on Michigan Avenue between Congress and Van Buren Streets. William "Deacon" Bross reported that the entire row vanished "quickly and grandly" as the flames "wrapped up the whole block and away it floated in black clouds over Lake Michigan." Bross's preoccupation with reporting the fire for the *Tribune* resulted in his being one of the best targets for plunderers. He sent his coachman to the lake shore with a buggy full of harness, coffee and other property only to have some friends foolishly turn it over to a stranger who said he had orders to drive it away. Bross never saw it again. Later, an express wagon pulled up to the door. Bross assumed his daughter had hired it and she assumed that he had. They both hurried to fill it; not until after the driver disappeared did they realize that they had been helping him rob them. Finding another stranger on his doorstep with "a considerable invoice" of his clothes and "the hunting suit outside," the usually volatile Bross could only comment, "Well, you might as well have them as let them burn."

The destruction of Terrace Row ended the threat of fire to the south but there was a new danger as the flames from the western edge of the business district threatened to backtrack across the river and destroy the West Division in the same way the area north of the river had been devastated. All the buildings on the west bank were soaked with water from the river; by Monday afternoon, while the business section was burning itself out, the fire continued to grow only to the north. By nightfall, the big fires were out except in the neighborhood of Clark and Fullerton on the northern limits of the city. The last house to burn was that of a doctor on Fullerton Avenue; it went up in smoke about 10:30—more than twenty-five hours after the start of the fire. Shortly before midnight a light rain started to fall. Between 2 and 4 o'clock Tuesday morning the fire died out, though from Harrison to Fullerton burning coal piles in the city's cellars cast a weird footlight of red on the panorama of the city's ruins.

In the area swept by fire only two homes had been saved—the mansion of Mahlon D. Ogden and the modest home of policeman Richard Bellinger. Ogden was away, but his friends kept the roof of his house covered with wet blankets and carpets, the same precautionary measure that had been tried and failed in hundreds of other cases. Bellinger was probably the only man to fight the fire directly and win. During the night he raked up his leaves and

BUSINESS DISTRICT AFTER THE FIRE, looking north from Harrison Street

burned his wooden fences and sidewalks. He kept a wet covering on his roof, first using water from his cistern and carrying buckets from a ditch two blocks away; then as a last desperate measure pouring his entire supply of cider over the roof and walls.

Tuesday morning Chicago counted its losses. The fire destroyed 2,124 acres in the central part of the city. It burned 17,450 homes, made ninety thousand homeless and destroyed property worth two hundred million dollars—one-third of the wealth of Chicago. At the customs house, James E. McLean waited forlornly for his "fireproof vault" to cool. Opening it, he found that a million and a half dollars in currency for which he was responsible had burned; it required an Act of Congress to wipe out his prodigious debt. There were more important tragedies. Nearly three hundred were known to be dead; how many more vanished in the crematorium of the city was never to be known. Parts of the picture of a sorrowing city appeared in the makeshift newspapers that were soon on the streets: "Mrs. Bush is at 40 Arnold Street. She lost her baby . . ."—"Henry Schneider, baby, in blue poland waist, red skirt, has white hair. Lost."

The destruction was comparable only to the great fires of London and Moscow. The London fire burned thirteen thousand houses and drove two hundred thousand from their homes but covered only five hundred acres of ground. That of Moscow burned over four hundred acres and destroyed twelve thousand houses. The area of the Chicago fire had been twice as great as the total of those of London and Moscow.

Chicago turned matter-of-factly to the problem of recovery. City offices were set up in the First Congregational Church and a relief program was started. In the first day, nearly five thousand special police were appointed to keep order and stop the looting. The badge of these new officers was a small white piece of cloth with the word "Police" printed on it. The badges had been printed on a boy's press by Allan Culver with the aid of Katherine Medill, whose father Joseph had already found a print shop from which to issue his *Tribune*. The mayor issued proclamations forbidding the sale of whiskey and fixing the price of bread. The army provided tents as temporary housing.

Most cheering were the immediate offers of help which came from over the nation. Two special trains with food and clothing were dispatched from New York. Special committees arrived from St. Louis and Cincinnati to find what was needed. From England came the offer of books to replace the library destroyed in the fire. Only one letter, published in the *Chicago Magazine of Music, Fashion and Home Reading*, showed little sympathy. It came from the literary editor of an Augusta, Georgia, newspaper: "I feel a deep interest in the misfortunes of your city and would fain help you all I can," the correspondent wrote. "And yet, do you know, we owe it—some of my friends and I—to the implacable temper of Chicago troops, during the war, that we are now exiles, impoverished and struggling, far from the sepulchres of our fathers and without a single heirloom sacred to past affection spared us. It was a Chicago soldier who threw into the flames the likeness of my mother, and tearing a box of invaluable literary memoranda from the person who held it, consigned the box to the same flaming bed." The fires of Sherman still burned.

Another Union hero, General Sheridan, was called upon by Mayor Mason after the fire to declare martial law and preserve order. During the first day several looters had been shot dead by angry citizens. The mayor's practical, if unconstitutional, action, angered Governor John Palmer. The governor considered it an invasion of state's rights and felt the city should have appealed first to the state government for aid. After an exchange of angry letters among the governor, mayor and President Grant, the troops were withdrawn. Then, within a few days, they were brought back without the accompanying onus of martial law.

One of the first Chicagoans to recover his composure and nerve after the fire was W. D. Kerfoot. While the ruins of the buildings were still too hot for handling, Kerfoot put up a wooden shack on the deserted street to house his real-estate office. Outside a sign proclaimed in black letters: "All gone except wife, children and energy." Chicagoans, conscious that during the same hours that they were having their ordeal, flash forest fires had killed 750 in Peshtigo, Wisconsin, and destroyed the Michigan towns of Holland and Manistee on the eastern shore of the lake, thought that Kerfoot had all that was needful.

John B. Drake, who had been considered so foolish as to pay an option on a hotel that was sure to be burned, walked down to the edge of the burned district; he found the Michigan Avenue Hotel still standing. He immediately wired New York for a loan and a few days later walked into the hotel lobby with the full purchase price in cash. The proprietor, who realized the hotel was the only one standing in the downtown district, refused to sell and said there was no law which could make him. Drake left and returned in a short time with three or four friends. He laid his watch on the proprietor's table and gave him five minutes to deliver possession. As the proprietor hesitated again, Drake's friends made some remarks about the proximity of Lake Michigan and the imminent possibility of the proprietor's bobbing about in the water. This show of determination settled the issue and the sale was completed. Drake renamed the hotel the Tremont House and kept possession of it until 1873—just one year before it burned down.

89 WASHINGTON STREET, by W. P. Burton. The first building erected after the fire

PART TWO *Enter the Ladies*

1871=1890

GEORGE P. A. HEALY, a self-portrait, 1867

Puritans on Prairie Avenue

CHICAGO, having once raised itself out of the mud, turned optimistically to the chores of creating a new city over the ashes of the old. Poetic tributes from Bret Harte, Will Carleton, John Greenleaf Whittier and many an amateur were a spur to these efforts. From the city's prolific songwriter, George Root, came a series of tunes on the same theme—"Passing Through the Fire," "Lost and Saved" and "From the Ruins Our City Shall Arise." Those fortunate enough to have saved their pianos were diverted by a nocturne composed by Clara E. Saylor and given the clangorous title of "The Chicago Fire Bell." The city was determined that it would not be, as Sir Christopher Wren had disdainfully characterized the officials of London, "unworthy of a great fire."

Wagons hauled bricks from the ruins to the lake-shore basin to make ground for a larger lake-front park. Other teams dragged the ruins of the Courthouse north on Clark Street to provide a more solid base for that busy thoroughfare. Thrifty Presbyterians took the tar-stained stones of the Second Presbyterian Church and used them for their new church building in Lake Forest. New and more solidly constructed buildings began to appear above the jagged profile of the downtown area. In the Kendall Building, George H. Johnson used the first hollow-tile floor construction and thus made complete fireproofing possible. Architects flocked to Chicago, drawn by the rare opportunity to remake a city.

There was not always time to rebuild. Marshall Field & Co. opened its doors in a former horse barn of a street railway company. South of the fire area, on the elegant residential streets of Michigan and Wabash Avenues, "trade walked into the houses with a yardstick for its stiletto and domestic life took up its pack and retreated." Merchants who had lost their stores opened for business in the front parlors of their homes. The piano, the gorgeous sofas, the medallion carpet and the clock of ormulu were carted to the upper floors while temporary showcases took their places in the drawing and dining rooms. Servants accustomed to performing polite services at formal dinners were drafted as clerks to sell hats, furs, shoes and jewelry in the hurly-burly of the new domestic competition. Handsome bronze-hinged front doors were cluttered with business notices. Broad windows where canaries once chirped were blocked out by garish signs lettered with various degrees of skill (and spelling accuracy) by sign painters whose services were suddenly at a premium.

On the east side of Michigan Avenue in the burned district, temporary pine buildings were erected after the Board of Public Works abrogated the rule the lake front could be used only for a park. The city issued temporary leases for these lots and extracted a guarantee that all the barrackslike buildings would be torn down within a year. The former residents of the avenue, either burned out or forced away by the exigencies of business, sought more tranquil surroundings. Only a few had any desire to return to their old location. Most sought to avoid harsh memories and the fear that a southwest wind might bring with it another wall of flame. Some stayed permanently in Riverside, where they had summer homes. Others moved to new areas of the city.

The pattern for most of society's migration was set by three men who were referred to, more in reverence than irreverence, as the trinity of Chicago business: Marshall Field, George M. Pullman and Philip D. Armour. When these three established their homes on Prairie Avenue, that once deserted street became the most fashionable address in Chicago. Within an area of five blocks, forty of the sixty members of the exclusive Commercial Club had their homes. The pride and interest of the city in these new mansions was intense. When the food commission merchant and banker, J. W. Doane, erected his Chicago palace, the newspapers sent reporters daily for accounts of the progress in its construction. Within a few years after the fire the scene along Prairie Avenue changed from one of wild grasses and grazing cows to a vista of towered mansions with great bay windows and spacious yards. Those who could not find places in the exclusive precincts of Prairie Avenue lived either on adjoining Calumet Avenue or farther south in "Millionaire's

REBUILDING CHICAGO. View at Lake and LaSalle Streets, by *Theo R. Davis*

Row" on Michigan Avenue. In the construction of the expensive homes on Michigan Avenue, there was a tendency to imitate the boulevard system of Paris, with blocks of adjoining houses of similar style and arrangement. But the owners did not always allow their architects to follow the Parisian taste. Efforts to achieve individuality or excel all others soon led to an excess of ornamentation that, unhappily for the city's reputation, was known as the Chicago Style.

Life in these mansions took on an elegance previously unknown. Stern puritan living gave way to epicurean enjoyment, though many New England households still frowned on the practice of serving wine with meals. The hired girl was replaced by a downstairs maid and a butler. No longer was dinner served at noon with the head of the family coming home from the office to do the carving. Ladies' luncheons and formal dinner parties at which the hour was set "as late as 7 o'clock," became popular forms of entertainment. Before calling on friends, a lady scanned carefully the newly published *Bon Ton Directory*, giving the "Names in Alphabetical Order, Addresses and Hours of Reception of the Most Prominent and Fashionable Ladies Residing in Chicago and Its Suburbs." That there was a certain uneasiness about adopting the more rigid rules was evidenced in the frequent notation, "Friends Always Welcome."

The chief characteristic of Chicago society was its newness. Most hostesses had little experience in entertaining formally. A guest from Boston was horrified to find her Prairie Avenue hostess serving dessert ices in the center of

MRS. IRA HOLMES, 1866, by George P. A. Healy. The mother of Burton Holmes

calla lilies, a horticultural innovation more magnificent than appetizing. More conservative hostesses relied on the catalogues of the fashionable caterer, Kinsley, for instructions on how to manage a "Kettledrum" (a word borrowed from English garrison life where the drumhead often served as tea tray), High Tea, Coffee, or an At Home. Kinsley's was Chicago's most fashionable restaurant and aspired to the title of The Delmonico's of the West. H. M. Kinsley had first maintained a restaurant in Crosby's Opera House. After the fire he erected a five-story Moorish castle on Adams Street, making it additionally conspicuous with red-and-white striped awnings which hung from every window. Here the diner might have a choice of a French or German café, a Ladies' and Gentlemen's Restaurant, a Gentleman's Restaurant or the option of using one of the private banquet rooms or the large ballroom. From this headquarters Kinsley issued the catalogues which determined the proper etiquette for Chicagoans in such matters as Afternoon Reception, Society Jewelry, The Art of Dressing and The Etiquette of the Ballroom. For those wishing to remain au courant with fashionable conversation or menus, Kinsley included a glossary of frequently used French terms. One of Kinsley's most famous performances was in connection with the driving of the golden spike which marked the completion of the Union

Pacific Railroad. Kinsley filled a baggage car with provisions, chafing dishes, cooks and waiters to serve a group of travelers which included Jay Gould, George Pullman, William H. Vanderbilt and other railroad kings going west for the ceremonies.

Summertime in Chicago found society activities at a minimum. Life along Prairie Avenue returned to an informality more like that of a small town than of a city approaching a population of half a million. On summer evenings the drawing room was moved to the front steps; the children sat on the family's stoop rug waving friendly greetings to passing friends while the adults sat in rocking chairs in the porch or vestibule. This flight from the drawing room may have been hastened by the styles in interior decoration which had been given a depressing tone by the Eastlake pattern popularized at the Philadelphia Centennial Exposition. In the name of art, houses were filled with ebonized furniture and fragile gilt chairs while flimsy curtains replaced traditional draperies. Under the influence of William Morris, many houses were given a dungeon gloominess by brown and green wallpapers applied in perpendicular patterns called picture screens and friezes. Another fad was for gilt milking stools, spinning wheels and chopping bowls which added an incongruous note to many a formal drawing room. Increasing the sense of melancholy were the dried cattails in upended sewer tilings which decorators preferred to more cheerful flowers. In personal dress, bangs and bangles were the fashion rule among debutantes, while their escorts tended to toothpick shoes and tight trousers. Matrons wore bonnets or mantillas, while men of substance identified themselves with massive rings in the pattern of their seals.

Culture was not neglected. The women of society formed a Fortnightly Club whose purpose was to be the dissemination of both "social and intellectual culture." Their husbands joined the Chicago Literary Club with much the same purpose. Both were to prove durable institutions. More transient was the Twentieth Century Club, patterned after the Nineteenth Century Club which Courtlandt Palmer had organized in New York. The newspapers, recording the founding of the Twentieth Century Club, said that "while there are many bright minds among its members, it is essentially a listening club and not a talking club, and in this respect it differs from any other social, scientific, or literary club in America."

Mrs. George Roswell Grant, who had the idea for the Twentieth Century Club, felt that "when a distinguished foreigner and people from other parts of the country come to Chicago, they want to meet the representative society people. They don't care about being bored with a lot of men who have a local reputation as men of genius . . . They want to meet people whose names are known as men and women of fashion." Despite such attractions as a lecture in Italian (reported as having been delivered "after a fashion like drawing long, tight-fitting corks"), the club was split by dissension. At the first annual meeting a group of rebels planned a protest against what they called "autocratic management" in the club's affairs. The women complained that only a few ladies such as Mrs. Pullman, Mrs. Doane and Mrs. Field had been allowed to entertain the club and that too many meetings had been held in the Art Institute. Speaking anonymously to a newspaper reporter, one of the insurgents explained the reasons for her stand: "Why did we go into the club if not to get a chance to entertain and be entertained by swells ... What we want is to have a provision inserted in the new constitution that the club shall meet only in the homes of its members." The lady also expressed disappointment in the club's choice of speakers. "There has been absolutely nothing sensational or interesting in the slightest degree in the lectures," she said. "We might just as well have had Carmencita and people of her sort who would give us something to talk about." The reign of Mrs. Pullman, Mrs. Field and their cohorts was not easily disturbed, however, and the rebels went meekly along with the established order.

The Marshall Field house was one of the dominant mansions on the Avenue. It was designed by Richard Morris Hunt, the same architect who built the New York residences of William H. Vanderbilt and John Jacob Astor. Field did not pick Hunt because of his New York reputation but because the architect came from Brattleboro, Vermont, and could therefore be counted on to plan a building expressing the Yankee virtues of "dignity, simplicity and common sense." Field's instructions to the architect were succinct: "No frills." The result was a house extraordinarily plain in its exterior where Mr. Field ruled, but sumptuous in its interior where Mrs. Field had her say. A spectacular circular staircase of carved wood spiraled upward from the end of the central hall. The ivory and gold drawing room with its high ceiling would have formed an appropriate setting for state receptions in a royal palace. Though undistinguished in appearance to the outsider, the house was one of the most costly in Chicago and was the first to be equipped with electric lights. (The power came from a privately owned electrical plant in J. W. Doane's stables.) Every morning at a regular hour Marshall Field left his home in his carriage for his store. But on arriving at

GOING TO THE RACES

State Street, he would get out of the carriage a short distance from Marshall Field Co. and walk the rest of the way. He thought it both bad taste and bad business to arrive at work in a fancy carriage with a coachman on the box.

Marshall Field prescribed this stern regimen only for himself. With his children he was overindulgent. The first "grown-up" birthday party of Marshall Field, Jr., was the most magnificent the city had ever seen. For several years Mrs. Field had made it a custom to give a Christmas party for young Marshall and his sister, Ethel. In 1886, when Marshall was seventeen, his mother felt it was time for him to have a more adult party. She planned a "Mikado Ball" around the theme of the Gilbert and Sullivan operetta which was currently the most popular stage success in America. Decorators were called in to transform the house into a miniature Japanese village. Not even Kinsley's was considered adequate for the occasion. Sherry's was engaged in New York to bring all the supplies of linen, silver and food from the east in two private railroad cars. The cost of the party exceeded $75,000.

On the night of the ball, Prairie Avenue was illuminated for several blocks with special calcium lights. A long line of polished carriages drawn by meticulously groomed horses began delivering the first of the five hundred invited guests at 6 P.M. the hour that the friends of fourteen-year-old Ethel had been bidden to arrive. Everyone was in a Japanese costume. The carriages stopped at the side entrance as the front hall had been blocked off with a reproduction of Ko-Ko's garden, the setting for the second act of *The Mikado*. On one side of the hall was a miniature pagoda which housed the musicians of society's favorite band leader, Johnny Hand, who wore a black silk ribbon dangling from his glasses. Valicia and his mandolin orchestra, the first unit of its kind ever heard in Chicago, alternated with Hand's musicians. The drawing room had been converted to an octagonal Japanese court. The doors had been removed and replaced with swinging fringe curtains of beaded wood, ivory and glass such as were used in doorways by the wealthy people of Japan. The walls of every hall were obscured behind satin and bamboo screens and the ceilings hidden by a profusion of Japanese lanterns and parasols. Expensive bronzes, tapestries and porcelains had been purchased to carry out the oriental motif. At one end of the ballroom stood

CARRIAGES ON DERBY DAY, 1893

KINSLEY'S RESTAURANT (From Kinsley's catalogue)

two Japanese flower trees, their artificial foliage carefully arranged by a Japanese artist. There were imported favors for every guest, Mrs. Field having scored a social and diplomatic coup by persuading the iconoclastic James McNeill Whistler to design two of the favors that were distributed along with toy animals, lanterns, parasols, Japanese slippers and the currently popular ornamental storks. As the younger guests left the party, their older brothers and sisters arrived to dance to "I've Got a Little List," "Willow Titwillow" and other Sullivan airs, which must have required complicated stepping. The dancing was managed by Eugene A. Bournique, whose parents ran the most fashionable dancing school in the city and where adults as well as children learned the intricacies of ballroom behavior.

Bournique's was more than a dancing school. Many society receptions were held in its richly furnished ballroom beneath brilliant crystal chandeliers flanked by a series of stained-glass windows. Most residents on Prairie Avenue had their own ballrooms but met at Bournique's for an exclusive dancing class organized by Mrs. Pullman. In this class were the first couples of Chicago's society, many of them in their fifties and sixties. They applied themselves to the problems of the schottische, the waltz, the polka, and a quadrille of local origin known as "The Prairie Queen" in the same methodical manner they had amassed fortunes. Among the students were the sons of two Presidents—Frederick Dent Grant and Robert Todd Lincoln. General Philip Sheridan was another member of the class. The hero of the Wilderness Campaign and the Battle of Five Forks, who had never learned to go any direction but forward and around the flank of the enemy on the battlefield, carried this military single-mindedness into the ballroom. When General Sheridan waltzed, he whirled his partner around and around without reversing his direction while the dizzying lady listened hopefully for the end of the dance. Jennie Otis Counselman confided after a series of turns with the general that "as he stepped on my toes and did not reverse until I was dizzy, I concluded many who were not heroes danced better."

As a feminine society began to develop, the men spent much of their time at the Chicago Club. Here a guest might see Marshall Field, George Pullman, N. K. Fairbank, John Crerar and T. B. Blackstone dining together or playing poker at the "millionaire's table"—which might more accurately have been called that of the multimillionaires. Many fortunes were still to be made. Gustavus Swift, who had come to Chicago to do the cattle buying for a packing firm and had since become head of the company, was to be found in the malodorous surroundings of his plant's sewage outlet watching for signs of fat that might indicate wastefulness on the production line. This frugality, engendered in part by ancestors who had fought an unequal battle with the miserly sands of Cape Cod, was to prove the basis of a fortune for this "Yankee of the Stockyards." It was also to give the industry a solid economic base and a notoriety for using everything of the hog but the squeal. Gustavus Swift had no reason to apologize for his role as sewer inspector. It was recognized as a sound business practice; and business success rather than an ancestral blood line was the only sure key to the portals of Chicago society.

One of those who dared to rebel against the stern rule of the city's business leaders was Mrs. Herbert Ayer, who "loved everything that was pretty and especially everything that was French." She was a student of ceramics and antiques. It was known—and discussed with disapproval—that she was fond of French novels and had even dared to act out French plays at parties in her home. She entertained unconventionally at Sunday-morning breakfasts, real French *déjeuners à la fourchette* at which she served *omelettes aux fines herbes*, chicken livers *en brochette*, *café noir* and a fine wine. Her guests were principally stage celebrities such as Edwin Booth, Lawrence Barrett and John McCulloch. If they found the breakfasts unusual it was only in the degree of pleasure they afforded. These violations of the social proprieties continued to disturb Chicago's society arbiters until Mr. Ayer's firm failed. It was felt this catastrophe carried a moral for the eccentric behavior of his pretty wife. But Mrs. Ayer was not prepared to accept an unhappy ending to her romance with life. Using her own name of Harriet Hubbard Ayer, she manufactured and sold a beauty cream of her own prescription.

She was soon the head of a prosperous cosmetics business. Moving to New York, she was hired as a columnist by Arthur Brisbane and became the highest paid woman journalist in the country. Although separated from her husband, she displayed a nobility worthy of a heroine in the French romances of which she was so fond. Learning that her former mate was dying, alone and without money, she returned to pay his bills and care for him. She sat holding his hand when he died. Gallic sentiment had given the story of Harriet Hubbard Ayer an ending of which not even transplanted Puritans could disapprove.

The most festive day for all of South Side society was Derby Day at Washington Park. The running of the American Derby was the signal for the fashionable world to display its summer finery. Shortly before noon the boulevards of the South Side began to fill up with lines of carriages. The horses' tails were docked and their heads held high; polished harnesses jangled cockily as the gay cavalcade of the best people, the finest horses, the handsomest phaetons, victorias, coaches, hansoms and even "just plain hacks" made its way south to the race track at Sixty-first Street and Cottage Grove Avenue. In the carriages sat the wives of the town's new millionaires, wearing summer gowns and holding brightly hued sun parasols over their heads. Frequently the women would be unaccompanied, their husbands preferring to ride out in one of the big drags or "Tally-ho" coaches filled with cronies from the Chicago Club or Calumet Club, the exclusive province of those who could claim a place among the first settlers. Mayor Carter Harrison usually galloped along on a Kentucky thoroughbred with Mrs.

RACECOURSE AT WASHINGTON PARK

Harrison and Carter, Jr., following more sedately in one of the small T-carts. The drivers of the fancier turnouts would frequently leave their female passengers at the clubhouse and spend another half-hour driving around the special paths to the left of the clubhouse. Here fancy-gaited animals were put through their paces, wheeling, turning, prancing high and flecking foam while an appreciative audience in the clubhouse applauded with discreet enthusiasm. Later the horses were driven to the rear of the club area where grooms unhitched the animals and took them to shaded stalls in the rear to cool and feed.

It was in their horses and carriages that fashionable Chicagoans first dared to compete for public attention. Hobart Chatfield-Taylor gave credit for this new air of sumptuousness to the English coachman who, "clean shaven and erect," sat upon the box where formerly there had been a mustachioed Scandinavian or a Negro with the sole responsibility of driving the horses. The English coachman, by his own impeccable attire and formally correct behavior, set a new standard for the occupant of the carriage behind him. To merit the approval of one's English coachman was the obsession of every socially ambitious Chicagoan, though more than a few among the city's first citizens found it difficult to resist grabbing the reins themselves. Their children were more adaptable and in many homes it was the children who insisted the coachman be added, proud to have him shout at less elegant modes of transportation, "Git out of the way and let the quality by!"

There was expensive competition to see who could have the flashiest horses and most expensive carriages. Charles Schwartz was the innovator, driving his Brewster drag and team of bays from one end of Michigan Avenue to the other. Hall McCormick was next in the contest with a London-built drag and a pair of roans. Both, however, were outdone by Potter Palmer, who surprised Chicagoans by appearing in a French char-à-banc with leopard skins spread over the seats. It was not the sole surprise Potter Palmer was to give Chicago.

MRS. POTTER PALMER AS A
YOUNG LADY, by George P. A. Healy

The Pride of Potter Palmer

IN THE summer of 1871, a few months before the great fire, Chicagoans learned to their astonishment that Potter Palmer had reserved the bridal suite of the Palmer House for himself. A bachelor of forty-four, Palmer had retired as a multimillionaire several years before when Marshall Field and a group of associates took over the management and a major interest of Palmer's dry-goods store. Palmer was not of a temperament to enjoy inactivity. After a short trip to Europe, he returned to Chicago and purchased a million dollars' worth of land along State Street. With typical audacity he set out to make it the principal street of Chicago. His first step was as farseeing as it was unconventional: he chopped twenty-seven feet off the front of his property and added it to the width of the street. Then, to demonstrate his own faith in the future of the street, he began construction of his Palmer House with the determination to make it the most elegant hostelry in the city. Chicago heard Potter Palmer liked to make frequent trips to Saratoga, where he acquired a reputation as a playboy and free spender. Stories filtered back to Chicago of late dinners, dashing rides behind four-in-hands, rivulets of champagne and gold coins dropped freely by the Quaker dry-goods prince into waiting hands. Occasionally he would shock Chicago by driving his

ENTER THE LADIES   124

buggy down the street with his feet on the buckboard and a lady of the demi-monde at his side.

The city's surprise over Palmer's decision to renounce the pleasures of Saratoga and similar pastimes was compounded when he revealed his bride would be Bertha Honore, a beautiful twenty-one-year-old daughter of a family from the city's aristocratic Kentucky colony. The courtship had been brief; this was explained on the grounds that Palmer was decisive in his actions. Those who knew Bertha Honore were as firm in their belief that the quick culmination of the romance could be attributed to the bride. They knew her as a girl of firm will and in later years had cause to suspect she immediately foresaw the potentialities of a union that was to prove illustrious for Chicago, and, to all appearances, as happy as less splendid romances.

Potter Palmer and Bertha Honore were married in July in the new Honore home on South Michigan Avenue. The bride wore a Paris gown of rose-point lace and white satin; orange blossoms were looped over her shoulders and a crown of the traditional flowers rested on the small wave in her long, dark hair. More than seven hundred guests attended the reception. Kinsley had exceeded his own high standards, replacing the customary cut glass with a complete service of sterling silver. The wedding gift of the groom to the bride was on the same fabulous scale; it was the new Palmer House, then valued at half a million dollars.

Palmer was in the East when the great fire obliterated his State Street investments. He lost ninety-five buildings in the flames and rents totaling $220,000 a year. Because of his heavy holdings in land, he fell $15,000 short of having enough money to pay taxes on the charred earth that represented his total assets. He was able to recoup because an insurance company, whose faith in his abilities must have been devout, gave him a loan of $1,700,000 with no more collateral than his signature. With these funds the Palmer House was rebuilt, more imposing than before. Its design was grandiose; before it was finished, Palmer told his bookkeeper to enter no more charges as he didn't care to know the cost. Even so, he pared no magnificence from his plans. He insisted that the hotel set a new standard for being fireproof and shrewdly used the fact to publicize his accomplishment. He offered other hotel owners the option of starting a fire in any room in the Palmer House. If the flames spread beyond the room within an hour, Palmer would pay for the damages; if not, the other hotel keeper had to pay for them. There were no takers for the offer.

Another bit of showmanship, on a level with the earlier innovation when he offered to let women take goods home on approval against the advice of such established merchants as A. T. Stewart of New York, was his order to have silver dollars embedded in the floor of the Palmer House barber shop.

His silver dollars meant as much to the men as his courteous store policies had signified to their wives; generations of farm boys in the Midwest were to grow up dreaming of the day they could walk on the silver dollars in the Palmer House barber shop, known also as the Garden of Eden in honor of its proprietor, W. S. Eden.

As Potter Palmer set out to remake the city physically and commercially, his bride was busy trying to remake it socially. Her first opportunity for a display of her talents as an architect of society on a grand scale came with the marriage of her sister, Ida Honore, to Lieutenant Frederick Dent Grant, the son of the President. The wedding was at the Honore home, relocated on Vincennes Avenue at Forty-fifth Street, but its sumptuous plans were in the determined hands of sister Bertha. On the afternoon of the wedding, the Palmers arrived in an elegance exceeding that of President Grant and his wife. Mr. Palmer was sartorially exact in a gray topper with gray gloves and wore in his gray cravat one perfect pearl. Mrs. Palmer, wearing her collection of diamonds and pearls, made a spectacular appearance as the rays of the sun caught the edges of the diamonds among the pink tea roses in her hair and her sedate gray gown flared out in a bold fringe of cardinal red. Even the couple's first-born baby, Honore, eight months old, was brought in suitable elegance to the wedding. He lay with appropriate decorum on a beribboned satin pillow in a handmade dress three yards long. The bridal couple knelt under a canopy of white flowers—camellias, orange blossoms, Cape jasmine and carnations. The cut flowers were of such a variety that when antiquarians attempted to reproduce the wedding table in later years, they found many of the flowers unobtainable.

No bride's costume was ever more explicitly described than that of Ida Honore, who wore, according to the next day's paper, "a Paris gown of lace and supple white satin d'orange, underneath which was a corset of the same satin, made to order with one hundred bones in it." Her petticoats ranged from a top one of soft imported muslin with a long train to a short white flannel "inside" with four petticoats between these two. In the bride's trousseau, according to the knowledgeable scribe, were a dozen more corsets, including one of lavender foulard with "matching underwear" and endless pairs of stockings classified as opera, carriage, reception, morning and evening. The groom created his own sensation by dashing up to the house in an open wagon drawn by four well-curried army mules with jingling harness and burnished hooves. On the second floor, the young couple's wedding gifts were on display, including $10,000 worth of diamonds that Potter Palmer gave his young sister-in-law and the pearls she received from her mother-in-law, the first lady of the United States, with whom the bride was to live at the White House.

Detailed reporting of society events was so uniquely a Chicago practice that the Philadelphia *Evening Bulletin* blamed it for "the annual crop of divorces in Chicago." The *Tribune* took exception to this theory, explaining the reason so many details were made available to the local press was that "the gentlemanly reporter is indigenous to Chicago. Nowhere else do travelers find the calm repose, the insouciance, the neatness and elegance of attire, the quiet, unassuming manner, the soft, smooth voice, the graceful, languid gait that conspire in the construction of the Chicago reporter."

The reign of Mrs. Palmer over Chicago society, which began with the Grant wedding, coincided with the rise of the feminist movement. There was evidence that Mrs. Palmer was more closely attuned to the real aspirations of this social revolution than was Amelia Bloomer. "One hears so much about the 'new woman' that one is in danger of being bored by her unless she arrives quickly," Mrs. Palmer said. However, she was a vigorous advocate of greater education for women. In a newspaper article, she discarded the platitude that "the fact of sex in women, instead of being fixed and unalterable seems to have been a variable condition," changing for the worse if a woman were educated. It was her theory that women "in a lucky moment found that men did not really admire the stupid, superficial fools they had trained us to become. . . . Woman is no longer frightened by the thought that man may not admire and love her, for she feels that he can't help it." This confidence in her own abilities and those of the rest of her sex brought her often to the lecture platform, where she discoursed on any subject from politics to art. Her theories of art were characteristically individual. "You women know how it is," she said in explaining art to a culturally avid audience at the Art Institute, "the more you put on, sometimes, the worse you look, and the more you take off, the better you look." That her audience was

GENERAL GRANT IN LINCOLN PARK, with Carter H. Harrison and Thomas Hoyne, 1879

not more shocked by such theories was explained by a writer in *The Woman Beautiful* who reported "people are concerned not so much about what she thinks as they are about her aloof manner, her stunning carriage, the smooth pink and white unwrinkled skin, the perfect teeth, wonderful hair, velvet gowns, her world famous furs and the sumptuous way in which she conducts her ménage."

Mrs. Palmer's ménage, as the magazine writer described it, was an innovation of her husband's as important as his development of State Street and his sponsorship of Chicago's boulevard system on the South Side. In the 1880's, Potter Palmer turned his attention to the neglected lake front on the North Side, then a wilderness of small dunes, stunted willows and pools of stagnant water. In this inhospitable setting, he planned to build the most splendid house in Chicago. His first problem was to fill in the marshy land. He disdained the use of waste material as both unsatisfactory and unhealthy. He ordered sand from the lake shipped in, hoping by this means to do away with any danger of malaria or the other diseases that were (probably erroneously) attributed to locating buildings on land made from waste and garbage. For the privilege of dredging this sand from the lake, he deeded his riparian rights to Lincoln Park, setting the pattern for a lake front development that was to be world famous.

He was less original in the architecture for his new home, choosing to pattern it after the imitation Rhenish castles popular with the rich and homesick brewers of Milwaukee. A high brownstone mansion studded with turrets, balconies and minarets, the house was finished in 1885. In a defiant gesture toward less affluent imitators, Palmer constructed the house without exterior doorknobs or outside locks; it was only possible to enter when a servant opened the door. For a visitor the test was as arduous as a diplomatic ceremony; his card had to pass through the hands of twenty-seven butlers, maids and social secretaries before he could be admitted. Even Mrs. Palmer's closest friends were required to write for appointments.

Upon being admitted to the Palmer mansion, the visitor stepped into an octagonal hall three stories high, its floor a mosaic of marble and its walls heavily obscured by large Gobelin tapestries. From the hall he might be taken to a French drawing room, a Spanish music room, and English dining room with a shiny dark sideboard of solid Dominican mahogany or through a Moorish corridor into a Turkish parlor or perhaps a Greek or Japanese parlor. Intimates of the family rode in one of two private elevators—the first installed in a private home in Chicago; on arriving at an upper level they stepped out across inlaid parquet flooring past the bedroom where Mrs. Palmer slept in a Louis XVI bed ten feet high. However, Chicagoans did not appreciate Mrs. Palmer's jade collection which she considered one of the finest in the world. When her guests continued to show lack of interest in

ROOF GARDEN AT THE PALMER HOUSE, 1873

it, she sadly moved it to Paris, commenting that "There is no use having it here, as no one ever looks at it."

Members of local society were more appreciative of Mrs. Palmer's abilities as a hostess, when she entertained at formal dinners in the ballroom and banquet hall for as many as fifty guests. Gowned in velvet and wearing a $30,000 collar of diamonds and pearls, surrounded by her collection of Monets, Degas and Corots, Mrs. Palmer presided with the demeanor of a queen. Foreign visitors were pleased and impressed that she could converse in French with them. The walls were loaded with art treasures that were to form the nucleus of the Art Institute of Chicago. Mrs. Palmer was an early collector of French Impressionists. By the time her house was built she had enough of these French paintings to fill a gallery, with sufficient Monets remaining to form a frieze on the walls of her ballroom. Potter Palmer was not always present at these stately dinners. He excused himself on the ground that he was not a society man, and often spent the evenings alone in a room in a tower of the house. He preferred an afternoon at the races or an evening with his business cronies planning a greater—and richer—Chicago.

Everything Mrs. Palmer did showed the results of careful planning. Self-control was her fetish. She believed that through strict self-discipline anything could be accomplished. Despite the luxury of her own position, she was an early champion of the rights and welfare of working women. In these activities she won the respect of Governor John Peter Altgeld, who wrote her at length and with a warmth that was as much a tribute to her charm as her politics. One letter he concluded: "Now please do not ask why I have written this letter, for all I could say would be that 'I could not help it.' I believe, however, that this is always a good excuse, especially if one is willing to take the consequence. I made frantic efforts to see you in the fall but the fates were against me. They guarded you jealously and spared you the affliction . . . Assuring you of my high regard as well as admiration, I am very respectfully yours, John P. Altgeld."

Mrs. Palmer's interest in politics was more than that of dilettante. She encouraged her son, Honore, to run for alderman of the Twenty-first Ward and when he announced for the office she became his political manager. Honore applied himself to the task of getting elected with the same discipline his mother practiced. He studied Italian so he could address the voters in his ward who spoke no other language. To the Germans he spoke a precise Harvard German and managed a passable French for the few voters of French origin. Honore's rival attempted to ridicule these efforts to meet the voters on their own level by circulating the report that Honore had joined the waiter's union. Honore heard the joke and hurried down to the Palmer House where he had himself photographed in a white uniform carrying a tray, much to the pleasure of the waiters in every restaurant and saloon in the district. The climax of Honore's campaign was the reception given by Mrs. Palmer for the ward workers and others supporting her son's candidacy. Many of the guests were more familiar with the lodging houses and saloons in the southern part of the ward than with polite society, but the doors of the mansion were opened to all. It was an unusual reception. The guests arrived in force, five hundred strong and led by a band. Mrs. Palmer received them wearing her most elegant gown. She shook hands with every guest, entertained the crowd with a brief concert and served them supper. The opposition was helpless before such tactics and Honore was elected. Much to the satisfaction of his mother, he was a diligent alderman and subsequently was returned to the council for a second term.

The great indulgence of Mrs. Palmer was jewelry. Her collection of gems and stones was exceeded only by that of Queen Margherita of Italy, who had a considerable ancestral advantage over the American newcomer. One of Mrs. Palmer's collars—given the appropriate if degrading name of a dog collar—contained 2,268 pearls and seven large diamonds. At a ball given by the Countess of Stafford, Mrs. Palmer wore a diamond-studded belt, a circle of diamond stars around her throat and a standing collar of diamonds. During a transatlantic voyage, she stopped Alois Burgstaller of the Metropolitan Opera in the middle of an aria by suddenly appearing in the audience wearing a tiara of diamonds as big as Tokay grapes, a corsage pinned to a base of diamonds, a sunburst of diamonds nearly ten inches in circumference, a stomacher of more diamonds and a collar of pearls. Mrs. Palmer crossed the Atlantic every year; when she traveled as a passenger on the maiden voyage of the Lusitania, she sent back daily reports of the trip for the Chicago *Herald-Examiner*. It was through the trips to Europe of Mrs. Palmer that society there was made fully aware of Chicago's great wealth, a bit of knowledge which was to have repercussions a generation later when Chicago heiresses entered the market for European titles with the same aggressiveness that their fathers had shown in gambling over land.

Abroad, Mrs. Palmer made her own rules of behavior just as she did in Chicago. When the opera *Salome*, which Richard Strauss had fashioned around a poem by Oscar Wilde, was causing a sensational controversy in Europe, Mrs. Palmer arranged to have it performed in her Mayfair house in London. Among the guests who saw the opera's London premiere, given by a cast imported from Paris, were King Edward and Queen Alexandra. At another party the entertainment was Pavlova dancing. When Mrs. Palmer gave a reception for Honore and his wife in Paris, the guests were offered as a diversion a performance of the Russian ballet.

In Chicago, the court through which Mrs. Palmer reigned over society was her New Year's Day reception. To be invited to this annual event meant that one was accepted in society during the following year. There was always trepidation that Mrs. Palmer, who believed in pruning her lists every two years, might drop a name from the list. The invitations were never refused. Those admitted to the New Year's reception were also reasonably certain to receive invitations to Mrs. Palmer's annual Charity Ball, usually held about a fortnight afterward. These Charity Balls were regarded as civic institutions rather than society affairs and were given a proportionate amount of space in the newspapers. Each year, from five to seven columns of the front pages of the newspapers were given over to the details of the evening as the new aristocracy of Chicago stepped out of polished carriages and walked under special awnings and over specially laid oriental rugs into the Auditorium, where the ball was held. Very few dared to be late. The boxes which overlooked the dance floor were filled with a promptness considered correct by the "personified millions of the West." Looking around him at one of the Charity Balls, a *Tribune* reporter saw "good, easy men in their somber conventional garb of black and white . . . yet what rich city of the antique world—Antwerp or Venice in her palmiest days," he asked, "could have shown an assemblage of burghers rivaling in gold power and gold necromancy the achievements of these decorous merchants?"

The grand march at the Charity Ball was the opportunity for Mrs. Palmer to acknowledge the authority of her deputies who ruled over the subdominions within Chicago society. One wing of the formal promenade was always led by Mrs. Palmer herself, appearing on the arm of someone such as N. K. Fairbank, the president of the Chicago Club, or General Nelson Miles, the hero of the Indian Wars. Leading the other column of Chicago's wealth might be either Mrs. William J. Chalmers, who reigned over the West Division from her Ashland Avenue home, or Mrs. Horatio O. Stone, whose authority was generally accepted as pre-eminent in the South Division.

The West Division had been the early home of Mrs. Palmer's family and remained a predominantly southern community. Originally Ashland Avenue had been known as Reuben Street, but when "Hey Rube!" became popular as a term of ridicule, the residents of Reuben Street found themselves being called Rubes. This was intolerable and the property owners asked to have the name changed to Ashland, after the country estate of Kentucky's Henry Clay. Their petition was successful and southern hospitality and customs continued to prevail along Ashland Avenue. The houses were spacious and the grounds nearly the size of country farmyards. Most families kept their own horses, cows and chickens and raised their vegetables in back-yard gardens. The squire of the avenue was Mayor Carter H. Harrison, who kept his black bay in a stable near his house and liked to ride up and down the street in the manner of a plantation owner looking over his acreage.

A self-contained segment of Chicago society was to be found west of the Potter Palmer house on the North Side, centering around the forty-five-room mansion of Cyrus Hall McCormick. The McCormick house, which required five years to build, was predominantly French in style, with a high

TALLY-HO PARTY GOING TO THE DERBY, 1870. Third from left is Carter Harrison I. Next and reading to the right are General Philip Sheridan, Potter Palmer and General John A. Logan

mansard roof and elaborate cresting. The interior was impressively decorated with banded columns, garlands and other features easily traceable to Charles Garnier's Nouvel Opéra, the architectural wonder of the world in the reign of Napoleon III. There was a private ballroom with a full stage in which the publicity-shy McCormick clan could enjoy its entertainment. The private auditorium may have been suggested by the family's experience during the Civil War; the former Virginians were so discomfited by the bloodthirsty denunciations of their southern kin from the pulpits that they finally quit going to church.

Around the mansion of Cyrus, the other members of the McCormick family built their homes. William Sanderson McCormick lived in a large house of yellow Milwaukee brick on Huron Street and Robert Hall McCormick lived a short distance away on Rush. When young Robert Sanderson McCormick married Katherine Medill the couple lived close by at the Ontario Hotel. Leander Hamilton McCormick, with whom Cyrus had made his home before marrying Nettie Fowler, lived a few steps away at Rush and Ontario. Passers-by, looking at the collection of the clan's mansions, named the area McCormickville.

The most ostentatious mansion on the North Side was that of Perry H. Smith, a vice-president of the Chicago & North Western Railway. The house was located on the northwest corner of Pine Street (now Michigan) and Huron, just a few blocks north of the river. White marble walls, a slate-covered mansard roof and the enormous size of the building gave it the appearance of a public institution. Inside, guests found a small theater with rising rows of permanent seats in the manner of commercial playhouses. The rooms were tremendous and appeared more spacious at night when tall mirrors were drawn across the high windows in place of the more conventional interior shutters. The highly polished mirrors, their edges concealed by velvet draperies, were hazards for guests unfamiliar with the house, who often took them for doorways. The housewarming for the mansion was scheduled for January 2, 1878, to avoid conflict with the traditional reception of Mrs. Palmer. Even with this gesture, Mrs. Palmer was for once the loser. The Smiths, determined never to be outdone, monopolized the attention of fashionable gossip for weeks by showing their guests three faucets in the butler's pantry—one for hot water and one for cold water; while out of the third poured bubbly, sparkling iced champagne.

Few families could hope to compete with the munificence of a Potter Palmer or Perry Smith. Competition among most hostesses took the form of seeking unique favors to distribute at their formal parties. European travelers sought original party mementoes with the same fervor they pursued antiques or shopped for Paris gowns. Frequently the favors were of a nature to be used during the ball—parasols to be spun during a dance, brightly colored hats for the girls, flower-trimmed harnesses with bells which tinkled delicately as the girls directed their escorts through the intricate patterns of a cotillion. On exceptional occasions, the men might also take home a remembrance such as the solid gold dresser boxes which Mrs. Pullman distributed at one of her parties.

Through these final decades of the nineteenth century and the early years of the twentieth century, the dominant figure who represented Chicago society to the world and whom the city itself recognized as its most illustrious hostess continued to be Mrs. Potter Palmer. One of the warmest tributes came from a newspaper in New York, a city that has never been lavish in its praise of things Chicagoan: "With levees, soirees and promenades now in the dim perspective, we can look upon Mrs. Palmer's time and see what will be missed in the new ensemble. For each age has its afterglow, and none more brilliant than the one just passed. Poets, painters, and novelists drew upon such as she to make lovely pictures of grandes dames."

MRS. POTTER PALMER,
1893, by Anders L. Zorn

GARDNER S. CHAPIN. A caricature by T. Wust from the Chapin and Gore Restaurant

The Sporting Life

A HISTORIAN of the police department, writing of Chicago during the 1880's, lamented that it had become known as a "fast" city throughout the land. "People of respectability tolerate things here," he wrote, "which are perfectly shocking to the moral sense of respectable people elsewhere. Men, reckless of public opinion, and women, regardless of feminine delicacy, are continually creating social sensations. . . . The painted woman drives an elegant equipage, paid for, perhaps, by some prominent citizen; whole thoroughfares are given over, nay abandoned, to bagnios and brothels." Scribner's Magazine, viewing Chicago about the same time, was in full agreement. "Chicago! The name has a strange fascination for the American people. The name is familiar in the remotest villages of all parts of Europe. The wickedness and piety of Chicago are in their way marvelous."

Perhaps most to be marveled at was the man who personified this combination of wickedness and piety—Carter H. Harrison I, who through four consecutive terms ruled over Chicago during the expansive eighties. Harrison's aristocratic background and southern upbringing, plus a period at school in Europe, had given him a sense of noblesse oblige toward the workingman and infinite tolerance for the weaknesses of all human beings. He believed that vice was as durable as virtue, that no law ever written could prevent gambling or prostitution and that a workingman had as much right to have a glass of beer on Sunday—his only day of leisure—as on any other day of the week. The mayor was not alarmed by charges that the city suffered from moral decay. He once declared in a burst of oratorical enthusiasm that "the young city is not only vigorous but she laves her beautiful limbs daily in Lake Michigan and comes out clean and pure every morning." Reformers, noting that in one year more than seven million bushels of corn were consumed in the manufacture of whiskey in Illinois, were not sure it was water which the city was using for its bath. But even Harrison's enemies, such as Senator John A. Logan, who charged that Harrison had made Chicago known as the Gomorrah of the West, conceded that the mayor had been good for business. His belief in progress and a wide-open town exactly suited the burgeoning city, where the aim of every citizen was "first to make money, next to spend it—how, where and when is nobody's business." Or as George Wellington Streeter observed shortly after he laid siege to the North Side lake front, "This is a frontier town and it's got to go through its red-blooded youth. A church and a WCTU never growed a big town yet." The city's tolerant and humorous view of crime was typified in a police-court item in the *Tribune* reporting that "Ben Hughes and George Carr, two youthful pickpockets, were sentenced to six months in the House of Correction by Justice Summerfield. They picked the pocket of Mrs. Alcina Riebeling in a bungling manner and were thus punished for their lack of skill."

There were so many vice districts that local baedekers were published to enable the visitor to find his way among the Black Hole, Little Cheyenne, the Bad Lands, Satan's Mile, the Levee, Dead Man's Alley or Hell's Half Acre. This last section of real estate was distinguished by the fact that every building was occupied by a saloon, a low gambling house, a concert saloon, an assignation house or a row of streetwalkers' cribs. It was not an area in which it was of much use to call the police, for they never entered it except in pairs and then only when on specific assignments. This caution was no reflection on the courage of the police. Applicants wanting positions on the detective force were warned that "the criminals of the Garden City are noted for their recklessness. They shoot quicker and with less provocation than in any other city and the detective who pits himself against these desperadoes and hopes to come out with a whole skin must be nervy to a degree and as quick as chain lightning in handling a gun."

One of the saloon proprietors of the day was an ex-pickpocket who owned the Lone Star saloon and Palm Garden at the southern end of Whiskey Row. His name was Mickey Finn. Among the drinks he offered to his patrons were a "Mickey Finn Special" and a "Number Two." The Mickey Finn Special was compounded of raw alcohol, water in which snuff had been soaked and a mysterious white ingredient Finn had obtained from a voodoo doctor. To those whose digestive apparatus was too sensitive for this fiery concoction, Finn serve Number Two, in which beer rather than alcohol was used to make the voodoo doctor's blackout pills more palatable. A Mickey Finn Special could render a victim unconscious for two or three days, enabling the ingenious Finn to stack up his dupes in the back room without missing a turn at the bar where other customers might be clamoring for one of the *specialités de la maison*. At his leisure Finn would rifle the pockets of the doped patrons and dump them into the street.

Another early entrepreneur was Johnny Harmon, who is credited with opening Chicago's first concert saloon at Madison and Peoria Streets. Here girls provided entertainment while dispensing drinks to thirsty patrons. Harmon fell victim to his own desire for efficiency. He placed a sign over the bar with the following legend: "Gentlemen will please keep their hands off the waiter girls, as it interferes with the discharge of their duties." This unamiable attitude caused a sharp drop in business and shortly afterward Harmon was forced to close his doors for lack of patronage.

Attempts to reform the city's vice districts either fell short of their mark or were sabotaged by the intolerant leaders of the temperance movement. The administration of Joseph Medill and his "fireproof ticket," elected to prevent the misappropriation of relief funds after the fire, was nearly wrecked by groups insisting that all Chicago's woes were directly attributable to the opening of the saloons on Sunday. However, one constructive reform was put through under Medill. A complicated tax-levy system was established which restricted the taxing powers of the city to only 2 per cent of the assessed value of the real and personal property. This tax program was based upon a combination of pessimism and realism—if the aldermen could not be kept from stealing, at least the city could limit the amount they could steal.

Political corruption was notorious. When a combination city hall and county building was constructed, the county-building portion cost a million dollars more than the city hall, though both were of the same dimensions and material. This was considered excessive graft, even for Chicago, and eventually several politicians were convicted for diverting the funds. One of these escaped before he could be taken to the penitentiary and fled to Canada. He did not die a fugitive but returned shortly thereafter to Chicago where he opened a saloon. As it would not have been considered sports-

A SUMMER CONCERT GARDEN

manlike to arrest him a second time, he was not bothered by the fair-minded representatives of the law.

In 1872, the city tried twice to establish a reform group, once with a Committee of Seventy and again with a Committee of Twenty-five. Both groups broke up in fights with the anti-liquor crusaders. When the temperance groups lost a public referendum on closing the saloons on Sunday, praying women began tours of the city's saloons. Kneeling in the sawdust and alternately weeping, singing and praying, the women implored divine assistance in leading the bartenders to repentance. When this widely dispersed attack failed, they marched in a body to City Hall to protest to Mayor Harvey Doolittle Colvin. As the mayor was no more than a hireling of the town's boss gambler, Mike McDonald, the mass demonstration only served to embarrass the clergymen whom the indignant ladies forced to accompany them on their foray. In 1874, another reform effort was made, this time with a Committee of One Hundred. Like its predecessors it dispersed without having disturbed the city's customary pattern of life. In 1877, the Citizens' Law and Order League, by concentrating upon the sale of liquor to minors and demanding court action against it, was able to accomplish some good in a limited area. But even these successes were achieved only because the saloon owners were willing to co-operate.

The ignominy of failure that haunted all Chicago reform efforts pursued the indefatigable Frances E. Willard, the devout lady who resigned as Dean of Women at Northwestern University to head the Women's Christian Temperance Union. Miss Willard's temperance crusade began modestly with a campaign to get Chicago women to replace the wineglasses on their parlor tables on New Year's Day with pledge books; in these gentlemen callers were to pledge their total abstinence. This crusade was to grow until it resulted in the passage of the Eighteenth Amendment, prohibiting the sale of alcoholic liquors. But Miss Willard, who was to have so much influence on American history, was to have less success in Chicago. She was not able to convert her own nephew, Josiah Flynt, to her cause. Flynt, who had been reared by Miss Willard, was a victim of what he called the "go-fever." He hopped a freight train for Buffalo, stole a rig, was caught, escaped from reform school and finally entered hoboland, where he became one of the important sources of information for Havelock Ellis in that author's *Studies in the Psychology of Sex*. From Josiah Flynt to Mayor Colvin, Chicagoans were more interested in the exploits of gamblers like Mike McDonald than in the earnest pleas of Frances Willard.

McDonald was the successor to Colonel Jack H. Haverly, who in the days following the Civil War had raised the gambler to the level of a businessman. Haverly preferred to refer to himself as an organizer or a promoter rather than a gambler. It was Haverly who expounded the idea that betting on the horses was no worse than gambling in wheat. As a demonstration of his principles, he sought to reduce betting on the races to a steady, dividend-paying basis. He formed auction pools to bet on the races precisely as the members of the Board of Trade formed pools to trade in wheat or pork. Soon the papers were sending reporters to the tracks to send back tabulated accounts of Haverly's "investments." These were reported in the same columns with statistics on the daily sale of carloads of wheat or cargoes of lumber. Unhappily, Haverly's system was no better than that of any other horse player—except on those days he had been given information on a fixed race.

McDonald went a step beyond Haverly. In addition to putting gambling on the same basis as a legitimate business, he entered into a working partnership with the politicians. During the time that Joseph Medill was mayor, McDonald had enough influence with the board of police commissioners to persuade them to fire the chief of police for, among other acts of which McDonald disapproved, barring the gambler from police headquarters. McDonald did not have any influence with Medill, however, and the mayor threw out the police board and rehired the police officer. The defeat was only temporary. When Harvey Doolittle Colvin was elected mayor, Mike McDonald became the boss of Chicago. It was during Colvin's regime that

McDonald built a four-story gambling house at the corner of Clark and Monroe Streets in the center of the business district and known as The Store. One of the gambler's partners was afraid that it might be too big. McDonald replied—in a phrase that takes a certain glory away from P. T. Barnum—"Don't worry about that. There's a sucker born every minute." Another reason for the gambler's confidence may have been the prowess with the dice of his one-armed brother-in-law, Nick Hogan. Gamblers said that if Hogan had two arms he would have all the money in the world. Throughout most of the 1870's and 1880's The Store was the largest of a group of thirty gambling houses which ran wide open on Clark, Dearborn, State and Randolph Streets. Anyone wanting favors from City Hall usually had to go first to the second-floor office of Mike McDonald at The Store. It was McDonald, along with Harry Varnell, who headed Chicago's first gambling syndicate. In a single year the pair made a profit of nearly a million dollars from the control of betting at northern Illinois and Indiana race tracks.

McDonald was also interested in boxing. It was he who gave John L. Sullivan the backing that enabled the Boston Strong Boy to make his bid for the world's heavyweight championship. Sullivan came to Chicago to ask the gambler to back him in a fight with Captain Dalton, then the leading contender for the heavyweight title held by Paddy Ryan. When McDonald said he didn't think Sullivan was big enough to whip Dalton, the fighter offered to take on three toughs from the stockyards at one time; he promised to lick all three in a bare-knuckle fight within an hour. Mc-

CHARLES COMISKEY. A caricature by William H. Schmedtgen from the Chapin and Gore Restaurant

Donald, who was sure of seeing a good fight one way or the other, agreed to the proposition. When Sullivan finished off his opponents in the specified period, McDonald gave the fighter the backing which enabled him to meet Dalton. After knocking out Dalton in the fourth round of a fight at Chicago, Sullivan won the world championship with a ninth round KO of Ryan in a ring in front of the Barnes Hotel at Mississippi City, Mississippi.

The favorite gathering place in Chicago for sports figures and gamblers was the restaurant of Chapin and Gore, on Monroe Street just west of State. Gardner Chapin and James Gore first met in California during the gold rush. Later they separated, Chapin coming to Chicago to open a small grocery store and Gore remaining in the West, where he grew wealthy as a salesman of mining stock. Gore visited Chicago later to repay Chapin a loan of $200 and stayed to go into partnership with his old friend. He persuaded Chapin to add a wholesale liquor store—which at that time meant selling whiskey by the jug—and in a short time the new branch was doing so well the grocery was abandoned. The liquor store was then expanded to include a restaurant where the finest steaks in Chicago were served. Behind the lunch counter was a series of ranges where the customers watched their meats roasting over the coals. If a patron failed to find a piece of meat that pleased him, manager Louis Pease hired a hack to go to the stockyards to bring back the desired cut. With such a high standard of service, Gore scoffed at all advertising, declaring that all he needed was a "walking ad," a satisfied customer. He would only break this rule, he told a salesman for Wilbur Storey's Chicago *Times*, if he could buy the entire front page of the paper. The salesman, either through shrewdness or lack of tact, told Gore he wouldn't pay the price for such an advertisement. "Name the price," Gore said indignantly. As a result of this conversation, the first full-page advertisement ever run in a Chicago newspaper made its appearance on September 4, 1875.

During the racing season the restaurant became the headquarters for the bookmakers. It was said that if a bookmaker wasn't at Chapin and Gore's, he must be either in the hospital or the morgue. As all transactions were cash, the bookmakers frequently found themselves with more money than it was wise to carry down a Chicago street. This money, locked in an individual tin box carrying the name of the gambler, was put in the restaurant vault. Often the vault contained as much as half a million dollars in cash. But in one of those uniquely inviolate agreements of the lawbreaking fraternity, it never was robbed. No women were admitted to Chapin and Gore's, but this was by choice of the proprietors and no reflection on its social status. The wealthiest Chicagoans were among its patrons. General Phil Sheridan, Long John Wentworth, Philip D. Armour, actor Joe Jefferson when he was in the city, the Pinkertons (when they were not looking for one of the restaurant's patrons), John W. "Bet-a-Million" Gates and Dr. Florenz Ziegfeld, the popular director of the Chicago Musical College, ate there often. Another popular table was that where General Nelson A. Miles and Colonel William F. Cody matched tales about Indian fighting during the times that Buffalo Bill's Wild West Show was playing Chicago. The wall of the restaurant was gaudily decorated with caricatures of famous guests and a painting of a fictitious "Chapin and Gore Butterfly Ball" which portrayed many of the town's more decorous citizens in undignified merrymaking. The canvas included such incongruous couples as Wilbur F. Storey and Lydia Thompson, whose closest actual relationship had been at opposite ends of a horsewhip.

Neither Chapin nor Gore was afraid of competition. With the profits from their restaurant they financed the establishment of the genteel catering firm of Kinsley's. Another restaurateur who profited from the partners' generosity was Charles Rector, a former dining-car superintendent who had caught their attention when he was working at the Boston Oyster House. With the financial assistance of Chapin and Gore, Rector founded his own restaurant. Until Rector moved to New York, it was the most popular after-the-theater eating place in Chicago.

A notable and unusual eating establishment was that of Ambrose and Jackson, founded by two runaway slaves who had arrived during the 1850's. Neither could write but both could cook. They did one of the largest businesses in Chicago. Among their regular patrons were Democratic stalwarts Stephen A. Douglas, Cyrus H. McCormick and William B. Ogden.

The gamblers, like the city's more respectable millionaires, had moved away from the downtown area after the fire. Many of their elegant homes were located on Drexel Boulevard, a street never mentioned without a disapproving shrug by the residents of nearby Prairie Avenue. No fancier carriages or dresses were to be seen than those on display along this boulevard when the gamblers took the fancily attired mistresses of demi-monde mansions out to the races or for a Sunday-afternoon ride. No violence ever sullied the streets of this neighborhood and every effort was made to keep it respectable.

Nearer the center of town crime and prostitution had been organized with the same business efficiency that characterized more legitimate activities in Chicago. The organization of the vice district was the equal of any neighborhood in the city. It had its own newspapers, published under such titles as *Chicago Street Gazette*, *Chicago Gazette*, *Chicago Life* and *Chicago Sporting Life*. One entrepreneur felt the business establishments were sufficiently permanent to issue a *Sporting and Club House Directory*. The publisher's chief difficulty was with saloon keepers who were patronized by the "sporting-house trade" but who would not advertise in the directory. With

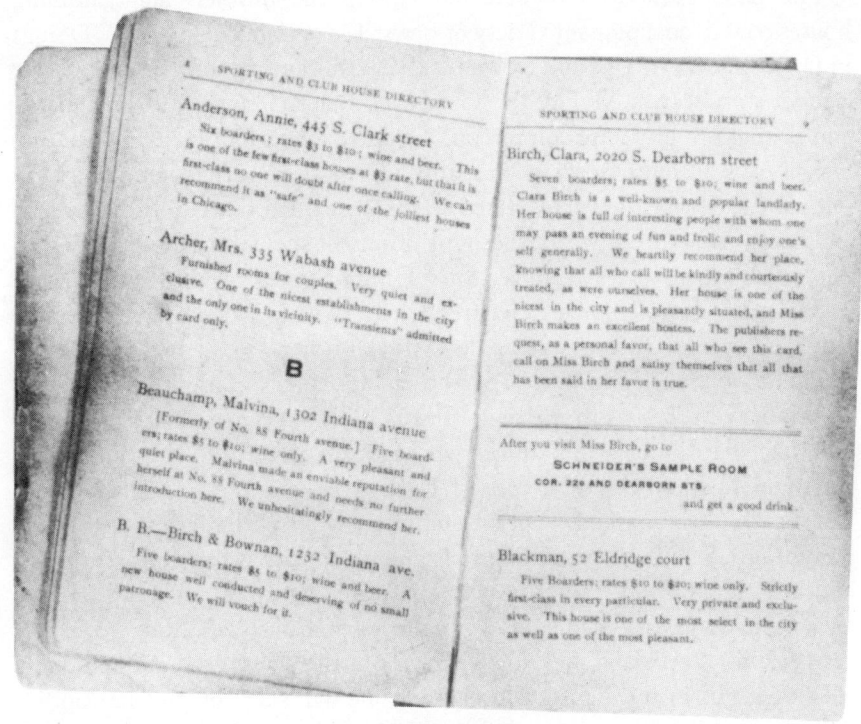

SPORTING AND CLUB HOUSE DIRECTORY

a fine feeling for delicacy, he avoided profanity and only quoted them as saying they didn't want their names in a "D——ed W—— House Directory." The book contained both the names of recommended houses and a listing of dives the publisher felt it was wise to avoid. There were advertisements for liquors, candies and for a medicine guaranteeing "the Opium Habit will be positively cured at home without interruption of business." Even with these gestures of co-operation, the publisher had to concede that "compiling a *Sporting and Club House Directory* is an undertaking beset with difficulties which are not to be met with in any other sort of compilation."

One of the directory's more eloquent listings was that of Mrs. M. J. Dean: "14 boarders, rates $5, $10, $15 and $20. Mrs. Dean's house is strictly first class ... on the first floor besides three magnificently furnished parlors is the handsome and well equipped cue and billiard room. There are two music rooms on the first floor and one on the second. ... The whole building from cellar to garret is pervaded with an atmosphere of quiet elegance. ... Most of Mrs. Dean's boarders are eastern people and while they are modest and ladylike they are still full of fun and music and entertain callers with a grace all their own."

The newspapers which circulated among the brothels and gambling houses contained a piquant variety of news. There were columns on "Doings in Dixie" and "The Ups and Downs of the Gay Sports in the Crescent City"; a serial story, "Irish Mollie, the Courtesan Queen"; and news of billiards and boxing. An etiquette column on "Good Manners and Household Decoration" was a regular feature. Probably the most popular column was the one called "Hot Turnovers." Here the reader learned that "Lottie Maynard should not be so fresh with other girls' lovers or she will hear something to her disadvantage" . . . "Emma, at 17 Union Street," could read that she had "better let up monkeying after Charley Todd, for he has a perfect lady, and everybody knows he is dead stuck on her."

There were also warnings of shootings and feuds. To Kit Morgan, on December 9, 1882, was a message from "One That Knows"—"There is no law that you cannot go up and down Madison Street all you want and if you want to stand on the corner of Fifth Avenue and Madison, that you can do. Don't be bluffed." Dick Remington was told he "had better keep away from 26 and not be pulling that gun or he may get more than he got and lose the gun too." Another warning read, "Murphy, you want to stay away from 529 Clark Street. Stay away from that old cat." And "Mike the Lusher must stop his monkeying with May of the Bon Ton . . . if you don't leave that girl in the Leland Hotel alone she will slug you and her both." There were probably many young men interested in the fact "They have two new strawberry blondes at the Hotel de Goodrich," or who might agree "There is a lot of snide young tidbits at 376 State Street." In the *Chicago Street Gazette* of October 20, 1877, the reader was informed "Harry Robinson's nose lights up the avenue elegantly these dark nights. Have another cup of bean soup, Harry." A domestic report revealed "Anna Wright is again happy. The old man is best after all, ain't he, Anna?" The creatures of this underworld society were traditionally peripatetic and it was unquestionably important to some to read "Again she's moved. Miss Lollie Whitney is now one of the flock of angels who flutter their wings and oil their feathers at the cage of [Carrie] Watson."

Carrie Watson applied to her institution the same principles that had formed the basis for many another Chicago fortune. She regarded prostitution as the "natural result of poverty on the part of the woman and passion on the part of the man." For her, it was not a matter of morals but of economics. Carrie was only eighteen and a virgin when she came to Chicago. She entered her profession not through necessity, as many girls did, but because of its business potentialities. After a talk with Lou Harper, Carrie became an inmate of the latter's mansion with the express purpose of learning the business. She must have been an apt pupil. Within two years, she leased a house on South Clark Street and opened an establishment catering only to society trade. Five years later she was ready to remodel the house into a resort that Herbert Asbury has termed the finest in America at the time. It was a three-story brownstone mansion with five parlors, more than twenty bedrooms and a bowling alley and billiard room in the basement for those bored or satiated with other entertainment. The halls were hung with expensive paintings and wine was brought to the parlors in solid silver buckets. The girls received their guests in fashionable and expensive gowns while a three-piece orchestra headed by a character known as Lame Jimmy provided music of an appropriate mood. There was no soliciting with the exception of what Asbury describes as an "ornithological pimp"—a parrot trained to say, "Carrie Watson. Come in, gentlemen."

The publisher of the *Sporting and Club House Directory* required a page and a half to list the attractions of Carrie Watson's. She had:

> 20 boarders; rates $5 to $50; pool rooms, billiard rooms, wine and beer. In fact, everything and plenty of it. This is one of the most widely known sporting houses in the United States or Canada. Nothing west of the Alleghanies [sic] begins to compare with it in brilliance or magnificence. In the basement are the billiard and pool rooms with perfect appointments. On the 1st floor are 5 parlors and a music room (at the latter of which competent musicians are constantly in attendance) and these parlors defy description. . . . A moment in the brilliantly lighted corridor, resplendent with bronze and crystal decorations and one is ushered into the far and justly famed "Mikado" parlor with its 4 walls and ceilings composed of solid French plate mirrors . . . the English language is inadequate to describe the feeling of one who enters this enchanted bower for the first time . . . the hand that writes this grows palsied at the recollection and these lines if longer drawn out will end in an inky blur . . . Miss Watson's is the HOUSE of the West . . . Her boarders are of such variety that any taste is sure to be suited and no living human being ever went away dissatisfied.

Carrie Watson's public appearances were as spectacular as her place of business. When she went out she drove in one of two snow-white carriages with bright yellow wheels. The carriages were pulled by four glistening black horses, probably the handsomest in the city. A measure of both her financial prosperity and the dubious operations of political favoritism was the fact she paid a larger personal-property tax than most of Chicago's millionaire businessmen. Her assessment was exceeded only by that of Marshall Field, George M. Pullman, Potter Palmer and J. W. Doane; it was equal to that of the fast-rising traction magnate, Charles T. Yerkes.

That Miss Watson had no regrets about how she became a woman of property was revealed in an interview in *Sporting Life* on December 9, 1882: "Miss Carrie Watson says she would be willing to reform but she can't think of any sins she has been guilty of. She charges regular prices for

ALL AROUND TOWN.

The Ball! The Ball!

NEWS ITEMS FROM THE *Street Gazette*, 1877

wine, never cheated a man or woman out of a cent, never told a lie, never starved her boarders, never got drunk, and never even took as much as a pinch of snuff. Now, what more could be expected of a good woman?"

Unique in this enterprising district was Waterford Jack, "the millionaire streetwalker." Like many another tycoon, she attributed her success to hard work and industrious application; it was her boast she had walked the streets every night regardless of the weather for more than ten years. Foot weary at last, she organized a company of streetwalkers and established them in a marble-front store, acting as their business manager. All the money the girls earned was turned over to her. She took a percentage for accounting and other expenses and banked the rest for the girls. If prudent enough to retire, they might have some reward to show for their labors. The *Chicago Street Gazette* paid this tribute to Waterford Jack early in her career: "Waterford Jack has $22,000 in the bank, every cent of which she has picked up on the streets of Chicago. Jack (her right name is Frances Warren) has made money. It is said to her credit that she never stole a cent and was never drunk in her life. She is a pug-nosed, ugly little critter, but for all that she has prospered in her wretched business and now stands before the world the richest streetwalker in existence."

No matter how illegal their business, the madames of the city's brothels felt entitled to the full protection of the law. One legal pioneer who called upon the law for assistance was Madame Hastings, who ran a notorious establishment where the girls were wakened in the morning with cocktails and usually followed this eye-opener with a breakfast of absinthe. The house was also believed to be a principal outlet for the white-slave trade. Even with such a reputation, Madame Hastings objected to being raided by police equipped with warrants made out against mythical personages such as Richard Roe or Jane Doe. She sued to have one such series of arrests set aside. A lower court ruled against her but upon an appeal to a higher court the warrants were ruled illegal and Madame Hastings took her historic place among the champions of law and order.

Among other famous houses of assignation was The Arena, on Michigan Avenue, distinguished by its many porches as well as by its reputation. Nearly as successful as Carrie Watson was Lizzie Allen, who ran a place known as the House of Mirrors. Lizzie Allen was famed for her liberal use of cosmetics as well as her business enterprise. In one of the district's newspapers it was announced that "Lizzie Allen has put on her fall coat of veneer and varnish and she is now the finest looking woman in Chicago." She remained in business for thirty-eight years before she retired. When she died, her estate was valued by a probate court at $300,000. She rests now in Chicago's Rosehill Cemetery under a tombstone inscribed "Perpetual Ease." Her house was taken over by two girls from Kentucky—the Everleigh sisters.

BOARD OF TRADE BUILDING, 1886, Scene of attempted demonstration by anarchists

The Melting Pot Explodes

CHICAGO was restless. During the seventies and eighties it had been a principal beachhead for the suddenly rising flood of immigration from Europe. This tide of new workers, following upon the unemployment which resulted from the panic of 1873, forced wages dangerously low. Resulting economic pressures on both the immigrant and established families increased the difficulties of assimilating a large foreign population. Language was another obstacle. The lack of communication among the rapidly growing alien groups led to an increase in resentment. Chicagoans (some of whom were only a few years removed from Europe themselves) blamed the later arrivals for cheapening the price of labor. The new workers, faced with the same poverty they had hoped to leave behind them, were bewildered and without leadership. The economic pressures of unemployment and poverty, built up over a period of years behind this barrier of language, were to explode finally in the most tempestuous decade of Chicago's history.

More and more of the new families arriving in Chicago spoke varied languages of southern and central Europe. Their common tongue, if any, was not English but German, the universal Latin of European radicalism. For entertainment the immigrants had to find places where German was spoken; their own language communities had not yet taken form. Enter-

ENTER THE LADIES 148

tainment in the German theaters was expensive; even the beer gardens were beyond the means of an unemployed worker who had spent his life's stake on the trip to the New World. The only diversions accessible under these conditions were the free labor meetings, in reality socialist rallies, where skilled orators spoke eloquently in German of the worker's millennium. A dramatist could not have created a more roseate picture than the visions of these outdoor spellbinders, who captured both the hearts and minds of their audiences. If the men who heard these speakers had not been out of work or isolated by the barrier of language, they might have found other sources of amusement. But they were essentially a captive audience and soon came to believe the speakers on the platform were the only real champions of the workingman.

Older Chicagoans referred to these speakers and writers, whose ideas were vigorously advocated in the columns of the German-language newspaper, *Arbeiter Zeitung*, as anarchists. It was a description less valid in the beginning than it was to become later. Most of the so-called anarchists were originally German socialists; they did not turn to anarchism until after a series of frustrations during the frequent battles of these bitter years.

The first mob made its appearance in the winter of 1872 in front of the offices of the Relief and Aid Society on LaSalle Street. The mob had been brought into being by a rumor that relief money had been embezzled by members of the society and withheld from the rapidly rising number of unemployed. Because the mob lacked leadership, the police were able to disperse it by driving it north through the LaSalle Street Tunnel and forcing the men to divide along the streets running east and west from LaSalle. No shots were fired and the incident, known as the "Bread Riot," was not regarded as serious. During the winter of 1873 unemployment (and with it, poverty) spread to such a degree that the first floor of City Hall was given over to families who had no other shelter. There was no serious violence, but the desperate figures huddling under their rags in the corridors of every public building were a reminder of the size of the problem which had to be solved.

Four years later, there was a hint of impending trouble when the newspapers reported groups of employes were quitting work along the line of the Baltimore & Ohio to protest a cut in wages. These reports caused little alarm at first, but concern increased when the items reappeared with nagging persistency and reported the spread of the strike to Pennsylvania and West Virginia. Reports of riots were frequent. Then, in the third week of July, the railroads with offices in Chicago followed the lead of the eastern lines by cutting wages 10 per cent.

The following Sunday, newspapers issued extra editions hourly with reports of the spread of the riot fever. Railroad shops were burning in Pittsburgh and the city was in the hands of a mob; there was rioting in Philadelphia, trouble was threatening in Cincinnati and tempers in St. Louis were at a "fever heat." In Chicago, the downtown streets were as crowded as on a business day. There were rumors that local railroad workers were about to join the walkout. By Monday, most of the city's railroad employes were off the job.

The socialist leaders were quick to exploit the situation. A mass meeting of workers was called for Monday night at Market and Madison Streets. An audience of nearly five thousand heard a series of speakers urge a march through the streets in support of a general strike. No specific program of action was adopted, but on Tuesday morning the automatic telegraph alarm at police headquarters rang continually as officers reported the movements of half a dozen different mobs through the city. Strangely, there was no evidence at the time or later that the striking railroad workers formed any significant part of these crowds. Workers were compelled to leave their jobs and join the roving gangs. In many cases employers anticipated the mobs by closing their factories and sending the workers home.

One group of rioters marched up Canal Street armed with clubs and sticks taken from the lumber yards along the river. While the police were attacking this gang, another had made its way to Remington's gun store on State Street. It was preparing to smash the windows to get at the guns and ammunition when the police arrived to break it up. An hour later the mayor issued a proclamation asking gun-store owners and pawnbrokers to take all the firearms and ammunition from display cases and lock them away. The mobs continued to roam the streets. By late afternoon the city's factories were shut down from the lake to Western Avenue near the edge of the city.

CHICAGO IN 1883, by S. D. Childs

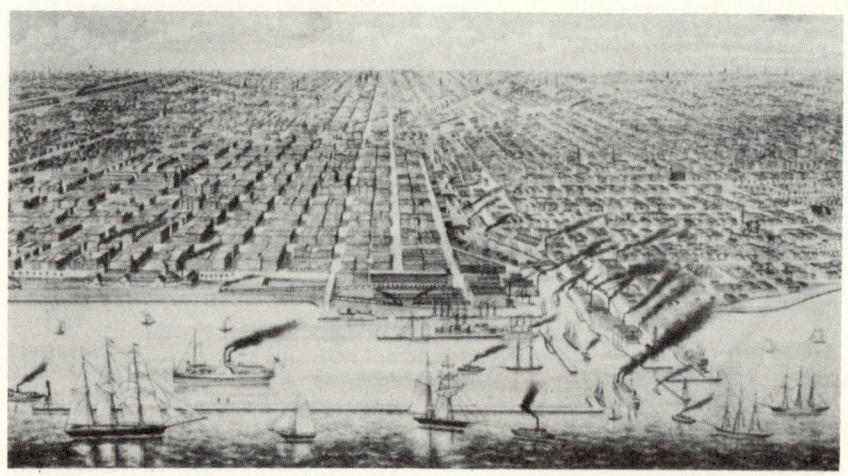

Every distillery, tannery and brick kiln on the North Side was closed. A circular was distributed calling a second mass meeting, but the police dispersed the crowd as it arrived and the meeting was never held. Mayor Monroe Heath ordered the saloons closed, but the proprietors interpreted the order as applying only to their front doors and a brisk business continued via the side entrances.

During the night the city prepared for civil war. More than three hundred special police were sworn in. Arms and ammunition were collected from the stores and an arsenal was established at City Hall. Cavalry companies were organized from private stables. Even the workhorses of the street railway company were saddled and used by police. In another proclamation the mayor asked the citizens to "organize patrols in their respective neighborhoods and to keep women and children off the streets." On the North Side, a group of young men from the town's wealthiest families formed a volunteer company and made their headquarters in the mansion of Perry Smith, hiding their guns in the basement coal bin. Military companies were organized by wards. On Wednesday morning the mayor was assured there were twenty thousand men under arms and ready to act if necessary.

The mobs had also gathered an arsenal and were brandishing revolvers, shotguns and rifles. Factories were set on fire. One crowd gathered at the McCormick reaper works, a favorite target for demonstrations. The police had to send twice for reinforcements before the men could be driven away. To increase the mobility of the police, the delivery wagons of Marshall Field & Co. and John V. Farwell were taken over as troop carriers. Even with this improvisation, it was difficult to keep up with mobs, who would disappear down a series of alleys and form again on another street.

The socialists, over the signature of "The Workingmen's Party of the United States," continued their strategy of calling a nightly meeting. Police who attempted to break up a crowd of about two thousand at Market and Madison were pelted with lumps of coal from nearby yards. Meanwhile, a more serious threat occurred at the shops of the Burlington Railroad, where a mob had joined with a group of strikers in an effort to burn the buildings. A crowd of about three thousand had ditched several cars and locomotives by the time the police arrived. When the police foolishly drove up in omnibuses and wagons they were beset with stones and pieces of brick. They opened fire in return and in a half-hour's fight seven of the rioters were killed and twenty-five seriously injured. Sixteen of the policemen were seriously injured and only two or three escaped without any injury.

While the police were battling the rioters, a mass meeting was being held in the Moody and Sankey Tabernacle. The mayor sent a message requesting the raising of "a force of five thousand good and experienced citizens," composed as largely as possible of ex-soldiers to put down "the ragged Commune wretches." Enlistments began immediately and the troops took up headquarters in the ornate surroundings of the Grand Pacific Hotel. More sensible was the action of the City Council. Realizing that the mobs were made up principally of unemployed workers, the aldermen voted half a million dollars to start construction immediately on a new Courthouse.

Thursday began quietly. The Workingmen's Party distributed a circular saying "the honest effort to increase wages depends entirely upon your good conduct and peaceable though firm behavior." Then came the unexpected arrival of two companies of United States troops, sent directly to Chicago from the Indian Wars. Every soldier wore a full cartridge belt at his waist and carried a rifle on his shoulder. The troops were tanned, grizzled and covered with dust, but as they marched down Madison Street to their headquarters at the Exposition Building, they were cheered more loudly than many a handsomer parade.

At police headquarters, Deputy Superintendent Joseph Dixon created his own mobile artillery by mounting a cannon on an express wagon. When a mob took possession of the viaduct over the railroad tracks on South Halsted Street, he rushed his new weapon to the scene of action. He found the mob stoning and firing upon the trains of both the Burlington and the Chicago and Alton as they passed under the viaduct. The police forced the mob off its vantage point and kept it away with the threat of Dixon's cannon. But the crowd continued to fight against a force of two companies of volunteer cavalry and two regiments of troops. The jails in the nearby police stations were full of rioters. Ten of those in the crowd were known to have been killed and nineteen of the police were injured or wounded.

That night another meeting was called for Turner's Hall. It had no significance, but the police decided to break it up on the grounds that "Poles and Bohemians were there in large numbers and the wildest threats were made." Two squads of police charged the meeting. A wild fight followed, with shooting on both sides. Stoves and furniture were thrown indiscriminately through windows to smash openings for emergency exits. Two policemen were wounded, one of the men in the hall was killed and an unknown number wounded. Later, those who held the meeting sued the police. The judge rendered a decision which said in effect that if every policeman in the attacking force had been killed, no member of the crowd could have been legally punished.

Possibly because of the arrival of the federal troops, the Turner Hall foray and the Halsted Street riot were the final outbursts of the week of disorganized violence. On Friday the riots stopped. After these defeats in the railroad riots, the socialists formed military companies and paraded the streets with their weapons under the banner of a red flag. A state law pro-

DRIVING THE RIOTERS FROM TURNER HALL, 1877

hibiting the marching in public of armed companies of men forced these activities underground. The groups continued to drill in secret, wearing rubber shoes so they would not be heard outside the gymnasiums where they trained and hiding their faces under black hoods so that no one could inform against his neighbor. About the same time the socialists turned to a weapon closely associated with the history of the anarchist movement—the bomb. They became in fact the anarchists they had been labeled. On week-end trips to the Indiana sand dunes, squads practiced with homemade bombs. Blast effects on the surrounding area of shrubbery and trees were carefully measured and recorded.

The opening of Chicago's new Board of Trade building was a symbol the anarchists were quick to seize as a provocation for a demonstration. The usual handbills were distributed—this time over the signature of the International Working People's Party—and a mass meeting called for the evening when the Board of Trade dedication was to be held. According to the circular, the plan of the evening was as follows: "After the ceremonies and sermons, the participants will move in a body to the Grand Temple of Usury, Gambling and Cut-Throatism, where they will serenade the priests and officers of King Mammon and pay honor and respect to the benevolent institute. All friends of the bourse are invited."

About five hundred men and women appeared for the meeting. After listening to denunciations of the Board of Trade, they started toward the building to break up the dedication ceremonies. Marching behind a group of red flags (for the common blood of humanity) and black flags (for starvation), the demonstrators sang the *Marseillaise* in English, French and German. At the head of the column strode Samuel Fielden, Albert Parsons and August Spies, a trio which Chicagoans suspected considered itself the Danton, Marat and Robespierre of the American Revolution. Because the column's intentions had been so well advertised, a force of two hundred police guarded the approaches to the Board of Trade, while another four hundred were being held in reserve. The police forced the singing and chanting paraders to turn north away from their objective. Unfortunately, the mob's surge trapped a late member of the Board of Trade and his wife. Their carriage was stoned and tipped over by the angry crowd in a scene reminiscent of the revolutionary days of Paris.

Later the same year the employes of the West Side Street Railway Company went on strike after the company violated an agreement. The public's sympathies were with the strikers. For several days Chicagoans from the West Division rode uncomplainingly to work in express wagons, hacks or other makeshift transportation. To break the strike, the company hired new drivers and attempted to run its cars along their regular routes. Almost immediately, mobs formed along Madison Street. They stormed the cars, stoned the drivers and conductors, and tipped over several of the company's vehicles. The mayor, faced with this recurrence of rioting, had no choice but to provide the police protection which the company demanded. Captain John Bonfield, who was in charge of the police in the district, believed the most practical solution to any problem was a show of force. He first tried a plan of stationing wagonloads of police at intervals along the route. This strategy was ineffective and drivers continued to be chased from their posts and cars toppled. Bonfield's next tactic resulted in a sight probably never duplicated in America—he formed an armored train of streetcars. From the company barns came a unit of three cars. The first was an open car loaded with armed policemen. The second was a closed car to be used either as a prison van or ambulance. Then came another car of armed men with their guns facing to the rear. As these cars moved away, another three followed, and then another three until there were about seventy-five cars in the line. Ahead of the leading car marched a force of police with the indomitable Bonfield out in front. The rioters, unable to attack the cars, piled obstructions on the tracks. On some corners barricades were erected and from behind them the mob threw stones as the police attacked with oversize billy clubs. No attempt was made to pick up passengers; the maneuver was purely a tactic to cow the demonstrators. The unusual cavalcade fought its way slowly from Western to Ogden Avenue, with the police under orders not to fire unless they should be fired upon. The show of force had its effect and the defeated mob vanished into the alleys and byways. But it was still to be heard from again, and more fearfully than ever before.

Despite these humiliations, the anarchists continued to plan for the day they would seize power. They experimented with more homemade explosives. Maps of the city were studied and intersections marked where properly placed dynamite could paralyze traffic. In January of 1886 a bomb was left on the doorstep of Judge Lambert Tree. A few days later, another was found in the Burlington Depot. Impetuous practitioners of the doctrine of violence were growing bolder.

In February the workers at the McCormick reaper factory left their jobs in a walkout in support of an eight-hour day and increased wages. During the following few months, as the McCormick strike dragged on without a settlement, it was followed by other strikes as the agitation for the eight-hour day in all industries increased. By May, the trend to the shorter work shift was conceded by all but the most stubborn employers. Even the generally intimidated employes of Pullman City had gone out to wait for the shorter day. At the stockyards, seven thousand packing-house workers had gone on strike at 7 in the morning and had been back on the job at noon with their requests granted. The Knights of Labor, the union organization of the time, was cautious about making claims of universal success despite these favorable signs. But the anarchists, who had first been suspicious of the eight-hour day movement, now embraced it as their own cause. A universal eight-hour day was inevitable, they told their faithful audiences; by May 1st it would prevail throughout the country and labor strife would be at an end. The millennium was at hand.

Like most millenniums, that of May 1, 1886, was slightly postponed. Because of the high expectations engendered by the writings and speeches of the anarchists, the absence of any significant change caused an emotional reaction of bitterness and frustration. The disappointment was particularly severe among the McCormick strikers, whose jobs were being taken by other workers, and among the freight handlers and switchmen who were hard pressed by the effects of a long strike. This was the atmosphere when a mass meeting was called for Monday afternoon at a prairie lot on Blue Island Avenue, then known as the Black Road because of its black cinder surface. Nearly five thousand men were in the field when the quitting bell at the nearby McCormick reaper works sounded and the gates swung open to let out the non-union workers.

These were the men who were being denounced by the speakers on the prairie for "taking bread from the mouths of children." Through coincidence or shrewd timing on the part of those who had planned the affair, the crowd needed no urging to seek vengeance. Shouting "Scab!" the strikers swarmed across the prairie toward the gate, forcing the workers back inside the plant. A policeman standing near the entryway fell with a bullet in his thigh. The crowd laid siege to the plant and, even after patrol wagons with police reinforcements arrived, a second attack was launched. In this assault half a dozen of the demonstrators were killed. A striker who attempted to leap on a patrol wagon was shot down in the street. The volleys from the guards successfully scattered the strikers, who moved away in small groups to the nearby saloons. A few minutes later, Mayor Harrison came cantering by on his Kentucky mare. It was not the least remarkable event of the day that the men on the street, who had just been fired upon and had had some of their number killed by the mayor's police force, showed no hostility toward him. The only taunts were those of an occasional wit calling upon the openhanded mayor to "set 'em up" for the crowd.

While the workers brooded over their misfortunes in the saloons, the editors and printers at the *Arbeiter Zeitung* were busy exploiting the day's drama. Circulars were printed and a few hours later a man on horseback rode through the North and West Sides scattering packages of them where-

THE FIGHT AT THE HALSTED STREET VIADUCT, 1877

ever a group of workers could be found. "Revenge! Workingmen to arms!" the pamphlets urged. "They killed six of your brothers at McCormick's works this afternoon . . . To arms, we call you; to arms!" It was signed "Your Brothers."

The circulars produced no upsurge of violence. Tuesday morning the Black Road was quiet. There was only the sound of noisy conversation coming from the overcrowded saloons. (Except for one grocery and an undertaking parlor, saloons were the only places of business in the area.) About noon the tranquillity was shattered by the sound of a yelping dog, running at full speed down the middle of Black Road with a can of pebbles tied to his tail. No political pamphleteer ever produced action as quickly as the frightened dog, which had been the victim of a cruel boy's prank. From every swinging door along the street small groups of men rushed out to see what had caused the disturbance. The surge was simultaneous and the nearly deserted street was transformed suddenly into a scene of action. As if by some common thought, the men started drifting toward the McCormick works. There, as no one moved to assume the role of leader, they milled about impatiently and waited for someone to signal the next move.

An objective unexpectedly presented itself when one of the detectives mingling with the strikers attempted to arrest a man carrying a pistol. Only the proximity of the police at the McCormick gate saved the impetuous officer from being beaten to death. Frustrated in its attack on one victim, the crowd scented another when someone shouted that a police officer had been seen using the telephone at Samuel Rosenfield's drug store at Eighteenth and Center. To the belligerent and excited crowd, this information made Rosenfield an agent of the police. The men moved quickly to the drug store, sending a shower of bricks and stones through the plate-glass windows at the front of his shop. The police were able to rescue Rosenfield and his family from their living quarters in the rear of the building but because of the narrow streets could not break up the mob which soon had stormed into the store and emptied the shelves. The next objective of the angry rioters was Weiskopf's saloon, located under a hall where the anarchists occasionally held meetings. Weiskopf was accused of being an informer. His place was reduced to a shambles in a few minutes while the less ferocious members of the attacking force rolled barrels of whiskey and beer into the street and cracked them open for the crowd.

During the day the anarchists kept up their barrage of propaganda. In Tuesday's edition of the *Arbeiter Zeitung*, August Spies had written an editorial calling upon the workers to take up arms and "rise in your might and level the existing robber rule with the dust." In the afternoon another circular was on the streets; it called for a "great mass meeting at Haymarket, Randolph Street between Desplaines and Halsted" and promised "Good

TRADING ON THE BOARD, 1891

speakers will be present to denounce the latest atrocious acts of the police—the shooting of our fellow-workingmen yesterday afternoon."

The night of the meeting—Tuesday, May 4, 1886—was a warm, damp evening. Dark clouds moved quickly across a somber, starless sky. At the time set, a crowd of about one thousand had gathered in the Haymarket. To the reporters the men seemed sullen and preoccupied. The boisterous, drunken outbursts which usually erupted in the early stages of such rallies were subdued and infrequent. A block away, at the Desplaines Street police station, officers and patrolmen were preparing for a battle. A force of two hundred men armed with new revolvers and "extra-long hickory clubs" was on the alert. A large number of detectives had been sent to mingle with the crowd.

The speakers who had called the meeting were late in arriving. Then, looking around for a suitable platform, they sighted an empty wagon standing near the entrance to the Crane factory half a block to the north. Following the speakers to the wagon, the crowd moved off of Haymarket Square and north on Desplaines Street. Finally the meeting got under way, though very much behind schedule. August Spies, the German-born publisher of the *Arbeiter Zeitung*, spoke first. He was followed by Albert Parsons, brother of famed Confederate general, W. H. Parsons. Last came Samuel Fielden, the Lancashire Englishman who made his living driving a stone wagon and who was as devout a Methodist as he was anarchist.

On the fringe of the crowd was Mayor Harrison. After listening to the first speeches he visited the police station and told the officers he did not think it necessary to break up the meeting. "I have no right to interfere with any peaceable meeting of the people," he said. "So long as they are orderly, I will not interfere." The mayor and chief of police then left the station, putting stubborn John Bonfield, now an inspector of police, in charge. Bonfield, without informing his superiors, had been making his own preparations for dispersing the crowd. When the detectives making periodic reports to the station told Bonfield that Fielden was saying "the law must be throttled, killed and stabbed," the inspector's temper gave way. Bonfield ordered his force into the street to break up the meeting. About the same time, rain started to fall and the crowd began to move away. But Bonfield insisted upon his victory. He turned his column of police from the broad Haymarket into narrow Desplaines Street, a maneuver which pushed the crowd back together.

A captain in the front rank ordered the meeting to break up. He was answered with a shouted reply from Fielden that it was a peaceable gathering. Then a bomb with a sputtering fuse appeared over the heads of the crowd and landed in the middle of the police. It exploded the instant it touched the ground and the front ranks of the police fell in pain and terror. Revolver shots rang out from both sides. Paul Hull of the *Daily News*, covering the meeting, said someone in the crowd cried "Charge" and the shots came "like the falling of corn on a tin pan or the roll of a drum." In five minutes the riot was at an end. The first Nihilist bomb in America—of the same pattern

ATTACK ON POLICE PATROL WAGON NEAR McCORMICK'S REAPER WORKS, 1886

as the missile which had killed Czar Alexander II of Russia—exploded with terrible effectiveness. Seven police officers died of their injuries and sixty others were wounded. It was impossible to tell the casualties among the crowd; most were dragged, helped or carried away by their friends. Best estimates were that at least two hundred were wounded; there was no way of registering the death toll.

The following day the police attempted to fix the responsibility for the bomb. The offices of the *Arbeiter Zeitung* were closed when large supplies of explosives allegedly were found there. August Spies of the *Arbeiter Zeitung* and Michael Schwab, its assistant editor who spoke in German at the anarchist meetings, were arrested. Albert Parsons, whose wife was to be known as the Jeanne d'Arc of Chicago anarchism, fled but later surrendered. Also arrested and accused of having a part in the plot was Louis Lingg, an organizer for the carpenters' union who was believed to have manufactured the bomb, George Engle, a painter, Adolph Fischer, a printer, Oscar Neebe, an organizer for the beer-wagon drivers' union, and Samuel Fielden. The police were unable to link any of these with the murder off Haymarket. But such was the temper of the times—and the courts—that all were convicted of murder on the ground that their inflammatory speeches and publications had incited the throwing of the bomb. Luther Laflin Mills, the prosecutor, erected a wire barricade at the second-floor landing of his home to protect his family from creeping intruders. At the trial, two factors in the prosecution's case were the handbill urging the workers to take up arms and the fact that the meeting had been moved to Desplaines Street from Haymarket. It was the police contention that this had been done to form a trap for the police, though the events of the night the bomb was thrown did not bear out the charge.

After the conviction, Judge Joseph E. Gary imposed the death sentence on Parsons, Spies, Fielden, Schwab, Fischer, Lingg and Engle. Neebe, whose crime apparently consisted of owning stock in the *Arbeiter Zeitung*, was given fifteen years in prison. After a request for a new trial had been refused, the condemned men asked for the privilege of addressing the court. Their speeches reflected the variety of their character.

Fielden was eloquent and forgiving in his three-hour oration: "I have loved my fellow men as I have loved myself," he said. "I have hated trickery, dishonesty and injustice. If it will do any good, I freely give myself up. I trust the time will come when there will be a better understanding, more intelligence, and above the mountains of iniquity, wrong and corruption, I hope the sun of righteousness and truth and justice will come to bathe in its balmy light the emancipated world."

Spies charged the penalty against him was a conspiracy to "stamp out the labor movement." Schwab tried to tell the unsympathetic court and audience exactly what anarchism was; he called it "a state of society in which the only government is reason." Lingg was defiant. "I die gladly upon the gallows," he said, "in the sure hope that hundreds and thousands of people to whom I have spoken will now recognize and make use of dynamite. In this hope I despise you and despise your laws. Hang me for it."

Parsons called the trial "the sum totality of the disorganized passion of Chicago" and charged the jury had been bribed. He went on to explain why he and his companions had chosen the techniques of the anarchists over those of the early labor leaders who relied on the peaceful techniques of trade unionism. Dynamite, he said "is democratic; it makes everybody equal. The Pinkertons, the police, the militia, are absolutely worthless in the presence of dynamite . . . Dynamite is the equilibrium. It is the annihilator. It is the disseminator of authority; it is the dawn of peace; it is the end of war. It is man's best and last friend; it emancipates the world from the domineering of the few over the many, because all government in the last resort is violence; all law, in the last resort is force . . . Force is the law of nature and this newly discovered force makes all men equal and therefore free."

Spies, standing on the gallows on November 11, 1887, cried out "There will be a time when our silence will be more powerful than the voices you hear today." Parsons pronounced his own benediction in the words "Let the voice of the people be heard." But with the explosion of the first purposeful bomb, the anarchists exploded any chance they might have had for political effectiveness. The bomb was considered by Americans an indiscriminate and unfair weapon; even those who protested the unfair trial of the accused could find little to defend in this philosophy of dynamite as the equalizer.

Fischer and Engle went to the gallows with Spies and Parsons. Lingg, who had been under sentence of death, acted as his own executioner by exploding a dynamite cartridge between his teeth in his jail cell. Schwab and Fielden had their sentences commuted to life imprisonment by Governor Richard Oglesby.

The identity of the bomb thrower was never firmly established. Most evidence pointed to the fact that he was once picked up by the police but released after being interrogated as a "mere windbag." All those who could settle the question with historical finality are dead, but their descendants say they heard from their fathers and others closely associated with the case that the actual bomb was thrown by Rudolph Schnaubelt, who fled to Europe, lived on anonymously and died quietly in his sleep.

The bomb throwing had one important aftereffect. To the members of the Commercial Club, the Haymarket episode was not an isolated phenomenon but a threat of revolution. They were aware no federal troops had been close enough to protect their interests if the anarchist strategy had been successful. To correct what they felt was a serious hazard, they offered to give the government six hundred acres of land along the shore of Lake Michigan, twenty-six miles north of the center of the city, if the government would establish a military base there. On March 3, 1887 the government accepted the offer and Fort Sheridan was founded. It was to remain long after it had fulfilled its original purpose of reassuring the newly wealthy Chicagoans that their property would not be subject to violent expropriation or destruction. More than a fort, however, was to be needed to bring tranquillity to turbulent Chicago.

"BRIDGED"—A FAMILIAR CHICAGO EXPERIENCE, by Charles Graham

Chicago Builds Its Parthenon

THE LOSS of Crosby's Opera House and the other concert halls in the great fire made it necessary for musicians and actors to use any setting available. The musicians made their most frequent appearances at the dedications of new buildings, ceremonies that were repeated with a kind of grandiose monotony as the skyline of a new city began to appear. One of the more spectacular of these concerts was presented at the opening of the depot of the Chicago, Rock Island and Pacific Railroad. The director was the ubiquitous P. G. Gilmore, fresh from a quantitative musical triumph in Boston where he had conducted an orchestra of more than one thousand pieces as part of the Boston Peace Jubilee. His performance at the Rock Island Depot, if less formidable, was still of a proportion to quell the timid. He augmented his own band with more than one hundred local musicians and supplemented these with a locally organized chorus of more than a thousand voices. This massive combination of musical talent presented a program ranging from "Anthem to Peace" to the "Anvil Chorus," the latter sung to the accompaniment of a collection of red-shirted firemen pounding rhythmically with sledge hammers on a row of blacksmiths' anvils. A local historian reserved his opinion about the musical merits of the performance but took sensible consolation in the fact that "The affair served its purpose in furnishing a harmless diversion and in advertising the fact that Chicago had any amount of spirit left, subject to call."

The most congenial home for good music during these years was under the domes and towers of the crystal palace erected for the Interstate Industrial Exposition. Chicago had always had a fondness for fairs and expositions. Shortly after the fire, Potter Palmer, Richard T. Crane and a group of business leaders were already planning an exposition to advertise the greatness of the partially rebuilt city. The exhibits at the exposition were intended to cover the entire field of human knowledge, but the emphasis was quite naturally on the subjects about which the founders knew most—industry and commerce. The plan of the exposition, which opened its doors in the summer of 1873, was a reflection of the culture and interests of Chicago. The main divisions listed displays of Food, Drinks and Tobacco, Products of Farm and Orchard, Instruments and Machinery of Useful Arts, Raw Materials, Minerals, Objects Used in Dwellings and for Personal Wear, Natural History and Fine Arts. The Fine Arts classification presented a unique definition of this hallowed phrase. It included, in addition to the usual subjects of painting, sculpture, architecture and stained glass, a further subdivision of the Liberal Arts classified by the catalogue as "publishing and instruments, surgical, musical and telegraphical." For those who wished to add to the horrendous collections which were a feature of every fashionable living room, there was an exhibit of bric-à-brac.

The exposition itself was open for only a few weeks each fall, when the interior of the building took on the appearance of a gargantuan general store in which it was possible to find anything from groceries to steam engines. Four years after the exposition's first show, the building was rented by the forerunner of the Chicago Symphony Orchestra as a temporary home for a series of concerts under the direction of Theodore Thomas. At the end of the long hall used for the concerts an attempt had been made to alleviate the barrenness with a semblance of a German garden decorated with evergreen trees sprouting from big wooden tubs. Around the periphery were small tables where good Milwaukee brew and other refreshments were served during the concert as well as at intermissions. The conditions in the temporary hall with its long rows of hard and noisy wooden chairs were far from ideal. The sound of a passing train on an adjoining lake-front railroad track would often obliterate the music. The residual fragrance of an exhibit of a vinegar manufacturer lingered in the building, leaving some Chicagoans with a permanent identification of good music and the smell of vinegar. Under such difficulties, Theodore Thomas introduced the city to fine music gently, filling his program with good standard works, providing at least one special "composer's program" and one full symphony (still a

INTERSTATE INDUSTRIAL EXPOSITION, 1884

novelty in Chicago) in every week's series of concerts. After a few years of this, he had the boldness to stage a Wagnerian festival which, possibly through the influence of the Teutonic scenery or refreshments, was given a more appreciative reception than Wagner received in more sophisticated musical capitals.

Another leader in the efforts to elevate Chicago's music was Dr. Florenz Ziegfeld, who with George F. Root had founded the Chicago Musical College. One of his apt students was his own son Florenz, though the boy often seemed to be more interested in showmanship than musicianship. When Florenz was thirteen he went to see Buffalo Bill's Wild West Show, then incongruously housed in the Academy of Music on Halsted Street. After a demonstration of marksmanship by Buffalo Bill, the plains scout challenged any member of the audience to try his skill. Young Flo Ziegfeld accepted the challenge, stepped on the stage and hit the bull's eye. Buffalo Bill, impressed as much by the young man's nerve as his shooting ability, offered him a job; when the company left Chicago on a three weeks' tour, Flo Ziegfeld had his first taste of show business.

Buffalo Bill, or Colonel William F. Cody, as he called himself on more dignified occasions, made his own stage debut in Chicago under the sponsorship of Ned Buntline, the famous dime novelist. In addition to acting as Buffalo Bill's manager, Buntline provided Cody with a plagiarized play under the title *Scouts of the Prairie*. It called for Cody to be supported by about twenty actors smeared with grease paint and billed as Indian warriors. On opening night Buffalo Bill had stage fright so badly he couldn't speak a line. The inventive Buntline stepped onto the stage and began questioning the star about his life on the plains—a subject of far greater interest to the audience than the pilfered drama. Under Buntline's questioning the frontier hero was more at ease. When the manager felt the audience had enough of talk, he signaled for the twenty actors; they came rushing on stage shouting for the scalps of Cody and his companion, "Texas Jack" Omonundro, who had been a scout with Jeb Stuart's cavalry. This cue was one to which the two scouts reacted easily and they swung into action, disposing of the supposed redskins with a ferocity that made their first night's efforts a popular triumph.

The arrival of Sarah Bernhardt on her first American tour presented more of a problem to Chicagoans than the simple heroics of Buffalo Bill. French art and literature were still suspect. From many of the city's pulpits came denunciations of the star and her art when it was announced that she was to appear at the McVicker's Theater. The annual reception given by N. K. Fairbank, the president of the Chicago Club and his wife, was scheduled for the night of her opening, but it would have been considered a scandal to invite anyone from the stage to so sedate a gathering. One man, however, was determined that Madame Bernhardt should have the finest reception possible. He was Potter Palmer, the proprietor of the Palmer House. There is no evidence that his wife made any effort to entertain the actress but Palmer himself could not have made more elegant preparations. A suite of rooms along an entire side of the hotel was set aside for her. A new "five glass landau" was placed at her command with Henry Wentsel, a "handsomely bearded veteran of the 197th Pennsylvania infantry," as its driver. All her meals were individually prepared in her rooms and only the French dishes for which she had a fondness were served.

A grotesque annoyance of her Chicago appearance, as it had been of every city in which she had appeared on tour, was the presence of a Yankee promoter named Henry Smith whom Bernhardt described with disgust as "the whale man." When she had arrived in Boston, Smith persuaded her to pay a visit to the harbor to see a whale which one of his fishing boats had harpooned. There he arranged for her to pull a small bone, of the kind from which women's corsets were made, from the whale. Smith lost no time in exploiting the connection of the petite Sarah and the mammoth whale. He immediately arranged for a tour that would coincide with her; when she arrived in a town, Smith and his whale would follow closely behind. In anticipation of the whale's arrival the city was plastered with signs which read:

> Come and See
>
> **THE ENORMOUS CETACEAN**
>
> which Sarah Bernhardt killed
>
> by tearing out its whalebone for her corsets

Other signs advised that the whale "is just as flourishing as when it was alive" and added that it had $400 worth of salt in its stomach and every day the ice upon which it was resting was renewed at a cost of $100. When Sarah Bernhardt stepped from her private railroad car at the station, her eyes fell upon Smith, who was there to greet her along with the French consul and a deputation of Chicagoans. Sweeping along in a light green coat trimmed with tawny fur and wearing a fur hat trimmed with plumes and a bird's head with glittering eyes, she mustered all her French invective to the task of driving him away. However, as few witnesses understood the cause of the clash, it served to advertise the whale further and increase the stature of the canny Smith.

At Bernhardt's opening performance an extra squad of police was required to handle the crowd outside the theater. There was not an equivalent rush at the box office, unfortunately, and there were empty seats in the rear when the curtain went up on *Adrienne Lecouvreur*, the first night's play. The distraction which the audience felt at hearing a play in French must have been matched by that of the actress at the peculiar sounds from the pit. A critic, in recording his reservations about Bernhardt's acting, admitted part of the effect might have been lost because so many members of the audience brought English copies of the play and kept ruffling the pages as they followed the plot. The *Daily News* critic found himself listening only half to the performance on the stage and giving the balance of his attention to the star's sister, Jeanne, and other members of the Bernhardt party who sat in the empty seats in the rear making uncomplimentary remarks about the audience as the play progressed. Another, more provincial critic, complained: "There are people who suppose Bernhardt is giving her performance in English. Whether any of them have paid $5 a seat to see it is not known, but the deep disgust of such an individual may be imagined. To give up an exorbitant sum for the sake of sitting four hours through an incomprehensible entertainment because the greatest actress in the world figures in it is one thing; to expend the same amount with the idea that the same result is to be obtained plus an understanding of what is spoken is something different."

As one play followed another at the McVicker's, the critic of the *Daily News* grew more enthusiastic about Bernhardt and that of the *Tribune* increased his reservations. This lack of approbation from the morning paper critic led to an editorial in the *News* commenting that "if the young men who 'do the dramatic' on the Chicago morning papers knew their business as well as Bernhardt knew hers, ah! then one might read 'criticisms' which appear daily and not be struck with apprehension that in many instances the plow has been forsaken for the pen by young men who would have made excellent agriculturists."

In order "not to meet the sandwich-men advertising the whale," Bern-

REPUBLICAN NATIONAL CONVENTION OF 1884. A Parade on Michigan Avenue

hardt permitted herself to be taken on a series of sight-seeing trips, including one to the stockyards. The evening of her excursion to the slaughterhouses she was to play *Phèdre;* but at curtain time she still found herself "trying to do everything to get rid of the horrible vision of the stockyards" and the "dreadful and magnificent sight" than which nothing could have been "more Hoffmannesque." So ardently did she throw herself into her role that at the play's conclusion she fainted and had to be carried from the stage.

The talented Bernhardt was an amateur painter and sculptress and an exhibit of her work was arranged for O'Brien's art gallery to promote her stage appearance. Hundreds of invitations were sent out. Although Chicago society had decided it would not receive her, the social ban did not extend to being received by her. The social predicament was noticed by at least one of the reporters on hand to watch Bernhardt, dressed in a clinging black gown, receive her guests. "There had not been time," he explained, "for social bread-and-butterdom to meet and formally resolve on a course. The result was that, each acting on her own impulse, hundreds of ladies decided with truly feminine curiosity to 'take it in' . . . There was no small room for amusement in watching the effect upon the ladies who came when they found themselves actually in the same room with The Naughty Sara against whose skirts they were liable to be swept at any moment by the almost resistless human eddy which surged around the room . . . For the most part . . . the women visitors seemed to regard [Sarah] somewhat in the light of an interesting but highly dangerous beast. They stood about her in rows four or five deep and watched the play of her features and her every movement, with mingled curiosity, admiration and fear, the last predominating and giving an expression which seemed to say 'Have a care! An accident is liable to happen any minute.'" The only person of consequence to have the courage and good manners to spend some time with Bernhardt was Amy Fay, a musician who had lived both in France and Germany and had been a pupil of Franz Liszt.

But if society shunned "the divine Sarah," there were others of possibly less status and more interests who did not. In her memoirs, Bernhardt was to look back on her Chicago visit as "the most agreeable days I had had since my arrival in America." She also gave evidence that she had observed Chicago as closely as the city had scrutinized her:

"First of all," she wrote later, "there was the vitality of the city in which men pass each other without even stopping, with knitted brows with one thought in mind, 'the end to attain.' They move on and on, never turning for a cry or a prudent warning. What takes place behind them matters little. They do not wish to know why a cry is raised and they have no time to be prudent: 'the end to attain' awaits them . . . Women, here, as everywhere else in America do not work, but they do not stroll about the streets as in other cities: they walk quickly: they also are in a hurry to seek amusement." Nor was this affection one-sided; when it was the time for parting, Bernhardt received from the "Ladies of Chicago" a collar of camellias made of diamonds.

The final chapter of this incongruous romance between the actress and the city she would not allow to reject her was written after she left town. To the bishop who had denounced her before she arrived came a note from her manager:

> Your Grace:
> Whenever I visit your city I am accustomed to spend $400 in advertising. But as you have done the advertising for me, I send you $200 for your poor.
>
> Henry Abbey

The year after the visit from Bernhardt, Chicago prepared to receive another celebrity in the person of Oscar Wilde. The poet was on a lecture tour arranged by Richard D'Oyly Carte to exploit the notoriety associated with Wilde's name as a result of the phenomenal success of Gilbert and Sullivan's *Patience*. Wilde was unquestionably the original of the operetta's esthetic hero, Bunthorne. The announcement of Wilde's visit created irresistible opportunities for provincial humorists. One cartoon showed a tailor's advertisement of "Wilde Oscar" labeled "Balaam, the Ass-thete." A *Daily News* writer turned to verse:

> He comes! The simpering Oscar comes.
> The West awaits with wonder
> As bullfrogs list to beating drums
> Or hearken to the thunder.
>
> The women pause with bated breath,
> With wild and wistful faces,
> And silent as the halls of death
> Seem all our public places.
>
> Here in the energetic West,
> We have no vacant niches
> For clowns with pansies in the vest
> Or dadoes on the breeches,
>
> We do not live by form or rule,
> We love our wives and lassies;
> We like to look at Western mules
> But not aesthetic asses.

The best that may be said of such humor is that it was no worse than Wilde had met in the other cities he visited.

OSCAR WILDE. A caricature by E. Jump from the Chapin and Gore Restaurant

The poet's first impression of Chicago after his arrival was a good one. He was taken directly to the Grand Pacific Hotel where John B. Drake had perfected a technique for receiving celebrities and where every clerk carried himself with the demeanor of a Lorenzo the Magnificent. After a dinner of brook trout, boiled quail, steak, sweets and champagne, Wilde confessed his amazement that "such good wine could be obtained so far west." He spoiled his host's triumph, however, by requesting Turkish cigarettes which were not available in Chicago. After dinner, Wilde received the press. When the reporters arrived he was lying on a large sofa pulled up before the fire and covered by a wolfskin and tigerskin. His head was resting on a gold-colored silk shawl. To the Inter-Ocean reporter he offered a handclasp that was "like the clinging of a vine." The Tribune interviewer was more impressed. He admitted that he "went to scoff" but "remained an hour" to hear such Wilde pronouncements as "life without industry is barren and industry without art is barbarism."

Wilde was faced with the necessity of being in top form. He was competing for public attention with John L. Sullivan, who had just returned to Chicago after hammering the world heavyweight title away from Paddy Ryan. While Wilde held court at the Grand Pacific, Sullivan received the plaudits of the crowd at Chapin & Gore's. It was a contrast which the Tribune found significant:

"Mr. Wilde represents a soulful past when military knights rode to the fray picking mandolins," the editorialist observed, "but Mr. Sullivan belongs to the rude present and fights in twenty-four foot tournaments unaccompanied by lutes . . . Mr. Wilde's school recognizes the ugliest flowers and birds, fills houses with uncouth jugs and bottles, covers wallpaper with geometrical impossibilities, covers floors with hideously figured, faded, colorless rugs. It destroys every curve, the lines of beauty, and substitutes an angle or a straight line. It clothes lean, lank women in draperies without a fold or curve, dishevels their hair and suggests uncleanliness. It changes the Venus de Milo into a clothes pole. Whatever is hideous, grotesque, bizarre and unreal and false it substitutes for the beautiful in aesthetics and from every art eliminates repose, which is the soul of art. As between the two schools it may at least be said for Mr. Sullivan's that it cultivates the muscle and develops a high type of physical manhood, however much we may be disgusted with the method of its use." The author of this artistic lament was probably a victim in his own home of the new vogue for the "esthetic" which had swept Chicago in the wake of the success of Patience. The sniffing of a rose or a lily "for bodily refreshment" was a matter taken seriously by many Chicagoans.

Literary notoriety being rated as less objectionable than that of the stage, Wilde was entertained by the same society which had avoided the lovely Sarah Bernhardt. Mrs. Horatio O. Stone gave a dinner at which he was the guest of honor. There was a large reception at the mansion of Mr. and Mrs. Franklin MacVeagh. It was at this reception that a departing guest gave a word of reassurance to a reporter by saying Wilde had talked "very pleasantly and sensible." Wilde was quoted as having expressed the view that artificial flowers should never be worn and that only an Oriental beauty should wear a sunflower. This latter advice was a hard blow to feminine Chicago, for sunflowers were at the moment the ultimate in fashion—a fact which may not have escaped the quick-witted visitor when he issued his dictum. The MacVeagh reception had an indecorous dénouement. A group of boy hecklers outside the house waved sunflowers and lilies and made it necessary to smuggle Wilde out through the stable and down the alley.

The lecture with which the poet was to enlighten Chicago was a discourse on the decorative arts. Wilde said much of the lecture had been written after his arrival and an audience of 2,500 packed Central Music Hall to hear his views. Their attitude, observed the Times, was the same as if they had paid "to see a two-headed Australian 'what-is-it' who would talk Greek or Choctaw." Wilde did not disappoint those who had come to look rather than listen. He appeared on the platform wearing black breeches tied at the knee with a black bow and black silk stockings and pumps. A fitted dress coat revealed a low-cut white vest and an expanse of white shirt front. His hands were encased in white gloves.

As might have been expected, what he had to say gave little excuse for ridicule. The audience tittered over his pronunciation of telephone; but his comment that "the value of the telephone is the value of what two people have to say" was worth the effort of remembering. His audience forgot his strange costume when he remarked that after the fire "the pouring out of the generous treasures of the world [for Chicago] was as noble and beautiful as the work of any troop of angels who ever clothed the naked." But a few minutes later the same audience was stirring in resentment as, after paying tribute to the waterworks as "simple, grand and natural," he went on to express his shock at the tower as "a castellated monstrosity with pepper boxes stuck all over it." He was amazed, he said, "that any people could so abuse Gothic art." Despite a vigorous attack by the newspapers, Wilde refused to recant his heresy about the city's beloved water tower that had survived as an ironic symbol of its own failure. He did consent to swell the city's pride with a departing interview in which he said that there was no "tinsel or shabbiness" about Chicago, that its women were handsome and well dressed and that it had been hospitable. To this a newspaper could only add as its au revoir, "Go, Mr. Wilde, and may the sunflower wither at your gaze."

Another celebrated visitor was Mme Helena Modjeska, whose conquest of at least one Chicagoan—a young columnist for the Daily News named Eugene Field—was complete. When Modjeska appeared in Camille, Field sat in the front row or a box during every performance. Wherever he sat, his large solemn visage had a fascination for Modjeska and she involuntarily played at him. It soon became a game between the two; Field attempted to adopt a facial expression exactly contrary to the sentiment the actress was portraying. After the theater, Modjeska would reproach him, "Ah, Meester Field, why will you seet in the box and talk with your overcoat on the chair to make poor Camille laugh, who is dying on the stage. You are a very bad man—but I lof you." It was a "lof" which was reciprocated appropriately in a verse:

> Nor will revolve, since rising sons are we,
> Round any orb, save, dear Modjeska, thee
> Who are our Pole Star, and will ever be.

The visits of Theodore Thomas and his orchestra, Sarah Bernhardt, Oscar Wilde and Modjeska were attractions which any provincial city might expect to have. Their performances emphasized to a small group of thoughtful Chicagoans that the time was near when Chicago should have its own culture with native artists, musicians and writers. One of those who dreamed of a more sophisticated Chicago was Ferdinand Wythe Peck, the son of a pioneer who had been a founder of the city's fire department. Peck envisioned one building that would be the home of opera and the arts, a Parthenon of modern civilization. To make his vision practical, he proposed

INTERIOR OF THE AUDITORIUM, 1889

the new home for opera be constructed in connection with a hotel and office building. He intended to make it self-supporting as Crosby had intended his opera house should be; profit was as important to Chicagoans as esthetic principle. Out of Peck's planning came the Auditorium. Its erection symbolized to Chicagoans the beginning of an era when they might add to the pleasures of accumulating a fortune the satisfaction of indulging in the pleasures it could buy.

Peck, after first presenting his idea to the increasingly important Commercial Club, had no difficulty in raising the money through the sale of stock. For his architects he engaged Dankmar Adler and Louis Sullivan, partners who were beginning to lay down basic principles for a new American architecture. The building which Adler and Sullivan designed could only have been erected in an opulent city expansive with new fortunes. The most expensive marble obtainable was used for the floors and thousands of man-hours were spent in forming it into intricate mosaics. The theater auditorium was based on a radically different principle; it was designed according to acoustical principles rather than sight lines. The floor rose much more sharply than was necessary for the audience to see; this arch, combined with the vault of the ceiling, provided nearly echoproof acoustical perfection. The equipment of the stage was as highly mechanized as any in the world. To permit the banking of the stage for concerts the floor was in sections which could be lifted separately by hydraulic lifts beneath the stage. Laid flat with an overlay of hardwood, it could be extended to a ballroom

ENTER THE LADIES 174

floor that would accommodate several thousand. The boxes were another departure from tradition and were only forty in number. It was Peck's idea that there was no place in Chicago for privileged classes; he said the city "regards the Metropolitan Opera House of New York where the whole structure is sacrificed to boxes with infinite scorn and patriotic dislike." Peck regarded boxes as a reflection of effete European ideas. If there was one thing he impressed upon the architects it was that he wanted the Auditorium to represent "the future and not the corrupted past." The hotel was also in a new tradition. Among the innovations was the location of the kitchens and dining rooms on the top floors. This, it was explained, enabled the wind to take away the cooking odors without offending the guests.

There were social questions as well as cultural problems to be solved when the Auditorium was erected. It was obvious that only the most formal wear would be appropriate for the members of society who appeared in the elegant surroundings of the Auditorium. To the ladies this meant the décolleté gown, still regarded as daring in Chicago and not suitable for public entertainment. To establish a standard in the matter for readers of the Tribune, a reporter made a survey among the city's social arbiters, who were ready to reveal their opinions if nothing more.

Mrs. William B. Howard expressed the majority opinion. "I think it would be too bad to do away with it," she said, "now that we have such a magnificent building to display it in. The luster of any evening is undoubtedly increased by the appearance of women in low-necked dresses." Mrs. Marshall Field felt the subject "one which every woman must decide for herself. I never wear a low-necked gown myself and hold that a slender woman's appearance is vastly improved by the Bernhardt style of dress. Of course it is all right for women who have handsome necklaces to cut the dress low enough to display them. But as I never wear jewelry of that kind myself I always have the necks of my dresses cut high. I really think that quite as dressy an effect can be produced by omitting the sleeves." Mrs. Carter Harrison said she felt that the low-necked gowns might be all right but that by the time a woman became a grandmother, she should no longer wear them. To this view Mrs. H. O. Stone, "the grandmother of a sweet little baby myself," took exception. She told the reporter her late husband had always wanted her to wear such gowns and she had no intention of abandoning the practice which she did not find at all immodest.

Economy and health also entered into the discussion. To Mrs. Fernando Jones the décolleté dress was "less expensive than the high-necked one, for it takes elegant material and a good deal of decoration to make the latter dressy enough." Mrs. Reginald De Koven, the wife of the composer of "O Promise Me," was another who gave her approval to the low-cut dress, disdaining charges that it was unhealthy. "Not in the least," she retorted.

"I have always worn low-cut bodices for evening since my coming out and I always shall wear them. I have a sensitive throat and take cold easily but have never been able to trace a single illness to the wearing of a low-necked dress." Mrs. John W. Jewett was also concerned with the issue of health. "For the years between sixteen and twenty-eight when the neck is plump and full and the skin like satin a dress cut modestly low is not in my opinion inappropriate provided the wearer has exceptionally robust health, but after that . . ." Here the reporter discreetly remarked that "an expressive gesture with the hands completes the sentence."

The question of ladies' dress having been aired if not finally settled, Chicago began to prepare for the dedication of the Auditorium. The event was considered worthy of the presence of the President of the United States and the Pecks rushed work on their new mansion in order to have it ready to entertain President and Mrs. Harrison as their house guests. But though the Auditorium was finished, the Peck house at 1826 South Michigan was not. With only three days remaining before the dedication, Mrs. Peck called upon Marshall Field and a few other business leaders to come to her rescue. Within an hour, contractors, painters and decorators began arriving at the house, which was finished and completely furnished in time to receive the Harrisons. The city took an immense interest in the Harrisons' entertainment. For breakfast, the newspapers reported, the President had eaten a parsley omelet, porterhouse steak, mutton chops, breakfast bacon, hothouse tomatoes and a baked potato—"No frills but good eating." By lunch the Chief Executive was at least moderately hungry as he sat down to a repast at the Union League of Blue Points, Schloss Vollrader, Crème de Terrapin, Sherry Solero, Fillet of White Fish, Roman Punch, Chicken Wings, Champagne, Larded Quail, Chateau Pichon, Cheese and Crackers, Fruit and Cake and Coffee. In response to a question, the President said he had been informed his coming to Chicago had been criticized in the East because the Auditorium was a private enterprise. "Such criticism," he said, "springs from those who have never seen your great buildings. It marks a period in the development of our country. Altogether exceptional itself, my presence at its opening can set no precedent." If there were those who did not agree with the President, they were not to be heard in Chicago.

The crowd that began to gather on the night of the opening had grown to about twenty thousand persons by curtain time. Attorney Wirt Dexter described it as "a well dressed mob and with wit enough to become exasperating." Its comments were loud and to the point. The *Tribune* reported the following morning that "whether the cream of society or only its boiled milk, all had to pass through the serried ranks of upturned, swaying, laughing, gibing, hooting faces." But if it was a noisy mob it was not unfriendly; every one felt that this was the greatest night in the history of Chicago.

The mob outside was as proud of the new symbol of the city's success as any of the select group which picked its way across the street through the lines of carriages while the rain dripped upon high-piled coiffures and made little furrows in brilliant complexions.

Once inside the Auditorium the members of the audience sat proudly through speeches by the governor, the mayor, the President and an address of dedication by John S. Runnells. They listened attentively as a "Triumphal Fantasie" was played and a chorus sang "America" and a cantata written for the occasion by young Harriet Monroe. But their great affection was reserved for Chicago's favorite singer, Adelina Patti, who had returned to sing "Home, Sweet Home" and the "Swiss Echo Song."

Patti, so the readers of the newspapers learned, had bleached her hair "red-gold" because her own dark tresses had "cast a depressing effect" on her feelings while she was in mourning for her sister, Carlotta, who had died six months before. She added in the same interview that she was to wear "half-mourning" in her appearance at the Auditorium—"a white brocade dress with black slashings and steel beads." That the feminine members of her audience took note of her appearance and particularly of her hair was indicated by an item in the newspapers several days later: "A State Street hairdresser says that many women of Chicago with black hair have called upon him recently and talked to him in a confidential manner which he is bound to respect." Chicago, no longer the young girl in gingham, was ready for a few frills.

PART THREE
The Spirit of Democracy

1890=1910

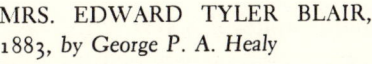

MRS. EDWARD TYLER BLAIR,
1883, by George P. A. Healy

Why Do We Need a Genealogy?

EVEN WITH the development of great fortunes there was no leisure class in Chicago. An air of continued striving and aggressiveness was still the chief Chicago characteristic. There was a general consciousness that the city lacked some sense of form or elegance of refinement not to be found in "her corn and railways, her hogs and by-products and dollars." Typically, or so it seemed to most visitors, the city was now striving to add this refinement with the same purposeful determination which had always marked its pursuit of wealth. And, as an English observer was quick to remark, although the city did not quite know what it lacked, it was determined to have it, "cost what it may." A *Harper's* correspondent in the nineties was more severe. He found that local conditions were "Arcadian"—or, as he expanded his theme, "part and parcel of the kinship that permits Chicagoans to bring their rugs out and to sit on the stoops in the evening."

The local press was not entirely in disagreement. The *Saturday Evening Herald*, which sought to chronicle the first movements of the embryonic society, lamented that "it has always been said of Chicago that it was impossible to conduct a grand fete or hold a grand function year after year (be it a charity ball, a Derby or a fete of any kind) without making it common inside of a few years." Even the Assembly Balls, which for a long period were the city's most fashionable affairs, originated as a protest against the more exclusive invitation list of the Entre Nous Club. The Entre Nous members had excluded most of the younger married couples from the list of those invited to their affairs. Rather than accept the principle of exclusion, the offended group banded together as the Assembly Association, inviting only enough of the Entre Nous members to split that organization's loyalties. The invitations to the Assembly Ball then became the most eagerly sought social honor, with a packing-company executive, Arthur Meeker, and his wife acting as final arbiters in dispensing them. Within a short time, the Assembly Balls had grown from a restricted four hundred to nearly eight hundred. The Charity Balls sponsored by Mrs. Palmer had far outgrown their original dimensions and were open to all who had the resources to contribute to charity. After the 1909 charity ball, where music was provided by the incongruous alternates of Johnny Hand's society orchestra and the First Regiment Band, the *Record-Herald* reported triumphantly that "all stiffness of formality was absent. It breathed the spirit of democracy, the spirit of the most democratic city of the most democratic nation of the world. There was no one who couldn't belong." Mrs. Walter Brewster, one of the leaders of society, was to sigh somewhat wearily that "if you are anybody at all, you are it. You are invited to every ball, wedding, debut, charitable entertainment and opening."

Not everyone was satisfied with the emphasis on democracy which had been characteristic of society from the earliest parties at Beaubien's Sauganash Hotel. The exclusive Fortnightly Club, distressed by the city's reputation, scheduled a discussion to determine "Is Chicago Provincial?" A society columnist suggested that the city needed a new club—one in which members could enjoy themselves "without thought of any useful occupation." But Joseph K. C. Forrest, who wrote a column in the *Daily News* which he signed "Old Timer," said he doubted "if those who have made business their chief end in life could transpose the order of their existence and make a business of pleasure." He was not sanguine about the chance of "even your retired, much less your active banker, your bloated speculator, your pork packer" developing into society leaders as long as they carried "the spirit of the store, the bank, the packing house and the mart of trade into society with them." A suggestion that ancestral blood lines and genealogies be referred to as a criterion of social standing met with a rebuff from Marshall Field. To a prospective genealogist who wished to prepare a chart showing the merchant's forebears back to the time in 1630 when they landed in Massachusetts, Field had a quick answer. "I have nothing to give you," he said. "Why do we need a genealogy?"

A catalogue of the standards of social acceptance more generally recognized than any kind of social register or genealogical bluebook was that found in the *Tribune* when the excitement over the Klondike gold rush was at its height. "Chicago is still the best Klondike," the *Tribune* proclaimed. "Today there live in Chicago over two hundred men whose fortunes reach and pass the million mark. Every large fortune was made here. What you need is an outfit of good sense, sobriety, industry, economy and stick-to-it-iveness. Without an exception, so far as can be ascertained, these millionaires started in without capital." Typical, the paper indicated, was Silas B. Cobb, who had arrived in the city without enough money to pay his fare to the captain of the schooner which brought him. Cobb went to work for John Kinzie, who had bought his release from the captain, and at fifty-five had been one of the richest men in Chicago. This model citizen, according to the account, "never kept a clerk or a bookkeeper, never asked any man to go on his note, never went to law in his life, never paid a lawyer or a doctor a cent. He had no extravagances and no dissipations." On the list of millionaires which accompanied the article, the paper listed Cobb's wealth at fifteen million dollars or as much as that of Potter Palmer. The richest man on the list was Marshall Field, whose wealth was estimated at seventy-five million dollars and whose firm was credited with making more men millionaires than any other one concern in the United States. Philip D. Armour, who was not only the world's largest packer but whose firm handled more wheat than any other single company in the world, was credited with forty million dollars. Calling attention to the fact that so many men on the list were Chicago pioneers, the *Tribune* explained that they "had survived the wear and tear of time so well" because they "led frugal and abstemious lives in their youth."

Though the city was young and its leaders durable, there were many names on the *Tribune's* list that reflected a changing leadership. The name of Montgomery Ward appeared on the list as having made his first one million dollars. William Deering, who had competed with Cyrus McCormick, had accumulated ten million dollars. But the new order was most readily seen in the growth of the stockyards which had been founded in 1848 and in the expansion of the packing houses which surrounded the yards. The third richest man in Chicago, according to the *Tribune*, was Samuel W. Allerton, who had operated his packing business on the credo that "nobody can succeed unless he can build up character and credit." At one time, Allerton had possessed enough of both these virtues to buy up all the hogs in Chicago and hold them until the price rose enough to satisfy him. Allerton, whose worth was listed as twenty million dollars, was less active in business. Allerton's contemporary, Nelson Morris, was also a less dominant figure. It was Morris who was credited with knowing more about buying cattle than anyone else in the United States. It was said he could tell from which

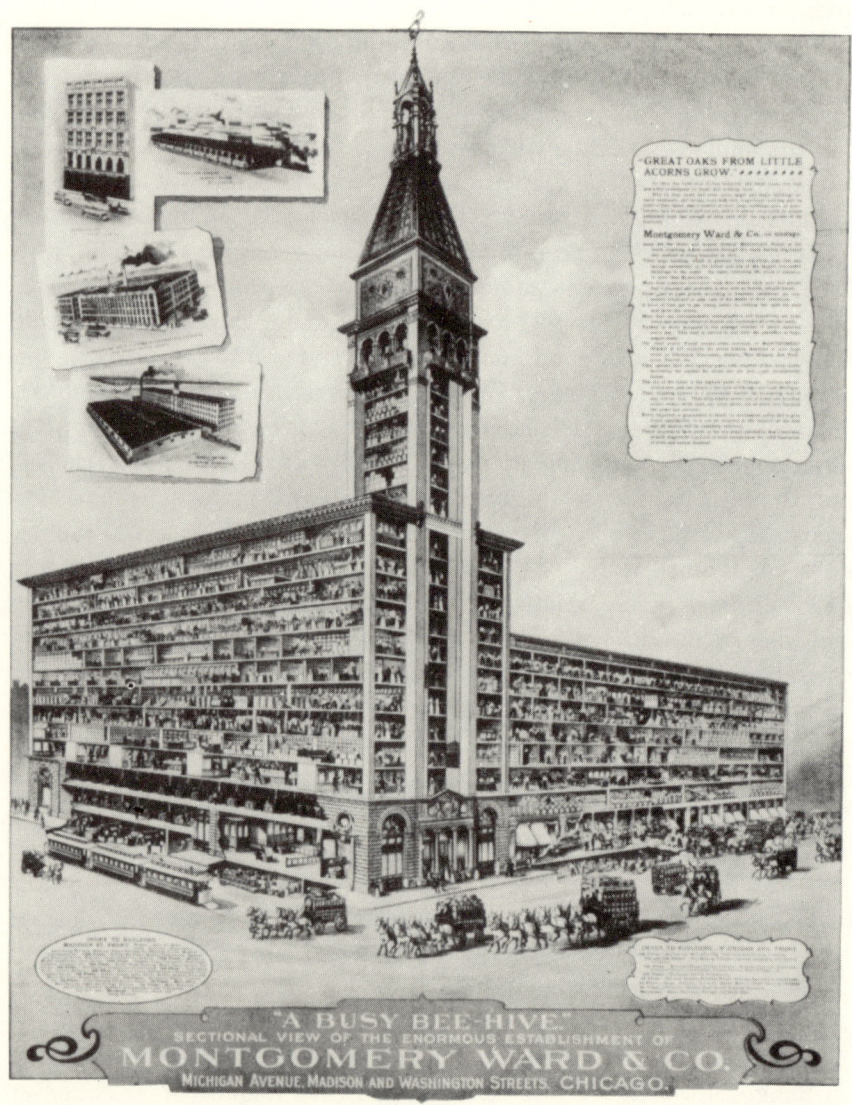

MONTGOMERY WARD & CO., about 1900. Lithograph published under the title "A Busy Beehive"

section of the country a steer had come by the taste of a steak after the animal had been butchered. Philip Armour still dominated the yards, but more was being heard of John and Michael Cudahy, who had formerly been Armour partners but had established their own chain of packing houses and accumulated a combined fortune of five million dollars. The real challenger to Armour, however, was Gustavus Swift, whose thrifty practices were reflected in a quickly accumulated fortune of ten million dollars.

THE SPIRIT OF DEMOCRACY   184

Gustavus Swift found Chicago a comfortable city in which to live. "A man can get wholesome food in Chicago more cheaply than he can in the East," he explained, "and he can live as well on a smaller amount of money. I can spend my money fast enough here." He thought Chicago "was the finest city in the world for the moderate, natural average man of affairs." Swift's idea of being moderate was firmly expressed in his personal life. For many years after he accumulated a fortune, he kept his family in a modest house near the stockyards on the ground that it was convenient to his work. When he finally permitted a move into a garish and monstrous yellow brick house at 4848 South Ellis, he saw no need of adorning it with such frills as draperies or lace tablecloths. He told his wife, Ann, who had been living without curtains for thirty years, that he would not permit them and yielded only after she threatened to leave him. But he still would not permit any curtains to be purchased for his own bedroom.

Swift, who told an interviewer that "no young man is rich enough to smoke 25-cent cigars" and that "no man, however, rich, has enough money to waste in putting on style," was under continuing pressure at home to add a bit of style. In the new house he discovered there were social rules to be obeyed as well as such fripperies as curtains and draperies to be tolerated. He was in the habit of sending for the cook to give her instructions about his food, but was prohibited from such informality by his wife. "We are doing things differently in the new house," she informed him. Stringent as were the prohibitions imposed by the family's social status, they did not

MASONIC TEMPLE, 1895

approach the business rebuke Gustavus Swift received from his brother, Noble. Swift & Company was preparing to bring out a new issue of stock and Gustavus wrote Noble to tell him that he might have some of the shares. "Brother Gustavus," Noble wrote in a tone of exasperation, "I do not care for any more Swift & Co. stock. Do you remember when we were boys, that everybody on the coast fished? What has become of the fish now? Fished out! Where will Swift & Co. be when the cattle are killed off? I don't want any more stock. Perhaps I have too much already."

There was some significance in the fact that Noble Swift did not live in Chicago. As novelist Henry B. Fuller observed, it was "the only great city in the world to which all its citizens have come for the avowed purpose of making money. There you have its genesis, its growth, its object; and there are but few of us who are not attending to that object very strictly." Philip D. Armour expressed the same Chicago philosophy in a slightly different way when it was suggested that he might retire. He explained he could not give up his business activities "because I have no other interest in life but my business. I do not want more money; as you say, I have more than I want. I do not love the money; what I do love is the getting of it, the making it. All these years of my life I have put into this work and now it is my life and I cannot give it up.... I do not read, I do not take any part in politics, what can I do? But in my counting house I am in my element; there I live and the struggle is the very breath of life to me." Armour was above worrying about criticism. "I can stand a lot," he said, "for my hide is thick.... That is the result of my early habits. I was raised like a farmer and I still have a pitcher of water in the center of the table as we used to at home."

The Reverend Dr. Frank Gunsaulus, the minister of the Plymouth Congregational Church which Armour attended, thought he might be able to persuade Armour to develop new interests. He announced as his sermon topic "If I Had a Million Dollars." When he mounted the pulpit to preach he saw that Armour, his richest parishioner, was in his regular place in the church. The minister's plan, as it was expounded in the sermon, was to establish a school to help young people help themselves. It would be an outgrowth of the educational plan developing in the Armour Mission. The mission had been founded with a $100,000 bequest in the will of Philip's brother, Joseph, and its operations had been continued with an equivalent grant from Philip. Julia Beveridge, the mission's librarian, was using the facilities of the building—constructed for a Sunday school—to teach woodcarving, drawing, designing and other manual arts to more than four hundred boys; an equal number of girls were learning dress-cutting and millinery work. Armour listened carefully as the Reverend Gunsaulus described the need for technical training on a higher level. After the sermon, he had a question for the minister. "Would you carry out those ideas if you had the means?" he asked. When the minister expressed his willingness to put his sermon into practice, Armour offered a million dollars if the minister would give "five years of your time." The bargain was sealed with a handclasp. Out of this Sunday morning colloquy came the Armour Institute of Technology, later merged with Lewis Institute to form the Illinois Institute of Technology.

Philanthropies such as that of Armour were remarkable because of their rarity. Rudyard Kipling, after a disapproving visit to Chicago, found nothing in it but an expression of materialism:

> I know thy cunning and thy greed
> Thy hard high lust and willful deed
> And all th' glory loves to tell
> Of specious gifts material.

There was much that Kipling missed. Had he been less prejudiced against what he called the "most American" of American cities, he would have seen the evidence of an esthetic revolution in architecture which had its origins in the materialism he deplored.

The preparations for the revolution had been going on for a generation. The first of the innovators was George H. Johnson, who had adapted an abandoned art of the Egyptians to create a process for making fireproof hollow tile. Another of the early arrivals was Louis Sullivan, who was to become the philosophic spokesman of the Chicago school of architecture. Sullivan, who had created the Auditorium in collaboration with Dankmar Adler, had an intense dislike of the classical style. During the 1880's he had become an advocate of the Romanesque, believing that its horizontal, low lines best harmonized with the prairie city and were best adapted to masonry construction. It was as a philosopher, however, that he had his greatest influence. He based his architectural ideas on two general principles. One was that architecture had no significance unless it reflected the life of the people. The other was that the form of a building should be an expression of its function. Out of these twin principles came the American skyscraper and modern functional design.

The function of a building in the business district was obviously that of multiplying as many offices as possible on valuable ground whose price had risen to several million dollars an acre. Multiplying offices required high buildings, but Chicago's swampy base provided a poor foundation for such structures. Once again Chicago had to conquer its notorious mud. The solution came from a new architectural firm formed by John Wellborn Root and Daniel H. Burnham. Root had the idea of floating "rafts" of crisscrossed steel rails and concrete in the subterranean gumbo and erecting the high structures on these. On a series of these rafts Burnham and Root put

NATATORIUM AT THE CORNER OF JACKSON AND MICHIGAN AVENUE

up the sixteen-story Monadnock Building, the highest masonry structure ever erected. The final step in the creation of the modern skyscraper was taken in 1884 by William Le Baron Jenney, a former army engineer. His design for the Home Insurance Building was aptly described by Carl Condit in *The Rise of the Skyscraper* as the step of evolution which "converted a building from a crustacean with its armor of stone to a vertebrate clothed only in light skin." The Monadnock Building had been based on stones six feet in thickness. The strength of the Home Insurance Building came not from such mass but from a skeleton of steel beams erected on floating foundations of the kind designed by Root. These were the first steel beams ever used in a building in America. Burnham and Root were quick to add Jenney's ideas to their own and in 1891 they erected at Randolph and State Street a twenty-two-story Masonic Temple, then the highest building in the world.

Paul Bourget of France was more perceptive than Kipling in noticing the changes that were taking place in Chicago. At first, he wrote, "you have around you only buildings. They scale the sky with their eighteen or twenty stories. The architect who has built them, or rather who has plotted them, has accepted the condition imposed by the speculator, multiplying the planned offices. It is a problem of interest only to an engineer, one would suppose. Nothing of the kind. The simple force of such a need is such a principle of beauty, and these buildings so conspicuously manifest that need that in contemplating them you experience a singular emotion. The sketch appears here of a new kind of art, an art of democracy made by the crowd, and for the crowd, an art of science in which the certainty of natural laws gives to audacities, in appearance the most unbridled, the tranquillity of geometrical figures."

It was not possible to rebuild the city in the nineties as completely as had been done in the seventies. Around the trim figures of the new skyscrapers were grouped a collection of buildings four and five stories high, dull in color and with no particular distinction of architecture. The pavement was of cedar blocks or cobblestones, the sidewalks mainly of stone with a few remnants of wooden walks which frequently gave way beneath pedestrians and formed a substantial source of income for lawyers adept at collecting damages from the city. A principal quality of the streets was noise—compounded from cable cars and street-level railroad tracks from which there was an "incessant tinkle of locomotive bells that seem to be sounding in advance the knell of those they are about to crush."

Horseless carriages were beginning to appear on the streets. In 1900, there were ninety permits for electric cars, fifty-five for gasoline vehicles and forty-four for steam cars. Among the licenses were ten issued to women who were bold enough to defy convention and to face the hazards of breakdowns from the capricious new carriages. There was already talk of a motorized bus line, a plan which the *Tribune* conceded might sound "chimerical, were it not for the fact that exactly the same thing, according to the *Scientific American*, is now being done in New York . . . Chicago, so the experts say, offers a much more inviting field [for horseless carriages] because of its level topography and long stretches of asphalt paved boulevards."

The South Park Board took a disapproving view of the new contraptions. In 1902 it banned from Michigan Avenue and Jackson and Washington Parks all automobiles which emit "spurts of vapor" (steam cars), "offensive odors" (gasoline cars) or cars with "a speed of more than eight miles per hour." All horns and whistles were prohibited.

The most popular form of transportation remained the bicycle. The Chicago *Post* reported in May of 1897 that all society was awheel and the boulevards and parkways gay with the latest model cycles. "The fashionable girl no longer lolls about in tea gowns and darkened rooms," the paper said, "but stands beside you in short skirts, sailor hat, low shoes and leggings, ready for a spin on the wheel." Every afternoon and evening cycling parties might be found at the Saddle and Cycle Club north of the city. A popular rendezvous for less fashionable cyclers was Fisher's Beer Garden at the north end of Lincoln Park. The Auditorium Hotel was another cycling

TOURING BY BICYCLE, 1896

center. Neighborhood clubs met at their own clubhouse, took a preliminary spin and then converged on the Auditorium for dinner. In the evening, there might be a spontaneous parade on Michigan Avenue, with the clubs moving in column down the street and then breaking ranks to move off toward their homes.

Cycling guides were best sellers. The books included such traffic information as a list of regulations prohibiting cyclers from riding at a speed exceeding eight miles per hour or riding more than two abreast, and requiring them to carry lighted lamps at night. Ambitious wheelmen could choose their objective from a distance table which indicated it was twenty-seven miles to Wheaton or Highland Park and seventeen miles to Western Springs. The ride to Aurora or Elgin and back was a hundred miles; those who made it in a day over the dirt roads were awarded a well-merited gold medal.

Cycling was not without hazards. A story by Poliuto, a popular newspaper columnist, told of a romance between one of the town's best cyclists and the daughter of a prominent family. The attachment had been suddenly terminated by the girl, who refused to give any reason for her action. The suitor was baffled until he found a newspaper clipping in a plain envelope among the letters and presents which, as propriety demanded, the girl had returned to him. The clipping explained his broken romance. It read: "Competent medical authorities have decided that serious results are caused by riding the velocipede. Among these, not the least is giving to Malthusian doctrines a practical and eminently undesired effect." Even a sheltered girl of the nineties could understand that this was reason enough to beware a young man on a velocipede.

Munsey's Magazine, looking at Chicago about this time, called it the "City of the Big Idea"—of the skyscraper, the refrigerator car, the mail-order store, the Pullman car and the packing house. At twenty-seven, Chicagoans would tell you, their city was as large as Athens or Damascus; at forty-three she had caught up to Rome; and at fifty she had surpassed Vienna, Constantinople and St. Petersburg, three of the empire centers of the world. The most remarkable portrait of the city, however, and one which rivaled anything ever produced by its native poets was the work of an English tourist, G. W. Steevens. "Chicago," he wrote:

> Queen and guttersnipe of cities, cynosure and cesspool of the world: Not if I had a hundred tongues, everyone shouting a different language in a different key, could I do justice to her splendid chaos. The most beautiful and the most squalid, girdled with a twofold zone of parks and slums; where the keen air from lake and prairie is ever in the nostrils and the stench of foul smoke is never out of the throat; the great port a thousand miles from the sea; the great mart which gathers up with one hand the corn and cattle of the West and deals out with the other the merchandise of the East; widely and generously planned with streets of twenty miles [in length], where it is not safe to walk at night; where women ride straddlewise and millionaires dine at midday on the Sabbath; the chosen seat of cutthroat commerce and munificent patronage of art; the most American of American cities and yet the most mongrel; the

"BEAUTY ON A BIKE," 1889

191 WHY DO WE NEED A GENEALOGY?

second American city of the globe, the fifth German city, the third Swedish, the second Polish, the first and only veritable Babel of the age; all of which twenty-five years ago next Friday was a heap of smoking ashes. Where in all the world can words be found for this miracle of paradox and incongruity?

To celebrate this "miracle" which had occurred in the quarter of a century since the great fire, it was inevitable there should be a parade. The plans for the parade were appropriate to a city where, as Steevens also noted, "if it is not the biggest thing of its kind that has ever been done, why then Chicago has lost a day." There was a practical end to be served by the mammoth demonstration. A national election was to be held in 1896. The candidate of the Republicans was William McKinley, who stood for the sound-money principles which were part of the basic inventory of the Chicago philosophy. The candidate of the Democrats was William Jennings Bryan, who had been nominated in Chicago a few months before after his famous speech in which he proclaimed "You shall not press down upon the brow of labor this crown of thorns, you shall not crucify mankind upon a cross of gold." The connection was obvious to the leaders of the business community; the parade would pay tribute to the principles of sound money from which the city's business prosperity stemmed and simultaneously advance the cause of McKinley. The Democratic city authorities were not hospitable to the idea of the parade and refused to proclaim an official holiday. The businessmen who formed Chicago's unofficial government declared a holiday on their own authority by closing the Board of Trade, the stockyards, the banks, the stock exchange, and most of the stores, offices and factories. When the day for the parade arrived, the theme of the fire anniversary was only an echo of the cries for sound money.

The parade began at 10 o'clock in the morning and lasted for five hours. The cable cars, horsecars and elevated trains reported they carried a total of two million passengers during the crowded day. The crush in the parade district was so great that twenty-four hours later there were still eight unclaimed children at police headquarters who had been lost during the day. The parade column was composed of more than 68,000 men and stretched out for thirteen miles. The Chicago Hussars led the groups and were followed by mounted police, floats, and charter members of the Lincoln Wide-Awakes walking with gold-painted canes rather than their oilcloth capes and torches. All the men in the parade wore some kind of gold decoration, either gold cords on their hats or colored sashes around their waists. A long section of Civil War veterans was followed by battalions of marchers regimented according to political clubs or business houses. Marshall Field, his partner, Harlow Higinbotham, and four other company executives rode abreast in the fore of an army of employes representing the firm's floorwalkers, salesmen, cashiers, porters and office boys. Just behind came the Carson Pirie Scott & Co. Sound Money Club, the first of several hundred such clubs to proclaim its identity in the parade. Following the business houses came the representatives of the stockyards and the packers—ten thousand men led by a brigade of stockyards cowboys sitting easily astride their mounts beneath capes of gold cloth and splitting the air with bugle calls. Megaphones appeared for the first time in Chicago, many of them mounted on the handlebars of bicycles, and increased the multiplication of noise. At the Chicago Telephone Building a huge telephone speaker was suspended from the building and into it the paraders shouted their cheers to be carried to William McKinley at Canton, Ohio, where the candidate was conducting his famous front-porch campaign. The parade over, the local papers counted up the marchers and the crowd; by their reckoning it was not only a record-breaker in politics, but the largest civil demonstration in the history of the world.

The Democrats celebrated the anniversary with a silver-metal parade the same night but could muster only a diminutive force of about fifteen thousand. The Democrats charged that many of their party members had been forced to march in the day's parade or be faced with the loss of their jobs. At night the darkness masked the marchers' identities while torches outlined a row of white-clad "ghosts" carrying placards reading "Murdered in Pennsylvania by Carnegie." There were other issues to be considered in addition to that of sound money.

Labor unrest was but one of the new currents flowing in society which

THE SLEIGH RIDE, Samuel W. Allerton and his son, by Henry H. Cross, 1879

were only partly understood by the titans who ruled the city. Another revolt came from the second generation, victims for the most part of their parents' success. Philip Armour's son, Ogden, returning home from a trip to England, told his father he did not much like the idea of going to work in the stockyards. The father, who prided himself on setting an example for the younger men coming up around him, did not share Ogden's enthusiasm that "so many Englishmen had a leisurely life on a small income." As the elder Armour put it, "Ogden thought there would be something he would like to do instead of grubbing for money. He thinks I should retire. I told him to be at the yards in his working clothes at seven on Monday morning."

Frazier Jelke, whose father made a fortune from oleomargarine, wrote in his autobiography that "this must be said of the Chicago tradition: it was hard on the second generation. . . . It is a matter of record that few sons of men of outstanding success made names for themselves or kept pace with their sires." The explanation lay in the fact that the fathers, who had little formal education, sought to give their sons the softening cultural advantages of college, art, travel and luxury. Then, on graduation, the sons were expected to go to work at jobs for which their training had not fitted them; they had been taught to live like gentlemen of leisure and unexpectedly found themselves put in the position of laborers or clerks or factory hands, as their fathers had been in their youth. As Jelke was to testify, "It didn't work."

Joseph Leiter, whose father had been the first partner of Marshall Field, was so brash as to challenge Philip Armour on the Board of Trade. Leiter attempted to corner the world supply of wheat by buying against Armour. When the chances appeared best that Leiter might succeed in his coup, Armour learned of seven million bushels of wheat in Duluth that had been passed over on the assumption it could not be shipped until spring. Armour, who assumed nothing, hired a fleet of ice-breakers and tugs to bring the shiploads of wheat to Chicago where he dumped it on the market. The price plummeted and Joseph Leiter had to take a loss on his buying of two and a half million dollars. To make good the debt, his father, Levi Leiter, returned to Chicago and sold some of his downtown real estate; for a Chicago businessman it was an act of desperation.

Leiter's sisters fared better by pioneering in a new area—that of marrying titled foreigners. After Marshall Field bought out Leiter's interest in the store, the Leiters took their three daughters to Washington, where Mrs. Leiter began an extensive campaign of elegant entertainments so that her daughters might meet titled suitors. Her average of success was high. Two of her daughters married English noblemen and the third married a cousin of the Duke of Argyll. Mary Leiter became the wife of the eldest son of the Fourth Baron Scarsdale, a bright young man who was to become Lord

Curzon, Viceroy of India. Daisy, whose baptismal cognomen was Marguerite, became the wife of Henry Molyneux Page Howard, who was twice an earl, being both the nineteenth Earl of Suffolk and the twelfth Earl of Berkshire. Nancy, the youngest daughter, married Major Colin Campbell, who overcame reported objections of his future mother-in-law against his lack of rank by proving a link to an Irish king. These marriages were proudly claimed by Chicago. Photographs of the Leiter girls were on sale in many of the stores which had not, as yet, Hollywood film queens to offer as models for young girls with the dual endowments of beauty and an ambitious mother. Mrs. Evelyn Clayton, a young Chicago widow, became a princess of Imperial Russia after her marriage to Prince Nicholas Engalitcheff, a Russian envoy. The union drew an added bit of attention when the new princess announced she was taking up cigarettes as the prince "loved to see a woman smoking."

There were other signs of sophistication. Rose Farwell, the youngest daughter of United States Senator Charles B. Farwell and a niece of John V. Farwell, in whose firm Marshall Field had once been a young clerk, wrote her graduating essay at Lake Forest College on "The Decay of Puritanism." This was strong language for a community still dedicated to the Yankee virtues. But even more indicative of a change was a newspaper's description of Rose Farwell on her wedding day. "Her father says she can ride any horse which she can mount," the *Journal* boasted, "and her latest acquisition in that line is a thoroughbred racer brought for her special use from Kentucky and which she handles with consummate ease. Add to that her proficiency in lawn tennis, her skill in handling the ribbons and she is a perfect specimen of a beautiful and accomplished daughter, the result of an education thoroughly American. And all this triumph of civilization has most fittingly chosen to adorn the home of the groom of today, Mr. Hobart Chatfield-Taylor, a young man whose wealth is counted among the millions and which he inherits from his father." The time of the pioneer was at an end.

Lake Shore Drive, 1889

A YOUNG STUDENT AT BOURNI-
QUE'S DANCING ACADEMY, 1881.
By Edward H. Hart

The Cultivated Class is Comparatively Small

THEODORE THOMAS, after moving west to establish the Chicago orchestra in 1890, indicated that he was thinking in terms of a combination of practicality and esthetics which was pleasing to Chicago. One of his objectives, he said, was to demonstrate the soothing qualities of fine music on the perpetually fatigued American business executive. "One reason I came to Chicago," he wrote in his autobiography, "was that I understood the excitement and nervous strain that everyone, more or less, suffered who lived there, and realized the consequent need of establishing a permanent musical institution in such a community."

Thomas, who had accepted the Chicago offer with the tart comment that "I would go to hell if they would give me a permanent orchestra," found quickly that he had not arrived in paradise. His first season was not a success. The programs were on a higher level than those of the summer concerts, for which he had offered music of a lighter character, with symphonies administered in very small doses. Although Chicago had the boldness to establish a permanent orchestra, it was still so uneducated in its tastes that it generally regarded symphonies as too severe. For this reason, Thomas arranged to give a large proportion of programs without a symphony in the second year and work the audience up to the symphonic standard a little more slowly. The conductor, conscious that most of his potential audience belonged "to the class employed in mills, factories and at all kinds of manual labor, while the cultivated class is comparatively small," arranged a series of special concerts for workingmen. Various schemes were adopted to raise money among them a benefit concert at which Thomas conducted the symphony orchestra for dancing at the conclusion of the concert. The orchestra protested this indignity but consented to play when Thomas threatened to mount the podium and conduct before the rows of empty chairs.

The Chicago music critics were another hazard. Thomas had once written George Upton, the *Tribune* critic (and later Thomas' biographer), that "I have no need to cultivate the critics for I know my work." Yet the critical onslaught against the orchestra's program was so intense that Thomas finally offered his resignation. He was persuaded to stay after a vote of confidence from the orchestra board, which indicated its faith in him by renewing his tenure without a written contract so that he would be free to do as he pleased. There were other difficulties. The members of the orchestra had to be assembled from all over the world, as there were few local musicians qualified to play symphonic music. Violinist Frederick Stock, hoping for a position with the new orchestra, had to switch to the viola because viola players were harder to come by than violinists. Many players were reluctant to come to Chicago because they thought there were so few families with an interest in music that the opportunities for earning extra money from teaching were too limited. Even the climate expressed its hostility to culture. "In many cases," Thomas wrote, "the men imported were unused to such a rigorous climate as that of Chicago and were driven away again by sickness and had to be replaced."

Meanwhile, Thomas resumed patiently his task of accomplishing the musical education of a city of almost two million people. A prerequisite of success was a concert hall; when the orchestra played in the vast Auditorium it was impossible to sell season tickets as audiences knew there were always seats available. A drive for a new building produced the first dividends from the efforts of Thomas to democratize the appeal of the orchestra. Contributions of scrubwomen and mill hands were listed next to those of the members of the Chicago Club. The total subscriptions surpassed the $750,000 it was expected to cost to erect the new building on Michigan Avenue with its twin stones bearing the name of Theodore Thomas. The impatient

THE WATER TANK LIBRARY, established in an abandoned water tank in 1871

conductor gave his first concert before the plaster was dry on the walls. The dampness, plus his exertion in readying the building, caused complications which resulted in his death within a month after the completion of the hall which was to be his monument. Cultural maturity, like wealth, appeared to have come rapidly to the young city. The successor to Thomas was found in the ranks of his infant orchestra; he was Frederick Stock, who after putting down his viola to take up the conductor's baton, became the symbol of the proudest moments of Chicago's musical history.

Two years after the founding of the symphony, a brilliant professor from Yale, William Rainey Harper, agreed to accept the presidency of the new University of Chicago. The city had known an earlier Chicago University which had been founded on ten acres of land donated by Stephen A. Douglas in 1856, but the recurrence of financial panics led to its closing in 1886. Thomas W. Goodspeed, then secretary of the Baptist Theological Seminary in Morgan Park and one of the university's alumni, immediately started to seek a means of re-establishing the school on a larger scale. The man to whom he turned for help was John D. Rockefeller, already an important contributor to the seminary. Rockefeller listened patiently to Goodspeed's ideas but took no action until Frederick Gates, secretary of the new American Baptist Education Society, added his pleas to those of Goodspeed for the establishment of a new denominational school at Chicago.

Rockefeller agreed to give $600,000 if another $400,000 could be raised by the Baptist churches of Chicago. It required long months of effort to raise the additional money and it was produced only after ardent solicitations to every church of the denomination throughout the Midwest. Marshall Field then aided the cause with a gift of ten acres of property just north of the proposed site for the World's Columbian Exposition and this was chosen as the location for the school.

The choice of the new president had been expected. Goodspeed had been urging the trustees to name Harper, who had the additional recommendation of being on friendly terms with Rockefeller. Both Harper and Rockefeller enjoyed cycling. When the Harpers visited the Rockefellers in Cleveland the cycling often took the form of a game of follow the leader with the entire Harper and Rockefeller clans pedaling through the countryside until dusk made it necessary for the leader to identify himself with a white scarf trailing behind. On these visits Harper would tell Rockefeller of his plans for a new college as he had outlined them in detail in his notebooks. Sometimes he would show the oil magnate the section of the book in which he had laid down additional plans for a great university which might be the outgrowth of such a college. As plans went forward for the first buildings of the new school, Rockefeller surprised the thirty-three-year-old president with a gift of an additional million dollars in bonds "as a gift to the Almighty God for returning health."

The extra million dollars made Harper turn from his plans for a college to those he had outlined for a university. He had written out in precise language the distinction. "A college," the notebook explained, "teaches; but a university teaches—and also learns." The principal effort of his university was to be directed toward graduate work and the training of students to push out along new lines of investigation. Many of Harper's ideas were new to education, among them the establishment of a junior college, a university extension course which provided home study and adult education, the creation of a university press and a special division of laboratories and museums which foreshadowed the university's emphasis on scientific research. All these plans were written out in detail before the university enrolled its first student. Not in the notebooks, but doubly welcome, were the victories of the University of Chicago football teams under Amos Alonzo Stagg. Harper was the team's most ardent fan; if he could not attend a game he would have the score phoned to him at the end of every quarter.

Harper applied the Chicago techniques of aggressiveness and "stick-to-itiveness" to higher education. He persuaded nine college presidents to leave their schools and be among the 120 faculty members who greeted the nearly six hundred students who entered the university on October 1, 1892. He used his persuasive abilities to instruct the newly rich Chicagoans in the practices of philanthropy; the endowment of the new school mushroomed beyond the reach of any financial panic. Harper was an amateur cornetist and when he practiced always insisted on every window in the house being shut, explaining "This is going to be noisy." He was just as noisy about his school but played with all the windows open. So much money poured in from John D. Rockefeller that the Standard Oil founder made a collection of cartoons showing Harper pursuing him for another grant. Rockefeller liked best those showing him "fleeing across rivers on cakes of ice with Dr. Harper in hot pursuit or perhaps he would be following close on my trail, like the wolf in the Russian story, in inaccessible country retreats, while I escaped only by the delay I occasioned him now and then by dropping a million-dollar bill which he would be obliged to stop and pick up." The university's chief benefactor visited it only twice, on one of his visits being so dismayed by the absence of enough clocks in the president's house that he slipped Mrs. Harper a check for a thousand dollars with instructions to "buy some more."

The cultural awakening extended to art as well. Martin A. Ryerson, seeking paintings for the new Art Institute Building under construction on the lake front, went about his task with "Chicago hustle" hardly to be expected of so soft-spoken and gentle a man. Chicagoans, it seemed, could find the same bargains in art as they did in wheat or corn or hogs. Ryerson studied art and the new catalogues as conscientiously as any member of the Board of Trade followed the weather and grain reports to determine the prospects for winter wheat. He secured a series of four art panels for the Institute,

THE PAVILION, JACKSON PARK, 1890, *by Charles Graham*

ardently desired by a European museum, by getting to the dealer's before European competitors were up and about in the morning; it was the same technique Gustavus Swift and Nelson Morris had used in outsmarting cattle buyers in the Chicago stockyards. Ryerson's companion on many of his buying trips was the president of the Institute, Charles L. Hutchinson, whose father had been a Board of Trade pioneer. Hutchinson did not have the educated taste of Ryerson, but by his enthusiasm and ability to raise funds for the paintings eased Ryerson's task. When Prince Demidoff was offering a group of Dutch masters for sale, Ryerson and Hutchinson rushed to the prince's villa near Florence and bid $200,000 for the cream of the collection. By this bold gesture they acquired fifteen prize paintings, including such names as Ter Borch, Hals, Hobbema, Van Ostade, Rembrandt, Ruisdael and Jan Steen. Among the treasures were Ostade's "Golden Wedding" and Rembrandt's "Young Girl at an Open Half-Door." Returning to this country after the purchase of the Demidoff collection, Hutchinson brusquely dismissed the questions of the New York ship reporters about the paintings. "They are corkers, every one of them," was all he would say, explaining that the details were too bothersome for a busy man. The New York Press of July 4, 1890 commented sarcastically:

> The hypercritical New York spirit that is tempted to revile Brother Hutchinson for not remembering what the Rubenses, Rembrandts and the Van Dykes were about deserves a stern and uncompromising rebuke. For our part, we have no doubt whatever these corkers are the largest specimens of the schools of Rubens, Rembrandt and Van Dyke that Mr. Hutchinson could find in Europe. He probably paid $1000 a foot for them and we presume the citizens of Chicago will give him a triumphal procession along the lake front when they arrive, carrying them and him in huge floats, drawn by a team of milk-white Berkshire hogs that have been newly washed with a ten-inch hose jet of water until their pink flesh shows under the clean bristles.

The ridicule was wasted. Ryerson augmented his coup with a trip to Spain where he bought El Greco's "Assumption of the Virgin"; he was the first American collector to recognize El Greco's genius.

The opening of the University of Chicago and the increasing interest in art among all classes of Chicagoans—some of whom collected French paintings when they went abroad much as they collected French clothes—encouraged Chicago's literary magazine *The Dial* to claim proudly that the city was "passing to a higher and maturer stage of civic existence." In an article on "Chicago's Higher Evolution" it cited such developments as the founding of a permanent orchestra, the establishment of the university, the founding of the Newberry and John Crerar libraries and the erection of the new building for the Art Institute. William Morton Payne, associate editor of *The Dial*, was less sanguine in an article written for the *New England Magazine*. "A chapter upon the books of native Chicagoans would be little less barren than the famous chapter upon the snakes in Ireland," he observed. It was his view that Chicago had but recently passed from the stage in which literature was regarded with "indifference or even positive contempt" to a level where there was a first awakening of interest in literary matters. As evidence of what he regarded as cultural barbarity, he alluded unhappily to the visit of James Russell Lowell, a recollection that made "most intelligent Chicagoans blush for their city [and] is too humiliating to be dwelt upon."

Lowell, whose expansive abilities embraced careers as poet, essayist and novelist as well as terms as minister to both England and Spain, had been invited by the Union League Club to give a public lecture on American politics as part of the observance of Washington's birthday. Chicagoans anticipated the event would be at a minimum historic; the *Morning News* reported that the audience which overflowed Central Music Hall represented the best of the "brains, fashion and wealth of Chicago society." To the great surprise of everyone Lowell announced he would not speak on politics but on literature. Specifically, he told his stunned listeners, he would discuss the principles of literary criticism as illustrated by Shakespeare's *Richard III*, a paper he had once delivered to the Edinburgh Philosophical Association. At this, said the *Times*, his audience "settled back into a fixity of intentness which only such a theme could inspire." The paper added that among the dignitaries on the platform there were some who "endeavored but ineffectually to refrain from a gentle but grateful slumber."

Lowell explained his change of topic by saying he wished to avoid controversy because he was a guest of the Union League Club. He hardly could have caused a greater furor than by his talk on what the *Tribune* described as "a singularly uninteresting subject." Many Chicagoans, always sensitive to the British influence, suspected that the speaker's associations with the English were responsible for his conduct. The *Morning News* reported that the organ had played "Yankee Doodle" because the organist "feared Mr. Lowell had forgotten it during his long sojourn abroad." An anonymous member of the Union League told the press that perhaps "Mr. Lowell prepared a speech in which he recognized our indebtedness to the English government—he is quite an Anglomaniac you know—and was advised or concluded that it would offend the Irish who have just had Justin McCarthy, the famous Irish editor, here, so he changed the subject." The Reverend Frank Briston, disappointed that Lowell's eloquence failed to keep its appointment with destiny, was of the opinion "he threw away the opportunity to make himself famous throughout the annals of American political history." The *Morning News* expressed the consensus of Chicagoans when it said "it was well for . . . the audience . . . that it went out to see James Russell Lowell rather than to hear him."

The unfortunate speaker, embarrassed and bewildered by the uproar, attempted to repair the damage by delivering his speech on politics at a banquet that evening in the Union League Club. In a room decorated by numerous flags and banners—"every one of them the Stars and Stripes of America; not a Union Jack was to be seen," noted a reporter—the poet spoke forthrightly on the need for independence in politics. The talk did not increase his popularity, as the club had recently expelled Lowell's Chicago host, Wirt Dexter, for rebelling against the dominant Blaine wing of the Republican Party. The *Tribune* dismissed the evening's talk more curtly than that of the afternoon, describing it as "a postprandial speech before a few college graduates." The other papers were as caustic.

The degree of anger at Lowell was a measure of the city's sensitivity over its own lack of men of letters and its resentment of a continuing dependency on eastern communities for intellectual leadership. The city was still too busy making money to have a literature of its own. George Horace Lorimer spoke for many in his *Letters of a Merchant Prince* when he had one of his characters say, "We don't have much use for poetry in Chicago, except in streetcar ads." It was a comment which gave some meaning to a later generation's discovery that the conductor of a West Side horsecar in 1889 was a young man who aspired to be a writer; his name was Knut Hamsun. The only Chicago novel to achieve any recognition before the 1880's had been Mrs. John Kinzie's *Waubun*, a fictionalized account of life in early Fort Dearborn and of the experiences of her father-in-law and family during their escape from the massacre. Stone & Kimball, Chicago's outstanding publishing firm, had no local authors of importance on its list, though it showed real literary awareness through such discriminating endeavors as the publication of the plays of Henrik Ibsen, the authorized American translations of the plays of Maurice Maeterlinck and the issuance of George Santayana's first book, *Sonnets and Other Verses*. Joseph Kirkland, an early midwest realist, was first published in 1888 and Mary Hartwell Catherwood was only at the threshold of her writing career. Most of the literary talent was expressed through the columns of the newspapers or magazines rather than in books.

The most widely quoted of the literary journalists was Eugene Field, whose "Sharps and Flats" column in the *Daily News* was the outstanding newspaper feature in Chicago. A favorite retreat of Field's was McClurg's bookstore, located in an old-fashioned red brick building at the corner of Monroe and Wabash. Field was to be found at McClurg's almost every noon, usually in a corner of the rare-book department where a verse of his was pasted on the bookcase:

> Swete friend for Jesus sake forbeare
> To buy ye boke thou findest here
> For when I do get ye pelf
> I mean to buy ye boke myself.

A small coterie met in the store regularly and the witty exchanges provided much of the material for Field's column. Among the members of the circle was the Reverend Frank Gunsaulus, whose varied accomplishments included the writing of a novel *Monk and Knight,* and whose presence among the free-spoken writers and reporters led Field to dub the meeting place the "Saints and Sinners Corner."

McClurg's took its name from General Alexander C. McClurg, a soldier-scholar who had had a remarkable career in the Civil War. He had been elected captain of a volunteer infantry company and after serving through a series of battles and marching with Sherman to the sea had been discharged as a colonel. He was devoted to literature and carried with him throughout the war a copy of *A Golden Treasury of English Verse.* Though he had his horse shot out from under him twice at Mission Ridge, the book was as spotless after four years in the field as if it had been kept under the glass of a museum. His wife was Eleanor Wheeler, a niece of William B. Ogden, whom McClurg met when she was acting as hostess for her bachelor uncle during a visit to Chicago. Her family in the East was so disapproving of her marriage to a midwesterner that they refused to enter her married name on the family plaque in the village church. After the war, McClurg had been promoted to general for organizing Dandy First, the state's first national guard regiment; he continued to maintain his literary interests by contributing articles to the *Atlantic Monthly* and the *Forum.*

The general believed that a classical education was the only proper one. He disapproved of the midwestern public-school system and imported two teachers from the Roxbury Latin school in Massachusetts to tutor his son, Ogden, and a few children of friends. When Ogden was old enough to be taken on a trip to Europe, McClurg thought it would be unfair to discharge the tutors. Feeling responsible for bringing them to Chicago, he arranged to finance them in setting up a Chicago Latin School for boys and a comparable school for girls. A man of strong opinions, McClurg welcomed the members of the "Saints and Sinners Corner" to the store but disapproved of the publicity the store received through Field's column, feeling that such notices were an "offense against the dignity of literature."

In the evenings Field liked to linger over a meal with other newspapermen at Billy Boyle's English Chophouse, a favorite rendezvous for gamblers. This diversion was spoiled when the intensity of the newspapers' attacks on the gambling houses led Boyle's patrons from Gambler's Alley to view the reporters as intruders and perhaps as spies and they were no longer wel-

SAINTS' AND SINNERS' CORNER AT McCLURG'S BOOKSTORE

comed. Another rendezvous of the literary journalists was the Press Club, founded two decades before by a group of newspapermen headed by Melville E. Stone of the *Daily News*. Impromptu entertainment or all-night poker games were the usual diversions at the Press Club. Among those to be found there regularly was George Ade, whose *Stories of the Streets and the Town* were running in the Chicago *Record* and whose books *Artie* and *Fables in Slang* were popular successes. Opie Read, who published his humorous weekly, *The Arkansaw Traveler* in Chicago, was an inveterate performer, always willing to stretch up to his six feet of height and drawl out a tale of Arkansas life. He was also one of the most prosperous of the writers. His novel, *The Jucklins*, was a favorite at railway newsstands and sold more than a million copies. Another of the Press Club group was Finley Peter Dunne, creator of Mr. Dooley, the loquacious saloon philosopher of Archey Road. Among the Dooleyisms were: "Trust ivirybody—but cut the cards . . . I care not who makes th' laws iv a nation if I can get out an injunction . . . Manny people'd rather be kilt at Newport thin at Bunker Hill . . . and Th' modhren idee iv governmint is 'Snub th' people, buy th' people, jaw th' people!' "

A successor to the Press Club was the Whitechapel Club, a dimly lit refuge existing in one room opening on an alley back of the *Daily News* office. It had neither janitor nor key. Its center table was a large coffin which had once served to carry a dead Indian to the Indiana dunes, where the

Whitechapel members cremated him with what they considered appropriate rites. The walls contained grisly relics of famous murders. Lamps had been fashioned from human skulls; in a place of honor was a skull claimed to be that of Waterford Jack, the millionaire streetwalker of early Chicago. When the club was in need of funds, the members put up Hobart Chatfield-Taylor, one of their number, for mayor. They raised $900 in campaign contributions but the money went directly into the club treasury. Chatfield-Taylor was given nearly as much space in the papers by his colleagues in the club as the legitimate candidates received. Running on a platform of "No gas, no water, no police," he polled about a thousand votes.

A more consciously literary group was that which met Friday afternoons after the symphony and went by the name of the Little Room. It was made up for the most part of professional writers and artists who hoped to develop interest in the genteel tradition of the East; it was self-conscious about its cultural standards and some midwesterners complained that it excluded more literary people than it admitted. Its name was taken from a short story in the *Atlantic Monthly* about a room which vanished and reappeared, reflecting the fact that the group originally had no special meeting place but gathered in the studio of any one of a number of artists. Among those who came regularly to the Little Room were Harriet Monroe, the young poet whose odes were a feature of every civic dedication; George Barr McCutcheon, whose melodramatic adventure novel, *Graustark*, was a best seller; novelists Edith Wyatt and Henry Kitchell Webster, critic Floyd Dell, cartoonist John McCutcheon, sculptor Lorado Taft, concert pianist Fannie Bloomfield Zeisler (Chicago's first virtuoso) and the poets Wallace Rice and William Vaughn Moody. Hamlin Garland, whose novels of the poverty and frustrations of midwestern farm life were setting the pattern for a new American realism, was a frequent visitor, but the dominating figure—and the one who best expressed the group's admiration for the literary standards of the East—was Henry Blake Fuller.

Fuller had been a precocious youth; at fifteen he published two controversial articles on "The Marriage Question" in the *Tribune* and found himself locally famous. His personal delicacy bordered on the effete. Hamlin Garland said Fuller regarded the chirp of a robin as a "yelp" and when at Garland's country home "carried wads of cotton with him so that he could stuff his ears against the 'drone of the katydids and the crowing of the roosters.'" Fuller's most successful novel, which won him the recognition he coveted from the critics in the East, was *The Cliff Dwellers*. In the phrase of its title, the book gave a name to the new society developing around the Chicago skyscrapers. But with this initial success, Fuller lost interest in the themes of Chicago and what he considered the crudities of midwestern living. Like Henry James, he sought the subject matter for his books in

Europe; he returned to Chicago only to accept the acclaim and tribute of his circle in the Little Room.

A group originally as peripatetic as the Little Room was the Attic Club, which in 1909 moved into its own clubrooms on the top floors of Orchestra Hall and changed its name to the Cliff Dwellers. The club was organized by Hamlin Garland, Henry Fuller, Lorado Taft, Charles Francis Browne and Ralph Clarkson as a counterpart in Chicago of the Players Club in New York. It did not, as is popularly supposed, take its name from Fuller's novel but directly from the cliff-dwelling Indians of the Southwest.

In later years the Little Room met in the Fine Arts Building, a center for the awakening literary and artistic interests of the young city. It was here Arthur W. W. Denslow had his studio and where, in collaboration with Frank Baum, he created probably the most immortal of Chicago books—The Wizard of Oz. Hobart Chatfield-Taylor and his wife, who were members of the Little Room, both had studios in the building as well. Chatfield-Taylor was the epitome of the sophisticated Chicagoan and for two decades there was scarcely a literary or social function of importance with which he did not have a connection. He had ambitions to write and had published a novel of merit called *With Edge Tools*, though his later books were to be in the form of personal memoirs. With a friend, Slason Thompson, he founded a short-lived literary magazine called *America*, which forever established its identity by publishing for the first time Eugene

THE CLIFF DWELLERS. An illustration for Henry Blake Fuller's novel

Field's "Little Boy Blue." Chatfield-Taylor after the turn of the century founded the Society of Midland Authors, still Chicago's most active literary group. Mrs. Chatfield-Taylor, the *Journal's* "perfect specimen of a beautiful and accomplished daughter," operated a craft bindery for fine books. Another tenant was Ralph Fletcher Seymour, who published illustrated books in the manner of a medieval craftsman.

The vitality of the activity in the Fine Arts Building had its origins in the interests and energies of the Browne family and the publishing activities which had grown out of *The Dial* magazine. Francis Fisher Browne was another of the transplanted New Englanders. For many years he had been an editor of the publishing division of McClurg's and in 1880 had persuaded General McClurg to finance a literary magazine which would stand "pre-eminently for objective and scientific criticism." Later, to avoid suspicions that McClurg books were given preferential treatment, Browne arranged for McClurg to withdraw and established *The Dial* as an independent magazine. Though *The Dial* was published in Chicago it was not in any way a regional magazine. Among the writers to whom it provided early encouragement were Frederick Jackson Turner, Woodrow Wilson, Norman Foerster and Henry Seidel Canby. Turner called it "part of my education" and Barrett Wendell was to describe it as the "most unbiased, good-humored and sensible organ of American criticism." Like the musicians of Theodore Thomas, Francis Fisher Browne found Chicago winters too rigorous and spent much of the winter in California when the active management of the magazine was taken over by various of his four sons. The consistency of *The Dial's* viewpoint was the work of the associate editor, William Morton Payne, who wrote most of the reviews of fiction and poetry. A self-educated man, Payne spoke four languages, had translated a number of books from the Scandinavian languages and later was to be elected a member of the National Institute of Arts and Letters. *The Dial* was the most durable of American literary magazines, surviving for thirty-eight years before expiring after its transfer to New York. Another of Browne's ventures was the establishment of a bookstore in the Fine Arts Building for which he had the foresight to engage a young Oak Park architect, Frank Lloyd Wright, to design the interior. Architecturally, and perhaps intellectually as well, the store was a generation ahead of its times. The walls were of a light oak plywood and dominated by the straight functional lines Wright was to make famous. In connection with the store was a reception room with a huge fireplace where visiting literary celebrities gave occasional talks. Although the store was located in the center of a nest of studios of Chicago's painters, architects, sculptors, cartoonists and musicians, and in the same building as the clubrooms of the Chicago Literary Club, the Fortnightly Club and the Caxton Club, which had been founded in 1895 for ". . . literary study and the promotion of arts pertaining to the production of books" the venture was not a success. On its closing, Jenkin Lloyd Jones said he feared its failure had been one of "an excess of excellence . . . Chicago has a way of killing things that are too good to be true."

One of the most important ventures in the Fine Arts Building was the Little Theater conducted by Maurice Browne (not a member of Francis Fisher Browne's family) and Maurice's wife, Ellen Van Volkenburg. This was the first little theater in America. It had only ninety-one seats in the miniature Grecian temple which served as an auditorium and its credo was "create your own theater with the talent at hand." It was primarily a theater for participation. On a stage not much bigger than a large dining-room table, the Brownes presented the plays of Shaw, Strindberg and Schnitzler and tested the acting theories of Stanislavsky and Reinhardt. The Little Theater of the Brownes had only an ephemeral existence but led to one important consequence for the commercial theater. Lawrence Langner, visiting Chicago on business as a patent attorney, attended a play staged by the Brownes; from their theater group he took the idea for the Washington Square Players that evolved into the American Theater Guild.

Yet it was not from the ferment of the Fine Arts Building but from the mind of a lonely figure walking the streets as an installment collector for an easy-payment furniture company that the most durable literary achievement was to come. Theodore Dreiser, after reading the column of Eugene Field faithfully for two years, was "beginning to suspect, vaguely at first, that I wanted to write, possibly something like that." To Dreiser, nothing else that he had so far read gave him quite the same feeling for "constructive thought" as Field's daily notes, poems and aphorisms. Dreiser noted particularly that they were mostly about Chicago, "whereas nearly all others dealt with foreign scenes and people."

To Dreiser there was no more romantic topic than the young city. "It is given to some cities and to some lands to suggest romance and to me Chicago did that hourly," he wrote in *Newspaper Days*. "It sang, I thought, and in spite of what I deemed my various troubles, I was singing with it. . . . Chicago was so young, so blithe, so new, I thought. Florence in its best days must have been something like this to young Florentines or Venice to young Venetians." Later, as a reporter for the Chicago *Globe*, Dreiser continued to store up impressions of his "metropolis of men and streets." Out of these observations he drew the material for *Sister Carrie*, a novel which shocked Victorian readers because Carrie, her virtue gone, did not meet the traditional tragic end but rather pursued her life of amoral independence "with as much success as attended any other human proceeding." There was little reason for Chicagoans to be shocked; in their papers they could read daily of the success of their own Mrs. Leslie Carter. It was a career of which Carrie might have been envious.

GRIPMAN ON CABLE CAR, 1893

An Ardent Temperament Rather Than a Weak Will

THERE WAS only one subject for Chicagoans in April of 1889—the marital difficulties of the Leslie Carters. Leslie Carter was a leading member of Chicago society, president of the Chicago Dock Company, and had been president of both the Chamber of Commerce and fashionable St. Luke's Hospital. Mrs. Carter was born Caroline Louise Dudley in Kentucky, the child of a British businessman and a daughter of the southern aristocracy. The father later took the family to Dayton, Ohio, where he held a position with the Standard Oil Company until his death. The Dudleys lived in the grand manner with tutors and maids, but Mr. Dudley left Caroline and her mother only the shadow of an estate. To maintain their social position a fashionable marriage was clearly necessary. When Caroline met Leslie Carter at a party in Chicago, it was not long before that fashionable marriage was arranged.

From the time of the marriage, the Carters spent much time apart. A son, Dudley, was born, but Mrs. Carter preferred a summer home in Cooperstown, New York, or traveling in Europe to domestic life in Chicago. The couple's friends, aware that Mrs. Carter's extravagances were a continual worry to Carter and that he had mortgaged his property to meet her bills, were astounded when it was announced he was the object of a divorce suit. As the legal maneuvering proceeded, the newspapers reported that Mrs. Carter's charges were too sensational to be printed. Before the case could be brought to trial, Mr. Carter brought a countersuit, asking the divorce be granted him and charging adultery, a prosaic accusation by the standard of Mrs. Carter's suit.

If, as was rumored, Mrs. Carter planned a stage career, her press notices on the first day of the trial were a favorable omen. The *Times* reporter noted as she came into the courtroom that "her hair was the color of an August stubble field and her lips red and inviting." The *Morning News* readers were told she was "a decidedly attractive woman of the blonde type" and that "her poses have a languorous sentimental air and her face suggests an ardent temperament rather than a weak will." The quality of her hair caused all the newspapermen to strain for hyperbole. To the man from the *Morning News* her hair was "a breath of autumn sunset, neither yellow nor red but pale auburn." His colleague on the afternoon editions, after noting that "from her swelling bosom" hung an oxidized silver scent bottle for use in case she should be compelled to faint, rhapsodized over her hair as "golden as the dandelions which dot the meadows on a fine spring day. It was not blonde under which come all colors from bright orange—falsely called 'red hair'—to the hue of dried hay. It was yellow,—yellow as a sunflower, yellow as a buttercup, yellow as yellow." The *Tribune's* fashion-conscious correspondent reported that Mrs. Carter was "fashionably attired in a rich, tight-fitting walking suit of black that showed her mature figure to excellent advantage.... Through a flimsy black veil her complexion seemed matchless.... One feature alone," he said with less gallantry than his colleagues had shown, "detracted from the beauty of the fair complainant—the mouth with its red, strawberry-like lips looked too coarse for the fairer emotions."

When the jury was selected, Mr. Carter's lawyers announced they would name five men as co-respondents in his countersuit for divorce. They added that it was only necessary to prove one case of infidelity, explaining with a show of magnanimity that while "propositions had been made to take the depositions of a number of gentlemen in Europe," Mr. Carter had preferred "to avail himself of proofs of her infidelity on this side of the ocean which were ample."

The first of the men in Mrs. Carter's life had been a D. S. Gregory. The attorneys charged that he had been "kissing in the roses" with Mrs. Carter outside a Cooperstown hotel when a chambermaid had interrupted the tryst with a well-aimed pitcher of cold water. The second man was State Senator James F. Pierce of New York, who, it was said, had sent Mrs. Carter love poems and had been found seeking inspiration for his muse near her room at Cooper House at three o'clock in the morning. The third name on the list was a doctor, J. B. Gilbert. The lawyers said they would produce witnesses from the room next to Mrs. Carter's who would testify in detail as to the noises and conversation which emerged from her room when Dr. Gilbert made a late-at-night call. ("He treated me like a gentleman," was Mrs. Carter's comment.) The fourth man named by the attorneys was Kyrle Bellew, the actor. It was charged that he had dined frequently with Mrs. Carter at Delmonico's and had found it convenient to have an adjoining room at the Colonnade Hotel in New York while giving her dramatic lessons at $25 each. The fifth name on the list was that of a mystery man, William K. Constable, who for reasons of his own had sent Mrs. Carter $45,000 for a trip to Europe.

Among those in the courtroom as these extended charges were presented was Edward Gilmore, a New York theatrical manager. He was believed to be ready to offer Mrs. Carter a stage contract. "I should be delighted to engage Mrs. Carter," he told reporters as he left the courtroom. "But if the trial moves as it moved today I shall have retired from the theatrical business long before she could make her debut."

Mrs. Carter was to require all her potential talents as an actress when she took the witness stand to match wits with her husband's lawyers. It was a drama, as the *Tribune*'s reporter saw it, to determine only one question: "Was the woman lying?" The climax came during her fourth day on the stand, when her husband's lawyers brought up the charge she had made against him. The accusation was too infamous for Victorian readers and the reporter could only hint that "after hovering awhile around the edge of the cesspool which furnishes Mrs. Carter's cause of complaint, Mr. Carter's lawyer made a dive into it, dragging the witness with him, and for a while there was in the room the oppressive atmosphere of Phallic rites and other bestialities." For hours the witness and the lawyer parried question and answer as he attempted to get her either to confess or deny that her husband had been successful in forcing her to participate in the unnatural act with which she charged him. The inquiry was one which might have defeated her; if she had admitted the participation, she would have appeared in the wrong for not bringing the charge before she did; if she denied it, her case would collapse.

When the cross-examination turned to other subjects, Mrs. Carter continued to evade skillfully the queries she did not wish to answer. One clue to her character emerged when she was forced to confess that she had signed her letters of credit in Europe as Louise Dudley rather than as Caroline Carter. "Caroline was simple, homely, American and therefore thoroughly objectionable," a reporter noted. "Louise was foreign, theatrical, operatic.

There was a dressmaker of the name in London. Queens had been called Louise. So Caroline Carter bought her letters of credit in the name of Louise." They had been impressive letters of credit, one of them having been used in buying a $10,000 cloak which, Mrs. Carter explained, had not been an extravagance but had been purchased in anticipation of taking up a career on the stage.

By the end of the week, the trial had become the outstanding theatrical performance in Chicago and the papers were running sketches of fictional billboards outside the courtroom. On Mrs. Carter's last day on the stand, a small program was handed about the courtroom which read:

> ## Positively Last Performance
> ## of
> ## Mrs. Leslie Carter
> ## The Beautiful and Accomplished Society Belle
> ## Accompanied by
> ## Mr. Kyrle Bellew
> ## And an Efficient Cast of Co-respondents
> ## Regular Prices

The *Morning News* reported the trial was such an attraction to "flashy young men known in common parlance as dudes" that the bailiffs were compelled to bar the doors against the crowd. Judge Egbert Jamieson, who was presiding, announced a minimum age limit of thirty-five for the courtroom audience—thereby, said the *Tribune*, "excluding most of the ladies." The age rule proved to be impracticable. As the trial entered its second week the judge was forced to take cognizance of the "number of graybeards and baldheads among the spectators." As the *Tribune* quoted him, "We have no desire to take the place of the departed Gayety Burlesque Company. An old curiosity monger is quite as reprehensible as a young curiosity monger." To this the chief bailiff added his own moral opinion. "We must check," he said, "the spread of immorality among the old and decrepit."

It required five weeks of daily court sessions for the lawyers to trace the travels and adventures of the peripatetic Mrs. Carter. Four of the five men named by the lawyers appeared to deny the charges. The fifth, Mr. Constable, was reported ill in New York; the case against him collapsed when his wife sent a statement saying it had been she who had given Mrs. Carter the $45,000—for what purposes she did not explain. Kyrle Bellew was the last of the co-respondents to appear. He combined an appearance in court with a professional performance at McVicker's where he had the role of Antony in Shakespeare's *Antony and Cleopatra*. In court he said "Mrs. Carter had some talent for a comedienne and I did not see why with some development she should not show talent for high comedy." In Shakespeare's play that night he was hissed—six times, according to the critic—despite his insistence that his attentions to Mrs. Carter, like those of Dr. Gilbert, had been professional.

The jurors were more critical of Bellew's performance than the McVicker's audience. After twelve hours of deliberation, they found Mrs. Carter guilty of the charges made against her and Bellew; they acquitted Carter of the accusations against him and granted him the divorce. Mrs. Carter wept in her hotel room when the jury's verdict was brought to her. A few days later she was sufficiently composed to set out for New York and a stage career in which she hoped to put the name of Mrs. Leslie Carter on every "billboard and fencepost in the country." Through the impatient Gilmore, then manager of the New York Academy of Music, she secured a letter of introduction to David Belasco.

Though Mrs. Carter had appeared in amateur theatricals, she had no professional dramatic training other than the few lessons from Kyrle Bellew. Her most valuable attribute was self-confidence. When Belasco asked whether she wished to appear in comedy or tragedy, she replied: "I am a horsewoman and wish to make my first entrance on a horse, leaping over a hurdle." This interview with the young producer-playwright was a failure. Hearing that Belasco had gone to a small country hotel for a rest, Mrs. Carter sought him out to plead her case a second time. Belasco granted her another interview, chiefly, he confessed later, because of the memory of her "bizarre and alluring appearance" and the "copious and resplendent hair" which had fascinated the Chicago reporters. At the second meeting, Mrs. Carter poured out the story of her life while Belasco, saying nothing, began to see "possibilities in her—if only she could act, on the stage, with the same force and pathos she used in telling her story." Though Belasco was already a successful director and playwright, he had ambitions of becoming an independent producer. To do this he needed a star; by making a star of Mrs. Carter he could establish himself without obligation to anyone.

The task was not easy. Mrs. Carter's training began with such funda-

MRS. LESLIE CARTER IN *Zaza*

mentals as physical exercises to increase the grace of her motions on the stage. Within the period of a year Belasco required her to learn more than forty roles and rehearsed her in every one. There was very little money; lunches at Delmonico's gave way to "25-cent table d'hôte on Fourth Avenue." There were also strong prejudices against Mrs. Carter because of the divorce trial. Charles Frohman wrote Belasco that "The stockholders request me not to have Mrs. Carter use our stage any more." When the producer sought to arrange for his star's first appearance in Chicago, he was turned down by the manager at Hooley's Theatre who wrote him: "This is the most fashionable theatre in Chicago; Mrs. Carter is not wanted here and we cannot afford to make enemies."

Financial help came surprisingly from N. K. Fairbank, who a little more than ten years before had been unwilling to receive Sarah Bernhardt at a reception in the Chicago Club. Both Fairbank and his wife had taken Mrs. Carter's side during the divorce dispute and he invested $40,000 in one of her plays before his lawyers persuaded him to withdraw the backing after the play had a disastrous tour. It was five years after her first interview with Belasco before success finally came to Mrs. Carter and the producer who had worked so patiently to make her a star. Her indebtedness to Belasco was measured by the fact she achieved stardom in *The Heart of Maryland*, a

Civil War romantic drama which he had written particularly for her. Even a Chicago critic conceded that there was not "the same amount of artificiality in her performance which would naturally suggest itself to those who were familiar with her more uncouth endeavors." *The Heart of Maryland* was followed by triumphs in *Zaza* and *Du Barry*. To those who suggested that these latter roles were much in character, Mrs. Carter replied, "I delight in such roles—especially when the tour takes us to Chicago." It was a tremendous triumph for the "fair defendant" whose face suggested "an ardent temperament rather than a weak will."

There are but two more chapters essential to the story. In 1906, Mrs. Carter broke with Belasco and said she would never have another thing to do with him. And while she won the world's acclaim for the name of Mrs. Leslie Carter, the man whose name it was—proclaimed innocent by the jury, but his fortune gone and mind slipping—turned on the gas in his wall lamp and quietly left the world behind. Chicagoans read the news and thought of Sister Carrie.

It was difficult to keep the theater out of the courtroom. A decade after Mrs. Carter established her reputation as an actress on a local witness stand, Samuel Eberly Gross, a Chicago real-estate man, came before the bar of justice to claim authorship of Edmond Rostand's *Cyrano de Bergerac*. Gross's basis for his suit was that he had written a play much like *Cyrano*, called *The Merchant Prince of Cornville*, which he had sent to the Porte St. Martin Theater in Paris, where it was held a short time before being returned. He charged that Constant Coquelin, the actor-manager and a close friend of Rostand's, had allowed the French playwright to purloin the essentials of the play. As evidence he cited the circumstances that both *The Merchant Prince* and *Cyrano* featured a character with a large nose who stood under a balcony impersonating a much duller but handsomer lover.

Gross asked for an injunction against any American performance of the play and sent a Chicago detective, W. J. Sutherland, to France for additional evidence of the alleged plagiarism. Sutherland returned with an affidavit from an English-speaking servant of Rostand's who contradicted the playwright's assertion that *Cyrano* had been written before *The Merchant Prince* was copyrighted in 1896. Sutherland had not obtained his affidavit without difficulty, for Rostand was then living in a chateau surrounded by a twelve-foot fence and well guarded by dogs and watchmen. That Sutherland, who spoke no French, was able to return with an affidavit on a literary dispute was hailed by the *Tribune* as a case of "Chicago hustle against French police, bodyguards, dogs, iron fences, and interpreters and Chicago won."

When an American tour was announced for *Cyrano* with Sarah Bernhardt and the same Coquelin in the principal roles, it was not known whether Chicagoans would get to see the play. This was but one of many difficulties confronting Bernhardt, who had sent ahead a white cabriolet with yellow wheels for her stay in Chicago only to have the rail car on which it was traveling attached to the wrong train in Washington and the coach temporarily unavailable to greet her with its similarly imported French driver on the box. Bernhardt, it was explained, had particularly wanted the carriage for use in Chicago because "the reports telegraphed East of the state of Chicago's health have troubled her. Of smallpox she has a horror and the grip she regards as an archfiend. Both maladies she thinks are more apt to attack her in this city of chilly winds than elsewhere." Ultimately the cabriolet arrived, as did word from Gross that he would not seek an immediate injunction against the performance of *Cyrano*. Part of his mellowness may have been the result of a visit Coquelin paid to the city's Art Institute. As the *Tribune* reported it, the actor spent the afternoon "unobstrusively flattening out the stigmas Henry B. Fuller has been throwing at Chicago." Coquelin's enthusiasm was difficult to resist. "Never outside my own France have I seen French art more nobly represented than in this Art Museum of yours," he told a reporter.

For his part, Gross assured the press that he did not desire "to interrupt the pleasures of the citizens of Chicago so I will not do anything which might prevent the play's being given. Besides I want to see the French version of the play to be performed here by M. Coquelin." He reiterated his

SARAH BERNHARDT

claim to the play, however, and promised that as soon as it was through being shown he would "carry the fight to the finish in true Chicago style." The finish was to be delayed for fourteen months while a master in chancery took a number of depositions, among them an indignant protest from Rostand that "there are big noses everywhere in the world." Finally, in May of 1902, Judge Christian C. Kohlsaat in United States District Court ruled that Gross was in fact "the author of *Cyrano's* being." An injunction was issued preventing Richard Mansfield from producing *Cyrano* and Gross was awarded nominal damages of $1, which he accepted as vindication and waived all rights to royalties.

In Paris, Bernhardt and Rostand laughed at the verdict, Bernhardt asserting that it must have been the first of April in Chicago. Mansfield suggested that the decision might result in the "great American and European artists overwhelming Mr. Gross with orders for plays and Chicago may in the future be the center of another new industry." The legal rights had been settled; but the question remained of whether, as the master in chancery asserted, it had been a case of "clear and unmistakable piracy" and that "the greatest dramatists have been the most persistent purloiners of literary property of those less gifted." George Jean Nathan, a friend of Gross, had his own views, which added artistic judgment to legal right. "I thoroughly believe Rostand swiped my friend's play," he said. "But Rostand made it into a beautiful thing, didn't he, so what's the odds?"

There always seemed to be something not in the script for a Chicago theater. When Jean de Reszke and Nellie Melba were singing *Romeo and Juliet* at the Auditorium, a psychopath rushed onto the sage and began threatening de Reszke who drew his sword and pinned the maniac in the corner while the rest of the singers on the stage retreated until the stagehands could come out to remove him. Melba was less calm, shouting for the manager to ring down the curtain because her voice was gone. De Reszke paused again to call up "For God's sake, keep quiet, Melba. Open the window and come out." The startled Melba, her fear gone, meekly complied and the pair ended the evening in triumph.

There was another unscheduled drama with no humor. On December 30, 1903, Eddie Foy was playing in *Mr. Bluebeard* to an overflow crowd of more than sixteen hundred at a special holiday matinee in the Iroquois Theater, a showplace of marble, plush and mahogany with an ornate lobby suggestive of an old-world palace. As a double quartet appeared on the stage for a number titled "In the Pale Moonlight," a flash of flame spurted from an overloaded electrical circuit and touched fire to a flimsy drapery at the side of the stage. The mishap was a repetition of an accident in Cleveland two weeks before, but the show's management had not dropped the dangerous practice of overloading the floodlight circuits for the number.

Chicago was not to be so lucky as Cleveland, where the fire was quickly extinguished. The flames skimmed over the flimsy stage decorations and within a minute were out of control. No adequate fire-fighting apparatus was on the stage and one box of fire powder—out of only two available—had no effect on the flames. A stagehand tried to lower the asbestos curtain but it snagged when only partially closed; the tunnel formed between the curtain and the front of the stage acted like a tremendous suction tube and swept a jetlike blast of fire out into the auditorium and up toward the galleries and balconies. The theater was in a panic. Except for a few unfortunate victims killed by hysterical spectators leaping from the galleries above, those on the main floor were able to escape. In the galleries and balcony there was a holocaust of fire and panic. Fire doors were locked and exits opened inward; before these inflexible barriers victims were piled five and six feet in depth. Others were still in their seats and sat glassy-eyed in death where they had been scorched to lifelessness by the jets of flame from the stage. The fire was out within half an hour; some firemen said it had been only ten minutes before the blaze was subdued. Yet the counting of the dead and the injured dragged on for a day and a night; there were so many that the toll was never exactly known. The newspapers said that 575 had been killed; the coroner insisted there were 601 bodies, only one of them unidentified. Most were women and children, trapped on a holiday adventure.

The managers of the theater and play and several public officials were indicted for the criminal negligence which caused the catastrophe but there were no convictions. Not a person was punished, although the fire did lead to the adoption of a new set of safety regulations for American theaters. Buildings were required to have ventilators covering 20 per cent of the roof over the stage to prevent a recurrence of the draft which swept the flame outward over the Iroquois auditorium, and automatic sprinklers were added as a second safety precaution. The safety innovations were commendable; but they obscured the fact that if the Iroquois had observed the minimum regulations in effect before the fire there would have been no tragedy to mar that Wednesday holiday in 1903.

A footnote to the history of the Iroquois: The archway which formed the stone front of the theater was a counterpart, except in minor details, of a monument that had been erected in Paris to commemorate the death of 150 victims in a flash fire at a charity bazaar there in 1857. It had been a prophetic design.

CARTER HARRISON. A caricature by William H. Schmedtgen from the Chapin and Gore Restaurant

The Glories of the White City

"GENIUS is but audacity," Mayor Carter Harrison told a gathering of mayors during the Columbian Exposition summer of 1893. "Chicago has chosen a star and, looking upward to it, knows nothing it cannot accomplish." The mayor chose an appropriate setting for his boast. The genius—or audacity—of Chicago was never more remarkably illustrated than by the World's Columbian Exposition, a bold scheme to bring to the attention of the world the accomplishments of the city by the lake.

The ostensible purpose of the exposition was to celebrate the four-hundredth anniversary of the discovery of America by Christopher Columbus. Chicago's claim was put forward first by the directors of the old Interstate Industrial Exposition. Nowhere, they argued, had American enterprise and ingenuity been better demonstrated than in the phenomenal growth of Chicago, which in sixty years had been transformed from a village by a swamp into a city of a million and a half people. A company was organized to raise five million dollars to underwrite the costs of the exposition and Senator Shelby M. Cullom of Illinois agreed to introduce a bill which would make the exposition an official project of the United States Government. It was at this moment that Chicago's aspirations were most seriously endangered. Cullom, in a moment of senatorial absent-mindedness, neglected to specify that the fair be held in Chicago. A vigorous competition immediately arose among New York, Washington and St. Louis, each of which wanted to take the honor of the fair away from Chicago. It was during the bitter exchanges over the site for the exposition that Chicago's sobriquet as the "Windy City" was popularized. Charles A. Dana, arguing the cause of his city in the pages of the New York Sun, admonished his readers daily to pay no attention "to the nonsensical claims of that windy city. Its people could not build a World's Fair even if they won it." When New York made a matching offer of five million dollars for the fair, Chicago offered to double that sum. At last the city had its prize. On April 25, 1890, President Benjamin Harrison approved an Act of Congress providing for an "international exhibit of arts, industries, manufactures, and the products of the soil, mine and sea, in the city of Chicago" and invited the nations of the world to take part. A national commission was appointed to supervise plans for the fair. Harlow Higinbotham, a self-made Chicagoan who had seen the city for the first time from the top of a load of hay being brought into market, was named president of the exposition and the architect Daniel Burnham was designated chief of construction.

Two years before the fair was to open, a group of architects met in Chicago to plan its buildings. Among them were Frederick Law Olmsted, the landscape architect who had laid out New York's Central Park and the Chicago suburb of Riverside; Richard Morris Hunt, Charles McKim, George B. Post, Henry Ives Cobb, Louis Sullivan and such sculptors as Augustus St. Gaudens and Lorado Taft. When the group met for luncheon at Kinsley's, St. Gaudens called it "the greatest meeting of artists since the fifteenth century." There was artistic disagreement at the luncheon. The Chicago architects wanted to express their functional ideas in the fair buildings; the eastern group insisted upon a classical theme. Burnham, anxious to secure the greatest possible participation in the exposition, prevailed upon his Chicago colleagues to accept a compromise. Louis Sullivan grumpily predicted that the harm done by the influence of the exposition would set native American architecture back by half a century. With the responsibility for designing the major buildings assigned, the work began of transforming a bleak South Side beach broken only by ridges of sand and wild oak into a landscaped park. It was soon evident that the grandiose plans of the architects could not be carried out in time for the fair to be held in the summer of 1892 and the date was advanced to 1893.

To pay proper tribute to the anniversary of the discovery of America, a special dedication was planned for October 20, 1892, within twenty-four hours of the time historians were agreed that Columbus set foot in the New World four centuries before. More than 150,000 curious Chicagoans—twenty-five acres of people according to official reports—tramped through the mud of the partially completed grounds to hear a series of dedicatory speeches and a concert by a chorus reputed to contain five thousand singers. The speeches were hardly audible beyond the platform, but this detracted little from the enthusiasm of the crowd, some seven thousand of whom jammed into the half-finished Manufacturers Building to partake of a free lunch.

There were other preparations to be made for the fair. It was time for a municipal election and the choice of a mayor to represent Chicago before the world. The Democrats named Carter H. Harrison—"Our Carter"—to run for a fifth term. The Republican candidate was packer Samuel W. Allerton, who promised to make Chicago a respectable city for the visitors to the exposition. The campaign was one of the bitterest ever staged in a city where unscrupulous political maneuvering was the norm. The press was almost unanimously against Harrison because of his outspoken sympathy for the men accused of the Haymarket bombing and his tolerance of gambling and segregated prostitution. To state his own case, he was forced to purchase the *Times* which, becoming a political organ, did not long survive the campaign. Harrison was elected by a narrow margin and his victory was taken as a sign that Chicago would be a wide-open town during his administration (except for those gamblers who had been so unwise as to oppose his candidacy). Down in Marion, Indiana, Otto McFeely heard two residents of the Hoosier State discussing Harrison's election. "I'm a goin' to Chicago to the fair," said one, "but I'm goin' to wear nothin' but tights and carry a knife between my teeth and a pistol in each hand." In Chicago the demand for roulette wheels became so great that the ordinary source of supply was inadequate and a new factory was started. At George Hawkins' gambling place a doorkeeper assured a reporter that there was no danger of a raid from the authorities: "We's the people," he explained. "We're all right." Mayor Harrison was quick to assure prospective visitors from over the country a genuine Chicago welcome. He promised the latchstring would always be out at the mayor's house. The city's hospitality might be rough, he said, but it would be genuine. He announced that he had purchased a supply of two hundred barrels of whiskey for official entertaining—adding a discretionary warning that Chicago whiskey could kill "at the distance of a mile."

In New York, Ward McAllister, counselor and chamberlain to Mrs. William Astor, whose edicts were the supreme law of New York society, was alarmed at the prospect of New Yorkers being treated with such boisterous informality. Through the columns of the New York *World*, he suggested to Mayor Harrison that "it is not quantity but quality that the society people here want. Hospitality which includes the whole human race is not desirable." He also conveyed some suggestions to Chicago hostesses. In New York, he explained, it was the custom to keep abreast of the times when entertaining. He recommended that Chicago women follow the practice of the East where "society supplies itself with a résumé of everything that is going on" before attending a dinner party. This, he said, explains the fact that "when you go into fashionable houses you will find a good deal of intellect."

Dining, McAllister explained, was a matter of great importance. "I would suggest that Chicago society import a number of fine French chefs," he said. "I should also advise that they do not frappé their wine too much. Let them put the bottle in the tub and be careful to keep the neck free from ice. For, the quantity of wine in the neck of the bottle being small, it will be acted upon by the ice first. In twenty-five minutes from the time of being placed in the tub it will be in a perfect condition to be served immediately.

AGRICULTURAL BUILDING, WORLD'S COLUMBIAN EXPOSITION, 1893

What I mean by a perfect condition is that when the wine is poured from the bottle it should contain little flakes of ice. That is a real frappé." The *Journal*, reporting a dinner which the mayor was giving for sixty foreign naval officers, assured McAllister that "the mayor will not frappé his wine too much. He will frappé it just enough so the guests can blow the foam off the tops of the glasses without a vulgar exhibition of lung and lip power. His ham sandwiches, sinkers and Irish quail, better known in the Bridgeport vernacular as pigs' feet, will be triumphs of the gastronomic art."

Not wishing New Yorkers to become excessively alarmed, McAllister assured them that "the women of Chicago are well-dressed and cultivated. They will do their best to entertain New York society and they will have plenty of money to do it with." He disclosed that "a number of our young men are already beginning to make their investigations as to the wealth and beauty of Chicago women with the result that they are now more anxious to go to the fair than ever." These matrimonial investigations were somewhat aided by the *Journal* which ran a story of "Eligible Maidens [who] Abound in This Fair City"; but, the paper warned, though many of the girls have wealth, "fortune hunters find them possessed of a keen instinct and plenty of common sense."

Chicago's replies to McAllister's views were rapid in coming. He was addressed by the local papers in such terms of disaffection as Singular Personage, Head Butler, New York Flunky, A Mouse Colored Ass, A Popinjay, A Delightful Duffer and by the *Times*, traditionally supreme in epithetical exchange, as The Premier of Cadsville. Gussie Gander, a columnist for the *Times*, submitted a list of questions which she thought applicants for high social position might be required to answer. One of them was: "Do you consider Ward McAllister a great man, a simple poseur, or an ordinary every day matter-of-fact damn fool?" To this McAllister replied haughtily, "I require no Chicago indorsement."

The uproar over McAllister's etiquette suggestions offended the New York *World*, which tried to explain with more condescension than good will that McAllister had only spoken "in a kindly spirit as one who is anxious to see the society of the West elevate itself by observing the society of the East." McAllister was almost pedantic in his detachment. "I never intended to convey the impression that any New Yorker as a man is necessarily superior to a native of Chicago," he said. "We in New York are familiar with the sharp character of Chicago magnates and many of us have learned to our cost that the Almighty Dollar is the trail they are following." But he did not think "these Chicagoans should pretend to rival the East and Old World in matters of refinement. Their growth has been too rapid for them to acquire both wealth and culture. . . . The leaders of society are the successful Stock Yards magnates, cottolene manufacturers, soapmakers, Chicago gas trust speculators and dry goods princes. These gentlemen are undoubtedly great in business but perhaps in some cases unfamiliar with the niceties of life and difficult points of etiquette which constitute the society man or woman. For several years, for example, society persons have always hired a man to lead their Germans. He gets $25. That, to a New Yorker, appears extraordinary. It is a little out of the line. Again, Chicago's most famous millionaires have a ballroom in the attic which is approached by an elevator. This seems to be an incongruity. Here, in the East, the opinion is that the approach should be as artistically effective as the ballroom itself."

Chicago was particularly vulnerable to the thrust about third-floor ballrooms. Putting these seldom-used party rooms on the third floor was the accepted practice in almost every Chicago mansion. The city's press defended its finest houses and their unusual features only to incur more of McAllister's disapprobation. Denying that he had ever said anything unfavorable about "ladies sitting on the doorsteps in summer," he repeated that his sole criticism had been about "the novel idea of putting a ballroom in a man's attic. In this city we don't go to balls in private houses by climbing a ladder or going up in an elevator. . . . A bowling alley," he added for the benefit of those who had cited these appointments as an indication of the luxurious quality of the dwellings of Chicago millionaires, "is also an objectionable feature in any house. Why not have a shooting gallery?" In hopes of terminating the dispute, he turned to a philosophical approach. "It takes nearly a lifetime to educate a man how to live," he said. "Therefore Chicagoans can't expect to attain social knowledge without experience and contact with those who have made such things the study of their lives. In these modern days, society cannot get along without French chefs. The man who has been accustomed to delicate fillets of beef, terrapin, pâté de foie gras, truffled turkey and things of that sort would not care to sit down to a boiled leg of mutton dinner with turnips. . . . One paper says it is evidently my opinion that cultivated society is one in which the entertainment of the stomach is perfectly understood. That is a sound maxim."

McAllister was more tolerant of the Duke and Duchess of Veragua, when they arrived in New York en route to Chicago for the opening ceremonies of the exposition. The Duke was the only living descendant of Christopher Columbus, and as such McAllister conceded the Duke should be recognized. "The line of descent from Columbus is rather remote but still it is the only link we have to cling to and we should therefore extend to him every courtesy," McAllister explained. He went on to say that Columbus himself "in a social way was an ordinary man, being born in a humble station in life. But he was born with genius. He discovered the New World."

Having been passed by McAllister, the Duke and Duchess arrived in Chicago where they were greeted at the station and escorted to their hotel

GRAND COURT AT NIGHT, WORLD'S COLUMBIAN EXPOSITION, 1893

by the yellow-plumed cavalry and blue-coated infantry of the United States Army. President Cleveland had also come to Chicago for the opening. On May 1, 1893, with a chilly spring haze still on the ground, a parade of twenty-three carriages carrying the President, Harlow Higinbotham, the Duke and Duchess and other dignitaries made its way southward to the White City which had been created on what had once been a wasteland and deserted beach. A crowd of 620,000 people followed the parade southward, jammed through the exposition gates and crushed toward the speaker's platform for the opening ceremonies, meanwhile battering each other with umbrellas and lunch boxes. Eighteen tightly corseted women fainted and a company of United States troops had to be called to bring an end to the pandemonium. The speeches once again poured unheard into the uproar; President Cleveland pressed a golden switch and the World's Columbian Exposition was officially under way. The only dissenting view in the jubilation over the opening was that of Red Cloud, appearing nearby in an arena with Buffalo Bill. "This big show all about pale face who found red men over here," he was quoted as saying. "Ugh! Bad medicine."

Chicago society competed for the privilege of entertaining the Duke and Duchess of Veragua. The Duke, given the place of honor at every dinner table and overwhelmed by the excess of attention he was receiving, showed an understandable reluctance to fix the date of his departure. The committee of the national commission responsible for paying his expenses was growing restive. The *Times*, in discussing the delicate problem of persuading the Duke he should make way for other expected celebrities, suggested that the visiting nobleman felt "it would be undignified in a guest of the United States Government to be in a hurry about making his departure." The Duke, who was in fact a farmer who raised prize bulls for the Madrid fighting ring, was unaccustomed to such public acclaim and found it difficult to comprehend the rapidity with which the American public tired of celebrities. After a month the commission felt it necessary to tell him his welcome, or at least the expenses-paid portion of it, was at an end. The blow to the courtly gentleman was made worse when a tactless officialdom made no provision to escort him to the station in a manner similar to that in which he had been received. Hobart Chatfield-Taylor, who seemed to be everywhere at one and the same time, took it upon himself to assuage the royal couple's feelings. When the time came for the Duke and Duchess to depart, Chatfield-Taylor appeared at their hotel with a group of amateur hussars mounted on shining black chargers and carrying polished sabers at their belts. The troopers were entirely without official status but to the uninformed Duke they represented the majesty of the United States Government and he departed as ceremoniously and gratefully as he had arrived.

The energies of much of Chicago society were taken up by the activities at the Woman's Building, the domain of Mrs. Potter Palmer and the Board of Lady Managers made up of feminine representatives from every state. The appointment of a woman to an executive position had been regarded as a radical innovation and Mrs. Palmer was determined that it should not be regretted. During the previous year she had toured Europe soliciting exhibits. The list of those upon whom she called read like the pages of Burke's Peerage and she persuaded many of the families of the European nobility to lend precious heirlooms for the exposition. From Italy, Queen Margherita sent laces from among the crown property which dated back to Roman expeditions hundreds of years before Christ; the laces had not been out of Italy since they had been brought back by Roman armies from Egyptian tombs.

The Woman's Building, designed by a feminine architect, Sophia G. Hayden, was more than an exhibit hall. It was, in the days before homemaking magazines and food columns in the daily newspapers, a demonstration laboratory to teach American women how to live. There was a model kindergarten, then still an innovation in education, and a kitchen in which ten girls in white caps and aprons—among them Alice Higinbotham, whose father was president of the fair—spent two hours every day demonstrating cooking methods and the most efficient ways of tidying up a kitchen. Exhibits on child care provided the first instruction on the subject that many women ever had. There were, of course, exhibits of what women had accomplished in the arts, sciences and professions. Concerts in the auditorium featured the works of women composers. And, at a series of "Congresses," women met to discuss the political issues of the day nearly thirty years before they were to be granted the vote.

The Woman's Building was opened in a special ceremony on the second day of the fair with Mrs. Adlai Stevenson, the wife of the vice-president, driving the silver nail which marked its symbolic completion. The address was given by Mrs. Palmer, who said bluntly that she did not have any use for the "chivalric type" of man who raised objections to a woman's finding a job. Perhaps, she said, "they might possibly consent to forgive the offense of widows with dependent children and of the wives of drunkards and criminals who so far forget the high standard established for them as to attempt to earn for themselves daily bread, lacking which they must perish. The necessity for their work under present conditions is too evident and too urgent to be questioned. They must work or they must starve."

Quite unexpectedly, on the fourth day of the exposition, the Woman's Building was the scene for an unscheduled exhibition of feminine temperament. A group on the Board attempted to rebel against the leadership of Mrs. Palmer in a meeting marked by "tears, flushed cheeks and excited speech." The discontent had been stirring since the opening ceremonies when some members of the board felt they had been given insufficient opportunity to meet the Duchess of Veragua, Lady Aberdeen and other distinguished guests. Another cause of dissension was Mrs. Palmer's plan to put the affairs of the building in the hands of a more manageable subcommittee once the exposition opened. The leader of the opposition was Miss Phoebe Couzins of St. Louis. After Miss Couzins stated her objections, Mrs. Palmer rose to reply. She was upset and spoke slowly so as to be sure her emotions were in restraint. "I presume that all this discontent cannot have existed without some reproach upon me," she said, "and I refer to that matter with the greatest reluctance and humiliation. I do not wish to make any defense or plea. Good intentions count for nothing. . . . Congress was paying these ladies a per diem for their subsistence and I felt that for us to send a bill to Congress for a luncheon provided for this board . . . would savor of junketing and we had no right to do it. . . . We have thought we were working together as a band of women for something fine, for representing the interests of women . . . that we mark an epoch. . . . If I am mistaken in that estimate and we are all torn up and pulling hair over an introduction to a Duchess, I have nothing to say to this board except that I feel deeply humiliated." By this time Mrs. Palmer's excitement had communicated itself to the audience and there was an unparliamentary rush of weeping delegates toward the speaker's stand. Katherine Minor, a delegate from Louisiana, cried out above the hubbub: "I boldly say for the state of

Louisiana that Mrs. Palmer is the only woman in the United States that can lead me and I bow to her . . . as our American queen." When the tears were wiped away and the women once more in their seats, a vote of confidence was moved and passed: only Miss Couzins and four colleagues expressed their dissent by not voting. The *Record* spoke proudly of Mrs. Palmer's victory as "a brilliant, sensational and bloodless coup d'état."

A series of similar minor explosions marked almost every week of the exposition. There was a demand that the fair be closed on Sundays, an issue which had to be fought through both Congress and the courts before the gates were finally opened. The French, who like the other nations, had a special exhibit, negotiated with Harlow Higinbotham throughout the summer in pressing a claim for additional funds to support their display. The greatest single *cause célèbre* was that of Paderewski's piano. The products of the Steinway Company and several other eastern music firms had been banned from the exposition after they refused to exhibit their products. The order caused little difficulty with the assorted musical organizations which were daily pouring out a "Columbian cyclone of harmony" with Columbus marches, Columbus galops, Columbus fantasies and Columbus nocturnes as well as more substantial music. Paderewski, who had been engaged to play a concert with Theodore Thomas and the official exposition orchestra, refused to play on anything but a Steinway. The issue was finally referred to the national commission which held there could be no exceptions to its ruling. Thomas, angered by the commercial aspects of the quarrel, smuggled a Steinway into the hall by night and gave the concert with Paderewski in defiance of commission orders. For his disregard of the ban, the high-principled Thomas was pilloried as an agent of the Steinway Company, a charge which ultimately led to his resignation as musical director for the exposition. The effect of the squabble on Paderewski was more enervating. He canceled a performance in New York with an emphatic declaration that "I'll shoot myself before I'll play tomorrow. Tell them to take all the money I've got but I won't play." When his secretary attempted to remonstrate with the soloist, Paderewski threw his unfortunate aid bodily out of the room, an episode which a reporter redundantly attributed to the circumstance that "great excitement was telling upon his mental faculties in a degree."

More subtle difficulties arose with the arrival of Her Royal Highness, the Infanta Eulalia of Spain, and her husband, Prince Antoine. All that Chicagoans knew of the princess was that the Duke of Veragua had said her name should be pronounced E-oo-la-li-a. There was a long debate in the newspapers over the propriety of shaking hands with a princess, which was firmly resolved by Mrs. Palmer, who said, "If she does not want her hand shaken like a pump handle . . . we [will] comply therewith." The Infanta

MRS. POTTER PALMER'S RECEPTION FOR THE SPANISH INFANTA, 1893

arrived in George M. Pullman's private car, after a trip in which she had ordered the train stopped in Pennsylvania while she sent out for a fresh supply of Spanish cigarettes. The carriage of Mrs. Palmer, drawn by four chestnut horses, was waiting for the Infanta at the station, as well as a reception committee of Mayor Harrison, Allison Armour and Hobart Chatfield-Taylor, who, among other functions, was serving as Spanish consul. The mayor had discarded his slouch hat for a silk topper, "the most sincere compliment he could pay the lady." Cavalry troops presented arms as the princess made her way to the carriage, but she was not at all pleased. She told Chatfield-Taylor that she wished only "to see the World's Fair in peace and comfort without an official in sight." She made one official visit to the grounds (when thirty thousand pansies were strewn in her path), but during most of her stay she made her trips to the exposition via the lake in Allison Armour's small steam yacht and disembarked away from the public piers. She usually avoided public recognition for an hour or two but the reporters were adept at learning of her whereabouts and the deception was only temporarily successful. Meanwhile the prince visited the stockyards, went shopping, had most of his beard trimmed off to look more like an American and spent such time as he could, according to Chatfield-Taylor, "roaming incognito through the streets of the city by night, like the caliphs of old."

The visit of the willful young Infanta might have attracted no more than an average amount of attention if it had not been for the social scandal she created by daring to arrive late and leave early at a reception given for her by Mrs. Potter Palmer. The story has persisted that the Infanta snubbed Mrs. Palmer after discovering that she was the wife of the proprietor of the Palmer House where the princess had her suite. As Chicagoans told the story the next morning, the princess had asked if Mrs. Palmer were "the wife of my innkeeper." Upon being informed that she was, the princess had at first refused to attend the reception and had only agreed to go later under duress. A review of the evening indicates the princess may have been guilty of capriciousness, but does not bear out the theory she was adamant about being received by the wife of her innkeeper. Her suite at the Palmer House was fitted out with furnishings more suggestive of an old-world castle than a modern American hotel. Massive antique furniture filled the suite; the Infanta slept in an oversized mahogany bed inlaid with pearl and covered with heavy draperies of gold cloth. Ornate vases decorated every corner of the apartment. The princess and Mrs. Palmer had met several times before the reception. So far as is known, Mrs. Palmer never referred to the episode and it is possible that the impatient guests—and the crowd of several thousand outside the brightly lighted Palmer mansion which was driven away by a torrential rain before the princess arrived—might have been seeking explanations for her tardiness.

One cause of her being late was that she was visiting with Adlai Stevenson, the vice-president, who had only arrived in the city at 8 o'clock. According to the newspapers, Stevenson was told that the princess wished to see him and he arrived at her apartment shortly before 9, the time at which Mrs. Palmer's reception was scheduled to begin. The princess' carriage left the Palmer House at about a quarter to 10, not excessively late for a guest of honor—at least by royal standards. The length of time the princess stayed at the Palmer mansion is in dispute. All are agreed that she arrived about 10:15, "blazing with jewels and radiating graciousness." Both Mr. and Mrs. Palmer came down from the front steps to greet her and escort her to the French room, where a small dais had been arranged for her to meet the guests. Some accounts say she stayed only an hour, others that she stayed until 1 in the morning. The time may have been short to Chicagoans, but it was at least sufficient for the Infanta to meet four hundred people, partake of a Spanish supper, listen to a short concert and watch the guests dancing in the ballroom, where the orchestras of Johnny Hand and the increasingly celebrated band of John Philip Sousa alternated in providing music. One account says the princess received the guests in "sullen, unbending silence" but the *Times* quoted the princess as telling one of the guests she looked exactly like the Infanta's favorite sister, hardly the remark of a rigidly formal guest.

The Infanta's popularity was not great. When she was presented with a featherweight dress of spun glass, the general hope seemed to be that she would wear it, fall and cut her throat. When the Infanta was invited to the Higinbothams' for dinner, she insisted on passing on the guest list, in advance. She did not object to the presence of Mrs. Palmer on the list, but did say she would sit only with the governor rather than the mayor. The governor at the time was John Peter Altgeld, however, and he avoided the social whirlpool of the exposition summer rather than embarrass those to whom he would have been an unwelcome guest.

Whether the story of the Infanta's snub of Mrs. Palmer was true or false, it could hardly have been comforting to the dignity of Chicago's society queen to hear it so often repeated. The opportunity to repay the Infanta in kind did not come until six years after the exposition when the United States was at war with Spain. Mrs. Palmer was invited to a reception in Paris which Sebastian Schlesinger of Boston and his daughter, Baroness de Reibnitz, were giving for the Infanta. The intensely patriotic Mrs. Palmer declined and there was much chuckling in Chicago where the *Tribune* quoted her as replying curtly that "I cannot meet this bibulous representative of a degenerate monarch."

Another royal visitor in the summer of 1893 was the Archduke Ferdinand, the heir to the Austro-Hungarian throne. He was so genuinely incognito that few Chicagoans knew he was in their midst. The Archduke's Chicago escort, unhappy that his titled visitor would not even visit the Old Vienna café, summed him up as "half-boor" and "half tightwad," unaware that the unsocial visitor was later to be considered worthy of a major war.

Meanwhile, as the exposition months passed by, more than twenty-eight million people strolled through the six hundred acres of classical white buildings, gazed at exhibits which told them how their life could be made better or easier or sought adventure among the international entertainments of the Midway Plaisance. Many of the visitors came to the fair on the new South Side elevated road with its steam "dummie engines." Others piled into the "cattle cars" which the Illinois Central had fashioned from boxcars and fitted up with wooden benches. Once the passengers were located in these cars, the conductor twisted shut a wooden gate, giving stockyards-conscious Chicagoans a feeling of kinship with the cattle who were penned in railroad cars in much the same fashion. Others came by the lake, disembarking at the eastern end of the fair grounds after a trip from the special piers erected opposite the Auditorium Hotel.

At the fair grounds, visitors saw an extended panorama of mammoth buildings that suggested a multiplication of the glories of the Acropolis. To the west the dome of the administration building rose higher than that of the Capitol in Washington. Immediately in front of the administration building was the spectacular MacMonnies fountain with its graceful rowing maidens, a work acclaimed by St. Gaudens as the masterpiece of masterpieces. Along the sides of the lagoons lay the showplaces of the exposition—the buildings for Agriculture, Fine Arts, Electricity and the Hall of Mines and Mining. The Manufacturers Building, designed by George B. Post, was not only the giant of the exposition but the largest building in the world. Visitors were told that "if the great pyramid of Cheops could be removed to Chicago it could be piled up in this building with the galleries left from which to view the stone." Statistics were awesome. Seven million feet of lumber were used in the floor and it required five carloads of nails just to fasten it down. There were eleven acres of skylights and forty carloads of glass in the roof. The iron and steel used in the frame would have provided two structures the size of the Brooklyn Bridge and the individual trusses in the ceiling were double the size of any that had been constructed before. All this, Chicagoans would remind you, was an exposition, a show, a flexing of the muscles to demonstrate what Chicago might accomplish if it had a mind for it. A gem in miniature was the Merchants and Tailors Building, which S. S. Beman had designed and which he was to adapt for the First Church of Christ, Scientist, in Chicago and make a model for such churches over the country. At night the white buildings were lighted by the greatest electrical display the world had seen, a spectacle with a special attraction for a young English immigrant named Samuel Insull, who had left a post with inventor Thomas Edison to become the new president of the Chicago Edison Company. In the shadows and waterways of the lagoons, visitors with more ordinary ideas

MIDWAY, WORLD'S COLUMBIAN EXPOSITION, 1893

of romance drifted along and talked of the newest sensation among the shows of the Midway.

The Midway Plaisance, a long stretch of land connecting Washington and Jackson Parks, was the playground of the fair. Here the tourists walked down the streets of a German or Austrian village, gazed curiously at a group of Dahomey huts with sixty native warriors, traded for knickknacks in a Chinese market or Japanese bazaar, listened to the chatter of the thousand parrots in the Hagenbeck animal show that had been imported from Hamburg or craned their heads for a better look at the captive balloon which carried twenty people to a height of six hundred feet. They stood in line for a ride on the newly invented Ferris Wheel, a monster "bridge on an axle" which George Ferris had invented to match the structural glories of the Eiffel Tower which dominated the Paris Exposition of 1889. The Ferris Wheel, like the Manufacturers Building, was a behemoth. It carried forty persons in each of its thirty-six cars; during the summer more than 1,750,000 people took the ride in the big circle. At the top of the ride they could look north to the outlines of first skyscrapers or peer downward, as did young Harold Swift, at the first buildings of the new University of Chicago.

Eugene Field sang the praises of the Midway in a short rondel.

> Come boys, let's away to the Midway Plaisance
> There are visions of loveliness there to behold
> Oh, the lithe Moorish maidens with bangles of gold
> And eyes that will set you afire at a glance.
>
> And the houris from Germany, Italy, France,
> And the Javanese maidens of minikin mold!
> Come boys, let's away to the Midway Plaisance.
>
> They discount the marvelous yarns of romance
> Ingeniously spun by the authors of old:
> Why the half of the charms of that place can't be told
> And hush, we will see that Algerian dance—
> Come boys, let's away to the Midway Plaisance.

The most famous attraction was not the Algerian torture dancer but a sleek Egyptian, Fahreda Mahzar, who had come to America with a troupe of Syrian dancers engaged for the Streets of Cairo and who was billed as Little Egypt. Although Little Egypt wore a full skirt, only semi-transparent, and an unrevealing brassiere, there were thousands willing to swear with a Chicago policeman that when she danced "you could see every muscle in her body at the same time." Her dance, which was exotic enough to reveal the diamonds on her garters, was the Midway's most talked-of attraction. Seeing Little Egypt became synonymous with going to the fair. (That the dancer did not share the public's opinion of her performance was evident a generation later when she sued a motion picture company for using "naked girls" in connection with a film portrayal of her dance.)

Passing through an Irish market town or perhaps stopping for a cup of coffee in a Tunisian café, the adventurer might then make his choice among one of the sideshows where models were grouped in "artistic poses" on the stage. For the gullible there was a "nudist colony," where a spectator peered through a small hole in the wall—and saw only his own reflection mirrored over an unrevealing painting of a nude body. There were occasional shows not on the exposition list—such as that which occurred when someone gave the dwarf elephant several buckets of beer and the intoxicated pachyderm escaped for a romp through the grounds. James J. Corbett was the star of his own show, *Gentleman Jim*, though his thespian efforts consisted mostly of punching the bag. Corbett was enchanted with the food at the Viennese café and spent so much time there—where the public could view him without buying a ticket to his show—that his manager threatened him first with "a Smith & Wesson" and finally with a lawsuit if he did not spend more time in the exhibition room of the theater. Nearby a young professor in white tights who gave his name as Bernarr Macfadden was flexing his lithe muscles and demonstrating a new exercising machine invented by his sponsor, Alexander Whiteley.

Florenz Ziegfeld, Jr., who had been assigned to procure military bands from the different countries of Europe for the fair, had brought back as an extra attraction Sandow, the European strong man, and was acting as Sandow's sponsor and manager. Amy Leslie, the drama critic for the *News*, described Sandow as a fascinating mixture of brute force and poetic sentimentality. On a walk through the Wooded Island (carefully arranged by the shrewd Ziegfeld), Sandow snipped a tiny cup from a stock of snapdragon. "Now, when we were little in Germany," Sandow told the astonished Miss Leslie, "we took these blossoms and pressed them so, and if the flower mouth opened, why that was a sign they were calling us at home." As Amy reported it, "he touched the tinted bud and its rosy lips parted in a perfumed smile." Just as Sandow finished his sentence, a Columbian guard shouted that he had violated the rule against picking flowers. To emphasize the reprimand, the guard seized Sandow by the elbow and attempted to push him away. At this effrontery Sandow lifted the surprised guard off the ground and held him at arm's length, examining him as though he were a curious discovery. Miss Leslie, more conscious of the dignity of the law, persuaded Sandow to put the guard down, which the strong man did with an outburst of German expletives and an explanation (in English) to Miss Leslie that he did not think much of humans as guards. "I prefer nice, well-bred dogs," he said.

Throughout the exposition summer the theaters downtown and on the Midway offered all-star bills. At the Columbia Theater was a former Chicago singer christened Helen Louise Leonard but more easily recognized as Lillian Russell. Lillian's father was an unsuccessful Chicago publisher who issued the works of Robert Ingersoll and other agnostic literature. Her mother had been an early and ardent feminist, who liked to discuss social issues at women's meetings which she usually called in an ice-cream parlor. After the Chicago fire Lillian's mother had founded the Good Samaritan Society to alleviate the suffering of shelterless prostitutes. Mrs. Leonard had aspirations toward authorship as well, one of her works being entitled *Failing Footsteps, or The Last of the Iroquois*. Helen Leonard gave her first concert at fourteen in Chicago's Kimball Music Hall but shortly afterward her mother found Chicago too limited for suffragist ambitions and moved to New York to join the ranks of the crusaders around Susan B. Anthony, taking Helen Louise with her.

In 1893, Helen Louise, now Lillian, was back in Chicago for a sixteen-week engagement at the Columbia Theater. One of those who followed her from New York was James Buchanan Brady, a wealthy salesman of railroad equipment who was better known as Diamond Jim. Brady, who was Lillian Russell's faithful, if platonic, admirer, divided his time between the theater, the Fine Arts palace at the fair and several restaurants where he could get an abundance of his favorite dish, sweet corn. The café owners competed to please Brady's gourmand's palate and the sight of Diamond Jim dining with Lillian became one of the most widely sought, if unofficial, attractions of the fair.

Derby Day at Washington Park was to be more festive than usual that summer and Lillian had changed her matinee day from Saturday to Thursday so that she might attend. According to her biographer, Parker Morell, her appearance in the Washington Park clubhouse caused consternation among the women and a few self-conscious members objected to her presence. The president refused to listen to the outraged ladies until the wives and daughters of the club officers were persuaded to join in the protest. Then the unhappy gentleman had to ask Lillian if she would accept a box in the grandstand. Lillian did occupy a box for the races but the *Tribune* described it as "one of the best in the grandstand." There was, however some evidence that Chicago society was too puritanical in its attitudes to receive actresses. The *Record*, in reporting the race, said Miss Russell held a levee between races and "all sorts greeted her" but chiefly members "of the profession which Miss Russell adorns." If society did snub her, its satisfaction must have been spoiled the next day when the democratic reporters put her name at the top of their lists of women at the races.

Despite this apparent show of morality at the race track, the city was

MAYOR HARRISON'S HOME ON
THE NIGHT OF THE ASSASSINA-
TION, 1893

like Monte Carlo. Carriages full of merrymakers rode up and down the boulevards through the late hours of the night singing "After the Ball." Roulette, chuck-a-luck and piquet flourished in the parlors of such gambling kings as Harry Varnell. Brothel rents were tripled and paid without complaint or hardship. The city, with every theater and café crowded, had never known such a spectacular night life; the carnival spirit was everywhere.

On Chicago Day more than three-quarters of a million Chicagoans—over half the population of the city—jammed, pushed and shoved their way into the exposition grounds. By October 28th, when Mayor Carter Harrison received the plaudits of his colleagues on Mayor's Day, the fair was a success by every standard, including the fundamental Chicago measure of showing a profit. That night, after Carter Harrison returned home, a psychopath took advantage of the latchstring that was always out; he called Carter Harrison to the door and killed him because of a hallucinatory grievance over not being appointed corporation counsel. The city grieved, but consoled itself with the knowledge that the world now knew of the greatness of Chicago. The work of "Our Carter" was done. There was good reason to believe he was satisfied.

A PATROL BOX ARREST IN CHI-
CAGO, 1893, by T. De Thulstrup

From Pullman City to Hull House

FIVE DAYS after the gates of the World's Columbian Exposition were opened; the stock market crashed, throwing the country into one of its recurring financial panics. Henry Adams wrote that "men died like flies under the strain and Boston grew suddenly old, haggard and thin." Chicago, bolstered by the influx of funds from exposition visitors, did not immediately feel the full effects of the economic recession. Philip D. Armour and Marshall Field told alarmed depositors standing in line for their money when a run started on the Illinois Trust and Savings Bank that all deposits would be personally guaranteed by the two richest men in Chicago. Harlow Higinbotham took time from his duties as president of the exposition to reassure the depositors further: when one woman would not be dissuaded from taking her savings out of the bank, he held her baby while she waited for the money. But the effects of the fair and the personal courage of the city's leaders could not offer permanent immunity to the blight of a nation-wide depression. The winter of 1893–1894 saw a widening of unemployment and poverty; starvation was averted in many instances only by the food on the free-lunch counters in the saloons of Democratic politicians.

The effects of the depression were most severely felt in Pullman City, the manufacturing town ten miles south of Chicago's business district

THE SPIRIT OF DEMOCRACY 238

where George M. Pullman had planned a community from which he had hoped to eliminate "all that was ugly, discordant and demoralizing." The nation's railroads, hardest hit of any industry by the panic, canceled a large part of their orders with Pullman. Because Pullman City was a one-industry town, the workers had to make railroad cars or starve. By 1894 they were starving.

Pullman City, which had been in existence for little more than a decade, was erected on a bold and original plan. After the fire, when Cyrus McCormick had moved his reaper works away from the business district to a sprawling plant on the West Side, George Pullman was seeking a similar location for his main car works. St. Louis, anxious for the factory to be located there, sought to lure Pullman with an offer of free land for the plant's erection. Pullman declined this immediate economic bonus for a long-term advantage; he preferred Chicago because he thought a man could do at least 10 per cent more work in the summertime where the lake breeze would serve as a natural form of air-conditioning. With this in mind, he purchased a tract of about three thousand acres on the shores of Lake Calumet, an area where Stephen A. Douglas had once made such extensive investments the lake had been called derisively "Douglas's Frog Pond."

With the site selected, Pullman engaged S. S. Beman to design a self-contained industrial city. The physical planning of Beman was elaborate and foresighted. The houses were built around a central arcade for the city's shops, theater and library, a design which anticipated other American suburban planning by half a century. All the buildings were of brick, which in turn was fabricated in the town's own brick kilns from clay taken from the bottom of Lake Calumet. Considerable care was taken in landscaping the community's small park. An elegant hotel was erected and given the name of the inventor's daughter, Florence. The streets took their names from such modern inventors as Stephenson, Watt, Fulton, Morse and Pullman himself.

It was Pullman's objective to demonstrate "that such advantages and surroundings made better workmen by removing from them the feeling of discontent and desire for change which so generally characterize the American workman, thus protecting the employer from the loss of time and money consequent upon intemperance, labor strikes and dissatisfaction which generally result from poverty and uncongenial home surroundings." He did not regard his five-million dollar investment as an altruistic venture. A separate Pullman Land Association was formed to handle the affairs of the model town. It was expected to show the same profit as the Pullman Palace Car Company, whose main manufacturing plant, dominated by a high clock tower that became the landmark of the town, was allotted five hundred acres of community property. "I have not contributed 50 cents to all that you see here," Pullman proudly told French economist Paul de Rousiers. "I have never had any idea of giving alms to my men and every dwelling pays the rent it ought to do to give the company a sufficient revenue for the money sank [sic] in building Pullman City." The industrialist did not understate his case. Gas and water bought from Chicago by the company were resold to the householders at a profit. Rents were high, investigators later establishing that the equivalent of a $15 a month cottage in Chicago rented for $18 a month in Pullman City. Even the sewage from the town's houses was collected in a reservoir to be pumped to a Pullman farm several miles away and used as fertilizer.

Pullman called his city self-governing; its critics called it feudal. As one resident put it, the citizens "paid rent to the Pullman Company, bought gas of the Pullman Company, walked on streets owned in fee simple by Pullman [and] paid water tax to Pullman. Indeed, even when they bought gingham for their wives or sugar for their tables at the arcade or market house it seemed dealing with Pullman. They sent their children to Pullman's school, attended Pullman's church, looked at but dared not enter Pullman's hotel with its private bar, for that was the limit. Pullman did not sell them their grog." All saloons and drinking resorts had been banned by Pullman on the ground he wanted to do all he could "to develop the better nature of our workmen." The man who wanted a glass of beer or nip of whiskey had to walk nearly a mile to a group of low-class saloons which had been thrown up at the edge of nearby Kensington to cater to the thirst of the frustrated Pullman workers.

Pullman was particularly proud of the town's theater and library, which he anticipated would improve his workers' "better nature." Special trains brought his Prairie Avenue neighbors to the opening of the theater in 1883. The entertainment was not a frivolous drama but a lecture by Stewart L. Woodford. The speaker found it easy to praise the munificence of Pullman but added a warning that "I do not dream that the millennium is about to dawn, even at Pullman. It will be strange," he told his audience of multimillionaires and carefully screened Pullman executives, "if the serpent does not hiss, even under the rose leaves of this Eden." The Reverend David Swing of Chicago's Central Church was more lyrical when he dedicated the library a few months later. It was his hope, he said, that "the rich men of the West will always prefer libraries, and parks and music temples and even good theaters to the perishable display of the ballroom. A library is almost as sacred as a sanctuary." To the Pullman workers the library was an expensive sanctuary. Only two hundred and fifty out of about five thousand families could afford the annual fee of $3 for adults and $1 for children which Pullman assessed those who wanted to use its facilities. Even the local church was expected to show a profit. A minister who hoped to lease the church for less than the established rent was firmly turned away. "When the church was built," Pullman told the astonished clergyman, "it was not intended so much for the moral and spiritual welfare of the people as it was for the artistic effect of the scene." For many years the parsonage stood vacant because its rent was more than a clergyman could afford.

When Pullman cut his workers' wages and hours after a falling-off in business, he refused to lower their rents. He insisted the rental of houses was a separate business from the manufacture of Pullman cars and there was no connection between the town's employer and its landlord. No one was allowed to fall behind in his bills; all charges against the workers were deducted by the company from the pay checks. Some workers in 1894 were getting as little as 7 cents a week in cash; others were in debt to the company and receiving no money for their work. Exasperated, and in many cases physically weak from hunger, the workers sent a delegation of forty-three representatives to discuss their plight with Pullman. He refused to meet the appointed committee, fired every one of its members and dispossessed them from their homes the following day. Fearful of more such reprisals, the workers turned to the American Railway Union in which many of them had taken out secret memberships since it had been founded a short time before by Eugene Debs. On May 11th, without consulting Debs or the union, the Pullman unit voted to go out on strike. The attitude of the workers as the walkout began was summarized by the strike chairman, Thomas Heathcote: "We do not expect the company to concede our demands. We do not know what the outcome will be, and in fact we do not care much. We do know that we are working for less wages than will maintain ourselves and families in the necessaries of life and on that proposition we absolutely refuse to work any longer."

When the strike was called, three thousand workers left their jobs and an additional group of several hundred was promptly laid off by the company. Debs, who had urged caution after being informed of the possibility of the walkout, hurried to Pullman City to see if a compromise could be found. He knew his young union was in no way strong enough to win a strike against Pullman and the forces which might be aligned with him. There was great pressure on Pullman to arbitrate the issues. The newly formed Civic Federation, through such spokesmen as banker Lyman Gage and Mrs. Potter Palmer, urged him to meet with the workers. The mayors of fifty-six American cities wired to urge arbitration. Pullman's stubbornness in the face of such appeals was so monumental it caused even Mark Hanna to explode in Cleveland's Union League Club that "a man who won't meet his own men halfway is a goddamn fool!" The stalemate dragged on. Pickets patrolled the gates of the Pullman Company but there was so little prospect of violence that the company did not ask for additional police protection. This was the situation when the American Railway Union opened its first convention in Chicago on June 12th.

The delegates demanded action against Pullman. Debs urged caution. When a motion was made that all Pullman cars be boycotted, Debs refused to allow it to be put to a vote. He insisted that another committee be sent to meet with Pullman, a move which failed when Pullman refused to talk with the group. A second committee, this time made up only of Pullman workers, was also refused an audience; the members were told they were "in the same position as the man on the sidewalk"—that is, no longer employes. There was no alternative but to ask for a plan of action. A committee recommended a boycott of all Pullman cars; the union voted unanimously to start the boycott on June 26th unless the Pullman Company expressed a willingness to arbitrate.

As Debs had foreseen, the boycott brought the union into conflict not only with Pullman but with all the nation's railroads, which uniformly refused to move trains without the Pullman cars. The General Managers' Association, a group of twenty-four railroads, saw in the strike an opportunity to break Debs's union in its infancy. On the sidelines were the comparatively young brotherhoods of conductors, switchmen, trainmen and engineers, craft unions which disapproved of Debs's attempt to unite all rail workers in one organization.

Clashes were inevitable as the railroad workers sought to cut the Pullman cars out of the trains. On June 30th, there was a minor disturbance at Cairo, Illinois, and, after an appeal from the local mayor and sheriff, Governor Altgeld sent three companies of militia to keep order. In Chicago, Mayor John P. Hopkins saw no need for troops, though the local United States Attorney was persuaded to wire Washington for authority to hire more deputies. The strategy of the railroads was to bring the federal government into the dispute; to do this they attached unnecessary Pullman cars to mail trains in order to provoke an interference with the United States mail.

In Washington, the situation was being watched closely by Attorney General Richard Olney, one of the founders of the General Managers' Association. He was not long in finding a pretext for action. On July 2nd, he secured an injunction to prevent the strikers from interfering with the mails or interstate commerce. Simultaneously, he recommended to President Cleveland that troops from Fort Sheridan be sent into Chicago to keep order. This idea was opposed by General Nelson A. Miles and Secretary of War Daniel S. Lamont and vetoed by the President. The following day, however, Olney produced a telegram predicting there would be disorders in Chicago on the Fourth of July and persuaded the President to send the troops into the city. Governor Altgeld was circumvented just as Governor Palmer had been by-passed after the Chicago fire. The fact that Alt-

THE FIRST MEAT TRAIN LEAVING THE STOCKYARDS UNDER ESCORT OF THE U. S. CAVALRY, 1894

geld had sent troops to Cairo when there was a necessity for it counted for nothing in the eyes of his political enemies; they insisted that because of his advanced social views he could not be trusted. To Altgeld's protests, Cleveland replied, "We are confronted with a condition, not a theory."

Olney was being much more solicitous about the railroads than he had been about the coal-mine owners a few weeks earlier. At that time, there had been widespread coal strikes in both Ohio, where William McKinley was governor, and Illinois. Twice Altgeld had sent state troops to keep order during the coal-mine disturbances. When a federal judge in Springfield applied for federal troops, Olney had wired: "Understand State of Illinois is willing to protect property against lawless violence with military force if necessary. . . . If such protection proves inadequate, the governor should be applied to for military assistance." The date of Olney's wire was June 16th; less than a month later he was willing to persuade Cleveland to call out federal troops not only in Illinois, but in Kansas, Colorado, Texas and Oregon—where the governors protested the disregard of their constitutional rights with equal futility.

Violence was at a minimum, although there were a hundred thousand men idle between New York and San Francisco. Without the intervention of the federal government, Pullman might have been compelled to arbitrate. But with the widespread hiring of deputy marshals recruited from the worst elements of every city—termed by the governor of Colorado a group of "desperadoes" hired "without any regard for their qualifications"—violence increased. Mayor Hopkins, Governor Altgeld and the Civic Federation denounced the turning of law enforcement over to toughs recruited in the Levee district. At Pullman City a bystander was killed by one of the temporary deputies. Chief of Police John Brennan charged that the deputies were shooting "innocent men and women" and said his men had arrested several deputies for stealing from the railroad cars they had been assigned to protect.

The test of strength moved rapidly toward a climax as the troops from Fort Sheridan pitched their tents around the public buildings and on the lake front. A major clash occurred when the soldiers tried to move a train out of the stockyards, shut down because the railroads could not deliver hogs and cattle. As the first train started to move out of the yards, the strikers overturned boxcars in its path and spiked the switches. The heavily guarded train was able to move only six blocks. Violence erupted all over the city. Executives trying to man switchtowers or locomotives were dragged from their posts and beaten by howling, brick-throwing mobs. The night sky was aglow with the flare of burning boxcars (some of which, according to Chief Brennan, had been fired by gangs in the employ of the railroads to rouse public opinion against the strikers). The carnage of war littered fashionable Grand Boulevard as an artillery caisson exploded, killing three soldiers and hurling fragments of metal into the drawing rooms of the mansions along the street. Suburban trains ran only irregularly. On one of the trains running the gauntlet of violence out of the city, young Cyrus Adams was warned to lie on the floor to escape the bullets and stones which the strikers were firing through the windows of the coaches and Pullman cars. After several days of rioting, President Cleveland warned that he would send in as many additional federal troops as were necessary to move the trains. On July 9th, realizing that his union stood alone against the federal government, Debs conceded defeat and the strike was broken without a single concession from Pullman. The defense of his citadel had brought death to more than a dozen men and caused property damage far in excess of half a million dollars. Debs and several others were sent to jail for violating Olney's injunction, despite the shrewd defense presented by Clarence Darrow, who had only recently left a position with the Chicago and North Western Railway, and D. S. Gregory, who was later to be president of the American Bar Association.

The Pullman plant reopened on August 2nd. Almost a quarter of the workers were new employes; all were required to sign pledges they would not join a union. Governor Altgeld appealed to Pullman to help more than a thousand men from the model city who were jobless and destitute; Pullman refused to accept the message until it was officially forced on him by a National Guard officer in full uniform. At last, despairing of dealing with Pullman, Chicago accepted the responsibility for the relief of the outcasts from the community where its founder had hoped to eliminate "all that was ugly, discordant and demoralizing."

Three years after the strike George Pullman died. His achievements in helping Chicago to raise itself out of its own mud, in founding one of its great industries, in planning a model community a generation ahead of its time in its physical conception and in leading Chicago to second rank among American cities merited a statue such as that to Stephen A. Douglas which scaled the skyline along the city's lake shore. His monument was to be of a far different kind, reflecting not affection but terror and fear. The funeral services for Pullman were held privately in his mansion on Prairie Avenue late in the afternoon. The funeral cortege pulled away from the house just at dusk. It was night when the procession arrived at Graceland Cemetery where elaborate preparations had been made to assure that Pullman was "more secure from the encroachment of the living world" than any of "the Egyptian monarchs supposedly resting under the ponderous weight of the pyramids." A pit as large as an average room had been dug on the family lot and lined across its base and walls with reinforced concrete eighteen inches thick. Into this the lead-lined mahogany casket was lowered,

UNITED STATES TROOPS ENCAMPED IN FRONT OF THE POST OFFICE, 1894

covered with a wrapping of tar paper and covered with a quick-drying coat of asphalt which would exclude all air from the casket. The balance of the pit was filled to the level of the casket with solid concrete, on top of which a series of heavy steel rails were laid at right angles to each other and bolted together. The steel rails were then imbedded in another layer of concrete. The work of filling in the grave required two days. Then "the sod was replaced, the myrtle planted" and the grave "differed in no outward respect from the thousands of others under the shadow of the trees of Graceland." Such was the price of victory in the Pullman strike. Pullman's will showed his estate to be about seventeen million dollars, of which more than a million was set aside for a manual-training school where boys might learn the skills of the hands. That George M. Pullman had never mastered the more difficult skills of the heart was evident from a further provision of the will. To his twin sons he left a pittance of $3,000 a year, explaining that neither had developed a sense of responsibility "requisite for the wise use of large properties and considerable sums of money." The regimen which pressed down upon the workers of Pullman City extended even to Prairie Avenue.

The Pullman strike emphasized the need for a boldness in social thinking which would match the originality in enterprise which had been a principal quality in Chicago's phenomenal growth. A pioneer in this more modern field was Lyman Gage, president of the First National Bank and founder of the Civic Federation, who had tried unsuccessfully to arrange for arbitration of the Pullman dispute. Gage had also urged clemency for the men accused of the Haymarket bombing, arguing that free speech and adequate discussion were better weapons than prejudiced courts in the defense of liberty. To implement his theory, he organized discussion groups in which speakers were allowed to express every variety of idea. The first meetings were held in his home but interest grew until it was necessary to transfer them to the recital hall of the Auditorium. At these forums everyone was allowed his time to be heard—speculators, clergymen, Republicans, Democrats, the few surviving anarchists and the Henry George single-taxers. Gage noted only one element absent at the meetings. "I am sorry to say," he confessed, "they are attended but feebly by the well-to-do people," adding an expressive comment that "higher classes" was not the best term for this group; he felt "self-satisfied is nearer." There was nothing self-satisfied about Gage. He persuaded Mrs. Palmer to take the post of first vice-president of his Civic Federation and as second vice-president he enlisted a union official, J. J. McGrath. On his various committees appeared the names of Marshall Field, Harlow Higinbotham, Cyrus McCormick, Jr., and Jane Addams, who had established America's first settlement house in the building once occupied as a home by Charles J. Hull and which more recently had been used by the Washingtonian home as an institution for "female inebriates."

To Jane Addams the Pullman strike was not an isolated phenomenon for which one man was responsible but a symbol of the growing demand for "a more democratic administration of industry." At Hull House, which she and Ellen Gates Starr had founded in 1889, she insisted that the real enemy of social progress was not so much deliberate aggression as brutal confusion and neglect. The area around Hull House afforded many illustrations of her thesis. The settlement was located in the vortex of the whirlpool of new immigration, an area of little wooden houses grimy with soot and often falling to pieces. The pathways were of rickety and worm-eaten planks and the streets quagmires of black mud. When the crown prince of Belgium paid a visit to Hull House he insisted that "such a street—no, not one," existed in all Belgium.

When Jane Addams began her work at Hull House, the feminist movement was growing rapidly. But the feminist movement in Chicago was to take on the individual characteristics of the city which had grown in the shadow of such giants as William B. Ogden, Long John Wentworth, Joseph Medill, Marshall Field, Philip D. Armour—yes, and George M. Pullman. Self-reliance was a cardinal virtue; the best way to get things done was not to wait until others were persuaded to do it but to do it yourself. This was a tradition suited to the temperament of Jane Addams. When a survey disclosed nineteen thousand people in one area of the city without any bathing facilities except those furnished in the warm months by the lake and river, her ire was so great that more than half of the city's sanitation-inspection bureau was discharged. When she saw that garbage collections were inadequate, she had herself appointed the ward's garbage inspector, taking a fat political plum away from the party bosses. Her supervision was more than nominal; after a few months her buggy became known as the garbage phaeton. She felt that education in esthetics was as important as cleaning up the streets and alleys. John Galsworthy's play *Justice* was given its American premiere on the stage at Hull House with Theodore Roosevelt mingling with the first-night audience of workingmen and their families.

An ally of Jane Addams in the war on brutal confusion and neglect was Louise de Koven Bowen, a third-generation member of one of Chicago's first families. Mrs. Bowen's grandmother had come to Chicago in a covered wagon with a rifle across her knee. Mrs. Bowen's mother had been the third white child born in the reconstructed Fort Dearborn. The family was fashionable and among the first in the city to have a uniformed driver and coachman on the box of its carriage. Although young Louise de Koven liked such shows of style, she had a strong social conscience. When only eight, she had seen a girl injured by a runaway horse in front of her home at Wabash and Monroe. Following the men who carried the victim home,

LINCOLN PARK, 1887, by *Charles Graham*

Louise de Koven found a miserable shack, with nothing but rags upon the girl's bed. She quickly returned to her own neighborhood, pounded on the doors of the big mansions and demanded contributions. Within an hour she had accumulated $57 which she gave to the injured girl. At sixteen, she had volunteered to teach a Sunday School class of boys with a reputation for being "bad." When one of her new pupils challenged her instructions she threw him bodily out of the room. Her authority established, she opened a boys' club in the basement of her parents' mansion and invited the class, most of whom were from poor homes, to spend their free time in the club. When Louise de Koven, then Mrs. Joseph T. Bowen, met Jane Addams, she was already practicing a philosophy of direct action. "When one of us became aware of the existence of a wrong," she was to recall, "we took down our bonnets, we put them on, we tied the strings under our chins, we got out a horse and buggy—if we had them—we put in a hitching strap with a weight on the end and we started off for the scene of the trouble."

Another of the women who joined the Hull House group was Dr. Alice Hamilton, who had been dissatisfied with the finishing-school education she received at Farmington, New York, and gone on to a study of medicine. Dr. Hamilton found time for elaborate medical investigations in the Hull House neighborhood. Her discovery during a typhoid epidemic in the 1890's that the common fly was a carrier of the disease was an important contribution to the ultimate control of typhoid.

Not everyone was as sympathetic with Miss Addams as Mrs. Bowen or Dr. Hamilton. The outspoken opinions of these three, plus the views of Florence Kelley on factory legislation and Julia Lathrop in the field of social welfare, gave the Hull House group what Jane Addams called "an early reputation for radicalism." Backers frequently withdrew their pledges because of the controversies this little group of individualists initiated; yet with Mrs. Bowen as treasurer some means were always found of carrying on. An honorary membership which the Daughters of the American Revolution had given Jane Addams was withdrawn after one such quarrel. "I thought it had been given for life," remarked Miss Addams, "but apparently it was only for good behavior." The Fortnightly Club, of which Mrs. Bowen was a member, withdrew an invitation for Miss Addams to speak because of alleged radicalism. Mrs. Bowen would tolerate no such nonsense and called a special meeting of the Fortnightly, more or less dragging Jane Addams to the platform so the speech could be given as scheduled.

It was Mrs. Bowen who acted as field marshal for much of the war on the political front. She supported Florence Kelley's efforts to secure the first factory-inspection law. She fought for and secured the establishment of the first juvenile court in Chicago and soon persuaded the county and city to co-operate in erecting a juvenile court building and detention home. In effect, she dictated the judges who were to be permitted to sit in the court as well. She organized the Juvenile Protective Association for the reduction of delinquency and it was at her insistence that policewomen and matrons were hired for the first time by the Chicago police department. She was practical enough in her sympathies to be among the first to hire a relief investigator to see that charity money was being properly spent. No subject was too indelicate for her consideration. As her agents brought in reports, Mrs. Bowen bombarded the city with pamphlets on "The Department Store Girl," "The Straight Girl on the Crooked Path," "Equal Suffrage," "A Study of Bastardy Cases," "Five and Ten Cent Theaters," "A Study of Public Dance Halls" and other such topics. Through it all, she bowed to no one in her fidelity to the Republican Party. When Presidents Theodore Roosevelt and William Howard Taft visited Chicago, it was Mrs. Bowen who introduced them.

The measure of Mrs. Bowen's influence was best illustrated when she came into conflict with the Pullman Company, almost as intransigent thirteen years after its founder's death as it had been during his life. At the time, Dr. Hamilton was making an investigation of industrial diseases for the federal government. She reported to Mrs. Bowen that conditions at the Pullman plant were substandard. Painters frequently contracted lead poisoning. Men who were hit in the eye by steel fragments or suffered any type of accident were all treated by an elderly doctor. Those with eye injuries frequently lost their sight as the result of such superficial treatment. Mrs. Bowen, a large stockholder of the Pullman Company, augmented Dr. Hamilton's findings with a private report of her own. Both reports were sent to the president of the company, who refused to acknowledge them. Then Mrs. Bowen wrote again, suggesting that the company take action or she would publicly refuse to take her dividends because of the poor working conditions at the plant. This threat brought action; the Board of Directors agreed to meet with Mrs. Bowen. The outcome of the meeting was an agreement by the board to invest $75,000 in new hospital facilities and the hiring of a competent medical staff. Special precautions were introduced to prevent lead poisoning and other safety recommendations adopted. This was only one in a series of victories which Mrs. Bowen scored as an individual arrayed against the power of the corporation. With Charles Cabot of Boston, she led an assault on the twelve-hour day which was then standard for workers of the U. S. Steel Corporation. Another time, a letter to her friend, Cyrus McCormick, Jr., brought an end to the practice of hiring women to work in the Harvester Company's twine mill at night and the establishment of a minimum wage for women in the company plants.

Throughout these social battles Mrs. Bowen held her place in society. Through the pattern set by her work at Hull House and the initiative shown by Mrs. Potter Palmer in the Civic Federation and at the Columbian Exposition, a new standard of social acceptance was established for Chicago women. A writer for *McCall's* found that while "the men busy themselves with speeches and the rebuilding of Chicago . . . and the making of more money, the women tend the poor and search out talent that should be encouraged and run baby clinics—all with a furious energy." Julian Ralph, writing in *Harper's*, confirmed this impression. "I do not believe," he wrote, "that in any older American city we shall find fashionable women . . . so forward in works of public improvement and governmental reform as well as of charity. Indeed, this seems to be quite a new character for the woman of fashion." No longer was it enough to contribute funds or lend one's name to the letterheads of genteel charity benefits. Social success was now subject to the same tests as economic success had been a generation earlier. Hard work and the Yankee virtues were still the criteria. There was no time to develop a café society; there was still too much to be done.

SCENE FROM THE FIRST WARD BALL, by John McCutcheon

Life Along the Levee

"CHICAGO presents more splendid attractions and more hideous repulsions close together than any place known to me," a correspondent wrote the London *Daily Mail* about the turn of the century. "It takes elaborate care to present its worst side first to the stranger. It makes a more amazingly open display of evil than any other city known to me. Other places hide their blackness out of sight; Chicago treasures it in the heart of the business quarter and gives it a veneer." Even the locally published Rand McNally guide suggested "entrusting your valuables with the clerk of your hotel" before venturing into the Levee district where an extraordinarily thin veneer covered the city's "worst side first."

The Levee, whose name was a heritage of the early influx of southern gamblers, was, of all the city, the area most careless of its morals. No one was quite certain of the exact borders of the Levee and equal doubt prevailed about the limits of Levee entertainment. It was always carnival time on the Levee. There were gambling houses, barrelhouse saloons, dance halls, pawnshops, tintype galleries, voodoo doctors, penny arcades, fake auctions and a few legitimate livery stables, blacksmith shops and oyster bays. Within the borders of a few blocks were located more than two hundred brothels. They ranged from low dives and panel houses, where robbers worked in collaboration with prostitutes, to elegantly furnished mansions governed by a strict code of conduct. A visitor who headed for the Levee usually said he was "going down the line"; he was lucky if he returned with his bait.

Exotic entertainment ranged from that at the French Elm, where the walls were covered with mirrors, to the attractions of John Williams' Opium Den or the House of All Nations where girls of a dozen nationalities—most of them born in Chicago—worked interchangeably between a five-dollar side and a two-dollar side, as economic conditions on any particular night dictated. At the Park Theater, boxes were available in which the actresses might be entertained between numbers and private wine rooms were provided for those who wished to enjoy a champagne tête-à-tête. Nearby was the California, a wide-open place which boasted of fifty girls and operated on a simple principle—keep moving. Frankie Wright also kept her house in the Levee, adding a collection of books and calling it the Library. Vina Fields, the exceptionally high-principled madame, was another who kept open house. She maintained decorum with a set of rules more strict, according to legend, than those of an exclusive girls' boarding school. A police matron testified that Vina Fields was a good woman. Vina herself had no illusions. It was misery that brought her girls to her, she said, "always misery."

The social center of the Levee was Freiberg's dance hall, the most notorious saloon in the city. Its manager was Ike Bloom, who insisted on only two things—decorous dancing and a prompt cut of his girls' earnings. Beyond that, anything went and often did. Bloom loved publicity and tried to make his dance hall a popular slumming spot such as the Moulin Rouge of Paris. He liked to recall the night Walter Shafter's horse had won the American Derby. Bloom, told that Shafter might pay him a visit, had decorated a box with the Shafter colors. The proud winner, out to make the rounds, tarried only to drink his glass of champagne. Then, according to Bloom, Shafter said: "Ring this up . . . and hands me 2500 iron men." An unexpected visitor at Freiberg's was Arthur Burrage Farwell, a cousin of the city's successful Farwell clan who, as president of the Chicago Law and Order League, devoted his energies to reform. Bloom received Farwell and the group with him courteously. "I tell 'em to go as far as they like," he told Ashton Stevens later. "I give them the freedom of the tables; I order the drinks all around—lemonade; and when they ask for the center of the dance floor to kneel down and pray and sing 'Washed in the Blood of the Lamb' I give it to 'em. I give 'em my jazz band too, which plays their accompaniment and plays it mighty damned well. One of the papers carried a story next day that was all straight except where it says I knelt and sang with 'em. That was an error, I don't sing."

The pride of the Levee and its showplace was the Everleigh Club, an elegant mansion under the direction of Ada and Minna Everleigh. The

Everleighs were two upper-class Kentucky girls with ambitions to go on the stage and a remarkable precocity for the profession of a madame. When the Everleigh Club opened its doors, Ada was twenty-three and Minna just twenty-one. Their scale of prices began at $50, unheard of even on the free-spending Levee. "I've heard of southern hospitality," one of their competitors sneered, "but not at these prices." Minna set the tone of the club. Girls were given daily instructions in etiquette and told to use the library which had been installed. "Be polite and forget what you are here for," Minna told them without conscious irony. "Stay respectable by all means; I want you girls to be proud you are in the Everleigh Club." She explained bluntly that the sisters had no time for the "rough element, the clerk on a holiday or a man without a checkbook."

Ada did the hiring. "I talk with each applicant myself," she said. "She must have worked somewhere else before coming here. We do not like amateurs. To get in a girl must have a pretty face and figure, must be in perfect health, must look well in evening clothes and must understand what it is to act like a lady." To this Minna added, 'Don't forget—entertaining most men at dinner is more tiring than what the girls lose their social standing over." Minna regarded her girls as members of a professional class. They accepted fees for services rendered, she explained, and did not sell themselves "as these eggheads keep shouting."

Patrons of the Everleigh Club were entertained genteelly in one of a number of elegant parlors bearing such names as the Moorish, Japanese, Egyptian or Chinese and decorated appropriately. There were Silver and Copper parlors for the mining kings who came to call and a famous Gold Room which was refinished each year in gold leaf and polished industriously

THE LEVEE AT NIGHT, 1898, by H. G. Maratta

every day. The sisters established these parlors on the theory that "the contemplation of deviltry" was more satisfactory than its performance. Dinners were sumptuous affairs and always accompanied by champagne. Although banjos were the favored instrument for music in many Levee houses, the Everleighs preferred a small ensemble of a violin, cello, piano and occasionally a harp. The piano player received sizable sums from music publishers for popularizing new songs with the select crowd which visited the Everleighs. Both sisters had a fondness for reporters. Newspapermen had the freedom of the house. The sisters let it be known that they preferred the reporters avoid the upper floors but there was no absolute rule even about this. On Christmas Eve there was always a party for the press with much champagne, dancing and small but valuable gifts for the guests.

The Everleighs were both sentimental. Their name was a pseudonym fashioned from their grandmother's letters which concluded "Everly yours" and Minna's fondness for the poems of Sir Walter Raleigh. The sisters were offended when no one praised them for "such noble gestures" as donating Sunday nights to old-fashioned romance. Sunday was Beau Night and the girls were permitted to entertain their sweethearts as if they had been receiving them in more conventional surroundings. Every Sunday evening a parade of swains bearing candy, perfume and flowers would file into the Everleigh Club, where the evening would be spent in the manner of much less sophisticated sweethearts.

The genteel approach of the Everleighs had its hazards. One of these was gambling. Realistic Minna thought that any man would rather gamble than spend his time with women. "Admitting that women are a risk," she told Charles Washburn, her biographer, "I still say that men prefer dice, cards or a wheel of fortune to a frolic with a charmer. I have watched men, embraced in the arms of the most bewitching sirens in our club, dump their feminine flesh from their laps for a roll of the dice." With such experiences in mind, Minna placed a half-hour limit on gambling. Besides, she said, it was illegal.

The sisters prospered. "If it weren't for the married men we couldn't have carried on at all and if it weren't for the cheating married women we could have made another million," they said when they balanced the books on their efforts. After ten years they had accumulated nearly a million dollars in cash, diamonds estimated to be worth $200,000 and books, paintings and tapestries worth $150,000 more. Even royalty came to the doors of the twin buildings at 2131–33 South Dearborn Street. When Prince Henry of Prussia came to Chicago he asked to be taken to the Everleigh Club and a special party was arranged in his honor. Minna, who had a professional interest in mythological revelry, had dressed all the girls in fawn skins and planned an orgy she considered worthy of the Roman gods. She had hoped to have her nymphs carrying torches but the flames smoked up the room in rehearsal and she compromised by dimming the lights. She taught the girls a ritualistic dance, the climax of which was the tearing to pieces of a bull (made of wood and cloth) in a frenzy of sexual excitement. After the dance, the girls went to their rooms and donned evening gowns, returning as fashionably dressed courtesans for a feast of steaks and champagne with the prince and his party. At first the dinner had all the formality of a royal banquet, with toasts to the prince and his brother, the Kaiser. When the table was cleared, a former dancer was lifted up for a schottische. During her dance a slipper flew off and hit a glass of champagne, spilling some of the drink into the dancing pump. "Boot liquor," said a quick-witted guest who deserves more than the anonymity which surrounds the incident. "The darling mustn't get her feet wet." He lifted the slipper to his lips and drank the champagne. The toast was imitated on the instant by almost every man in the room, who seized his partner's slipper, filled it with champagne and—according to the Everleighs—drank toasts "to the prince—to the Kaiser—and to beautiful women the world over." The episode at the Everleigh Club popularized in America, if it did not actually originate, a toast which was to be repeated a thousand times by gallant libertines.

The sisters had only one narrow brush with scandal. That they were not directly involved was attributable to their high standards and the loyalty inspired by their determination to make their girls "proud you are in the Everleigh Club." Nathaniel Ford Moore, the son of a Rock Island Railroad executive, was a frequent visitor to the Levee and a lavish entertainer. But

MUSIC ROOM AT THE EVERLEIGH CLUB (From Minna Everleigh's brochure)

when a narcotics peddler came to the door of the Everleigh Club after Moore arrived one Saturday night, he was politely asked to leave. The Everleighs banned drugs because narcotics mixed with champagne, the only drink they served, sometimes slowed the heart to the point of death. The sisters were less polite with the girl who had been entertaining Moore and who had violated the rules by making contact with a dope peddler. As a result of the quarrel, the girl quit and transferred her few belongings and talents to Vic Shaw's, a popular resort for young society men.

The incident was not considered serious until the following afternoon when Minna received a telephone call. "They're framing you," the caller told Minna. "They've got a dead man at Shaw's and they're going to plant it in your furnace. It's Nat Moore."

Minna quickly sent an emissary to Vic Shaw's. He forced his way in and found a group of madames and saloon owners meeting in one of the parlors. All were known to be hostile to the Everleighs. Minna's envoy, charging them with murder, threatened to call the police if they did not report the dead man. Vic Shaw first denied Moore was in the house but finally capitulated and asked Roy Jones, a saloon keeper who was also her liaison man with the police, to call and tell them Nat Moore was dead. The suspicion of murder did not prevail long. It was revealed that Moore had been treated in the house by a doctor that Sunday morning after a heart seizure and had died from a heart attack while sleeping in the afternoon. The police refused to become excited about a mysterious broken window in the front of Vic Shaw's. It had nothing to do with the case they said; Moore's death was "a plain case of going to the limit in the gay pace that kills." The surprising twist to the case was that Minna's caller had been the girl expelled the previous night; but she was loyal in her own way to the trademark of quality which the Everleigh Club had become in her sordid profession.

There were other hazards facing the Everleighs and the Levee district. A strong reform movement was taking shape. The man who first aroused the reform forces was not a Chicagoan but William T. Stead, English reformer and editor of the *Review of Reviews*. Stead had been among the millions attracted to Chicago by the World's Columbian Exposition. His methods were dramatic. When he was invited to give a lecture at the young University of Chicago, he sighted a pitcher of ice water near the speaker's lectern. He plunged his hand into the pitcher, seized the ice and flung it to the floor. "You Americans overheat your houses and freeze your drinking water abominably," he shouted at his startled audience. He was to be shocked by more than ice water. After a few months he called a conference of civic and religious leaders at Central Music Hall to discuss the flagrant vice, crime and political corruption. Knowing the city's traditional lack of interest in doing anything about such matters, he wakened its curiosity by promising a recital of what might happen "if Christ came to Chicago." The meeting was held without important results, but a year later when Stead published a detailed extension of his findings in a book called *If Christ Came to Chicago*, sentiment began to solidify behind a genuine effort toward reform.

Stead's principal target was political corruption which, because of a general indifference, allowed vice to flourish. He was in full agreement with another English tourist, G. W. Steevens, who found that "everybody is fighting to be rich, is then straining to be refined and nobody can attend to making the city fit to live in." Gambling was so widely tolerated that *Harper's* commented "the man with the slightest drop of sporting blood in his veins never descends to the depths where he buys his cigars. He shakes dice for them with the proprietor of his store." The Reverend Hugh F. Given of the Second Presbyterian Church thought it necessary to warn a new pastor at a public installation that "Chicago people are money and pleasure mad. In other cities the question is 'Does reform help the community?' In Chicago it is 'Does it pay?' " To this Stead added that "Here we have asserted in its baldest and plainest form the working principle on which the smart man of Chicago acts. Everything that is not illegal is assumed by him to be right . . . so long as it is permitted by law or so long as they can evade the law by any subterfuge, they consider they are doing perfectly all right. They believe in the state; they have ceased to believe in God."

The religion of the church, Stead found, had been replaced by that of the Democratic Party. It was a faith, he said, "built upon bribery, intimidation, bulldozing of every kind, knifing, shooting and the whole swimming in whiskey." Stead, who was the shrewdest kind of reformer, was aware that such political power did not survive without a better side. He found the basis for that power in talking with Democratic precinct workers. "I attained a clearer view and a surer hope for the redemption of Chicago than anything I had gained from any other conversation," he said of these talks with the party rank-and-file. "Here even in this nethermost depth was the principle of human service, there was the recognition of human obligation, set in motion, no doubt, for party reasons, and from a desire to control votes rather than to save souls. But whatever might be the motive, the result was unmistakable. Rough and rude though it might be, the Democratic Party organization and of course the Republican Party organization to a lesser extent are . . . setting in motion an agency for molding into one the heterogeneous elements of various races, nationalities and religions which are gathered together in Chicago."

The instruments of this unifying process were described by Carter Harrison II, Chicago's first native-born mayor, as a "motley crew." Looking over the Council of Aldermen with which he was supposed to administer the affairs of the city, he described it in his autobiography as a collection of "saloon keepers, proprietors of gambling houses and undertakers." As he saw the council, it was "a rare conglomeration of city fathers [that] ruled Chicago in the nineties, a great growing energetic community, whose citizens for years from lack of interest, supineness, from absolute stupidity had permitted the control of public affairs to be the exclusive appendage of a low-browed, dull-witted, base-minded gang of plug-uglies with no outstanding characteristic beyond an unquenchable lust for money, with but a single virtue, and that not possessed by all, a certain physical courage which enabled each to dominate his individual barnyard." The Herald, a Democratic newspaper, wrote that "the average Democratic representative is a tramp if not worse."

Not the least remarkable feature of the council was that it could still be sensitive of its honor in the face of such testimonials. In 1902, Alderman Nathan T. Brenner of the Ninth Ward asserted in the heat of an argument that there were only three aldermen in the entire group of sixty-eight who were not able and willing to steal a red-hot stove. The aldermen, who were quick to realize the futility of stealing a red-hot stove (as it would not serve as a container for currency) demanded a retraction. Otherwise, they said, they would appoint a committee to investigate Brenner. One alderman suggested however, that "if a red-hot stove has been passed around and he [Brenner] did not get a piece of it, let him speak out and tell us about it." It was necessary for Brenner to submit a written denial of the statement—which had been heard by every member of the council and a gallery of witnesses—before the bruised honor of the aldermen could be assuaged.

Subterfuge was the normal procedure for doing business in the council, one such instance providing Chicago with a subway it was unwilling to construct by legitimate methods. An ordinance had been passed permitting an independent telephone company to bore holes beneath the streets to install cables and wires for automatic telephones. The dirt was to be used in filling in more of the lake between the Illinois Central tracks and Michigan Avenue. As caravans of wagons made their way steadily toward the lake front, it was evident the quantity of dirt they were removing was far in excess of that required for the laying of a telephone cable. An investigation revealed the ordinance permitting the boring was altered after it left the council chambers and before it was legally recorded. The modified statute permitted a group of eastern speculators to dig a tunnel twelve feet wide, fourteen feet high and many miles in extent. The telephone company had served as a façade for a group planning to establish an underground freight railway on which downtown stores would be dependent for the delivery of much of their merchandise. A roar of protest was raised and charges filed against the officials responsible. As was expected, the proceedings against those accused of duplicity in the case failed and the defendants "went free and enjoyed a good lunch at Vogelsang's." The earth kept coming up until there were sixty miles of tunnel under the business district which connected the freight terminals with the principal stores.

It was generally believed that the first digging for the tunnel was done in the rear of an emporium owned by Alderman John Powers, better known as Johnny de Pow. Alderman Powers, who represented the Irish-Italian Nineteenth Ward, had an inordinate fondness for funerals and was proud to be known as Prince of the Boodlers. Boodle, or graft, had been developed to a high level of artistry at City Hall. The Civic Federation, slightly more generous than Alderman Brenner, estimated that fifty-seven out of the sixty-eight aldermen representing the city's thirty-four wards were grafters. The boodle value of an alderman's job was variously estimated at between $15,000 and $25,000 a year. For one important ordinance, a group of leading aldermen were said to have been paid $25,000 each while a larger group received a minimum of $8,000 each. On unimportant matters, an alderman cast his tally for as little as $300 or $400. Utility companies using the city's streets and alleys were the largest sources for graft. When the rights to the streets had been sold, the inventive Powers devised a method of setting up dummy competing corporations which were granted franchises. The operating companies were then forced to buy up these dummy corporations—owned in large part by the aldermen—in order to protect their established investment. Another device of the rapacious "gray wolves" of the council was to force the transit companies to "buy" new franchises when the method of operation was changed from horsecars to cable cars or electric trolleys. Powers' only difficulty in handling these matters was that of keeping the boodlers in line; some of them could only be persuaded with difficulty that it was unethical to sell out to two competing interests simultaneously. Powers' authority stemmed not only from his intellectual ingenuity but from the fact he was the representative in the council of Charles T. Yerkes, the city's traction magnate and most generous contributor of boodle. "You can't get elected to the council unless Mr. Yerkes says so," Johnny de Pow once told his constituents and there was every reason to believe it was true.

Yerkes was from Philadelphia but had more than an ordinary connection with Chicago. As a young man he had made a fortune as a flour commission merchant. When Philadelphia issued bonds which could find no purchasers at the legally established price, the city treasurer asked Yerkes to sell the bonds. Yerkes agreed, forcing the price up with his own purchases and disposing of eleven million dollars worth of the bonds in a year. The flaw in his technique was that he had been forced to buy back five million dollars worth of these same bonds to keep the price up. He might have been successful if the Chicago fire had not caused such heavy losses in the East that his loans were called sooner than he had expected and he was unable to pay. He was convicted for misappropriation of funds but pardoned upon the petition of the businessmen of Philadelphia. To his credit, he later repaid all his obligations though freed by the City Council of any legal obligations to do so. It was perhaps natural that Yerkes should think of Chicago when planning a new start.

Shortly after his arrival, he began a series of investments in street railways. After a succession of financial manipulations, he assumed control of the city's transit system and was again a multimillionaire. Operating in the council through Powers, he received his franchises at a fraction of their value. When no more revenue was to be obtained from the streets he began the construction of the elevated railway that was to form a circle around the business district and give the downtown area its characteristic name of the Loop.

Yerkes built his fortune by inflating the value of his companies' stocks rather than by service to the public. "Buy old junk, fix it up a little, unload it on the other fellow" was his expressed standard of operation. To a suggestion that he run more cars on his lines, he replied, "Why should I? It's the straphangers who pay the dividends." These and other practices met cold disapproval among the established members of the community. "He shocked me," Marshall Field told a friend after a business conference with Yerkes: "He is not safe." Such disapproval would have carried enough weight to put Yerkes out of business if the transit speculator had been dependent on local capital. But as the midwestern representative of an eastern traction ring with unlimited resources he was able to disregard public opinion with impunity in gaining control of the local transit lines. Keeping control was another matter.

To protect the value of inflated stock holdings by assuring themselves continuing franchises, Yerkes and his backers put through the state legislature a group of "Eternal Monopoly" bills which would have given Yerkes unquestioned rights to the streets for ninety-nine years. After turning down a bribe of half a million dollars from Yerkes, Governor Altgeld vetoed the bill. At the next session of the legislature, Yerkes had a new plan which would have extended his franchise for fifty years without additional compensation to the city. This bill failed in the legislature but Yerkes did succeed in putting through another bill, the Allen Law, permitting the City Council to give him the rights which the legislature had refused. Even this gesture cost him several hundred thousand dollars in bribes.

The battle shifted to Chicago, where Carter Harrison II promised to eat his brown fedora if Yerkes could pass the ordinance over the mayor's veto. The struggle was fierce and expensive. Harrison spoke in every neighborhood of the city, campaigning harder against the ordinance than if he had been

BATHHOUSE JOHN, by John McCutcheon

running for office. Yerkes bought a newspaper, the *Inter-Ocean*, and imported an editorial writer from New York to attack Harrison and the other newspapers. After a long tussle, the ordinance was defeated and the power of Yerkes broken. In Harrison, who, like his father, was considered a man of the people, Yerkes had met an opponent whom no amount of money could defeat.

The traction king acted quickly to sell his inflated holdings before they should collapse. He left the city for the four-million-dollar brownstone mansion he had built in New York with profits from his Chicago enterprises. There he could contemplate his collection of paintings in the largest private art gallery in the country or stroll over fine Persian rugs purchased at a cost of a million dollars to gaze at a $30,000 portrait of himself.

It was one of the recurring anomalies of Chicago politics that the defeat of Yerkes had been as much due to the efforts of two representatives from the lawless Levee district as to the forces of reform. John "The Bath" Coughlin and Michael "Hinky Dink" Kenna, the two aldermen from the First Ward, which included the Levee, were both skilled practitioners of the art of boodle. But when Yerkes came to them with an offer of $150,000 as well as other inducements for their votes, they turned him down. They had explained their reasons to Mayor Harrison at a conference a few days earlier. "Mr. Mayor," said The Bath, "I was talkin' a while back with Senator Billy Mason and he told me, 'Keep clear of th' big stuff, John, it's dangerous. You and Mike stick to th' small stuff; there's little risk and in the long run it pays a damned sight more.' . . . Mr. Maar, we're with you. An' we'll do what we can to swing some of the other boys over."

What the pair could do was considerable. Their ward was the most solidly Democratic in the city. Hinky Dink tended to the details of political organization, dealt with the police, devised strategy and worked out improved systems of chain voting. The Bath, who derived his nickname from the bathhouses of which he was proprietor, was the spokesman for the two, arguing the cause of "the people" in florid language in the council chamber and troubleshooting when collections went awry in the Levee vice district. "I formed my philosophy," The Bath soliloquized, "while watching and studying the types who patronized the bathhouses. I met 'em all, big an' little, from LaSalle Street to Armour Avenue. You could learn from everyone. Ain't much difference between the big man and the little man. One's lucky, that's all."

When The Bath and Hinky Dink attended the special convention called by Governor Altgeld in Springfield to put the state Democratic Party behind the free-silver boom, an eastern reporter wrote "These Chicago Democrats are for 16 to 1—sixteen parts whiskey and one part water." The sentimental oratory of William Jennings Bryan made a great impression on The Bath, who returned to Chicago and opened a saloon called The Silver Dollar. The walls and ceiling were adorned with gargantuan replicas of silver coins. The opening of The Bath's saloon attracted every politician in the city. As the guests arrived, they were welcomed by one-eyed Jimmy Connelly, already famed as a gate crasher. Connelly translated the *E Pluribus Unum* on the painted dollars as meaning "He brews us new rum" and assured anyone who would listen that "Dis is de proudest moment dat me an' de city of Chicago ever witnessed."

Hinky Dink customarily remained in the background, though he did consent to be interviewed after a trip to Europe. "Rome?—Most everybody in Rome has been dead for 2,000 years. . . . Monte Carlo?—Great place. I spent two days there an' broke even. I didn't play. That song about the man who broke the bank is just a bedtime story. The bunkerino. . . . Paris?—You sure get a run for your money in that man's town. There is no lid on that burg. Even th' stoves don't have lids in Paris."

The Bath was flamboyant enough for both men. He pretended to be a poet and frequently amused the council with his non-scanning verses, composed for him on dull news days by a newspaper reporter. The climax of his vicarious career came when he claimed authorship of a song called "Dear Midnight of Love" and arranged a special concert at the opera house where it was sung by May de Sousa, whose father was then a detective on the Levee beat. The only time The Bath was known to be reticent was when Theodore Roosevelt condescendingly remarked that the selection of Chicago for the site of a Republican convention was more a question of bathtubs (i.e., hotel rooms) than politics. "I ain't going to be unethicult for nobody," The Bath told a *Record-Herald* reporter who asked his views on the Republican feud over bathtubs. "It wouldn't be professional for me to butt in."

The Bath's wardrobe was even more expressive than his vocabulary. For his first appearance in the council he donned a coat of gray with matching trousers set off by a dark green waistcoat checked with white—his racing colors, he explained. His shoes were a yellow-hued tan and his shirt of brown silk. For a trip to Saratoga, he took a mountain green dress coat "cut in conservative fashion," a striped Prince Albert coat with plaid vest and plaid trousers. He augmented this basic wardrobe with a red vest with white buttons and six double-breasted white vests and a four-button cutaway. Notable among his collections of shoes were a pair of patent leather pumps with dark green tops and a pair of russet shoes with bulldog toes. Giving the press the details of his sartorial plans as he set forth for Saratoga, he explained, "I'll show them a thing or two in dress reform for the masculine gender. I want to be strictly original. I think the Prince of Wales is a lobster in his tastes. He may be all right playing baccarat and putting his coins on the right horses at the races, but when it comes to mapping out style for well-dressed America, he's simply a faded two-spot in the big deck of fashion. People have been following his lead because no other guy has the nerve to challenge him for the championship. But I'm out now for first place and you'll see his percentage drop."

The social careers of The Bath and Hinky Dink reached their apex with the First Ward Balls, annual masquerades to raise funds for the ward Democratic organization. The idea for the balls came from the annual benefit party for Lame Jimmy, the violin player at Carrie Watson's. For fifteen years Jimmy had been honored with an annual benefit, where, in the words of Carrie Watson, "joy reigned unrefined." But in 1892 when a member of the police force offended Levee proprieties by critically wounding another officer in a dispute over the attentions of a charmer, an edict went out to Lame Jimmy that he could stage no more parties. The Bath, pondering the loss of Jimmy's convivial entertainment, thought perhaps he was the man to sponsor a function to replace it. He was not thinking in terms of a party for three or four hundred people such as Jimmy had held; he thought the Seventh Regiment Armory was about right to hold the crowd he intended to invite. When the invitations were issued, saloon keepers and madames were apt in realizing it would be wise to accept and buy tickets; most freely welcomed the opportunity to renew their annual frolic. Brewers, wine merchants, distillers and other merchants dependent upon the good favor of the council were quick to volunteer supplies of liquor at special prices and buy large blocks of tickets. Waiters stood in line to pay $5 for the privilege of serving a party where tips were expected to be plentiful and large. The armory was subdivided with boxes which The Bath sold with the same enterprise he might have shown in disposing of real estate.

The ball was set for 8 o'clock but it was after midnight before the consci-

HINKY DINK, by *John McCutcheon*

entious ladies of the Levee began to arrive. They found a large crowd jammed around the doors to the armory but The Bath had thoughtfully arranged for a police escort. All the girls wore costumes, most of them preferring the scanty garb of Egyptian dancers, Indian maidens, geisha girls, gypsies and other guises which would justify wearing an abbreviated skirt. The *Tribune* reporter, noting a certain similarity in the costumes, reported that only a few of the dancers were hampered by long skirts, "it being considered bad form to wear anything that would collect germs from the floor." The Bath had banned *Black Crook* tights of the kind worn in America's first musical comedy, however, with the explanation that they were "too indecent."

The First Ward Ball was such a success that it had to be transferred in subsequent years from the armory to the larger quarters of the Coliseum. At the 1907 ball, a statistically minded reporter counted two bands, two hundred waiters, one hundred policemen, thirty-five thousand quarts of beer and ten thousand quarts of champagne "before they sent for reinforcements." The Bath reported that every alderman was there except those "who are sick abed." In the boxes, champagne was a favored trouble chaser while at three bars in the annex a battalion of bartenders was emptying seventy-five mammoth kegs of beer. Over a hundred square-shouldered ushers with greased hair and full dress suits were kept busy punching guests in the ribs to keep them in line. On the dance floor, a solid jam of merrymakers danced to a program of tunes that skipped the musical gamut from "Tipperary" to the "Teddy Bear's Picnic" and Franz Lehar's "Merry Widow Waltz." Hinky Dink was moved to hyperbole. "It is far ahead of anything I saw in

Paris," he said. "There is nothing like it in the world." The Bath promised that in 1908 the ball would be even more grandiose.

There were others who had plans for 1908 which did not include another First Ward Ball. One of these was Arthur Burrage Farwell, who presented a description of the 1907 affair to Mayor Fred Busse with a demand that the mayor refuse to issue a liquor license for the 1908 ball. One of the sections in the Farwell report was a *Tribune* story which said that "if a great disaster had befallen the Coliseum, there would not have been a second story worker, a dip or plug ugly, porch climber, dope fiend or scarlet woman remaining in Chicago." When the mayor told Farwell the liquor license had already been issued, the reform groups sought to get the Coliseum management to refuse The Bath and Hinky Dink the use of the auditorium. This failing, an injunction against the holding of the ball was asked. It was not granted, the judge holding that the contract with the Coliseum was sacred and inviolable. Despite the victory in the courts, the pressure was building up on The Bath to tone down his celebration. "All right, we'll compromise," he shouted at a reporter. "We won't let parents bring their children. There!"

Meanwhile, both aldermen increased their efforts to make the 1908 ball a success. Extra precautions were taken to see that nothing happened which might be considered disorderly, at least by Levee standards. (One precautionary measure was the establishment of a squad of pickpockets to mingle with the crowd and spot troublemakers.) The Bath even produced a poem for the occasion, the most pertinent portion of which read as follows:

> On with the dance
> Let the orgy be perfectly proper
> Don't drink, smoke or spit on the floor
> And say keep your eye on the copper.

More than fifteen thousand people tried to force their way into the Coliseum on the night of the ball. Traffic was at a stop in the surrounding streets and alleys. The crowd swarmed into all the bars, pushed into the annex and overflowed into the basement where an additional source of supply for beer quaffers had been established. "So close was the press," recorded the *Record-Herald*, "that even those already drunk were forced to stand erect." The ball degenerated into a riot. Tables were upset, glasses smashed and chairs broken as the more timid climbed the iron girders of the Coliseum in an effort to get out of the way. The doors and exits were firmly locked to prevent gate crashers but the pressure on one of them was so terrific that when it gave way more than fifty celebrants were dumped into the alley. The mêlée continued until midnight when it was temporarily stilled by the flourish of trumpets for the grand march. The Bath and Hinky Dink, each with an Everleigh sister on his arm, started down the floor followed by the members of the First Ward Democratic Club twenty-six abreast—the pride of Levee society and its shame. Outside, those who had not been able to get in charged the police and slugged and scratched each other until hats, bracelets, scarf pins and furs were scattered over the sidewalk. Inside, the revelry resumed after the grand march. "It's a lollapalooza," said Hinky Dink. "There are more here than ever before. All the business houses are here, all the big people. Chicago ain't no sissy town."

In an obscure box, escorted by a detective from the city's dance hall and amusement detachment, sat a spectator who was less approving of what he saw. He was Dean Walter Sumner of the Espiscopalian Cathedral of SS. Peter and Paul, newly designated chairman of the vice commission appointed by Mayor Busse. Sumner spoke affably to the Levee celebrities who greeted him and they found him "a decent fella," but he reported angrily to the mayor the next day that "The ball is a disgrace." He conceded that the demi-monde in large cities almost invariably had a yearly celebration but found "Chicago is unique in holding this revel of the underworld in a downtown building of great capacity and wide reputation." Sumner's report, plus a threat of the Roman Catholic archbishop to order a denunciation of the ball from every pulpit of his faith in the ward, forced Mayor Busse to order the balls stopped. "I'm an optimist," said The Bath, when he heard his $20,000-a-year privilege had been canceled, but his optimism ignored a growing number of omens which foreshadowed the end of the Levee and its pattern of segregated vice.

The groundwork for reform had been carefully laid by the Civic Federation under the direction of Lyman Gage. It had maintained a steady attack upon public gambling, payroll stuffing, fraudulent street paving and sweeping, registration and voting frauds, crooked assessors and collectors, opium dens and many other municipal evils. Police raids on gamblers were such a farce that the Civic Federation staged its own raid upon Harry Varnell's gambling parlors where twenty-four faro dealers, twelve croupiers and sixty other employes catered to a never-ending stream of customers. The outcome of the raid was not surprising to experienced Chicagoans—the raiders were the ones taken to jail. The law also intervened to thwart a Civic Federation raid on Condon's gambling rooms, known as the House of David. Big Jim O'Leary, whose mother's cow had started the great fire, was the proprietor of a palatial gambling temple and saloon on South Halsted Street. He boasted that "I been raided a thousand times but I've never had a real raid." After operating a gambling house all his life, Big Jim was finally subjected to a real arrest at fifty-three; he was convicted of gambling and fined $100 as a first offender. He died three years later, never having been caught in a second offense.

In addition to a frontal assault upon gambling and related evils, the Civic

THE FIRST WARD BALL, by *John McCutcheon*. "Led by Bathhouse John, Ten Thousand Joyless Reveling Pickpockets, Bartenders, Prostitutes and Police Captains Celebrate the Reign of Graft, While Grief-Stricken Hinky Dink Sways in the Corner."

Federation organized a division known as the Municipal Voters League to try to interest public-spirited citizens in accepting public office. The attitude of most Chicagoans was expressed by Joseph Medill when he resigned shortly before the end of his term as mayor. "Politics and office-seeking are pretty good things to let alone for a man who has intellect and individuality," Medill said. "Generally, he will get more happiness out of life, I am sure, tending his business, respecting God, his conscience and the grand jury and doing only what those powers will let him."

The man who accepted the responsibility for persuading like-minded Chicagoans to change their views and enter the fray of politics was George E. Cole, a stationer who described himself to Lincoln Steffens as a "second-rate businessman" but who looked to Steffens more "like a sea captain and he worked and talked like one. He picked a crew of nine and shouted that he was going to beat the crooks up for re-election." Cole didn't quite do all of that, but he did succeed in getting a number of young men with independent financial resources to enter public life; among them were a grandson of Joseph Medill, Robert Rutherford McCormick, who won election as alderman from the Twenty-first Ward and William E. Dever, afterward mayor. The league also secured the election of other reform candidates; if it did not change the nature of Chicago politics at least it provided a temporary leavening which made it possible to do away with the worst abuses of the past.

There were other evidences of a revolt against lawlessness, not all of them of equal significance. Carrie Nation visited the First Ward saloon of Hinky Dink and announced she had come "to pray not to smash." Virginia Brooks, who had led a chopping expedition against the red-light district of Hammond, Indiana, transferred her energies to Chicago. She organized an anti-vice parade in which five thousand people marched despite a downpour of rain. Lucy Page Gaston carried her anti-tobacco crusade through the doors of the Everleigh Club. "There is something you must do," she told Minna. "You alone can stop your girls from going straight to the devil. You must make them stop smoking cigarettes."

Evangelist Gypsy Smith led a crowd of several thousand into the Levee and held a series of prayer meetings in the street, one of them in front of the Everleigh Club. All the brothels were shuttered and dark while the evangelist and his followers held their meeting but as soon as they left the lights went up and the Levee was as wide open as ever. Many sightseers who had come in the wake of the reformers entered the portals of the Levee houses. "I was sorry to see so many young men coming down here for the first time," Minna Everleigh said the following morning.

The most effective ammunition against the Levee was that provided by Dean Walter Sumner and the Vice Commission which Mayor Busse had appointed. The commission's 311-page report was so specific and sensational that it was barred from the mails. The commission found that the profits of the red-light traffic amounted to more than fifteen million dollars per year. For the benefit of the practically minded city, the commission computed the capitalized value of a prostitute at $26,000. This compared with the $6,000 value of a girl clerking in a store, computed on the same basis. Madames in the brothels could count on an income of from $100 to $500 a week. At the Everleigh Club, the commission estimated the sisters cleared about $100,000 a year. Minna confirmed that it was a good guess, saying the figure was actually $120,000.

Although the Everleighs were the most powerful madames of the Levee, their house was the first to be closed. The immediate cause of their downfall was the desire of Minna to be an author. Not content with the generous publicity given the club by the newspapers, Minna prepared an illustrated brochure describing the attractions of the Everleigh Club and including pictures of its many parlors. (The second edition added a suggestion that the visitors might like to see the stockyards, another great Chicago attraction.) The brochure was so widely distributed that Mayor Carter Harrison II, who succeeded Busse, found himself chided about it by every visitor. Like his father, Harrison had believed that segregated vice was inevitable, but after a narrow victory over the reform candidate, Charles E. Merriam, whose campaign was shrewdly run by Harold Ickes, Harrison saw that new forces were at work. He ordered all vice flats off Michigan Avenue and followed this with an order closing the Everleigh Club because of the flagrant publicizing of the city's evil through Minna's brochure.

The police hesitated to enforce the closing order, even though it had come from the mayor himself; that night the Everleigh Club was still open. The sisters had been tipped off, however, and there was a desperate gaiety animating the celebrations as lights blazed in every parlor, music rang through the tapestried halls and wine corks popped in every room. Shortly after midnight a police lieutenant and a squad of patrolmen knocked at the door. "From downtown," explained the lieutenant. "Nothing we can do about it." Minna was not perturbed. "If the mayor says we must close, that settles it," she said. "I'm not going to be sore about it either. I never was a knocker and nothing the police of this town can do to me will change my disposition. I'll close up my shop and walk out of the place with a smile on my face."

There was no excitement. The patrons had been forewarned and they left quietly. A line of carriages and cabs, their drivers informed of the potential closing through their own sources of information, waited in line much as they might have before the curtain was to be rung down on a play. At the door, well-dressed gentlemen lingered over their farewells; optimists like The Bath, they did not believe the order was irrevocable. But the Everleighs themselves made no effort to reopen. They lived quietly on the West Side of Chicago, coming downtown only for trips to the theater or to McClurg's bookstore, where Minna was a frequent visitor, her literary bent still unsatisfied.

With the passing of the Everleigh Club, such glamour as had affixed itself to the shoddy traffic of the Levee vanished. The following year the State's Attorney, John E. Wayman, caught in the crossfire of the city's war over reform, issued 135 vice warrants for houses in the Levee. When the city's police served only twenty of the warrants, Wayman ordered his own men into the city with instructions to raid all the brothels and gambling parlors they found open and to keep raiding them until they remained closed. With Wayman's action, segregated vice in Chicago came to an end.

PART FOUR *The Inheritance*

1910=1930

CARL SANDBURG AS A YOUNG MAN

One Ecstasy After Another

AFTER THE turn of the century a new kind of commerce animated Chicago. From the prairie states that produced the grain and livestock which funneled through Chicago for the East came a sudden outpouring of writers, all of them attracted by the vigor and promise of the young city by the lake. These new arrivals traded as voraciously and as greedily in ideas as any early speculator dickered in real estate. They found in Chicago an eager if often uninformed audience, willing to tolerate artistic experiment and to give an unprejudiced acceptance to artistic forms which represented a break with the traditions of older communities. The period of their activity was brief. Like the hundreds of trains which daily snaked into Chicago's rail terminals, many paused only long enough to refuel—or perhaps to switch tracks or change to another line. But no one was to forget they had passed by.

There was always to be a transient quality about Chicago's relations with the arts. A few years earlier young George Spoor and Maxwell Anderson had been among the experimenters with a new kind of drama which could be represented by moving figures on film. In their Essanay (S and A) studios on the North Side, they had formed the nucleus of a film colony that brought to the screen Wallace Beery, Gloria Swanson, Lewis Stone, Colleen

Moore, Edward Arnold and Tom Mix. By 1910 one-fifth of all the movies in the world were being made in Chicago. Carl Laemmle, hearing of the opportunities in the young film industry, sold his clothing business in Oshkosh, Wisconsin, to open a Chicago movie theater. Adolph Zukor gave up the fur business he established in Chicago after the World's Columbian Exposition to investigate the possibilities of these new films. But as soon as the industry prospered it fled its North and West Side studios for California. There, the owners explained, it was possible to make motion pictures outdoors without the expense of artificial lighting—an economy necessary to pay the salaries of such stars as Francis X. Bushman who demanded and received $125 a week. Bushman was so popular that the department stores discouraged his visits—they were afraid he would distract their girl clerks and shoplifters would have a holiday. The hostile Chicago climate was another factor in the move. In the winter, the actors, like the musicians of Theodore Thomas, suffered too much from colds and coughs. Even the growth of the city militated against the screen pioneers. The prairies used in the western films which formed most of the industry's product were vanishing in the ever accelerating expansion of the city itself.

The literary journalists, who as in earlier years formed the center of the new writing ferment, were a hardier strain. They brought to bear on the problems of writing a fresh view, based on the reporter's traditional disrespect for authority and a skill in dealing with the raw materials of the drama to be found in ordinary daily life. They worked individually, but because there was a fundamental similarity in their approach they came to be known as the Chicago school. Together they formed an academy from whose writings the best authors of the twentieth century were to acquire their precepts and maxims.

Because it was a time for muckraking, there was a strong tone of social protest in much of the writing. Frank Norris, famous as a war correspondent, was drawn back to the city of his birth to write *The Pit*, a fictional account of the gargantuan manipulations in grain and dollars on the Board of Trade that was intended to be part of an epic trilogy on wheat. Theodore Dreiser, gone on to New York but remembering his Chicago newspaper days, drew on Chicago's Charles T. Yerkes to create the character of Frank Cowperwood, hero of his novels *The Financier* and *The Titan*. The stockyards were the magnet for the young social rebel, Upton Sinclair, who wrote with sociological meticulousness and called his novel of stockyards life *The Jungle*. No sociological tract was ever so effective in dramatizing the need for reform as his novel. Robert Herrick, a professor at the new University of Chicago who claimed the city as his permanent home, took a skeptical look at politics in *The Memoirs of an American Citizen*. In the novel, he told of the accepted devices by which a poor Indiana boy might rise to the heights of the

United States Senate. Some readers called it cynical; others saw in it an effort to unmask some of the hypocrisy of politics.

The revolt against the old order in society extended to a rebellion against traditional forms in expression. It was here that the Chicago influence was to be greatest. The first prophet of this revolution in language was Harriet Monroe. Bored with composing odes for civic dedications and teaching elocution to the children of wealthy families, she announced a new magazine, called with a poet's economy of words, Poetry. It was to be centered entirely around poets and their work. There were many reasons why poets could look to Harriet Monroe for leadership. One which was basic was her unique ability to make poetry pay in the best Chicago business manner. When she was asked to write a Columbian Ode for the exposition of 1893, she demanded twice the sum the national commission offered her and held out until the committee of businessmen met her terms. When the New York World published the ode prematurely, she sued that publication and collected an additional $5,000 for her efforts. She did not compromise easily. A portion of her ode was a tribute to her brother-in-law, architect John Wellborn Root, who before his death had sketched out the ground design for the Columbian Exposition. The national commission did not think it should subsidize eulogies to relatives, however distinguished, and asked to have the lines deleted. Miss Monroe refused, fighting her cause with such fervor that the commission finally conceded defeat and voted to let the verses remain. It was not surprising that when Harriet Monroe founded Poetry, she specified that it would pay its poets.

The disrespect for established precedents, a Chicago trait, was important to Poetry's success. "The old prosody is a medieval left-over," Harriet Monroe proclaimed. "It is as completely out of relation with the modern scientific spirit as astrology would be if solemnly enunciated from the summit of Mount Wilson. All the old terms should be scrapped and a modern science of speech rhythms should be built up." Fortunately for Miss Monroe's aspirations, there were in Chicago two young writers with the ability to express in poetic form the substance of her editorial theories. They were Carl Sandburg, soon to be a movie critic and later an editorial writer on the Daily News, and Edgar Lee Masters, a law partner of Clarence Darrow who was experimenting with a number of free verse styles that he was to merge into the form of his Spoon River Anthology, published in 1915.

Sandburg's Chicago Poems were the signal of a break as defiant as Dreiser's Sister Carrie had been. William Morton Payne, defending the old order in The Dial, read Sandburg's verses with horror. Most of Sandburg's lines, he said indignantly, "were nothing less than an impudent affront to the poetry loving public." Payne refused to recognize the Chicago Poems by the name of poetry, calling them only a "collocation of words descriptive of Chicago."

To those who questioned his ideas about poetry, Sandburg replied: "Here's the difference between us and Dante: He wrote a lot about Hell and never saw the place. We're writing about Chicago after looking the town over."

Sandburg, going his independent wanderer's way, insisted that the spoken language of the people was the only proper language for poetry. The artist, he said, should express his sympathy for people by speaking with their tongues and out of their hearts. "Unless we keep on the lookout," he warned, "we write book language and employ the verbiage of dead men instead of using the speech of people alive today, people whose tools, games and sacrifices are wearing out an old language and making a new one." Of style, in his *Chicago Poems*, he said this:

> Style—go ahead talking about style.
> You can tell where a man got his style just
>   as you can tell where Pavlowa got her legs
>   or Ty Cobb his batting eye.
>
> Go on talking.
> Only don't take my style away
> It's my face.
> Maybe no good
> but anyway, my face.
> I talk with it, I sing with it, I see, taste and
>   feel with it, I know why I want to keep it.

Sandburg was a radical in the American tradition of Thomas Paine (one of his early jobs had been as secretary to the socialist mayor of Milwaukee). His poems were filled with protests against social injustices and he defied all those who called them propaganda. Because of his Whitmanesque style, his liberal social ideas and his solid Scandinavian stubbornness, he became the foremost target of traditional critics attacking the new free verse ideas being expressed by the contributors to *Poetry*. But as Sandburg stood almost alone, he was less alone; more and more writers sent along their own experimental ideas to Harriet Monroe. T. S. Eliot, Robert Frost, Ezra Pound, John Masefield and Edna St. Vincent Millay were among those who forwarded contributions. A new language was in the making in the crude commercial city of Chicago; out of this new kind of melting pot was to pour the bright, fresh metal of a modern American literature.

It was a time for individualists. Vachel Lindsay, a friend of Edgar Lee Masters who chanted poems aloud for a free meal or a night's lodging, was another of the experimenters. Lindsay was an odd combination of poet, evangelist and troubadour. He dressed carelessly and his hair was usually tousled; but his face was keen and there was the aura of an inner peace that gave him dignity, even when he chose to address audiences on such a topic as the Anti-Saloon League. Abraham Lincoln, whose mark and memorials were everywhere in Springfield where Lindsay was born, was the poet's idol, an emotion which was to find its artistic expression in "Abraham Lincoln Walks at Midnight." Lindsay's poetry was written to be read aloud and he did not stir up the intellectual controversy which Sandburg evoked. But as Lindsay spoke the lines of "General William Booth Enters into Heaven" or "The Congo" he echoed the ideas of the literary rebels.

The Dial stood disdainfully apart from this clangorous new literature. A new critical magazine soon erupted, however, whose mood was suited to the bold and often wild experimentation of the Chicago school. It was The Little Review, founded by Margaret Anderson—just turned twenty-one years of age and feeling "it was time to confer upon life that inspiration without which life is meaningless." The Little Review, she announced, would be a new kind of critical journal and "the most interesting magazine that had ever been launched." She tossed out the "objective and scientific criticism" which had been the goal of The Dial's editors. She accepted or rejected manuscripts on only one basis: art as the person. "An artist is an exceptional person," she wrote. "Such a person has something exceptional to say. Exceptional matter makes an exceptional manner. This is 'style!' In an old but expressive phrase, 'style is the man.'"

The first issue of The Little Review had only a slight relation to Chicago. Its most notable contribution was a letter from John Galsworthy. "It seems you are setting out to watch the street of life from a high balcony where at all events the air should be fresh and sunrise sometimes visible," he wrote. "I hope you will decide to sleep out there under the stars, for what kills

MARGARET ANDERSON'S CAMP AT BRAESIDE

most literary effort is the hothouse air of temples, clubs and coteries." Margaret Anderson, with no source of funds for her magazine, was to be taken literally out under the stars of which Galsworthy wrote. All the money which she and Jane Heap, her chief collaborator on the magazine, could raise went into assuring its publication. When there was no money remaining to pay rent for the home which she occupied with her sister and two little boys, Margaret Anderson, "feeling that inspiration was demanded of me and that it was about to descend," followed Chicago custom by seeking a better place to live along the lake shore north of the city. At Ravinia, she walked east to the lake near Braeside, where she found a wide strip of beach that had not been claimed by any summer colony. Returning home, she loaded her few possessions, her family, and the oriental rugs which were her particular delight into a wagon and headed for the lake shore. En route, she acquired some tents and a few dollars worth of lumber for floors on which to unroll the expensive oriental rugs. In this sandy atmosphere the little group spent the entire summer, living like gypsies and roasting corn over the campfire and baking potatoes in its ashes. Each tent was equipped only with a soldier's cot, a deck chair and an oriental rug. After an early-morning swim by moonlight, Margaret Anderson commuted to Chicago to work on *The Little Review*. Her wardrobe consisted of a blouse that did not need to be ironed, one hat and one blue suit. The blouse was washed at night and donned again in the morning after being dried over the open fire. The campers stayed on the beach until the middle of November when, after a final cold swim, they moved to an empty and furnitureless apartment in the city.

The Little Review was as unorthodox financially as artistically. A luncheon date with a stranger might produce a check for enough to publish one issue. The next issue would be published the same way. Eunice Tietjens, the poet, came bearing a diamond ring. "I don't want this any more," she told Margaret Anderson. "Sell it and bring out an issue." Frank Lloyd Wright gave a hundred dollars. Contributors went without pay; Margaret Anderson believed magazines which paid writers could not afford to publish the material which went into *The Little Review*. She assumed in her confident and exuberant way that writers agreed it was better to be published without pay than to remain unprinted. Her contributors were the measure of her foresight. They included Sherwood Anderson, Malcolm Cowley, Gertrude Stein, Wyndham Lewis, Hart Crane, T. S. Eliot, Aldous Huxley, Marianne Moore and Ernest Hemingway. Sinclair Lewis was not completely happy with her ideas. He wrote that her theories of art for art's sake were too remote from the common herd and urged her to become interested in the psychology of the average person as well as that of the exceptional person. Upton Sinclair was more disapproving. "Please cease sending me *The Little Review*," he wrote. "I no longer understand anything in it, so it no longer interests me."

To this Margaret Anderson replied: "Please cease sending me your socialist paper. I understand everything in it, therefore it no longer interests me."

Margaret Anderson and Jane Heap were never at a loss for a means of getting attention. When there was nothing of interest to publish, they produced an issue of sixty-four empty pages, stating that since no art was being produced they could not publish any. Only the two center pages of the magazine contained some sketches of their activities—the Mason and Hamlin piano Margaret played, anarchist meetings (she was a disciple of Emma Goldman), horseback riding, fudge breakfasts and intellectual combats. "Life," said Margaret Anderson about this time, "is just one ecstasy after another."

Sherwood Anderson, restless in his job as an advertising copywriter, used *The Little Review* to set out his goals as a writer. "What I quarrel with is writers who look outside themselves for their material," he wrote. "It is the most unbelievably difficult task to catch, understand and record your own mood." His statement was a reiteration of the right to personal judgment characteristic of the Chicago school. "In the trade of writing the so-called new note is as old as the world," he wrote another time. "Simply stated, it is a cry for the re-injection of truth and honesty into the craft . . . In all the world there is no such thing as an old sunrise, an old wind upon the cheeks or an old kiss from the lips of your beloved; and in the craft of writing there can be no such thing as age in the souls of the young poets and novelists who demand for themselves the right to stand up and be counted among the soldiers of the new."

Anderson was less agile than Dreiser or Sandburg in finding his place among the soldiers of the new. He wrote of ordinary men in average situations within a framework of form so loose as to be in some cases unrecognizable. Publishers for his books were found with difficulty, and then only after the insistent recommendations of Dreiser and the Chicago critics. Anderson tried to break away from his advertising job but was forced to return to it. Then suddenly, stimulated by the experimentation of the other writers in Chicago, he burst forth with the luminous *Winesburg, Ohio*, a book conceived in a form so distinctively individual there was never to be a name for it. *Winesburg* had been written out of the conflict between materialism and the creative instinct which Anderson recognized in his dual personal life as an advertising writer and novelist; it was a conflict accurately mirrored in the city around him. Yet with the establishment of his reputation as a writer Anderson lost interest in the struggle which had produced *Winesburg* and sought to escape it. "Great projects arise within me," he wrote. "I have a brain and it is cunning and shrewd. I want leisure to become beautiful and there is no leisure." Like many others, he left Chicago in search of beauty unmarred by paradoxes. It was too late for

Anderson to be persuaded that the material out of which he created beauty lay all about him in Chicago—the "grotesques," as he called them, of *Winesburg*, were the same awkward mortals who formed the throngs of Chicago's streets.

Margaret Anderson, too, was ready to move on to New York. "I found my reasons for wanting to go," she wrote in *My Thirty Years War*. "Chicago had all it wanted from me and we had all that it could give. It was time to touch the greatest city of America. It would then be time for Europe. We hadn't as yet met all the interesting people of the world." In New York there remained only one final, glorious chapter for *The Little Review*. Month after month for a period of three years, the magazine published the first installments of James Joyce's *Ulysses*, and four times the post office seized and burned the copies as obscene. Margaret Anderson called it "a burning at the stake." Brought into court by the Society for the Suppression of Vice for having published Joyce's Episode XIII, Margaret Anderson was as irreverent as the pages of her magazine. She was found guilty and given a light fine, thereby establishing indisputably her claim to having introduced America to the most influential novel of modern times. *The Little Review* finally faltered and failed, joining the many magazines of which Keith Preston wrote:

> Among our literary scenes
> Saddest this sight to me;
> The graves of little magazines
> That died to make verse free.

The emigrants to New York were many. They had been touched by Chicago and having, as Margaret Anderson said, all that it could give, went on to touch the greatest city of America; some of them went on with the editor of *The Little Review* to Paris. First had gone Dreiser, then Francis Hackett, the brilliant literary editor of the Chicago *Evening Post*. Ring Lardner, who had given up conducting his column "In the Wake of the News" for the *Tribune*, was writing his baseball stories in New York. The diamond-sharp Percy Hammond, drama critic on the *Tribune*, had been hired away to New York, to be followed in less style by the incisive Burton Rascoe after he was fired from the *Tribune* for a slighting reference to Mary Baker Eddy, but taking with him a reputation made by his perceptive discovery and popularizing of James Branch Cabell and from his literary feuds with Ben Hecht and Henry Blackman Sell, then literary editor of the *Daily News*. Edna Ferber, walking miles and miles along the lake and "finding it exhilarating," had taken the typewriter she pounded in an isolated South Side room and moved to the East; but not without a note of affection for one of the "most vital, unformed, fascinating, horrible, brutal, civilized and beautiful cities in the world." Floyd Dell, the protégé of Francis Hackett on the *Post*, was gone, too. It was Dell who planted the seed of *The Little Review*'s flowering with his instruction to Margaret Anderson, then one of his apprentice reviewers: "Here is a book about China," he said. "Now don't send me an article about China but about yourself." The departure of Dell left a void in the Bohemian colony which had grown up in the group of low red buildings which clustered around the corner of Fifty-seventh Street and Stony Island as dilapidated reminders of the World's Columbian Exposition for which they had been erected. To the colony of which Dell and his wife, Margery Currey, were the central figures came Sherwood Anderson, Sandburg, poet Eunice Tietjens with her oriental dances and Thorstein Veblen and Robert Morss Lovett from the nearby University of Chicago. It was here that those free spirits, Maxwell Bodenheim, universally known as "Bogie," and Ben Hecht, indulged their whims and fantasies as well as their fondness for obscene poetry and practical jokes.

Hecht and Bodenheim, drifting between the city's bohemian clubs and the bookstore of Pascal Covici and Billy McGee on Washington Street served as a rear guard for the army of writers which conquered Chicago and then moved on toward the citadel of New York. Remaining in Chicago were only the deep-rooted Sandburg, Vincent Starrett, who penned shocking lyrics for relaxation, made scholarly investigations of Sherlock Holmes and wrote detective stories, poet Lew Sarrett, young Harry Hansen, the precocious war correspondent who patrolled the borders of new literature for the *Daily News*; and the two Bohemians, Bodenheim and Hecht.

Hecht, a child prodigy who had given his first violin concert at the age of ten, was a columnist on the *Daily News*. An irrepressible prankster, he dominated the gatherings at Covici and McGee's bookstore that were reminiscent of the crowd at the Saints and Sinners Corner of McClurg's a generation earlier. In 1923, Hecht persuaded Pascal Covici to underwrite a publication which he called the *Chicago Literary Times* but which was chiefly an outlet for Hecht's Rabelaisian humor. The first issue offered this salutation: "Chicago, the jazz baby—the reeking, cinder ridden, joyous Baptist stronghold, Chicago the chewing gum center of the world, the bleating, slant-headed rendezvous of sociopaths and pants makers—in the name of the seven Holy Imperishable Arts, Chicago salutes you." It was a tenet of the paper that headlines should be unconnected with the stories which followed them. Neither Hecht nor Bodenheim had the talent to make purposeful use of their ardent iconoclasm; when they tired of their efforts to shock Chicago they moved on to New York as the other writers had done.

There were traces of earlier glories. A few writers, most of them from the *Daily News* where Sandburg, Henry Justin Smith, Keith Preston, Lloyd Lewis and Harry Hansen still held forth, met for luncheons at Schlogl's and

LUNCH AT SCHLOGL'S, 1925. Seated, left to right: Philip Davis, Alfred MacArthur, Ashton Stevens, William F. McGee, Charles Collins, Harry Hansen, Leroy T. Goble, John Gunther, Peter Hecht, Dr. Morris Fishbein, J. U. Nicholson, Lloyd Lewis. Standing: Richard Schneider, Dwight Haven, Keith Preston, Pascal Covici, Ben Hecht, Vincent Starrett, Henry Justin Smith

exchanged wisecracks with visiting authors, Clarence Darrow, Senator J. Hamilton Lewis or other celebrities who had a tolerance for artistic eccentricities.

Jack Jones, a member of the International Workers of the World, or Wobblies, organized the Dill Pickle Club in a "deverminized garret" at 18 Tooker Street near the city's Gold Coast area of elegant apartments. Here speakers were invited to be insulted and wit more rude than original was poured out in a loud stream. A more sedate literary center, a favorite with such visitors as Rabindranath Tagore and John Masefield as well as many local poets, was the home of Harriet Moody, the widow of William Vaughn Moody. In a large brick home in a section of Chicago no longer fashionable, Mrs. Moody entertained genteelly with butlers and maids, winning such a reputation as a hostess that she was able to expand her income by founding a catering service.

By the early 1920's, most of this literary activity had receded. When H. L. Mencken bestowed the accolade of literary capital of the United States on

Chicago, most of those who had been the legislators of the new rules of literature were gone. Among the leaders, only Sandburg and Anderson remained. Yet Mencken's words, if read more closely than Chicagoans eager for honors were inclined to read them, took cognizance of this, too. "In Chicago," he wrote in an effort to explain the city to English readers of *The Nation* of London, "there is the mysterious something that makes for individuality, personality and charm. In Chicago a spirit broods upon the face of the waters. Find a writer who is indubitably an American in every pulse-beat, snort and adenoid, an American who has something new and peculiarly American to say and who says it in an unmistakable American way and nine times out of ten you will find that he has some sort of connection with the gargantuan and inordinate abbattoir by Lake Michigan—that he was bred there, or got his start there or passed through there in the days when he was young and tender." It was a city, Mencken said, which offered "free play for prairie energy ... some imaginative equivalent for the stupendous activity they were bred to."

Although Mencken was to repudiate this tribute in a few years, his initial instinct had been right. Not all the writers he praised were Chicagoans, to be sure, but it took very little to put the mark of Chicago on a man or woman who had once been part of the teeming city. The entire literary upheaval that was in later years to be called a renaissance was concentrated in less than ten years; the founding of *Poetry*, *The Little Review*, and the publication of Sandburg's *Chicago Poems* had been concentrated in less than five.

When the writers left, the jazz musicians came. Their stay was equally brief. Louis Armstrong, following King Oliver from New Orleans to the Lincoln Gardens in Chicago, knew "it was just an accident that swing and I were born and brought up side by side in New Orleans, traveled up the Mississippi together and in 1922 ... were there in Chicago getting acquainted with the North and the North getting acquainted with us." It wasn't Chicago jazz that Louis Armstrong played but New Orleans jazz—and yet it was Chicago that put his name in lights for the first time. It was in Chicago too that young Muggsy Spanier, Frank Teschmaker, Jess Stacy and George Wettling sneaked in to hear Armstrong play. It was in Chicago that young Bix Beiderbecke skipped his classes to play the cornet in prohibition dives. And it was in Chicago that five kids from Austin High School—Jim Lannigan, Jimmy McPartland, his brother, Dick, Frank Teschmaker and Bud Freeman—took New Orleans jazz and gave it the beat that was recognizably Chicago jazz. It was a town where Benny Goodman learned to play the clarinet—but a town that wouldn't listen to what he had to say about how it ought to be played.

For movie-makers, writers or musicians Chicago was a town where somebody was always coming or going—going down to the shadows of those skyscrapers that were a tribute to the imagination of Chicagoans of nearly half a century before. It was a city that had ideas too big for any but the largest city in the land; and it wasn't quite that big yet.

AL CAPONE

Nobody's on the Legit

THERE WAS always an irony about Chicago's efforts at reform. The Municipal Voters League, seeking a nominee for alderman in the Second Ward in 1902, had accepted the recommendations put forward for the son of a prominent citizen. The league was told the young man was able to finance his own campaign and could do no harm. "The worst that you can say of him is that he's stupid," the league was advised. The young man, who won a place in the council with the league's backing, was William Hale Thompson.

Bill Thompson had shown very little aptitude for education as a youth and was sent west to a ranch where he substituted the uninhibited pleasures of cowboy life for more arduous intellectual pursuits. Back in Chicago, he found the rough-and-tumble of Chicago politics a congenial activity. Forming an alliance with the least desirable faction of the Republican Party, he was able to emerge as the Republican candidate for mayor in the election of 1915. His Democratic opponent was Robert Sweitzer, who with the support of the German communities had wrested the Democratic nomination from Carter Harrison II. The campaign, in a city in which nearly a third of the population was foreign-born, carried bitter echoes of the fighting which had broken out in Europe after the assassination at Sarajevo. As anti-German sentiment increased, Sweitzer's German associations were transformed from

BIG BILL THOMPSON

an asset to a liability. Thompson, with the aid of disgruntled Harrison forces, was able to win the mayoralty.

The mayor soon established a reputation for unpredictability. First, he opened the door for unrestricted gambling and then, to satisfy the reform element, he ordered the saloons closed on Sunday. One of the persons to profit from this abortive reform effort was George Wellington Streeter, a soldier of fortune who had staked out a claim to Chicago's lake front and who for thirty years was able to defy a city grown to two and a half million people. Streeter, a former Mississippi River steamboat pilot and circus proprietor, had run aground on a sandbar off the shoreline in 1886 while testing, more or less soberly, a craft named *The Reutan* with which he hoped to make a fortune running guns for South American revolutions. Unable to dislodge his ship and separated from land by only a shallow strip of water, Streeter decided to make his home on the *Reutan*. Through the years the water separating him from the shore filled with sediment until the *Reutan* rested on the mainland. This suggested to Streeter that he might claim the land as an annexation of the island where the *Reutan* was lodged, basing his assertion on an 1821 survey which showed the shores of Lake Michigan to be much farther to the west. Christening his land the District of Lake Michigan, he announced he owed allegiance only to the federal government and named a crony, William Niles, as military governor of the district. With a battered top hat perched on the back of his head and wearing a stained frock coat, he opened offices in the Tremont House and spent his days exhibiting to gullible purchasers the documents on which he founded his right to the valuable lake front property.

In 1889, five constables sought to evict Streeter, but he drove them away from the "deestrict," as he called it, at the point of a rifle. Ten years later, after extended litigation in which Streeter challenged such formidable opponents as Potter Palmer and N. K. Fairbank, a group of policemen managed to capture the squatter but were routed by a kettleful of boiling water thrown by his loyal wife, Maria. On another occasion, Streeter sent two bullets crashing through the buggy of a police captain and a force of five hundred police was sent to the shore to capture him. Learning of the prospective attack, Streeter moved in an army of hoboes and squatters who dug in behind a series of driftwood barricades. The arsenal of Streeter's defense force consisted principally of rocks, stones and clubs with just enough rifles to make an attack dangerous. When the police charged, a volley of rifle fire caused the attackers to fall back for further orders. The delay in the battle worked to their advantage; by nightfall a large part of Streeter's unstable army had been demoralized by rumors and deserted. Cap Streeter was taken the next day, but the police found they had no specific charge on which to hold him—firing at a Chicago police officer not being considered a crime at the time. When Streeter later shot an intruder in his district with a load of buckshot he made such an eloquent defense as his own attorney that the jury acquitted him. But when he killed a night watchman whom he accused of being a trespasser, Streeter was finally sent to the penitentiary. His term was a light one and he returned to re-establish his claim to the district. The ludicrous spectacle of a squatter defying the entire city continued until the advent of Thompson. Then Streeter incurred the mayor's wrath by doing a lively Sunday business in beer and whiskey after the saloons were ordered closed. The District of Lake Michigan became a favorite resort for thirsty Chicagoans. The mayor ordered the liquor sale stopped and erected a fence to keep Streeter out of his lake-shore shack, but Streeter hacked it down. Finally, exasperated, the police dispossessed him and burned his shack and all its trimmings. The farce was over—though Streeter continued to press his ludicrous claim in the courts.

Thompson's eviction of Streeter and his closing of the saloons on Sunday—which was soon dropped—were about his only gestures in the direction of law enforcement. Slot machines appeared in such numbers that the saloons took on a frontier aspect. Gambling houses were running wide open. Graft piled into City Hall just as it had in the worst days of the gray wolves.

Meanwhile, there were formidable problems to be faced. The United States entered the war in 1917 and the large foreign and German population of Chicago was watched closely for any signs of disaffection such as had occurred during the Civil War. Frederick Stock, the city's beloved symphony conductor, resigned because he had not taken out his naturalization papers. Technically an alien, he did not wish to embarrass his sponsors (who rehired him immediately after the armistice). Thompson was so openly hostile to the war effort his opponents called him "Kaiser Bill." He spoke out against the national draft law and opposed supplying food to America's allies. When Marshal Joffre of France visited America, Thompson refused to invite the French hero to Chicago. "Are these foreign visitors coming here to encourage the doing of things to make our people suffer further or have they some other purpose?" he asked rhetorically. The City Council, not yet powerless, rebuked him by issuing a unanimous invitation to Joffre to come to Chicago. The war was to cause no harm to Thompson's political fortunes, however. When the draft took thousands of men from Chicago industries, Thompson was quick to exploit the new voters from the South who arrived to take the empty places in Chicago industries. The southern Negro, a free man for nearly sixty years but never recognized as an equal by his former masters, rushed to Chicago in such numbers that the Negro population quadrupled in only two years. Thompson, sensing the voting power of this largely uneducated group, established himself as its political champion.

Thompson counted heavily on these new voters when he ran for reelection in 1919. To get the city's mind off such troubles as a treasury in which a three-million-dollar surplus had been dissipated and turned to a four-and-a-half-million-dollar deficit, Thompson organized the Chicago Boosters Club. Businessmen were asked, under the threat of facing difficulty in having their licenses renewed, to contribute a million dollars to help "publicize Chicago." The cry was, "Throw away your hammer and get a horn." Big posters went up all over town. "A booster is better than a knocker!" Others said "All hats off to our mayor, Big Bill, the Builder."

A report on Big Bill's term of office had this to say: "Caesar Augustus found Rome a village of wood and brick; he left it a marvelous city of stone and marble. William Hale Thompson found Chicago with many unsightly spots, congested streets and a lack of recreation facilities; he is making it a city beautiful with wider thoroughfares, monumental buildings and all modern conveniences." The achievements of which Thompson boasted were in reality those of Daniel Burnham's Chicago Plan; they had been accomplished in spite of the fact he was in the mayor's chair rather than because of it. Chicago must have sensed this truth beneath the propaganda; though Thompson won his second term, his margin of victory was measured in his plurality in the poverty-burdened wards of the South Side where Chicago's new workers had been forced to settle in a black ghetto.

Thompson's interest in the new arrivals was only political, and he made little effort to ameliorate their conditions. On a July Sunday in 1919, a Negro boy who crossed an invisible line at a bathing beach used by both Negroes and whites was stoned and drowned. A policeman was called but he passed by the white man accused of starting the stone throwing and arrested a Negro. Trouble signals went out. The Negroes, fearing a recurrence of the terror under which they lived in the South, rushed to the beach. Police reinforcements arrived simultaneously. A Negro fired at the police and was shot down. The following day there were riots on the crowded streetcars; before the disturbances were quelled, thirty Negroes were injured and four Negroes and one white man were killed. At midnight, the streetcar workers went out on strike (over issues unrelated to the riots). With the public vehicles gone from the streets, automobiles filled with young hoodlums and race-crazed fanatics sped through the Negro area, shooting capriciously at anyone in sight. Two Negroes were murdered on downtown streets. Mayor Thompson, their champion, consented to ask Governor Frank O. Lowden for state troops only after a series of delaying actions. The arrival of five thousand state troops, most of them only half-trained recruits, was a sufficient show of force to stop the riots.

It was an era for madness. In 1924, two University of Chicago students, Richard Loeb, seventeen, and Nathan Leopold, eighteen, committed the purposeless thrill murder of fourteen-year-old Robert Franks. Trapped through an unusual pair of eyeglasses dropped by Leopold, the two young murderers were brought to court for trial. Defending them was Clarence Darrow—"sixty-eight years old and very weary . . . tired of standing in the lean, lonely front line and facing the greatest enemy that ever confronted man—public opinion." Darrow, champion of the workingman, was moved to take the case because of the same sympathies which had led him to identify his own cause with that of the poor. "In a terrible crisis, there is only one element more helpless than the poor," he wrote. "And that is the rich." His skillful defense enabled Loeb and Leopold to escape execution in the electric chair and they were given life sentences. Darrow thought the verdict just; he was convinced that except for the wealth of the families, a plea of guilty and a life sentence would have been accepted without contest.

From the time of Mike McDonald, there had been a close link between Chicago's criminals and politicians. But with the amoral Thompson in the mayor's chair, the alliance flourished as never before; its operations were marked by a new brazenness and by a new ruthlessness and efficiency. The era of the gangster in Chicago is often attributed to prohibition. It is true that the sale of illegal liquor constituted a sizable proportion of the gangsters' activities. But the genesis of their power could be traced back along before the advent of the Eighteenth Amendment.

The successor to Mike McDonald as kingpin of the underworld and the founder of the criminal dynasty which ruled Chicago during the Thompson regimes and much of the 1930's was Big Jim Colosimo. Big Jim's was a Levee success story. He made his first appearance in Chicago carrying a water pail to quench the thirst of section hands working on the railroad.

Later, he ascended the social scale to a job as a street sweeper, showing such political aptitude in organizing the sweepers that he won the sponsorship of The Bath and Hinky Dink. He also came to the attention of Victoria de Moresco, owner of a series of Levee brothels who admired his way with the politicians as much as his ability to break open a locked door with a shove of his huge shoulders. Thinking he might be a handy man to have around the house, she married him, elevating him to a position of money and power. As a gesture of his appreciation, he sentimentally named one of their brothels the Hotel Victoria. Soon he ranked second only to Ike Bloom in his influence in the district. Big Jim continued to prosper, not only operating Victoria's resorts, but taking over the Italian national lottery and the illegal wine industry, farming out carloads of grapes to Sicilian families and then selling the wine they made without paying the government tax. He assumed control of many of the Italian immigrant laborers, hiring them out for a fee to railroads or other industries in need of unskilled labor. All these activities brought him into frequent contact with the Unione Siciliane and the Mafia. Neither organization was easy to do business with and frequent extortion demands prompted him to import a bodyguard in 1910. The gunman he chose to protect him was John Torrio, member of a notorious New York gang.

Big Jim displayed other evidences of success. His dress became flashier. Diamonds were his trademark. He wore diamonds on his fingers, diamond studs on his shirt, a diamond horseshoe on his vest, diamonds on his belt and suspender buckles; even his garters were studded with diamonds. After the closing of the Levee resorts, Big Jim opened a café on Wabash Avenue; it soon was drawing a fashionable trade because of its exceptional food. Colosimo was a restaurateur at heart. Even when running a Levee resort, he prided himself upon the quality of his food and the discriminating choice of wine he offered his patrons. Though Colosimo's Café was only a front for Big Jim's more extensive illegal business activities, its standards were high and it became a favorite rendezvous of theater and opera personalities. Colosimo was a regular attendant at the opera and opera music was a frequent feature of the café entertainment, attracting such stars as Galli-Curci, Tetrazzini, Caruso and the opera's maestro, Campanini. George M. Cohan was a regular patron when a show of his was in Chicago.

The power of Colosimo reached its peak with the coming of prohibition. As a man who knew how to do business with Mayor Thompson at City Hall, Big Jim took control of the bootleg industry. He might have ruled it for a dozen years if it had not been for his fondness for opera—a fatal indulgence, as matters turned out. It was a desire to offer the patrons of Colosimo's the best in singing which led Big Jim to hire Dale Winter to sing in his café. Dale Winter was not a cabaret entertainer and didn't like to be called one—

she was a former vaudeville singer whom a Chicago reporter had found singing in a church choir and recommended to Jim. She was another diamond for Jim and a polished one; her qualities, by the testimony of all who heard her sing, were those of a fine, gentle-bred girl. Morris Gest traveled to Colosimo's to sign her to a Broadway contract and Ziegfeld also came with an offer. But by the time Dale Winter's reputation was made, she was in love with Big Jim and refused to leave. Every night she pitted her voice against the cabaret racket of noisy merrymakers; during the day she took singing lessons from Big Jim's friends at the opera. Colosimo asked Victoria for a divorce. "I raised one husband for another woman and there is nothing in it," Victoria said sadly and gave him the divorce without protest. When Big Jim and Dale were married, the groom promised his bride she could resume her singing career without the strain of the nightly appearance in the café. "You don't have to earn a living now," Jim said. "You can rest and study and rest and sing and rest and perform roles in the Auditorium." Dale Winter said "That was the thing we were silliest about—my being a great singer some day."

John Torrio, busy managing many of Colosimo's enterprises and establishing his own control over the city's gambling, had no time for silliness. Worried that Colosimo's marriage to the high-principled Dale Winter might result in the weakening of the empire that had been established, Torrio decided to eliminate Colosimo from the top spot, a feat only possible through murdering him. Although a professional killer, Torrio imported a special gunman from New York to take care of Big Jim. Setting a time for the assassination, Torrio told Colosimo that two truckloads of whiskey from Jim O'Leary's would be arriving at the café at that time. When Colosimo arrived to check the shipment, he was dropped to the floor with a bullet behind the ear and the way was clear for Torrio to take over.

Colosimo's funeral was a gaudy event which paraded the intimate relationship between the city's criminals and its political leaders. The honorary pallbearers included three judges, an assistant state's attorney, two congressmen, state representative Michael L. Igoe, who later became a federal judge, and numerous aldermen, including James P. Bowler, later a wheelhorse for the Kelly-Nash machine. The Roman Catholic Church refused Colosimo its rites because of his divorce; a Protestant clergyman conducted the service—after which Alderman John "The Bath" Coughlin knelt at the bier and recited the Catholic prayer for the dead. The assassination of Colosimo was believed to have cost $150,000, of which $20,000 went to the killer and the balance into the treasury of the Mafia. The friendship of the leading politicians for Colosimo did not prevent their being realists; with their acquiescence, Torrio succeeded to the command of the army of the underworld.

As chief of staff in maintaining discipline among the various forces involved in liquor traffic, prostitution and the gambling rackets, Torrio picked a twenty-three-year-old killer named Al Capone, a quick man with a gun who had been trained as a member of New York's tough Five Points gang. Torrio established his headquarters in the Four Deuces at 2222 Wabash Avenue, a combination saloon and brothel. The Four Deuces was never visited by the fashionable slumming parties which had found amusement at Colosimo's; a dozen murders were said to have been committed there and Chicagoans were already finding it unhealthy to be a witness to a killing. Though Torrio was not hesitant to order a murder, he avoided open clashes with a combination of compromise and threats as astutely employed as the diplomatic maneuverings of a European statesman. His authority was so complete he walked the streets alone. He carried a gun only infrequently; some people said he never carried one.

The gang chief with whom Torrio was most careful to maintain a delicate balance of power was Dion O'Banion, who bossed a North Side gang from his flower shop near Holy Name Cathedral. O'Banion, a former altar boy, was the son of an indigent plasterer and had been reared in poverty. In his youth he peddled papers on the Loop streetcars; an accident in a fall from one of the cars had left him with one leg shorter than the other. He graduated to employment as a terrorist during a newspaper circulation war and then to bootlegging and killing for a fee. He had killed two men in the entrance to the LaSalle Theater and had not been prosecuted for the crime. He carried three revolvers in specially constructed pockets of his tailor-made clothes and could shoot with either his right hand or his left. He was surrounded by a bunch of humorless thugs. When Samuel J. "Nails" Morton, a member of the gang, was thrown and kicked to death by a horse in Lincoln Park, the gunmen vowed vengeance. They kidnapped the unfortunate horse, led it to the spot where Morton's body had been found and solemnly "rubbed it out" in gangland fashion. O'Banion was also a political power, controlling the vote in the area of the Gold Coast and the slums behind it just north of the Loop.

The truce was broken when O'Banion became involved in a feud with the six Genna brothers, who amassed a five-million-dollar fortune by hiring hundreds of Sicilians and Italians to cook alcohol for them in West Side apartments. The Gennas—Angelo, Sam, Jim, Pete, Tony and Mike—had five police captains and four hundred patrolmen regularly on their payroll. When Angelo Genna married, he ordered a wedding cake which required four days to bake; it contained four hundred pounds of sugar, four hundred pounds of flour and seven cases of eggs. The opulent Angelo had dropped $30,000 gambling at The Ship, a Cicero gambling establishment in which O'Banion shared an interest with Torrio. Torrio wanted to cancel the debt, but O'Banion refused and issued a telephone ultimatum to Angelo to pay up within a week. Angelo, a powerful leader in the Unione Siciliane, did not like such treatment; he was also smoldering with resentment over the hijacking of a truckload of his whiskey by O'Banion's gang.

O'Banion's assassination had been planned several times with the full assent of Torrio, but was always stopped by Mike Merlo, the first president of the Unione Siciliane. Then, in May of 1924, O'Banion knowingly let Torrio get caught with thirteen truckloads of beer in a raid which was turned over to the federal government for prosecution. Torrio's fix did not extend that high and he was indicted for bootlegging with thirty-seven other defendants. It was a humiliating experience for the powerful gang boss. A short time later, Mike Merlo died and Torrio gave Genna the go-signal for the murder of O'Banion. While his death was being plotted, O'Banion was doing a rush business in flowers for Merlo's funeral. A hundred thousand dollars' worth of flowers were sent to Merlo's home and overflowed onto the lawn outside; one floral tribute contained a life-size wax effigy of Merlo. Torrio sent a $10,000 floral piece from O'Banion's and Capone ordered an $8,000 tribute from the shop. Even one of the Gennas called for a floral piece.

On the morning of November 10, 1924, while O'Banion was busy with

THE ELEVATED AT NIGHT, by Aaron Bohrod

the flowers for Merlo's funeral, three men stepped out of a car and went into his shop. O'Banion came out of the back room; apparently recognizing the visitors, he stepped to the front of the shop with a carnation in one hand and scissors in the other. One of the visitors grabbed his arm and pulled him forward, another held him and the third pumped five bullets into him, including a coup de grace to the head. O'Banion's funeral exceeded the splendor of Merlo's. He was buried in a $10,000 casket, bought in Philadelphia and shipped to Chicago in a special car. At his funeral there were so many flowers it required twenty-six trucks to transport them to the cemetery. Among the mourners at the funeral were Torrio and Capone, both conscious they were being blamed for the killing which could hardly have been done without their approval. The actual killer was believed to have been one of the Gennas, who had been looking at more than flowers when he ordered Merlo's wreath.

Hymie Weiss, a Polish boy who had shortened his name from Wajciechowski, took over the O'Banion gang and promptly ordered the murder of Torrio. The gang boss fled the city, with Weiss and his gunmen in pursuit; the chase led to several southern resorts and then across the Florida keys to Cuba and back again to Chicago. Torrio's pursuers caught up with him at the entrance to his Chicago home just before he was to start his sentence in the Lake County jail for bootlegging. He was severely wounded and lay for a long time near death in Jackson Park Hospital, guarded by a dual watch of police officers and personal bodyguards. A witness identified the man who fired on Torrio as Bugs Moran, a Weiss ally, but Moran was not indicted. Slowly recovering his health, Torrio went from the hospital to the Lake County jail where he had the sheriff install bullet-proof shutters on his cell windows and hired three extra deputies to guard him during the period of his incarceration. A free man at last, he decided to leave Chicago for reasons of health; he had an estimated ten to thirty million dollars in banks in New York and Europe. As far as was known, he never returned to Chicago, but rose to a new eminence in the more gun-free rackets of New York. In Chicago, his chief of staff, Al Capone, assumed Torrio's place as ruler of the underworld.

Capone, without the imagination or the keen business mind of Torrio, ruled by the bludgeon and the gun rather than by the arts of diplomatic strategy. Finding that Angelo Genna had installed himself as new president of the Unione Siciliane without Capone's permission, the gang chief moved quickly to show his anger. On May 26, 1925, Angelo Genna was killed; a month later Mike Genna was shot down and in July Anthony was trapped and killed. The remaining Gennas departed for Sicily.

The empire which Capone inherited was organized with the businesslike efficiency of a legitimate corporation. The Better Government Association wired the United States Senate that "Chicago politicians are in league with gangsters and the city is overrun with a combination of lawless politics and protected vice." Capone lacked the executive ability to keep this alliance running smoothly, however, and had to enforce his edicts by indiscriminate murder. The corruption of the police had been pushed to the point of saturation under the two terms of Mayor Thompson and the city was paralyzed. In an aldermanic election in one ward—the Nineteenth—a candidate for alderman and three of his aides were killed while two captains of the perennial alderman "Johnny de Pow" Powers were mowed down. Massacre was the only word for the Capone rule. During the first four months of 1926 there were twenty-nine gang killings in Chicago; the total for four years was more than two hundred—and all without a single conviction for murder.

When Mayor Thompson conceded he could not win a third consecutive term and withdrew from the race for mayor, Capone sought a stronghold outside the city as protection against any reforms introduced by Mayor William Dever, who was trying to beat down the criminals with a demoralized police force and courts riddled by Thompson appointments. The location Capone chose was Cicero, where the syndicate already had made sizable inroads. His first move was to take over the city government. He secured the nomination on the Democratic ticket of a group of subservient politicians and on election day moved his army of ex-convicts and aliens into Cicero in the manner of a latter-day European dictator.

The Illinois Crime Survey recorded in a matter-of-fact way that "automobiles filled with gunmen paraded the streets, slugging and kidnapping election workers. Polling places were raided by armed thugs and ballots taken at the point of the gun from the hands of voters waiting to drop them in the box. Voters and workers were kidnapped, taken to Chicago and held prisoner until the polls closed." Three men were killed, another had his throat slashed and a Cicero policeman was blackjacked. Late in the afternoon an appeal for help was sent to County Judge Edmund K. Jarecki, who swore in seventy policemen as special deputies and sent them to Cicero. When a police squad came upon Al Capone, his brother, Frank, and Charles Fischetti standing in front of a polling place, Frank Capone opened fire and was shot dead by a patrolman. Al fled down Cicero Avenue, fighting off another squad of police with a pistol blazing in each hand, and finally escaping. The rescue attempt had come too late. Cicero was taken.

Capone ruled the town of fifty thousand as firmly as he had bossed Chicago under the acquiescent Thompson. When an alderman opposed one of Capone's projects, the gangster waited for him and beat him up outside the council chambers. Another time Capone knocked down and kicked his hand-picked mayor while a Cicero policeman stood by, afraid to intervene. The federal constitution said there could be no sale of alcoholic liquors in the United States; but in the Capone-run town of Cicero there were 161 bars open day and night. At the Hawthorne Smoke Shop, a handbook for bets, the play totaled $50,000 a day. Capone himself was the heaviest bettor. He estimated that he lost nearly a million dollars a year to the bookies. Incongruously, he had never invested a dollar in the stock market. "It's a racket," he said.

Open warfare existed between Capone and the Hymie Weiss gang on the North Side. At noon on September 20, 1926, eleven cars of Weiss gunmen roared down the main street of Cicero. As the cars approached a restaurant where Capone was having lunch, a fusillade from machine guns, pistols and shotguns poured into the restaurant and nearby Hawthorne Inn, Capone's Cicero headquarters. Capone dropped to the floor and escaped unhurt but thirty-five cars parked along the street were raked with bullets. A woman sitting in a car with a baby in her arms was grazed over the eyes, damaging her sight. Capone made the headlines by paying all the hospital expenses of the woman—the first innocent bystander to be hurt in the wars (not counting the police heroes who paid with their lives). Capone ordered an immediate revenge. On October 11th, Hymie Weiss and a beer peddler were killed by a spray of machine-gun bullets as they stepped from their car near O'Banion's former flower shop; the assassin's bullets ricocheted and chipped the stones on Holy Name Cathedral. Chief of Police Morgan Collins did not arrest Capone. "It's a waste of time to arrest him," Collins said. "He's been in before on other murder charges. He has his alibi. He was in Cicero when the shooting occurred." A short time later, Antonio Lombardo, who had been placed at the head of the Unione Siciliane by Capone, was shot down and killed as he was walking with two bodyguards near State and Madison—famed as the busiest corner in the United States. The killers disappeared in the crowd.

In 1927, the voters of Chicago returned Big Bill Thompson to the mayor's seat for a third term. Al Capone, who had underwritten the mayor's campaign expenses and provided an army of hoodlums to "guard" the West Side polls on election day, moved back to Chicago. Thompson by this time had a new tactic to divert attention from his alliance with criminals; he declared war on England. He uttered his notorious threat to "punch King George in the snoot" and issued scholarly ukases about the alleged pro-English bias of the textbooks in the Chicago schools. He pushed through the state legislature a bill which said "The official language of the State of Illinois shall be known hereafter as the American language." A wit said later, "Mayor Thompson was for America First and Capone was for America's Thirst. Maybe they weren't so far apart at that." The Reverend John Thompson of the Chicago Methodist Temple found nothing humorous in the city's tawdry reputation; at a service he offered up this prayer:

THE FUNERAL OF ANTONIO LOMBARDO

"O, Thou that didst care for Nineveh and didst spare it, and Thou that didst weep over Jerusalem, dost Thou still brood over these great modern cities? We pray Thee to rule over Chicago, this young and strong, good and bad, city—and out of man's worst to bring Thine own."

Capone was difficult to reach, even by prayer. After Mayor Thompson's return to power, the gang chief set up a Chicago headquarters in the Metropole Hotel, 2300 South Michigan. His entourage occupied fifty rooms on two heavily guarded floors. They had their own service bars and operated their private elevators. The hallway outside Capone's suite was patrolled by gunmen as alert as military sentinels. In a large office, calculated to awe visitors, Capone sat beneath photographs of three men he considered great Americans: George Washington, Abraham Lincoln—and Big Bill Thompson. The offices of the Capone bootleg syndicate, methodically organized by Jacob "Jack" Guzik, whose brother was in charge of the white-slave traffic, were located in a nearby doctor's office whose pharmacopoeia of bottles and vials was composed of stock samples of the liquors handled by the syndicate. In the office files were the names of several hundred prominent Chicagoans who were customers, the list of police officers and prohibition agents who were receiving pay-offs and a record of the channels through which liquor was brought from New York, New Orleans and Miami. A special looseleaf ledger was set up to show the cost-accounting procedures followed in the brothels under Capone control.

Incredibly, while Capone terrorized the city—there were sixty-two bombings in 1928, many directed against reform leaders—he was being painted as a kind of public hero. When Commander Francesco de Pinedo, the round-the-world flyer, landed in Chicago in May of 1927, Al Capone was among the official greeting party. The police explained that his presence was requested to prevent possible anti-Fascist demonstrations against Pinedo's sponsor, Mussolini. The law could not preserve order—but Al Capone could. When the depression hit, Capone was the first to establish soup kitchens; hungry men murmured "Good Old Al" as they waited in line for their handout. Meanwhile, John Gunther in an article in Harper's was estimating that the sixty or more rackets then in operation in Chicago were costing its citizens thirty-six million dollars a year—enough to feed a good many more hungry men than those who stood in line waiting for Capone's charity.

The gangster boss lived lavishly. He was childish in his emotions, quick to anger and had to seek frequent stimulation in betting huge sums on the races or rolling dice for nothing less than a thousand dollars a pass. He had a flat nose, thick lips, the short neck of a night-club bouncer and a scar on his left cheek which he claimed was a war memento but was actually the reminder of a brawl in a Brooklyn dance hall. When he attended a play in the Loop, he went in the company of eighteen bodyguards, all in tuxedos, who were seated at strategic points around the theater. When he left his headquarters, he rode in a seven-ton bullet-proof car with fenders of steel it was nearly impossible to dent. Machine-gun bullets would have splattered harmlessly off its surface. Its doors were equipped with special combination locks so his enemies could not jimmy the doors and plant a bomb under the seat. Even so, he was not careless. When he drove, a small scout car always preceded him and a touring car of bodyguards protected him from the rear. When Capone entered one of the city's seven thousand speakeasies his hoodlums took up posts at the doors and no one was allowed to enter or leave while he was there. As compensation, he frequently bought drinks for the house.

The Fish Fans Club, a schooner clubhouse in Belmont Harbor owned by Big Bill Thompson, was a favorite speakeasy for politicians. It was organized supposedly to encourage the propagation of fish in American waters, but was in fact a part of the Thompson promotion machine. The club was padlocked by federal agents, but reopened; it came to a humiliating end when so many people crammed aboard to celebrate Big Bill's election to a third term that it became overloaded and sank. Fred Mann's Rainbo Gardens was another big speakeasy. Mann was a friend of the Mayor's and when federal agents padlocked his place he made a personal appeal to Secretary of the Treasury Andrew Mellon, in charge of the revenue agents, to be permitted to reopen. Mellon, however, did not intervene. In all the speakeasies, shootings were frequent; but as Eddie Condon was to recall later, "in all the joints the bands kept playing no matter what happened." He said the gangsters liked jazz. "It's got guts and it don't make you slobber," one of the gunmen said. The favorite speakeasy of the musicians was the Three Deuces (not to be confused with the Four Deuces) at 222 North State Street. It was here that Mezz Mezzrow says the nation's first jam session was staged, with Bix Beiderbecke and Bing Crosby, both appearing at the Chicago Theater nearby, as its principal participants. Entertainers had to bow to the wishes of their gangster bosses. When Joe E. Lewis notified the Green Mills Gardens he was leaving to play the Rendezvous, he was slashed on the face, throat and tongue by Machine Gun Jack McGurn.

McGurn was later arrested but never prosecuted for the greatest bloodbath of the Capone era. It occurred just a year before the gang wars sputtered to an end with Capone in complete control of the city. On St. Valentine's Day of 1929, a squad of four killers disguised as policemen and detectives ambushed with machine guns seven members of the Bugs Moran gang, successors to the interests of Dion O'Banion and Hymie Weiss. But while the gang wars were proceeding without letup in Chicago, Philadelphia nabbed Capone on a gun-carrying charge and sent him to the penitentiary. Even in Pennsylvania, Capone's influence was sufficient to procure a transfer from the strictly disciplined Holmesburg jail to Eastern Penitentiary where he was given his own cell, permitted to make long-distance telephone calls and allowed the use of the warden's office for running his illegal enterprises.

Always, he protested he didn't want to be in the rackets. "You fear death every moment," he said in one of the hundreds of interviews which were glamorizing his shoddy murders. "Worse than death you fear the rats of the game who would run and tell the police if you didn't constantly satisfy them with favors." He forgot easily about his murders. "All I ever did was to sell beer and whiskey to our best people," he said with a total disregard of facts. "All I ever did was supply a demand that was pretty popular. . . . They talk about me not being on the legitimate. Nobody's on the legit. You know that and so do they. Your brother or your father gets in a jam. What do you do? Do you sit back and let him go over the road without trying to help him? You'd be a yellow dog if you did. Nobody's really on the legit when it comes down to cases."

It sounded noble but it was wrong. A few people were "on the legit," even if they didn't count for much in local politics. The federal government put an investigator to work on Capone's tax returns. The investigator narrowly missed being assassinated at least twice, but finally found what he was seeking. Capone was brought to trial for income-tax evasion. The witnesses against him had to be hidden and shifted from place to place;

Capone was not beneath threatening the Government of the United States. But in 1931, after a long presentation of evidence, Capone was found guilty and sentenced to ten years in prison, a year in jail and $50,000 in fines.

The organization survived Capone just as it survived Mike McDonald, Big Jim Colosimo and John Torrio. In 1950, James M. Ragen, Sr., proprietor of a racing-news service which provided race results for handbooks, said, "The Capone syndicate is just as strong as it ever was." Three weeks later Ragen was shot to death on the streets of Chicago; the murder weapon, once found, vanished from the custody of the Chicago police department.

MARY GARDEN, 1935

Grand Opera — A Libretto for Romance

THERE WERE great plans for the future. Daniel Burnham, buoyed by his triumph at the Columbian Exposition, urged the powerful Commercial Club and the Merchants Club to form plans for Chicago as great as those that had been made for the temporary white city on the South Side. His arguments were practical. "Beauty has always paid better than any other commodity and always will," he said. "We have been running away to Cairo, Athens, the Riviera, Paris and Vienna because life at home is not so pleasant as in those fashionable centers. . . . No one has estimated the millions of money made here in Chicago and expended elsewhere but the sum must be a large one. What would be the effect upon our retail business at home if this money were circulated here?" Burnham had other words which matched his dream. "Make no little plans," he urged the city. "They have no magic to stir men's blood and probably themselves will not be realized. Make big plans; aim high in hope and work, remembering that a noble, logical diagram once recorded will never die but long after we are gone will be a living thing, asserting itself with growing intensity."

Mayor Fred Busse, a crude and rough product of professional politics, heard Burnham's words, shared his vision and appointed a Chicago Plan Commission to lay out the objectives of the city of the future. Busse was not a reform mayor; but it was under Busse that the two greatest reforms of twentieth-century Chicago politics were originated—the Chicago Plan and the Vice Commission, which laid the groundwork for the destruction of segregated vice. Inexplicable? Just Chicago, people said.

A new pattern of cosmopolitan living was emerging too. The pattern of homes with wide lawns—a heritage of "The Garden City"—was giving way reluctantly to the new apartment houses. Ogden McClurg, nurtured on a classical education but grown to be a bold promoter and planner, built his first apartment house at the far end of a sandy strip reaching eastward to the lake from the Harold McCormick mansion. McClurg numbered the building 999 Lake Shore Drive, indulging the same superstition which led him to locate McClurg's wholesale store at 333 East Ontario because of a belief that nine was his lucky number. When 999's ornate walls towered lonely against the lake sky, the area was considered desolate; maids refused to cross the windy stretch to go to work. But in a few years there was a row of buildings in the area, numbered 179, 199, 209 and 219, carrying out the theme of nines and confusing Chicago taxi drivers for all time.

On the night of November 3, 1910, the city felt it had actually achieved the cosmopolitanism and sophistication which had so long escaped it. "Everybody's happy," Harold McCormick, the son of the reaper king, told the reporters. "We could not ask for more." There was much to be festive about. At the Auditorium the new Chicago Opera Company was presenting *Aida* to a brilliantly dressed first-night audience. The nucleus of the company was an inheritance from Oscar Hammerstein's Manhattan Opera, which had gone bankrupt in its war with the Metropolitan; yet Chicagoans were already claiming the opera company as part of their own cultural garland. "The success of Chicago opera means the success of all culture in this city [and] the establishment of a finer standard of art than has ever been known here before," music critic Felix Borowski wrote in the *Record-Herald* the following day. There were few to disagree with his prediction. Arthur Meeker, the governor of the Assembly Association, pronounced the evening's performance a triumph. "I never saw the opulence of the East better staged than right here," he said. There was a democratic note about the opening night's crowd as well. Clarence Mackay, president of the Postal Telegraph Company, had come out from New York and given one hundred of his messenger boys opening-night tickets. Every Chicago employe, he announced, would be given a pair of tickets for at least one opera performance.

The impetus for bringing opera to Chicago had come for the most part from Harold McCormick and his wife, the former Edith Rockefeller, who was rapidly assuming the social power which Mrs. Potter Palmer relinquished through her long absences from the city. Two of Rockefeller's daughters had married Chicagoans. Alta Rockefeller had married Ezra Parmelee Prentice, a brilliant young lawyer, but the couple moved to New York shortly after their marriage. Edith and Harold settled in Chicago in 1897 in a turreted mansion at 1000 Lake Shore Drive which had been erected in the 1880's by S. S. Beman for Nathaniel Jones, a wealthy member of the Board of Trade. Surrounding the house was a high iron fence which had been designed to match a pair of gates purchased from the German exhibit at the Columbian Exposition.

From this gray stone palace on the lake shore, the McCormicks dominated Chicago society. Mrs. McCormick carried out her social program in a regal manner; no queen or ruler of a court could have been more rigid in attention to protocol. Even her children, when they were grown, could see her only by appointment. She required that printed menus in French be provided for every meal; at formal dinners there were menus and place cards engraved in gold. A butler stood behind every two chairs at dinner. Four men were required to serve a luncheon for two. Her large household staff included a first and second butler, two parlor maids, a coachman, footman, houseman and six detectives. Her personal maid had a helper, a sewing woman, who in turn had an assistant, described as a mending woman. In the kitchen were a chief cook and a second cook in addition to more menial help. The cooks had a coal stove; they were not permitted to cook with gas. Mrs. McCormick allowed herself to speak to only two servants—the chief steward and her personal secretary. Through these she ruled her entire household. When she called for her carriage (and later for a car) the coachman was given detailed instructions for the trip before he left the house. He was never addressed directly during the trip; the time at which he was to return for his passenger was set before he left, eliminating the need for Mrs. McCormick to speak to him.

The furnishings of 1000 Lake Shore Drive were in fact those of a ruler's palace. Most were selected because of Mrs. McCormick's belief she was descended from the La Rochefoucauld nobility of France. (Actually the Rockefeller family was German in its origins.) One or her rugs, purchased for $185,000, had been sent by the Shah of Persia as a present to the Winter Palace of the Czars at St. Petersburg during the reign of Peter the Great. Subsequently, before finding its way to a London auction, it was given to the Emperor of Austria in gratitude for Austrian aid to destitute Russians. In a huge chamber called the Empire Room, Mrs. McCormick installed four of Napoleon's royal chairs, two marked with the crest initial N and two with a B for the family name of Bonaparte. On the fourth floor was a fifteen-thousand volume library with such collector's treasures as the *Night of* the *Swan* valued at $30,000; *Histoire Héliodore*, worth $6,000; a *Patissier François* dated 1655 and a Byzantine manuscript of the New Testament in Greek valued at $14,000. In her bedroom, Edith Rockefeller McCormick slept in an enormous Louis XVI gilded bedstead and walked to a directoire loveseat across an ornate Aubusson carpet. On her dressing table was a small oblong box in gold with the diamond-encrusted initials "M.L.," believed to have been a gift from Napoleon to the Empress Marie Louise. In the halls and parlors were Buddhas from Chinese temples, tapestries from Brussels and English silver dating back to the time of Oliver Cromwell. For her large dinners, which might have an invitation list as large as two hundred, Mrs. McCormick served the guests on a golden service which Napoleon had given his sister, Pauline. It consisted of one thousand pieces and contained more than eleven thousand ounces of precious metals.

Mrs. McCormick's jewel collection, though not as extensive as that of Mrs. Palmer, contained single pieces of such great value they could never be sold. An emerald necklace, formed from jewels collected by Cartier at a cost of nearly $600,000, came to be valued at more than a million dollars. Ten large emeralds were the central features of the necklace and were spaced on a rope fabricated of 1,657 small diamonds. Another necklace was believed to be made in part of Russian crown jewels. It was made up of twenty-three large pearls, twenty-one large diamonds of various shapes and one hundred lesser diamonds. A slip of a woman with exquisite feet and ankles, Mrs. McCormick frequently wore a tiny golden anklet. Her formal dinners were so much like affairs of state that it was often said "she taught Chicago how to wear and to own a dress suit." The formality, however, never called for champagne. She was a "dry" and never permitted cocktails or liquor in her home. In later years she said that her father had made her promise that she would never serve a drink of liquor in her home. Recalling her first formal dinner, she said "my party was not very well under way before I noticed a certain lack of spontaneity that had marked the other dinners I had attended. The gaiety seemed forced and formal . . ." When the young bride asked her husband the cause of it, he replied, "My dear, don't you realize that these red-blooded young Chicagoans are used to having their liquor? They simply must have their cocktails, their wine, their highballs and cordials." The pledge, if it existed, was never broken, and no alcoholic liquors were ever served at 1000 Lake Shore Drive.

Mrs. McCormick, who hated hymns because her pious father had made her sing them so much as a girl, had a great devotion for the opera which was shared by her husband, Harold. The pair entertained frequently on opera nights. Mrs. McCormick sat at the end of the table with a jeweled clock beside her and insisted that a strict schedule be kept so that no one would be late for the performance. Those who did not eat quickly might expect to have their plates snatched away when Mrs. McCormick signaled the end of the time allotted for a particular course.

It was at such a fabulous dinner party that tragedy struck close to the heart of Edith Rockefeller McCormick. Her first-born son, John Rockefeller McCormick, was ill with scarlet fever at the family home in Lake Forest. During dinner, Mrs. McCormick's secretary received a call from the McCormick country home. The message was of such importance that the imperious rule against interruptions during dinner had to be broken. The secretary whispered to Mrs. McCormick that her son was dead. The shock was one from which most Chicagoans believed Edith Rockefeller McCormick found it hard to recover. It was also the beginning of an era which found both Edith and her husband playing roles as baroque as any in the repertoire of their beloved Chicago Opera Company.

The opera itself was to lead a tempestuous career. Three weeks after its opening it incurred the wrath of the moralists with a presentation of *Salome* with Mary Garden in the leading role. Mary Garden had been one of Hammerstein's stars at the Manhattan Opera but it was to Chicago that she owed her opportunity to sing. As a young girl she had been discovered singing in an afternoon recital by Mrs. David Mayer, wife of a partner in the Schlesinger and Mayer clothing store and a patroness of the arts. Mrs. Mayer, attracted by Mary's personality and voice, took Mary into the family, where the young singer served as nurse for the Mayers' boy, David, Jr., and continued her vocal training under professional instructors provided by Mrs. Mayer. Subsequently, Mrs. Mayer agreed to finance Mary's studies for two years in Paris. The relationship of sponsor and protégée was abruptly terminated before Mary returned to Chicago for an engagement with the new opera company. Mary charged that Mrs. Mayer had withdrawn her support because of a rumor that Mary had borne an illegitimate child in Paris. Mrs. Mayer, explaining frankly she had had the rumor investigated but did not give it any credence, pointed out that she had extended her support of Mary from two years to three. The break came, she said, when Mary, tasting intoxicating success at the Manhattan, had refused to recognize the woman who made her career possible. Because of this, Mrs. Mayer asked Mary to return the $20,000 advanced for the Paris training. Mary complied and Mrs. Mayer immediately turned the money over to charity.

This mild controversy was obliterated by the furor over *Salome*. Miss Garden always made it clear that it was not "Come and hear Mary Garden" but "Come and see Mary Garden." She insisted she was a "singing actress and not a singer." Percy Hammond, after watching her in *Salome*, was in full agreement. He called her "the feminine colossus who doth bestride our operatic world" and found her performance a "florid, excessive, unhampered tour de force, lawless and inhuman."

MRS. HAROLD McCORMICK
(Edith Rockefeller) *From a painting by Frederic August Von Kaulbach*

Chief of Police LeRoy T. Steward, who was also in the audience for *Salome*, was of a different opinion. "It was disgusting," he said. "Miss Garden wallowed around like a cat in a bed of catnip. There was no art in her dance that I could see. If the same show were produced on Halsted Street the people would call it cheap but over at the Auditorium they say it is art. Black art, if art at all. I would not call it immoral. I would say it was disgusting."

Miss Garden, who made a special study of the dance because, as she said, "I want the dance of the Seven Veils to be drama and not Folies Bergère," was astounded—but not so much she was at a loss for a reply. She dismissed the police chief by saying, "I always bow down to the ignorant and try to make them understand, but I ignore the illiterate."

To the second performance the police chief sent his chief censor, Detective Sergeant Charles O'Donnell, who wore "a black suit he usually reserved for funerals." Arthur Burrage Farwell, who had been denouncing the opera but had not seen it, was given a ticket but refused to go, terming Mary Garden a "great degenerator" of public morals. "I am a normal man," he said, "but I would not trust myself to see a performance of *Salome*." The *News* commented that if "curiosity caused the fall of man, it also led to the progress of the race and it continues a duality of service . . . it also produced the best crowd of the season." In New York, Oscar Hammerstein facetiously suggested that Mary wear some flannel petticoats in her veil dance because "when she worked for me she had a deadly fear when singing *Salome* of getting cold feet."

The second performance intensified the moral outcry, aided by an adverse report from Sergeant O'Donnell. Chief Steward offered to compromise if Mary would "tone down the head business" when she danced with the severed head of the prophet. Mary would have none of it. "If there is any more of this twaddle about immorality I shall leave Chicago and go to Philadelphia or some place where art is appreciated and viewed as art," she said. The Board of Directors, motivated by a desire to shelter their infant opera company, suddenly terminated the quarrel by withdrawing the third performance. In her autobiography, Mary Garden was to charge that the cancellation was ordered by Edith Rockefeller McCormick. According to Mary, Mrs. McCormick sent for her and said, "The truth came to me after your third [sic] performance . . . I said to myself, Edith, your vibrations are all wrong." As there were only two performances of *Salome*, there is at least one inaccuracy in this account; it seems more probable the cancellation was due to a recurrence of Chicago's unpredictable puritanism—which tolerated the nation's largest vice area on the edge of its business district but rose up in horror over a sensuous work of art.

It was apparent to Chicagoans that a mutual interest in the opera was about the only one shared by the McCormicks. In 1911, hopeful that a house in the country might provide a happier atmosphere, they built Villa Turicum, a forty-four room mansion in Lake Forest, but the housewarming was abruptly called off without explanation. Several barrels of French china stood unpacked for thirty years; two massive chairs from the Italian renaissance period, purchased for the marble-walled drawing room, were set in place but never uncrated. An unusual feature of the mansion was that the thirteen master bedrooms were identical and furnished in the same way, varying only in the color of the walls. Villa Turicum was seldom visited and never for an overnight stay; the McCormicks were reminded of it only by a purple truck with "Villa Turicum" on its panels which brought fresh flowers to the house in town every day. Harold McCormick developed an enthusiasm for flying and sponsored the first international aeronautical show in Chicago. Planes were paid $2 for every minute they could remain in the air and some of the builder-owners were able to make as much as $8 or $9. McCormick also established the nation's first aeronautical research laboratory at Cicero and built a field for a flying club there. In 1913, he made news by flying to work and landing on the waters off Grant Park in his aeroyacht.

It was in 1913 that Mrs. McCormick confirmed the rift in her marriage by leaving Chicago for Switzerland where she planned to study psychology—then called "synthetic psychology"—with Dr. Carl Jung. She did not return for eight years. Meanwhile Harold McCormick continued to bolster the tottering Chicago Opera Company with new transfusions of funds. Through his interest in opera he was to be led to the greatest romantic adventure of his life.

The opera company, under Cleofonte Campanini, scored a series of brilliant triumphs but was unable to avoid overshadowing headlines of an entirely different kind. When the company presented *The Secret of Suzanne*, an inconsequential farce, Lucy Page Gaston stalked out after the third cigarette lighted by one of the singers. "Horrible," she said. "Horrible. One after another. I saw her with my own eyes. It is enough to turn one forever against grand opera. An artful embellishment of a pernicious vice which should receive the stamp of disapproval from every true American woman."

Carolina White, the soprano who replaced Mary Garden when the latter was on tour, made the front pages by going on strike, adding that general manager Andreas Dippel was a slave driver. To this, Dippel replied, "The prima donnas do not work too much; they eat too much. It is terrible the way they have been entertained by society here in Chicago. Too many dinners and too many late hours. I eat too much—we all eat too much—but I don't complain."

There were many exciting moments of a better kind. There was the time, for example, when Chicago first heard Maggie Teyte, the mite of a soprano who talked with a touch of a Cockney accent. There was the memorable Saturday matinee in 1916 when an unheralded singer named Galli-Curci made her local debut in *Rigoletto*. Her triumph was so great that the audience would not go home but shouted, cheered and stamped its feet while Campanini hurried backstage to sign up the new star for more appearances before other managers should hear of the ovation. Galli-Curci was involved in a more disturbing drama when she was singing *Dinorah* on the opening night of the season in 1917. She had just left the stage when the sound of a hissing flame and a sudden stench startled the audience in the Auditorium. Campanini ordered the orchestra to strike up "The Star Spangled Banner"; Galli-Curci, who did not know a word of the anthem, rushed to the front of the stage to send its notes ringing through the hall and still the threat of a panic. Meanwhile, Battalion Chief Michael J. Corrigan of the fire department (later the city's fire commissioner) rushed to the bomb, wrapped it up in his coat and ran with it to the street where it sputtered out. The bomb was the work of a crank, later apprehended and found to have the operatically appropriate name of Faust. It was wartime, however, and there was little comfort in thinking of what might have occurred if the maniac had been slightly more skilled in devising his contraption.

The success and prestige of the Chicago Opera Company, which for a time neared that of the Metropolitan in New York, was largely the work of Cleofonte Campanini. A measure of his thoroughness was the time he called for twenty-seven full rehearsals of an opera before he considered it ready to be presented. When he died in 1919, his funeral was held in the Auditorium which had been his own temple. The stage was set for the transformation scene from *Parsifal*. In the center of the stage lay the body of Campanini, with a lone candle at either side and his baton and an opera score resting on his conductor's stand nearby. Rosa Raisa sang the "Inflammatus" from Rossini's *Stabat Mater* and the orchestra played the final movement from Tchaikovsky's *Symphonie Pathétique*. It was an impressive farewell.

With the passing of the brilliant Campanini, Harold McCormick lost hope that he would be able to establish a native opera company on a paying basis. By 1921, he was confiding to Mary Garden that it was going to be his last season and he asked her to become the director. "We want to go out in a blaze of glory," she remembered his saying, "and we need your name." Mary accepted, stipulating that she be known as "directa," which she considered the feminine of director, and that "you don't give me a business manager with whiskers."

Blazing was the appropriate adjective for the season; but it applied more to tempers than to glories. Conductor Giorgio Polacco tossed the score of *Louise*, Miss Garden's favorite opera, into her lap and shouted, "Lead your own orchestra. You don't sing with me." The feud was carried to the dressing rooms and ended with the petite Mary pushing Polacco bodily out of the room. Another day, when the French conductor, Henri Morin, was conducting a rehearsal of *Aphrodite*, Mary grabbed the baton, twisted it from his grasp and, when she had finished tussling with him on the podium, denounced him for knowing nothing about music. Lucien Muratore, one of the company's leading singers, said "it was impossible to come back under the management of Mary Garden." Miss Garden, unperturbed by either the charge or the fact she herself had kept her British citizenship and was not an American citizen, filed a counter blast asserting, "Foreign dictation is a thing of the past. We are to have a little American dictation for a while and see how that will work out. It is a great pity to see an artist of the value of Signor Muratore so badly counseled"—the last comment a slap at Muratore's wife, Lina Cavalieri. Muratore and Mary were reconciled in Paris the following season; by the time Mary wrote her autobiography she remembered the fuss as just a feud in the newspapers.

The "directa" signed up so many artists there were not enough nights in the season for all of them to perform. As she said of herself, "There never was anything tentative about Mary Garden. She was always out in the front of the picture." (Or as the *Tribune* remarked, "Somebody is always running Miss Mary through a printing press.") She had an instinct for publicity. When Emile Coué, the French exponent of "Every day in every way I am getting better and better," came to this country, Mary announced that his formula had cured her of bronchial pneumonia, buzzing in the head, little colds, irritability and depression. Such loquaciousness had its hazards. When she appeared at the Stock Exchange to auction off boxes for a charity affair, a revolver fell at her feet and the police seized an awkward assassin who had been determined to shoot her. After he had been locked up, a friend of Mary's visited the man in his cell to ask him why he wanted to kill the opera star. All that could be gotten out of the demented man was one statement: "She talks too much."

Mary's artistic standards were high. Among her accomplishments was the staging of the American premiere of Prokofiev's *The Love for Three Oranges*. But by the end of the season her temperamental outbursts had resulted in the resignations of her business executive, artistic director and many of her important singers. She left by mutual consent, saying "I am an artist and my place is with the artists." Her own estimate of the season, in *Mary Garden's Story*, is this: "The newspapers said that the company lost one million dollars during the season I was director. I don't know because I had nothing to do with the business end of it. It was news to me. It may very well have happened, but I didn't know. I do know we finished the way Mr. McCormick wanted us to finish—in a blaze of glory. That's what he asked for and that's what he got. If it cost a million dollars, I'm sure it was worth it."

By the time Mary Garden finished her term as "directa," Harold McCormick was thinking more of a Polish diva than of the Chicago Opera Company. He had become enamored of Ganna Walska, a singer of little ability with an astonishing predilection for extraordinarily wealthy husbands. She had taken up singing, she said, because the first man to attract her (whom she conscientiously described as the "second richest man in Russia") had been given an honorary appointment to the Maryinski Imperial Opera House and she wished to impress him by appearing on that stage. She first married the Baron Arcadie d'Engor, but he was killed in World War I. She came to New York, where she was engaged to sing at the Century, a French-language theater subsidized by Otto H. Kahn. She told Kahn she was having trouble with her throat and he sent her to Dr. Joseph Fraenkel. Dr. Fraenkel, a man much older than she, was so interested by her resemblance to Frau Gustav Mahler, for whom he bore an unrequited love, that he proposed on their second meeting and was immediately accepted. When Dr. Fraenkel died a few years later, he left Ganna Walska an estate of half a million dollars.

Ganna Walska met Harold McCormick while still married to Dr. Fraenkel. Her own account is that when she was sitting in her "regular front-row seat" at the opera, she observed a gentleman who seemed to be looking at her persistently throughout the performance. The next day she learned, or thought she did, that it had been Harold McCormick. Because he was identified with the Chicago Opera Company, Walska was eager to meet him. She called him at the Plaza Hotel. He said he was catching a train and could not meet her, but the determined Walska intercepted him in the lobby. To her "amazement" he was not the man who stared at her, she said. She was not too abashed to notice his "wonderful boyish blue eyes," however, and to confide to him her ambition to sing with the Chicago Opera Company. At the next meeting, Harold McCormick brought his son Fowler, a precaution he might have been wise to follow on subsequent occasions. Gradually, Walska won his confidence and when she sailed for Europe after Dr. Fraenkel's death, Harold McCormick was on the *Aquitania* with her.

Another passenger on the *Aquitania* was Alexander Smith Cochran, whom the papers of the day described as the "world's richest bachelor." When Ganna Walska met Cochran, whose wealth was estimated at eighty million dollars, she thought she recognized him as a man "who had made me aware of himself" at a wedding reception several years before. Cochran proposed to her the night he met her. Later he gave her a pearl ring, saying, "If in January you still do not want to marry me, send me back this ring. I will understand that Harold McCormick is too much on your mind." As the days passed, Cochran was less noble. While Harold McCormick was in Switzerland seeking his freedom from his wife, Cochran and Ganna Walska were married in Paris. Though Mrs. McCormick reluctantly agreed to a divorce, Harold arrived in Paris with her consent only to learn of Ganna Walska's marriage to Cochran.

For the events of the next few days, the historian has only the remarkable testimony of the new bride. "While Mr. Cochran was still sleeping in the next room in his first day of married life," she wrote later, "I was pouring coffee for Mr. McCormick." Apparently the unhappy suitor needed a cup of coffee. "After my sudden marriage I was more preoccupied with Mr. McCormick's helpless state than with my own thoughts," she said. Her distraction was such that she "did not react at all" when at breakfast Cochran told her he was giving her a house on the Rue de Lubeck, formerly the home of James Gordon Bennett, and invited her to pick out anything she wanted at Cartier's for a wedding present. Even his "businesslike announcement" that she would receive $100,000 a year for "pin money"— "All that went by me without actually touching my inner being," the bride wrote in her autobiography, *Always Room at the Top*. Life with Cochran was to be a great trial for the sensitive Walska. Immediately, she says, she was "so crushed by cruel reality" that she was unable to preserve the "image my illusion had created." An excruciating experience, according to Walska, was that when Cochran gave her a present done up in "ugly looking rubber bands." To her "great surprise," she found that "eight or nine" bracelets she had seen at Cartier's fell onto her desk and her heart "stood still in disgust." When Cochran went hunting, he offended her with the gift of "a beautiful Rolls Royce; forced me to accept a sable coat worth a million francs and so big, so heavy it made me look old and fat; reserved almost an entire floor at the Carlton Hotel in Cannes and sent me there alone with half a dozen servants to enjoy the grand season on the Riviera." He was so insensitive, she complained, that he failed to realize Walska did not want to cover the "natural beauty of [her] delicate wrists with artificial beauty of rubies, diamonds and emeralds."

Walska did not permit the indignities of her marriage to Cochran to interfere with her plans for a debut with the Chicago Opera Company, scheduled for December 21, 1920. She was to appear in the title role of Leoncavallo's Zaza. The house was sold out and she was to come out in triumph. Then, without explanation, a few days before the performance, she fled the city for Europe. Opera director Herbert Johnson would say only that the opera was not ready, that they could not get it ready and so the

GANNA WALSKA AND HAROLD McCORMICK, 1929

performance had been postponed. Those who had been present at Mme Walska's final rehearsal were able to provide more details, though few found their way into print. At the first rehearsals, Gino Marinuzzi, who had succeeded Campanini as musical director, pleaded unsuccessfully with Walska to raise her voice so it could be heard beyond the orchestra pit. Seeing the cause was hopeless, he absented himself from rehearsals and turned the responsibility for the opera over to Pietro Cimini, who for four years had been conductor of the Warsaw opera. The singers were still using their books and were sitting in a small circle on the stage. Cimini, after stopping Walska several times, finally implored her, "Madame, please sing in your natural voice." She looked into the deep vaults of the balconies, then down at the grim conductor. Crying out, "Pig, you would ruin my performance," she rushed from the stage. Later she found Johnson and Marinuzzi together in the opera office. "Gentlemen," she announced, "I am packing my bags. At the end of this season you will be packing yours."

With that she was gone. Publicly she blamed her failure to appear on Cochran, saying he had reneged on a promise to let her have a stage career because he had heard reports of scanty costumes and long stage kisses.

Cochran, at the time of the canceled debut, fled Chicago in a huff just a few hours ahead of his wife. He was angry because he found her registered at the Blackstone as Mme Walska rather than Mrs. Cochran. Later he obtained a divorce. Walska had planned a counter suit but dropped it and allowed Cochran to give her a cash settlement of $200,000. (There is no record that she complained about this insensitive gesture.)

In the meantime, Harold McCormick had been granted his divorce and was free to marry the diva. For her birthday, he sent to her chateau near Versailles one of every kind of machine which International Harvester produced. When she arose on the morning of her birthday she saw "to my great surprise . . . a whole regiment of robot soldiers." But if Harold was free to marry, he did not feel ready for the step. In the summer of 1922, he entered Wesley Memorial Hospital for a secret operation by Dr. Victor D. Lespinasse, a widely known specialist in gland transplantation and the author of the aphorism that "a man is as old as his glands." The surgeon refused to confirm the exact nature of the operation but the newspapers speculated that the glands of a young man were transplanted to McCormick. It was rumored a cable had been sent to Ganna Walska notifying her of the success of the operation about a week after it was performed. McCormick then asked to have the records of his divorce settlement brought to his hospital room, indicating he was interested in determining if he was free to marry.

Harold had been interested in the operation by a European doctor. The doctor, informed of the strict regimen of exercise and diet through which Harold hoped to keep young—he claimed to be able to do fifteen handsprings in succession—had advised him it was too strenuous for a man over forty. The doctor recommended instead a gland transplantation from a younger man, an operation it was believed would prolong life as much as ten to fifteen years. While Harold looked hopefully forward to his recuperation, the newspapers sought ways to describe the operation and evade the penalties for invasion of privacy. The *Journal* suggested that McCormick, who was fifty-one, was "a leader in the Boy Scouts and wants to be a boy as long as possible." In society's drawing rooms, a paraphrase of Longfellow was making the rounds:

> Under the spreading chestnut tree,
> The village smithy stands;
> The smith a gloomy man is he;
> McCormick has his glands.

Harold McCormick married Ganna Walska in Paris, calling for her at the house Cochran had given her and riding to the mayor's office for the ceremony in the limousine which had been a present from Cochran. Floyd Gibbons, in reporting the wedding for the *Tribune*, wrote that there was some doubt about the legality of the marriage as Harold was not supposed to marry until a year after his divorce; his lawyers assured him, however, that the law meant only that he could not marry in Illinois until a year had elapsed.

The final disappointment was still ahead for the rejuvenated bridegroom. Ganna Walska, writing of the marriage later, said, "When still very young, Harold's pockets were already filled with pills of every kind. In later years his blind submission to the disciples of Aesculapius became absolute to the point of hypochondria. Unfortunately, the same idiosyncrasy led him to idolize the physical expression of love. Nature in her wisdom having fulfilled him by giving him four children had chosen for his second wife an idealist who was able to put so much value on the richness of his soul that she could not even imagine the possibility of his preferring to seek further for a gross and limited pleasure rather than being satisfied with the divine companionship of the spiritual love she was willing to share with him."

While Harold McCormick pursued Ganna Walska to Europe, Edith Rockefeller McCormick returned from Switzerland, bringing with her Edwin Krenn, a young architect she met at the psychological clinic where she studied. "It was pointed out to me that psychologically Chicago will be the greatest center in the world," she said on her arrival. "That is why I have come back here to live. That is why I have planted my roots in the soil, hoping they will grow deeper and deeper. I am vitally interested in psychology."

With Krenn, Mrs. McCormick developed a new social pattern. At 9:15

each morning, she would phone Krenn at the Drake Hotel, across the street from her home. With Krenn she mapped out the day's routine. Shortly after 1 o'clock in the afternoon, Krenn appeared in one of the two hundred suits he was acquiring and the pair had luncheon, speaking German if no other guests were present. The early afternoon was usually devoted to language tutors. At four o'clock Krenn reappeared and he and Mrs. McCormick usually had tea and then went to the movies, sometimes taking in two or three in an evening. A car with a chauffeur and footman always waited outside even if it were only a low-priced neighborhood theater. She seldom went south of the river, however, except to go to the symphony or opera. After the theater, the car took Mrs. McCormick home; unless it was unusually early Krenn did not enter the house. Two butlers always had to be on duty at the door. Usually it was only necessary to bow Mrs. McCormick in, but some evenings she would decide to rearrange the furniture, joining in with the two men at the door in moving it around, an informality she would never have permitted before her trip abroad.

Mrs. McCormick became a student of the occult and once paid $25,000 for a horoscope. She also developed interests in philosophy and poetry. "My object in the world is to think new thoughts," she told an interviewer. Occasionally she entertained on a scale approaching that of her early years in Chicago. One such occasion was the visit of Queen Marie of Rumania when Mrs. McCormick was hostess to eighty for luncheon.

One of her unfortunate ambitions was to prove to her father that she was his equal in business acumen. She formed the Edith Rockefeller McCormick Trust and installed Krenn and Edward Dato, Krenn's prep-school classmate who had followed him to Chicago, as managers. To finance the operations of the trust she pledged five million dollars of Standard Oil stocks. She sent a copy of the trust prospectus to her father, who wrote in reply: "While you are a brilliant and mature woman of great mental capacity, I cannot forget you are my own flesh and blood. Therefore, it seems to be my duty to warn you of the pitfalls and vagaries of life. I would urge you to select an honest, courageous and capable man to advise you in these affairs."

His daughter thought she had such a man in Edwin Krenn, but she refused to allow him to leave the city to inspect any of her properties. When he suggested he give her a receipt for several million dollars in bonds, she said it was not necessary, that the business would be successful only if it were built on mutual trust. She never entered the office of the trust or looked at its books. Her supervision went only far enough for her to walk past the office one day and tell Krenn to stop the salesmen from smoking. One of her plans was the creation of a dream city of millionaires on the shores of Lake Michigan which she would call Edithton. As the site for the city, she purchased more than fifteen hundred acres of land south of Kenosha,

Wisconsin, for more than a thousand dollars an acre. Four million dollars were spent in landscaping and building a yacht harbor. The town was to be designed by Krenn in the style of Atlantic City and Palm Beach with homes like the castles of Spain. To prevent deviation from the Spanish style no building could be erected without approval from Krenn. The project was stopped by the stock-market crash of 1929 which brought an abrupt end to the Edith Rockefeller McCormick Trust. After the failure of the trust, Mrs. McCormick's brother salvaged what he could of the estate, arranging for her to move to a suite at the Drake where she was given a generous annuity of $1,000 a day.

Harold McCormick and Ganna Walska, who had spent only a slight amount of time in Chicago, separated in 1931. The cost to Harold was six million dollars—one fourth of his Harvester holdings. Having given up his professional sponsorship of opera to Samuel Insull, Harold took up whistling and became proficient enough to offer a whistling recital over the radio. His name was linked with a protégée, Betty Noble, and with a motion-picture actress, Pola Negri. He was also a good friend of Baroness Violet Beatrice von Wenner, a portrait painter and harpist, who frequently accompanied him on the harp when he gave a whistling concert.

In 1932 Edith Rockefeller McCormick died in her suite at the Drake Hotel. Her former husband, who had sent her a single rose every year on her birthday, rushed from California to be at her bedside. Then it was revealed that for years Mrs. McCormick had kept a room for him at 1000 Lake Shore Drive in the hope he might return. It was a story worthy of the opera they both loved so well.

SAMUEL INSULL AS HE APPEARED WHEN HE ARRIVED IN CHICAGO

Insull Builds His Empire

By 1910 the giants were gone. Before the turn of the century William B. Ogden, John Wentworth, Cyrus McCormick and George M. Pullman had yielded to the exigencies of time. Then, after 1900, with a kind of mournful regularity, had come the deaths of Philip D. Armour in 1901, of Potter Palmer in 1902 and of Gustavus Swift in 1903. Prairie Avenue, once the dwelling place of power and wealth, became a shadow street of widows and widowers. In 1906, President William Rainey Harper of the University of Chicago and Marshall Field I, the city's patriarch after the departure of Ogden, were taken by death.

During the hours when the death of Marshall Field was expected, a Chicago business executive was dictating a letter to a friend in France. "I expect from hour to hour to hear of the death of Mr. Marshall Field," he wrote. "Long before you get this letter you will know the result of the attack of pneumonia from which Mr. Field is suffering. It seems to me very deplorable that Mr. Field's life should not be spared for years to come as he certainly is the most prominent citizen of the western country and represents the very best element of American business life." If the writer of this letter was aware that Marshall Field I was the largest taxpayer in the United States, he gave no indication of his knowledge. "I do not suppose," he continued, "his death will hardly make a ripple in business affairs. It

317 GRAND OPERA—A LIBRETTO FOR ROMANCE

certainly will not bring securities on the market as he is not considered in any way a great leader in financial affairs. While he is a great leader in his own business, in corporative affairs I look upon him as just an investor." The letter was signed "Samuel Insull." A postscript added that Insull had not seen "a single statement to change the idea that Marshall Field's career is a great example to all those who desire to become successful by legitimate business methods."

Insull's own career had been a remarkable success story. He was born in England, where his father was a moderately successful manufacturer's agent (salesman). Both his parents were temperance crusaders and for many years his mother conducted a temperance shelter. At fourteen, young Sam Insull had gone to work as an office boy; at nights he learned the Pitman shorthand system. When Insull's employer replaced him with a rich man's son who was willing to work without pay for the experience, Insull advertised in the paper and had a new job within two days. His new employer was Colonel George E. Goraud, English representative of the Thomas A. Edison Company, who was at the time in the middle of a campaign to install Edison telephones in England. When Goraud set up his first telephone exchange, Samuel Insull sat at the switchboard and thus became the first telephone operator on the eastern side of the Atlantic. (Taking care of the batteries for him was a bright, irascible youth named George Bernard Shaw.) Insull's progress in the London office was rapid; soon he was sent to America to serve as Edison's confidential secretary. A year later he was directing the inventor's business affairs, keeping his bank account, signing his checks and exercising Edison's authority through a power of attorney. When the Edison manufacturing plant was erected at Schenectady, it was Insull who supervised the construction. But when the firm was merged with the Thomas Houston Company to form General Electric, Insull's precociousness placed him under suspicion from the other partners and members of Edison's family. He was relegated to the position of second vice-president in charge of manufacturing and sales.

Insull's demotion had hardly been accomplished when he received a letter from banker Byron Smith and investment broker Edward Brewster asking him to recommend a president for the Chicago Edison Company. The Chicago Edison Company was only one of a number of firms selling electricity in the Chicago area, as four blocks was the extent of economical power transmission for the early generators. But Samuel Insull, remembering a remark of Edison's that Chicago was "one of the best centers in the country for our line of business," recommended himself for the post and was accepted.

Soon after his arrival Insull took steps to revolutionize the distribution of electric power. From General Electric he ordered the largest power generator ever built; when the factory suggested a generator with a one-thousand-kilowatt capacity, he instructed them to construct one with a five-thousand-kilowatt output. The new unit was the first in the world entirely dependent on steam turbines. When the untested generators were installed, the engineer, Frederick Sargent, tried to dissuade Insull from standing by for the tests. There was a loud scraping on the casings and Sargent was afraid of an explosion. "That's all right," Insull said. "If this thing doesn't work, I'm dead anyway." The plant did not explode; and from the moment it started to produce power, the wheels of Chicago industry were dependent on one man—Samuel Insull. At once Insull made it clear he not only wanted to sell electricity in the Chicago area; he wanted to sell all of Chicago's electricity—and more of it than any man had dreamed.

He did not hesitate to express his ambitions of establishing a monopoly although monopoly was politically unpopular. "Ours is a business that is a natural monopoly," he said with some foresight. "It matters not what the legislation of the moment may be, what the opinions of the politicians may be, what our own opinions may be; eventually all the electrical energy for a given area must be produced by one concern." He was not worried about government regulation. "If there is anything wrong with my business I want to know it," he said. "And the best way for me to know is to have a public official who has the right to look into my affairs in a position so he can employ the highest class of talent to help him." He conceded that "regulation interferes with arbitrary action, and that is very unpleasant to a man of positive character. . . . On the other hand I think it is very good discipline. One of the great disadvantages the world over is that the human being when he is working for a little larger corporation or business than the average man in the community works for gets very much 'sot up.' I often think I have to take that criticism myself." And he added, "If public regulation fails, public ownership ought to come."

There was no reason during the first quarter of the twentieth century to think that private ownership under Samuel Insull was going to fail. His plans went beyond the city limits of Chicago. In 1902 he took over a group of struggling companies which provided sporadic electric service to the communities along the North Shore; many of the towns had service only from dusk to twilight and were forced to burn candles or lamps during frequently recurring power failures. Insull joined these companies together in the Public Service Company of Northern Illinois, extended his power lines to small communities in nearby Lake County, which had previously been without any service, and in two years was providing the entire area with dependable electrical power twenty-four hours a day. In Chicago, he persuaded the street railway companies and elevated railroads that it was cheaper to buy power from him than to manufacture it themselves. To convince the streetcar lines they would be saving money, he had an analysis made of their power costs and his own; he then laid it on the president's desk without a word of comment or salesmanship. All the transit systems were operating on temporary franchises, but Insull was bold enough to spend eleven million dollars for plants to supply them power. He had no guarantee they would be permanent customers except his own conviction he could sell them electricity cheaper than they could make it themselves.

It was soon an accepted tenet of Chicago business life that Samuel Insull was the man to get things done. When the Chicago, Aurora and Elgin suburban railroad went into bankruptcy, Insull took it over; he converted it to electrical power and soon was running it at a profit. He did the same for the Chicago North Shore and Milwaukee Railway and the Chicago, South Shore and South Bend Railroad when those lines collapsed into bankruptcy. To the North Shore he added a special Skokie Valley Route which cut the time of a trip to Milwaukee and provided a close link to the city for the new suburbs which grew up along the right of way. The transportation industry gave him two of its prized Coffin medals for the most efficiently operated electric lines in the United States. Like William B. Ogden, who built his first rail lines to the West away from the centers of population, Insull was building his power and rail lines to serve the cities of the future. It was this far-sightedness that led John T. Flynn to call Samuel Insull the commercial pioneer of electric power just as Thomas Alva Edison was its scientific pioneer.

The gains were not won easily. Insull, boasting that he had never touched a drop of liquor, found little time for social life. His seeming infallibility gave determination the quality of ruthlessness; he was arbitrary and expected to be obeyed rather than consulted. His days began nearly as early as those of the meat packers who rushed to the stockyards to buy cattle before the less ambitious merchants were awake. Insull's secretary was under orders to pick up the mail at the post office shortly after 6 o'clock in the morning; Insull himself arrived at 7:10 A.M. He expected to find waiting on his desk an operating report of the previous night for each of his power plants with an account and explanation of any power failures. The banker, the investment broker, or the stockholder who called up to inquire why his lights had failed was always able to get a detailed explanation from Insull himself; it was the shrewdest kind of salesmanship. By 8:45 Insull expected all the mail to be sorted and on his desk. He read first any clippings about himself from the newspapers. Though he was never friendly with the reporters, hated to have his picture taken and was curt with photographers, he was conscious that his customers formed their impression of him through what they read in the newspapers. For this reason he always took care to inform himself as to what the papers were saying about him—though he never admitted the fact. Any gifts in the mail were returned unopened. "Don't accept anything from anybody," he told his aides. Even a box of cigars was not acceptable.

The day was usually filled with meetings and conferences at which Insull kept his own notes by scribbling in his Pitman shorthand. Later these notes would be given to his secretary for transcription, one of the secretary's qualifications being an ability to transcribe the uncommon Pitman script. On Sundays Insull climbed into his electric car—later a Buick—and headed for the country to inspect new routes for power lines or possible sites for electrical generating plants. He had to see the physical expression of his plans in order to comprehend them. Though his ability to show a profit on all his ventures had given him a reputation as a financier, he had little interest in balance sheets or columns of figures. When he spoke it was not in terms of costs but with a map on the table where he could trace the physical growth of his expanding power and transportation companies.

It was a lonely life and not entirely satisfactory. Insull was self-conscious about his lack of a family and patiently looked forward to the day he would find a woman who could provide him with a son and heir for the industrial empire he was creating. When asked about his antecedents, he would only say, "My family tree is so short I can't tell. All that I know is that my parents were good Presbyterians." Typical of the prejudices of the day was a widely held opinion that Insull's tremendous successes were due to his "Jewish blood." To this Insull replied, "If I have some Jewish blood, I should not be ashamed. Some of England's greatest men were Jews." Then he met Gladys Wallis, a dark-eyed, white-skinned actress known as the "Pocket Venus" because of her exquisite features. This was the kind of perfection he had been seeking. When Gladys Wallis came to Chicago in *The Squire of Dames* with John Drew and Maude Adams and young Ethel Barrymore, Insull began a persistent stage-door courtship. He wooed the actress with the same intensity that characterized all his business dealings, even following her to New York, where she lived at Helen Windsor's theatrical boarding house with Maude Adams, Ethel Barrymore, Minnie Dupré, Edna Wallace (Hopper) and other promising young actresses. While Insull was proposing marriage, Gladys Wallis was made the star of her own stock company, but the power magnate persuaded her to relinquish her theatrical ambitions to share the unofficial throne from which he ruled Chicago. About a year after their marriage, a son, Samuel, Jr., was born and Insull turned with renewed fervor to the establishment of a durable inheritance for his family.

Chicago continued to regard Insull as the man to rely upon when there were big tasks to be done. In 1917, when the United States entered World War I, Insull was named by Governor Frank O. Lowden as chairman of the Illinois State Council of Defense. His performance was unique. The defense groups in other states spent sums of from $100,000 to $500,000 in carrying out their duties. Insull, given only a modest appropriation of $50,000, spent none of it and returned the state a profit of $300,000. He issued a patriotic cookbook which became the envy of publishers by selling 300,000 copies and showing a profit of $15,000. He made $150,000 by selling seed corn. People said that if he had been running the war he could have made it pay a dividend. A contemporary biographer wrote that Insull displayed "financial ability of a high order and inspired the confidence of bankers and investors. As a result, his securities are becoming widely known and are sought after in all parts of the investing world."

No additional assignment was too large for Insull to accept, although he was already the most powerful man in Chicago. After the war, the People's Gas Light & Coke Company was completely disorganized. Hundreds of thousands of Chicagoans were getting the wrong gas bills every month and only a fraction of the bills were being collected. The directors asked Samuel Insull to take over; he accepted the presidency, subjected the company to a drastic reorganization, straightened out the billing department and launched a typical Insull program to replace the antiquated gas plants with modern equipment. In a short time the company was prosperous.

The size of Insull's accomplishments was to be measured in the circumstance that Chicago, a city of two million people, was in many ways as much of a one-man town as the community erected by George M. Pullman. Samuel Insull provided it with its gas, furnished its electricity and ran the elevated system and suburban railroads which carried a high proportion of its commuters to and from their work. As Edgar Lee Masters dramatically pointed out, "with a flick of his hand he could plunge the city into darkness or in cold." Still Insull was not satisfied. He continued to be, as he had expressed himself nearly a quarter of a century before, "a great bull on Chicago." In 1926, two decades before the city was willing to take on the job, Insull was pressing for permission to build a passenger subway. He was not interested in owning the new transit facilities as Yerkes might have been; all he asked was a permit to build and operate it. "If the city is unable to [build it] and will give me an ordinance on which I can finance it, I will undertake the job," he told the City Council. The aldermen turned him down.

By the end of the war, Insull's horizons had expanded far beyond Chicago. His companies were operating in eleven states and furnishing power to 385 cities of which little more than half were in Illinois. He was always looking for new customers and wise enough to see that eventually women would be the greatest users of his electrical power. He outlined and put into effect a broad public-relations program, furnished speakers and literature to women's clubs on electrical living and in two years distributed more than five million pamphlets and broadsides.

Because of his visual approach to a problem, Insull's greatest interest was in the firms which served the Chicago area. The other businesses and the holding company of Middle West Utilities, which served to combine them into a single operation, were entrusted in large part to his brother, Martin. To Martin was also left most of the responsibility for arranging the financing with the bond houses which made possible the acquisition of these properties in distant states. Martin, who was often photographed in English riding clothes and who raised fine horses on his farm near Highland Park, was not popular with Chicagoans. Most of them distrusted him because of his pronounced preference for the English way of doing things; it was frequently pointed out that Samuel Insull had become an American citizen in 1896 but Martin never took the step. There was no one who dared criticize Martin to his brother, for Samuel resented a slur on Martin more than any attack upon himself. Yet one reason for Martin's rapid expansion of Middle West Utilities was to escape the shadows thrown by the reflected glory of Samuel Insull's name. It was this jealousy, of which Samuel Insull was unaware, that provided the flaw in his plans for a family dynasty.

When the personal direction of Samuel Insull was absent there was a tendency for trouble to develop. He was in Europe in 1926 when Frank Smith was running against William McKinley, a downstate utility owner, for the Republican nomination to the United States Senate. Insull's subordinates and Martin were eager to defeat McKinley because of a personal feud between the McKinley and Insull families. A cable was sent to Insull asking for a decision on how to defeat McKinley; Insull sent a reply giving Martin and the others carte blanche. Under the delusion that money was all-powerful, the aides dumped $125,000 into Smith's campaign. He won the nomination but his victory in the fall elections was nullified when he was turned back at the Senate door because of the excessive amount of money spent in his behalf. The incident gave Illinois the besmirched distinction of having two senators turned down because their victories were bought; Senator William Lorimer had been expelled from the Senate on much the same grounds a little more than ten years earlier.

Much has been written of the dealings of Insull with the Chicago politicians on whom he bestowed great quantities of money. Like many of the Chicago businessmen who preceded him, he erroneously considered a politician an item for sale on the same terms as any other commodity. There is a legend that Insull was contemptuous of politicians. It would be nearer the truth to say they were among his few friends. He dined often with the family of Roger Sullivan, the Democratic boss. Dinners with politicians provided an important part of his social life. Most of the time he came alone.

That ambitious men do not always make satisfactory husbands had been represented theatrically so often that Gladys Wallis must have been aware of her risk when she married Chicago's fast-rising young utility executive. By 1926, there were signs she felt the risk had been a poor one. She lived on a five-thousand-acre estate in a $125,000 Italian villa near Libertyville. A sliding roof which rolled back to reveal the canopy of stars on summer nights was little consolation as she read of the rise to theatrical stardom of her companions at Helen Windsor's theatrical boarding house. Walking through the baronial grounds of the estate with its artificial lagoons, monstrous goldfish, or pinning up the ribbons of Insull's prize Brown Swiss cattle or Suffolk Punch draft horses soon palled. Margaret Bird Insull (Gladys Wallis was her stage name) dreamed of hot, crowded dressing rooms and the discomfort of grease paint and quick changes in the wings. She told her husband she wanted to return to the stage. She had faithfully kept her bargain to relinquish her career. Her only stage appearances had been in 1905 in an amateur performance of Edmond Rostand's *Les Romanesques* in Winnetka and in 1908 when she gave a reading of Maeterlinck's *Pélléas* and *Mélisande*—to the accompaniment of what the papers called soulful music—to the Friday Club.

When Mrs. Insull announced her return to the stage, it was twenty-five years after Samuel, Jr., had been born; Chicagoans, reading of the role Mrs. Insull had selected, wondered if she had forgotten to count them. She would play, she said, Lady Teazle, the lively, innocent country maiden in Sheridan's *The School for Scandal* who marries a man old enough to be her grandfather. Insull, disapproving of his wife's plans, nonetheless consented to them, hoping that the magic of a stage success might restore some of the warmth which had disappeared from his relationship with his wife. Always

MRS. SAMUEL INSULL IN *The School for Scandal*

one to guard against failure, Insull suggested that his wife appear first in a series of charity performances for St. Luke's Hospital. He guaranteed the hospital $125,000 from a two weeks' run at the Illinois Theater. On opening night boxes went for $500 to $1,000 and no seat sold for less than $5. In two weeks the play netted the hospital $140,000, a sum which probably caused several other theater managers to be hospitalized with envy.

The local success of the play prompted Mrs. Insull to take it to Broadway where it had a short run. It then returned to the Selwyn in Chicago for another four weeks. Tasting triumph, Mrs. Insull leased the Studebaker Theater for five years and announced plans for the establishment of a repertory company in Chicago. After appearing in *The Runaway Road*, she retired to the role of director and producer, presenting *Heartbreak House* and *Mr. Pim Passes By* before she was forced to announce the closing of the theater. Her remarks on terminating her plans for the Studebaker were more familiar to theatrical managers than her two weeks' profit of $140,000. "I have reluctantly reached the belief that my ambition was misdirected, my plan a mistake and my money wasted," she said with commendable directness. "I'm not crying; indeed, I feel proud that I'm quitting with a laugh! I've learned that Chicago is not a marketplace for the raw materials of a repertoire theater such as I hoped to make of the Studebaker. I can easily have scenery painted here and properties manufactured here. But dramatists do not send their plays here to be read and actors do not walk Michigan Boulevard looking for Chicago engagements." Yet there was a trace of permanence even in this Insull failure; it was Mrs. Insull who persuaded the Theater Guild to start its touring subscription series with a Chicago engagement that opened with Alfred Lunt and Lynn Fontanne in *Arms and the Man*. Insull, who underwrote the costs of the engagement, made a profit on it, a token of success from the battery boy named Shaw who had proved so inefficient at the Edison Company switchboard in London he had been discharged.

During the twenties, Insull no longer had to sell securities in his companies. Customers fought for the privilege of sharing in his money-making magic. He continued to concentrate upon his Chicago interests. Mornings he spent at the People's Gas Light & Coke Company and afternoons in his offices at the Commonwealth Edison Building. The stock market, buoyant about every issue, could not be restrained in its enthusiasm for Insull. In 1922, when the country was still recovering from the post-World War I slump, Commonwealth Edison shot up to $122 a share. Royal Munger, then a financial reporter on the *Daily News*, called on Insull to ask what favorable factors Insull believed were responsible for the advance: "I will not say one word that will send that stock a point higher," Insull snapped. "It is too high now. That is more than the stock is worth." One of the privileges of owning Insull stock was that it carried rights to buy more Insull stock whenever additional shares were issued. Insull also had a preferred list of sixteen hundred Chicagoans who were permitted to buy new issue of stocks below the market price. To those who objected to this favoritism, Insull had a blunt answer: "It is not worth more." Even when it was known that those on the preferred list were getting stock for $12, the same shares were bringing $30 on the market. The plush carpet to Insull's office was being worn thin by people of every kind, all seeking market tips to make a clean-up.

Perhaps Insull's most audacious act was to accept the responsibility for making a paying proposition of Chicago opera after the "blaze of glory" season directed by Mary Garden. Before giving up the opera, Harold McCormick had generously paid all its bills and made it a gift of scenery and other properties worth approximately a million dollars. When Insull was given control he formed a committee willing to pledge $500,000 a year for five years to support opera. He also issued a statement that "no contract will be signed by any general director or business manager or any other individual from this day on. Every contract in the future must bear the signature of the chairman of the finance committee and one member of the Board of Directors. We will spend our own money." There were some objections to such a businesslike approach. Many of those who had a professional connection with the opera subscribed to the view of Oscar Hammerstein that opera should be run not as a business "but as a disease." Insull did not think opera stars would object to dealing with him. If the singers "want to stay at home and receive stage money," he said, "they may do so, but they'll have to come here to get real money.... One cannot ignore the dollar without getting into trouble." It was recognizably the Chicago approach.

Then, in a curious way, history began to repeat itself. Insull, like Uranus H. Crosby and Ferdinand Wythe Peck, conceived the idea of combining an opera house with an office building, convinced that office rents would pay for the opera. Insull attributed the fact Peck's scheme was not working at the Auditorium to the antiquated building. He made up his mind to erect a new home for opera on the banks of the river at the western edge of the business district, an area which the Chicago Plan Commission had designated as the site of a great Chicago civic center. The fact that not a single building rose in the area to confirm the Plan Commission's hopes did not deter Insull; he liked to be a generation ahead. He dispatched a group of architects to Europe to study the opera houses there. After they returned, he announced plans for a forty-five-story, twenty-million-dollar office building, opera house and theater on Madison Street near the river. The financing had that clarity and boldness typical of all Insull enterprises.

GRAND FOYER AT THE CIVIC
OPERA HOUSE

He sold ten million dollars' worth of stock among the "music lovers of the city" and gave the Metropolitan Life Insurance Company a mortgage on the remainder. If the entire income of the building had gone to wipe out the debt, the property would have been fully owned by the opera in about twenty-five years. Eventually, Insull envisioned a twenty- to thirty-million-dollar property, debt free, with its income supporting the opera. To make the task easier, he made a gift of the $300,000 in stock he had purchased to the opera company. All that was necessary, he told audiences throughout Chicago, was "reasonable foresight and management such as you would give to any other business." Opera was also to be democratic. It was one of the few points on which he agreed with Mary Garden, who said that the supporters of opera ought to be found in the telephone directory rather than the social register. In the new opera house, Insull said, boxes would be only at the rear. Society people who wished to wear their diamond tiaras and fine clothes would not be allowed to detract from the spectacle on the stage. It was his opportunity to put Chicago society in what he considered its proper place.

The building went up with amazing speed. The first ground was dug in February of 1928; by November 4, 1929, the opera house was ready for its grand opening—despite such a touch of local color as the theft of a large tapestry worth $4,000 from the stage. The opening night, with Rosa Raisa singing the traditional *Aida* was one that "disarmed criticism," according to a helpless critic. Samuel Insull stood in the foyer and greeted as many of the opening-night crowd as he could. The *Times* said Insull and Stanley Field had done everything that day to get the opera house in order but "dust off the seats," adding that "rich and poor mingled in the milling mob before the doors of opera gone democratic." James O'Donnell Bennett of the *Tribune* called the cavernous auditorium a "jewel casket"; he then switched metaphors to describe the hydraulic mechanism necessary to lift the enormous curtain as on the scale of machinery in the locks of the Panama Canal. Even a city which worshipped big figures found it hard to visualize an elevator seventy-five feet high which carried the scenery to storerooms beneath the stage. Mary Garden was not to be as impressed. She said "it wasn't like an opera house but more like a convention hall" and complained there was absolutely no communication with the public.

The opening of the opera house, just a few days before Insull's seventieth birthday, was the climax of his career. He was not as rich as either John D. Rockefeller or Henry Ford, but through his subsidiary companies he was the most powerful businessman in America. He sat on the boards of eighty-five companies, was chairman of the board for sixty-five, president of eleven and through his holding companies controlled six thousand power units in thirty-two states. With investments worth only twenty million dollars, he controlled a group of properties worth four hundred million. And still bankers competed for the privilege of extending him credit.

Insull had hoped that the opening of the new opera house would serve as the closing chapter of the forty years in which he had dominated the Chicago scene. There were many signs that he planned to abdicate his power, give much of it over to his son and play the role of elder statesman and patron of the arts. This plan was knocked askew less than a month before the grand opening by the crash of the stock market on Black Friday. Insull decided to stay on until economic conditions were more stable.

Insull's principal concern was to keep the price of Middle West and his holding companies high enough to cover the loans at the banks which had been necessary to finance Martin's extensive acquisitions. A few years before, Insull had been so seriously ill that he had gone to Arizona for a long vacation to recuperate. Returning, he found Middle West in such a groggy condition that he reorganized it, arranged new financing and left it with ten million dollars in the bank. He left soon afterward for a trip to Europe; when his boat docked a cable came from Martin asking for authority to raise fifty million dollars more which he asserted Middle West needed. Insull did not answer his brother, but sent a cable to his son, whom he had named vice-chairman of Middle West. "If you and Uncle Martin want to fail, do what you want," he wrote. "I am only an old man." In a few years he was to be fighting desperately to prevent that failure.

The Insull properties weathered the early years of the depression better than most companies. The banks still had money to lend Insull, although they refused to take a chance on the tax warrants of the city of Chicago. "Do you mean to tell me that the credit of the city of Chicago is not as good as that of Samuel Insull?" an alderman demanded at a public hearing. "Exactly that," replied Silas Strawn, who was on the witness stand. Like William B. Ogden, Samuel Insull was a big man to Chicagoans.

There were those outside Chicago who saw the weaknesses in Samuel Insull's position. One of these was Cyrus Eaton, the Cleveland financier, who had learned Insull was borrowing and buying heavily to keep up the values of his stocks. Eaton knew the stock-market game and Insull didn't. Slowly Eaton accumulated a large holding of Insull stocks, buying them when the stock fell and throwing just enough of the shares back on the market when the price rose to test Insull's strength. When he saw that Insull was committed to keeping up the price of his stocks, he showed his hand: unless Insull took over his holdings at a price far above that of the market, Eaton would dump the stocks, force the price down and put Insull in a position where the banks would call his loans and force him into bankruptcy. Insull was trapped; he had to pay Eaton forty million dollars for the stocks to keep them off the market. The move was that of a man playing desperately for time in the hope that normal conditions would return; but, as he was to learn, normal conditions as he understood them would never return.

Despite Insull's purchases, the values of the stocks continued to slip past the point where they would cover the bank loans. The banks, in their cautious but ruthless way, stepped in to take control, intending to leave Insull as their administrator. But there was one more revelation to come; it brought the Insull dream of empire and dynasty crashing to the ground. Martin Insull had taken more than half a million dollars of company funds to cover the margin on his personal brokerage account; and the man who had signed the check to give him that money was Samuel Insull.

On July 5, 1932, Samuel Insull sat in his paneled office in the Commonwealth Edison Building waiting to receive the directors of corporations who for years had done no more than nod assent to his every idea. There was a long directors' table in the room and from early in the morning until late in the afternoon groups formed, dispersed and formed again around the table. Secretaries carrying the bulky minute books of the various corporations hurried in and out of the room. At the head of the table sat Samuel Insull; near him was his son, his head erect and face taut, struggling to control his emotions over the collapse of his father's world. In an outer room the newspapers kept a death watch, the reporters noting that some of the directors had tears in their eyes as they left the room. As the meetings progressed, Samuel Insull resigned from every one of his positions and turned all his assets and those of his family over to the directors.

After the last directors' meeting, Insull asked his secretary to get his wife on the phone, adding "Do not disturb her if she is resting." When the call was put through, he said, "Well, it is all over. . . . It was a very tiring day. After dinner we will take a drive. Good-bye." At the table an office aide blurted, "You will be back in six months, Mr. Insull. Your stockholders will demand it." But the white-haired man at the phone could be ruthless with himself as well. "No," he said, "I will not come back. I am through." On the way out, he stopped to say a word to the newspapermen, his traditional enemies. "Here I go, gentlemen," he said, "after fifty years a man without a job."

The crash of the Insull stocks closed a Chicago bank and brought ruin to hundreds of small stock owners, many of whom had been pressured into buying stocks during the final days when Insull was using gas and electrical repairmen, clerks and even janitors as salesmen of his stocks in order to keep their value high. His opera stars suffered with the rest. Augusta Lenska, a retired contralto, attempted to commit suicide by throwing herself in front of a streetcar. Only shrewd Mary Garden lost no money. "I never accepted favors from Mr. Insull, which turned out to be rather fortunate, didn't it?" she said. Those who had doubled their fortunes with Insull stocks were often most bitter at the man they considered infallible.

SAMUEL INSULL AT THE HEIGHT OF HIS POWER

There were many explanations for the Insull crash. Royal Munger, in the most dispassionate analysis, said that if Martin Insull "had spent less time on Pullman trains [that is, in expanding into all parts of the country] and more studying figures he would still be on top." As it was, Munger said, Martin's lack of sound business principles produced results "for both himself and his stockholders [that] can only be called ghastly." Much of the blame was of course Samuel Insull's, who was probably not familiar with Lord Acton's comments on the corruptive possibilities of absolute power but was just as much a victim of that corruption.

More than three hundred thousand stockholders could not be deprived of their savings without a demand for retribution. A series of charges were brought against Samuel Insull, Martin Insull, Samuel Insull, Jr., and a group of executives for various alleged illegal manipulations. In addition, Cook County charged the brothers with embezzlement because of the use of the money for Martin's private stock accounts. In the midst of the investigations which preceded the filing of the charges, Samuel Insull slipped quietly out of the country for Europe and Martin fled to Canada. The flight was the least creditable act of Insull's life. It would have been better, a newspaper editorialist reminded him, to remember the words of Plato: It is better for the wrong-doer to be punished than to escape punishment. It is less evil to suffer wrong than to do wrong.

The story strays then from Chicago to Paris and Greece. After many legal maneuvers, Insull lost his asylum in that country and fled ignominiously in disguise, being finally apprehended in a ship off the port of Istanbul. He was brought back to trial on a series of charges and in every case acquitted. The jurors at the final trial told reporters they had known what their verdict would be six weeks earlier, even before Insull took the stand. The Chicago *Times*, exuberant over the promise of President Franklin D. Roosevelt's New Deal, summed the verdict up: "Insull and his fellow defendants—not guilty; the old order—guilty. That was the Insull defense and the jury agreed with it." Mrs. Insull, reunited with her husband in his moment of tribulation, paid him her own compliment. "He has been a great sport through it all," she said. "It is character that counts and not money."

John T. Flynn and other reporters converging on the scene of the titan's debacle found it difficult to explain the absence of bitterness toward the man who had wiped out the savings of so many. The directors of his corporations had only been dissuaded on grounds of public policy from voting him a pension of $100,000 a year; he was given instead an employe's pension of $18,000 annually. The answer, perhaps, lay in a letter written by a stockholder to Edward Brewster when Insull had reorganized Middle West utilities. "It reminds me of some of Shakespeare's plays," he wrote. "No matter how many times you read it, each succeeding time finds new beauties. . . . I take off my hat to the geniuses (or genius) that constructed that set-up. . . . We built better than either of us knew, I am sure, when we hitched our wagon to the Insull stars. All we have needed was faith and not understanding. We let Sam do it and I must say he did a mighty fine job. . . . I see no more reason for selling Commonwealth Edison at $400 than I did at $300. . . . I am still inclined to pin my faith on that genius of faith, Mr. Samuel Insull, who still commands us to 'Sail on, sail on, and on!' "

Samuel Insull's great journey, as he realized after his trial, was nearly over. Chicago saw little of him. He spent much time in Europe. In 1938, while walking across a subway platform in Paris, he suffered a heart attack and died. It was some hours before police were able to identify him as the man who bossed Chicago with an arbitrary rule, built the dynamos which gave it power and laced the countryside with the 125,000-volt lines that formed the life arteries of the Midwest.

The Paris police report before Insull had been identified was worth quoting:

> An unidentified man was found in a state of collapse on the platform of the Tuileries subway station near the Place de la Concorde. He was neatly dressed in a gray suit with red stripes, wore a brown felt hat and had 7 francs, 7 centimes [about 85 cents] in his pocket. He was of medium size with white hair. He had no identification papers but the initials "S. I." were on his handkerchiefs and underclothing. Agent 2023.

A man, after all, like any other man.

PART FIVE *The New Chicago*

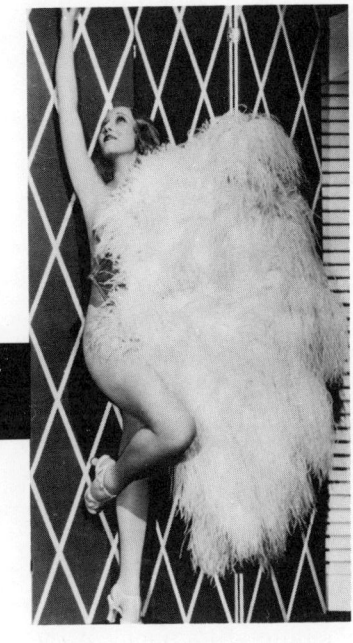

SALLY RAND with her fans at A Century of Progress

More Than a Century of Progress

THE effects of the Depression fell as heavily upon the city government as upon Samuel Insull. The municipal government was bankrupt, and the banks refused to extend it credit. In 1930, there was no money to pay Chicago's policemen, firemen, schoolteachers, janitors or clerks. But even with these formidable problems, the city refused to abandon plans to celebrate the one hundredth anniversary of the incorporation of Chicago as a village.

The originator of the new exposition was Rufus C. Dawes, who first advanced the idea in 1923. The theme of the fair, he suggested, should be a demonstration of what mankind had been able to accomplish through a mastery and understanding of nature, a subject dramatically demonstrated by the phenomenal growth of Chicago on swampland obviously not intended as a dwelling place. Plans for the fair, inaugurated under Mayor Dever's administration, were temporarily abandoned when Mayor Thompson returned for a third term in City Hall. As soon as the city accustomed itself to living with Big Bill again, the plans for the fair were reactivated and a corporation organized to stage a fair to be known as "A Century of Progress." The organizers specified that the fair was to be built without any taxation or federal, state, city or county subsidy. It was to be wholly a project of the unofficial government of Chicago businessmen to which all matters of importance traditionally were entrusted. Though several members of the committee lost their businesses and their fortunes in the stock market crash, they did not waver in their intention of celebrating A Century of Progress.

The fair, located on more than four hundred acres of artificially created land bordering the lake, was opened on April 29, 1933. Appropriately, it was the scientists rather than the more customary politicians who dominated the opening day. The most spectacular feat was the turning on of the lights at the fair with energy from the rays of the star Arcturus, focused on photoelectric cells in a series of astronomical observatories and then transformed into electrical energy that was transmitted to Chicago. Arcturus had been chosen because its distance of 240 trillion miles most nearly corresponded to forty light years; those at the fair liked to think the varicolored incandescent lights and miles of neon tubing at the 1933 exposition were set aglow by light that had been leaving Arcturus at the moment the Columbian Exposition was opened forty years earlier. Chicago, having only a brief century of its own history, sought by this gesture to identify itself with the infinite age of the universe.

The secretary of the new fair formed a closer link with the past. He was Daniel H. Burnham, Jr., whose father had been responsible for the architectural splendor of the 1893 fair. But the classical motif of that earlier exposition was replaced in 1933 by the severe modern architecture that had developed from the ideas of the Chicago school of half a century before. The philosophy of Louis Sullivan that "form follows function" was brilliantly expressed in a series of stark white buildings set with geometrical precision along the Lake Michigan shoreline and as purely functional as the machinery on display within their walls. Rufus C. Dawes, who had been elected president of the fair, described it as "the spontaneous expression of the pride of citizenship of Chicago." The exposition illustrated, he said, "the dependence of modern industry upon scientific research"—and provided evidence of man's achievements in the realm of physical science —"proofs of his power to prevail over the perils that beset him." The words were an echo of those of the founders of the Interstate Industrial Exposition. The abstract matters of esthetics or art had little interest for the leaders of Chicago. They were practical men, proud of their accomplishments in making knowledge useful and in finding profitable applications for the discoveries of science.

Some of the exhibits at A Century of Progress were reminiscent of the

Columbian Exposition. Among them were the partial reconstruction of a walled city of China, a golden-roofed lama temple from Jehol, a picturesque nunnery of Uxmal representing the zenith of Mayan culture and a teahouse from Japan. Other displays, such as the bathysphere that took William Beebe 2,200 feet beneath the surface of the ocean and the aluminum globe in which Auguste Picard soared 54,000 feet into the stratosphere, were awesome symbols of the daring exploits that were pushing out the frontiers of science. Other unusual attractions included an operating diamond mine in conjunction with a million-dollar display of diamonds, and a mechanical robot who gave lectures on diet that were illustrated by the workings of his own illuminated interior.

It was at A Century of Progress that Americans first became knowledgeable about dinosaurs and other prehistoric monsters. The world as it might have been a million years ago was represented in a series of dioramas before which visitors with no interest in archeological skeletons gazed with fascination at life-sized reconstructions of the hairy mammoth, the pterodactyl, the massive brontosaurus, triceratops and dimetrodon. Chicago had come a long way from the zeuglodon that once awed visitors in Colonel Wood's Museum.

The Transportation Building, its roof supported by a series of fingerlike skyhooks, was one of the dominant buildings of the fair. The exhibits of America's largest automobile manufacturers underscored the accomplishments of the engineers in transforming the country into a nation on wheels. A pageant, "Wings of a Century," recounted the advances of transportation from the days of prehistory. Against the ever-changing blue, gray or green backdrop of Lake Michigan, actors on an open stage reenacted the principal dramas in man's attempt to conquer the spaces of the earth. The pageant had a special meaning for Chicago, for it was from the city's place as a transportation center that Chicago derived its existence. First had come the Illinois and Michigan Canal, establishing Chicago as the port at the junction of America's two great inland waterways. The canal and lake traffic were followed by the engines and boxcars of the railroads; whether the trains ran south, north, east or west, Chicago was their terminal, the greatest rail center in the world. Finally had come the airplanes. Chicago became the stopover point for those who traveled by air as it had been the junction for those who journeyed by rail and water. Three times within a century one form of transportation had superseded another; yet Chicago remained for them all the crossroads of America.

Dominating the fair was an effort to anticipate another form of transportation. It was the Sky Ride, whose two gaunt towers stretched sixty-four stories high and were connected at the twenty-fourth floor by cables from which "rocket cars" were suspended. Before the possibilities of air travel were fully appreciated, it was believed the cities of the future would be joined by such suspended monorails. Although the phenomenal development of aviation outmoded such transportation, the Sky Ride gave those at the fair a view of the city as impressive as the one their parents had been able to obtain from the "bridge on an axle" that George Ferris designed for the exposition of 1893.

No Chicago fair would have been complete without a Midway. The Midway of the 1933 fair was less extensive in area but equally as provocative of comment as its predecessor of 1893. The Streets of Paris replaced the Streets of Cairo as the popular attraction; instead of Little Egypt, there was Sally Rand. Sally was an unemployed silent film actress who burst unexpectedly on A Century of Progress in the role of Lady Godiva astride a white horse. When this sensational bid for employment failed, she gave up her horse to buy two ostrich feather fans—on credit, she insisted later—and persuaded a manager to hire her as a fan dancer. She needed no help in publicizing her act. She first attracted attention by announcing she would not wear clothes because they interfered with the movement of the fans. The inspiration for her dance, she said, came from a childhood memory of "white herons flying in the moonlight" above her grandfather's farm. Whatever the inspiration, it was a profitable one. By the end of the summer she was drawing $3,000 a week and had all but pushed into obscurity the scientific theme that was intended to dominate the fair.

There were several attempts to subdue Sally by making her don some clothing. Judge Joseph B. David was asked to issue an injunction forbidding "lewd and lascivious dances" in the Streets of Paris attraction. The judge, indignantly remarking that "some people would like to put pants on horses," listened unsympathetically as an attorney charged that "one woman dances with nothing but a pair of fans about her. It's disgraceful!"

The judged interrupted. "Honi soit qui mal y pense," he said. "This court holds no brief for the prurient or ignorant. Let them walk out if they wish. If you ask me, they are just a lot of boobs come to see a woman wiggle with a fan or without fig leaves. But we have the boobs and we have a right to cater to them." Denying the injunction, Judge David dismissed court with the comment that "The Streets of Paris could starve to death for all of me. I go where there is a good glass of beer."

The moralists had little luck in imposing restrictions on the Midway until the city's mayor, Edward J. Kelly, visited the Oriental Village—presumably in quest of a good glass of beer. The mayor, according to the following day's newspapers, turned a "bashful pink" at seeing a number of seductive oriental houris clad in "purely hypothetical costumes." As quoted by the reporters, he ordered that the "nudity be denuded" and instructed all managers to make their performers put on clothes. Sally

Rand, after a thirty-five-minute argument with her manager, reluctantly appeared in a transparent gauze costume. Jack Hardy, production manager of the Oriental Village, sought to deprecate the importance of the mayor's order. "We're going mostly on class, not nudity," he said. "I don't think the mayor is a reliable weather vane when it comes to art and morality."

Texas Guinan, who was running a night club called the Pirate Ship, took a more realistic view. Protesting that the fair officials were "trying to put fun and pleasure on a business schedule," she closed her night club and left the fair. (Tragically, after she left, she became one of the victims of an epidemic of amoebic dysentery that marred the first summer of the fair.) Only Judge David continued in his role of defender of the arts. In September, he issued an injunction restraining the South Park Board (which had jurisdiction over the fair grounds) from draping artificial flowers over the bosom of a living model in the representation of Manet's painting, Olympia, in a peep show in the Streets of Paris. Noting that the model's bosom was already shielded by her strategically placed hand, Judge David warned, "I'll issue the injunction—but heaven help the lady if she moves her hand." As far as can be ascertained, she never did.

The well-publicized arguments over the morality of the fair's attractions increased rather than diminished the public's interest. By the end of the summer more than twenty-two million people had visited the fair grounds and it was decided to extend the exposition for another year. "However," said General Manager Lenox R. Lohr, "we believe that next year the pendulum will swing to finer things." He announced that a concentration of villages—Swiss, Black Forest, English, Early American, Venetian, Spanish, Irish and Tunisian—would replace much of the 1933 Midway. The Streets of Paris, an official statement promised, would be "more elaborate and more accurately representative of Parisian atmosphere than it was in 1933." In any case, the fair avoided the courts while another sixteen million visitors were drawn to the more substantial evidences of A Century of Progress.

The South Park Board, prohibited by Judge David from acting as moral censor at the fair, made its way into the headlines with an order prohibiting members of the Chicago Artists Equity from displaying nudes in their annual outdoor show in Grant Park. The board was compelled to withdraw its order, however, when a public protest was organized under the direction of Mrs. Frank G. Logan, wife of the honorary president of the Art Institute and one of the sponsors of the show. Though Mrs. Logan was tolerant of nudes, she was less satisfied with certain other forms of artistic expression. In particular, she disliked modernism. She was one of the principal benefactors of the Art Institute and with her husband had endowed an annual prize for work shown there. After a series of prizes had gone to paintings employing unconventional techniques or perspectives, the Logans unhappily confided to their friends that there had been "a miscarriage of artistic justice." When the Logan Prize went to Francis Chapin's *Pink House*, Mrs. Logan noted unhappily that it was drawn "on a bias." In 1935, when a jury picked Doris Lee's whimsical *Thanksgiving* as winner of the Logan Prize, Mrs. Logan publicly expressed her dissatisfaction. "The paintings [in the show] are trash," she said. "I am incensed. After a visit to a museum one should have a glow, should be uplifted. But a sane person leaves the exhibit feeling the art unleashes the jitters or delirium tremens. I defy anyone to find more than six or eight normal pictures in the whole show."

Kate Buckingham, one of the five or six most generous donors of funds to the institute and a woman whose philanthropies included the Buckingham Fountain with its multicolored water displays on the lakefront, echoed the views expressed by Mrs. Logan. "I haven't seen the Art Institute show and I don't want to," she said. "I don't intend to go, as from what I heard it's so dreadful that I'd be too disgusted ever to go back to the Institute." Chauncey McCormick, then the vice-president of the institute, attempted to soothe the dissident factions. "A newspaper does not endorse murder when it prints the news of a murder," he said. "We are recording the times, giving a cross section of what is happening in America."

The explanation did not satisfy Mrs. Logan. She reprinted with approval an editorial asserting that juries gave prizes only to pictures that would stir up controversy and stimulate attendance among a public curious to discover if a painting was "as bad as they say it is." She sought to have Jules Breton's *Song of the Lark*, one of the most popular paintings displayed at the Columbian Exposition, taken from a storeroom and restored to the walls of the institute. She was as disapproving of the politics of the modern artists as of their techniques. "In Chicago today few conservative artists have been making their expenses," she complained, "and all the radicals are working for the PWA [Public Works Administration]. Many excellent painters are so discouraged that they have not touched a brush for months. If insanity is essential to true art, there should be a lot of it produced." Noting that only one painting in an institute show had been sold, she said, "That went to Philadelphia, I am happy to state."

An outgrowth of Mrs. Logan's campaign against modernism was the organization of a Society for Sanity in Art. Its purpose, according to its laws of incorporation, was to "further rationalism in painting, sculpture and allied fields and to encourage the teaching of a saneness as a constituent element of creative endeavor." Sculptor Gutzon Borglum contributed an introduction to a slim volume titled *Sanity in Art*, in which Mrs. Logan published her own ideas and correspondence from those who agreed with her. For her it was purely an artistic crusade. She firmly resisted those who wanted her to identify modernism with immorality. "Morals have nothing to do with it," she said, adding that her purpose was only "to help rid the museums of the modernistic, moronic, grotesqueries of so-called modern art." A few members of the board of trustees of the Art Institute were among those who joined the Society for Sanity in Art. A trustee who declined was Chauncey McCormick, who commented, "Sanity in art—sanity in anything—is indeed a fine goal at which to aim; but the question immediately arises—whose sanity?"

COLONEL ROBERT R. McCORMICK

The Ghost and the Colonel

A CENTURY OF PROGRESS, effective as it was in drawing the attention of the world to Chicago's achievements, also left unanswered some questions about the land created for the fair and in particular about the future of the entire lakefront.

In the end, it came down to a contest between the ghost of a pioneer merchant and the very live and powerful publisher of the *Chicago Tribune*, Colonel Robert Rutherford McCormick. The lakefront, and in particular Grant Park with its long swath of green at the edge of downtown Chicago, exists as it does because of the battle waged by a strong-willed merchant, A. Montgomery Ward, founder of the department store chain that bears his name.

He was another of Chicago's self-made men. At eleven he had been working in a barrel factory and at fourteen in a brickyard. He came to Chicago in 1865 and took a position as a clerk in the store of Field, Palmer & Leiter. Seven years later he established the world's first mail-order house in the loft of a Chicago barn. When his business prospered, he bought property on Michigan Avenue for his company offices. He was shocked to find the building overlooked a wasteland of railroad tracks, dumping grounds, ugly armories that housed some of the city's National Guard regiments and other unsightly buildings. All the structures had been put up in defiance of an ordinance of 1837 requiring that the area east of Michigan Avenue from Randolph Street to Park Row was to be kept free of buildings forever. Ward, acting as a Michigan Avenue property owner, sought the help of the courts in restoring the area as a park. "Without recourse to the courts," he said, "there would be merry-go-rounds and what-nots all the way to Park Row. They have made a dumping ground of the park, allowed circuses, masked balls and anything else there." Ward, whom the Tribune described as "a human icicle, shunning and shunned in all but the relations of business," needed all the iron in his character to withstand the onslaught against him when he asked and secured a court injunction and order clearing the area of buildings and forcing the removal of eight railroad tracks.

For thirteen years, Ward fought in the courts at his own expense to have the injunction made perpetual. Finally after the victory was won, he granted the only newspaper interview of his life to a reporter for the Tribune. "Had I known in 1890 how long it would take me to preserve a park for the people against their will," he said candidly, "I doubt if I would have undertaken it. I think there is not another man in Chicago who would have spent the money I have spent in this fight with certainty that even gratitude would be denied as interest. I fought for the poor people of Chicago—not the millionaires. In the district bounded by Twenty-second Street, Chicago Avenue and Halsted live more than 250,000 persons, mostly poor. The city has a magnificent park and boulevard system of some fifty miles but the poor man's auto is a shank's mare or at best the streetcars. Here is a park frontage on the lake, comparing favorably with the Bay of Naples, which city officials would crowd with buildings, transforming the breathing spot for the poor into a showground of the educated rich. I do not think it is right." Ward did not expect any laurels for the litigation that earned him the title of "Watchdog of the Lakefront." "Perhaps I may see the public appreciate my efforts," he said, "but I doubt it."

The court's order upholding Ward was so sweeping that at first it was feared that the Art Institute would have to be demolished. Ward indicated he was willing to let the institute stand, but it was only with the greatest reservations that he finally consented to plans to erect the Field Museum of Natural History in Grant Park. The museum, with exhibits in anthropology, botany, zoology, and geology that place it among the finest institutions of its kind in the world, was founded with gifts of nearly ten million dollars from Chicago's merchant prince Marshall Field. Across the drive is the Shedd Aquarium, a gift to the city from a merchant who made

FIELD MUSEUM OF NATURAL HISTORY on the lakefront. The Great Hall

his fortune as a partner of Marshall Field. The aquarium, first and largest of its kind in America, was given to the city by John G. Shedd, a New Hampshire Yankee who became president of Marshall Field & Company after Field's death and a man whom Field once described to a United States Senate committee as "the best merchant in the United States." Shedd was conscious of the public responsibilities of a merchant. "The merchant is the pathfinder in art," he said. "Allow that the artist produces art, it is the merchant who exploits it, taking the initiative and taking the risks. To meet the necessities of the people is the first demand of the merchant; to deal in the demands for the artistic is the second and no less important office. Today the modern great merchandise house is international in scope and art and business success can go hand in hand. Too many men have made fortunes in Chicago and while making them have left the city to grow as it would. If some of these had found a little time for audience with men who had the welfare of the future city in mind and heart, fewer would have fancied need to take up residence in more beautiful and ripened environments."

A merchant who did have the "welfare of the future city in mind and heart," was Julius Rosenwald, who gave away sixty-three million dollars because he believed in "giving while I am alive." He began his business career as a manufacturer of men's clothing. One of his customers was Richard W. Sears, who with Alvah C. Roebuck had established a small mail-order house in competition with that of Montgomery Ward. In 1893 Rosenwald bought a half interest in Sears, Roebuck; by 1910 he was the firm's president. As Sears, Roebuck expanded under his direction, he became the richest man in Chicago. He showed little interest in maintaining any such distinction. He created the Rosenwald Foundation with a gift of thirty million dollars. Specifying that the money be used "for the well-being of mankind," he also set a time limit for its total expenditure so that no bureaucracy of officials or administrators would siphon off funds from worthy projects. He built more than five thousand schools for Negroes. He gave five million dollars to the University of Chicago. When the stock market crashed in 1929, he personally guaranteed the investments of all Sears's four thousand employees in the company's pension fund. But his visible memorial is the Museum of Science and Industry, which stands near the lakeshore just east of the University of Chicago. According to Sewell Avery, Rosenwald first thought of the museum when his son William, then only eight years old, wandered away from his parents in Munich, Germany, and was found in an industrial museum there. As the location of the museum, Rosenwald selected the Fine Arts Building of the Columbian Exposition. It had been used as a temporary home for the Field Museum, but when the new edifice was erected in Grant Park the old one was abandoned. Rosenwald reduced the building to its original steel skeleton and brick walls and reconstructed it in permanent stone, thus preserving for future generations the architectural masterpiece of the 1893 exposition. From the 1933 fair came many of the industrial and scientific exhibits that were to be displayed, forming a single memorial to two of the proudest moments in Chicago's history. Today, as exhibits are shifted and added to keep pace with the discoveries of science, the unchanging classic lines of the museum itself remain a perpetual reminder of the durability of beauty.

The fourth great public building of the lakefront, the planetarium, was a gift of Rosenwald's brother-in-law, Max Adler, also an executive of Sears, Roebuck and Company. The Adler Planetarium (1930), like the aquarium near which it stands, was the first building of its kind in America. Adler explained his gift in simple terms. "I wanted to give some evidence of my feeling for Chicago, and of my pride in the city which made it possible for me to accumulate my modest fortune."

Daniel Burnham's "Plan for Chicago" had generally provided that the lakefront should be "forever open, clear and free." Unfortunately for

Burnham's aspirations, Chicagoans also loved a fair. In 1948 and 1949, the former site of A Century of Progress was used for the Railroad Fair, which for two summers intrigued Chicagoans with antique locomotives, the latest in streamlined trains and diesel engines. When it appeared that another season of the Railroad Fair would lose money—including the dollars invested in it by the *Tribune*—Colonel McCormick decided that it would be the appropriate site for a new Exposition Hall to attract convention visitors to Chicago.

The planning authorities were against it and the State Street merchants were against it, preferring a location closer to the business center. The *Chicago Sun-Times*, under publisher Marshall Field IV and its editor, was mounting an increasing challenge to the *Tribune*'s dominance, and fought vigorously against this new incursion on the lakefront, as did a coalition headed by civic leader Benjamin F. Gingiss. But it was no match for the *Tribune*'s historic downstate relationships and the skills in lobbying of its political editor, George Tagge. The legislature passed the necessary bills and, after a series of legal maneuvers to block the project failed, Mayor Daley and Governor William G. Stratton broke ground for the new hall on September 17, 1958. It was appropriately named McCormick Place.

From the beginning, it looked more like the colonel's tombstone than an exposition hall. Squat, plain and made of concrete panels to save money, it lacked both grace and style. When, on January 16, 1976, a short in an electrical connection started a fire that burned it to the ground, Chicagoans were more inclined to celebrate than to mourn. Unfortunately, the financial obligations were such that it had to be reconstructed on the same site, though with a design that was at least acceptable from an esthetic point of view, if not from its location.

THE ORIGINAL McCORMICK PLACE. Looking north

JACOB M. ARVEY, ADLAI STEVENSON, AND JOHN S. BOYLE. Three powerful Democrats

"Chicago Ain't Ready for Reform Yet"

NOVELIST Mary Borden, when she visited Chicago, found it, as always, a city in ferment. "No one is ashamed of anything in Chicago," she wrote in *Harper's*. "Everything is moving too quickly, everyone is too specialized and it is all too much fun. Each one, whether crook or politician or expert gunman, is too good of his kind to be conscious of anything less positive and less exhilarating than his own power."

A. J. Liebling noted in the *New Yorker* that Chicago's citizens had an inverse pride in how bad things were, whether it was civic corruption or the weather. "The contemplation of municipal corruption," he wrote, "is always gratifying to Chicagoans. They are helpless to do anything about it, but they like to know it is on a big scale. . . . Ambivalence is a Chicago characteristic. People you meet at a party devote a great deal more time than people elsewhere to talking about good government, but they usually wind up the evening boasting about the high quality of the crooks they have met."

Reform in Chicago, on those rare occasions when it was successful, usually came not from some idealistic surge but because it was good politics. The successful architects of reform, in turn, usually were cradled by the same forces that created the need for reform. Such men, having been intimately acquainted with the problem, usually have had a clear view of what is needed to achieve a solution.

No one would have suspected when Lieutenant Colonel Jacob M. Arvey returned from war service in 1945 that he would soon be heading a reform movement within the Democratic party. Arvey was a product of Chicago's West Side and had been the alderman from the Twenty-fourth Ward whose astounding majorities for Democratic candidates (usually upward of 95 percent) had brought it national attention. It was a ward where charges of fraud on election day were as much a part of the Chicago scene as City Hall itself.

During his years in the mayor's office after Anton Cermak fell victim to an assassin's bullet, "Big Ed" Kelly had fashioned a formidable political machine in partnership with Patrick Nash (to whom Kelly also threw the most lucrative of public construction contracts). But during the war and following the death of Pat Nash in 1943, the Kelly-Nash machine had lost some of its vitality. When the war was over, Kelly chose Colonel Arvey to take control and rejuvenate the party.

At the time, Chicago was paying the penalty of more than a decade of corrupt government. Basking in the city's reputation for hospitality to GIs during World War II, Kelly blithely ignored the dirty streets, loafing payrollers and open corruption of everyone from City Hall clerks to the police force. Chicagoans routinely carried five or ten dollar bills in their drivers' licenses, which would just as routinely be removed when a car was stopped for a traffic violation. (This led comedian Mort Sahl to describe Chicago's Outer Drive as "the last outpost of collective bargaining.")

Every tavern had its dice table or "26" game, and bookmakers operated freely in barely disguised storefronts. Author Len O'Connor estimated that the mob was laying out almost $20 million a year for protection for projects ranging from elaborate gambling palaces to houses of prostitution or illegal slot machines and the lucrative numbers racket among the Negroes on the South Side.

Arvey quickly learned that the traditional Democratic voter—white and Catholic or Jewish—did not care for Ed Kelly. Peculiarly, it was not the corruption alone that turned them against him, but also his courageous stand on open housing in a white area called Morgan Park, which bordered on the Negro ghetto on the South Side. "As long as I am mayor," Kelly said, "any person will be allowed to live where they want to and can afford to live." He was ahead of his time.

Working the precincts in their door-to-door canvass before the midterm election of 1946, Arvey's captains found their voters deserting their party because of Kelly and vowing never to vote for him again. Arvey discussed the problem with two other party chieftains, Clerk of the Municipal Court

Joseph Gill and Chief Bailiff Al Horan, two men who controlled much of the party's patronage. It was their collective decision that Kelly would have to go.

Together, the three men called on Kelly at City Hall and asked him to step down. Kelly's reply was of the stuff of which heroes are made in the Democratic party of Cook County: "The Organization made me. It built me up. It put me where I am. If it's better for the Organization for this thing to be, then so be it." As Arvey was to recall, the mayor was absorbed in his own thoughts for a moment and then snapped out in a cheerful voice, "Hey, let's run Kennelly."

Martin H. Kennelly was a distinguished looking, white-haired, middle-aged bachelor and the head of a successful moving and storage company. A. J. Liebling was later to describe him as looking "like a bit player impersonating a benevolent banker." He had been on the fringe of politics as a supporter of Governor Henry Horner when Horner challenged the Kelly-Nash machine and had also been a supporter of State's Attorney Thomas J. Courtney in Courtney's unsuccessful attempt to unseat Kelly as mayor. His candidacy seemed ideal—a white Roman Catholic who would not be tainted with the Kelly-Nash label. As the reform candidate, he piled up a majority of 300,000 votes, and Arvey was hailed as a political genius.

Having ensconced his choice as mayor of Chicago, Arvey turned his attention to the national scene. By 1948, he had added the title of Democratic National Committeeman and in this capacity was searching for an alternative to President Harry S. Truman, who seemed doomed to defeat in the 1948 election. Arvey's selection was a war hero—Dwight David Eisenhower. Arvey called upon him to try to persuade him to run on a sort of national unity ticket, naturally under the Democratic label. Eisenhower however declined, and Arvey then turned his attention to what could be done to salvage the Illinois ticket.

Arvey's choices were to make national headlines. For governor he slated Adlai E. Stevenson, whose grandfather had been vice-president of the United States and who had come to Arvey's attention through his public appearances at the Chicago Council on Foreign Relations. To run for senator, Arvey tapped an old opponent from his days in Chicago's city council, Paul H. Douglas, the independent alderman from the Fifth Ward who was also a University of Chicago economics professor. Again it was an Arvey triumph. In the fall election, both men rolled up majorities of approximately half a million votes, pulling Truman along with them and enabling him to carry the state by a narrow 30,000 vote margin.

Two years later, Arvey was not to be so lucky. As candidate for sheriff, the Democrats picked Police Captain Daniel Gilbert, then chief investigator for the state's attorney office. Gilbert was not only politically well-connected, he was a flamboyant character with great confidence in his ability to "fix" anything. When a United States Senate committee headed by Senator Estes Kefauver was holding hearings on the possible alliance between crime and politics in major American cities, Gilbert walked into a closed-door session (without requiring a subpoena) to explain how he had earned the sobriquet of the "world's richest policeman."

After showing the senators his tax returns for the past six years, he boasted that he had made his money through utility bonds, the grain market, the stock exchange—and gambling. "I am a gambler at heart," he told the committee. There the matter might have rested if it had not been for Ray Brennan, an enterprising crime reporter for the *Chicago Sun-Times*. Posing as the representative of a stenographic service, Brennan obtained the transcript of Gilbert's remarks, which was promptly spread out under big headlines on the front page of the newspaper.

The results were disastrous. It was obvious that no one would believe a policeman could become as rich as Gilbert by honest means. Most of the Cook County ticket went down to defeat. More significantly, the failure of the Cook County organization to deliver its usual majority resulted in the defeat of the Senate Majority Leader Scott Lucas by a downstate politician from Pekin, Illinois, with the fine Republican name of Everett McKinley Dirksen.

Arvey promptly resigned as Cook County Democratic chairman, telling a reporter that it would not have been proper for him to stay on. "In politics, everything depends on your judgment, your judgment of people," he said. "There is no machinery or equipment you can use to avoid human error. Because I was shaken in my judgment, I thought it best to resign." Joseph Gill, by then a political elder statesman, was chosen as acting chairman while the various factions of the party maneuvered for position.

For the next three years, Gill ran the party with the assistance of a hard-working Irish lad from Bridgeport who was usually not far from his side; observing, learning and making himself a vital part of the organization. His name was Richard J. Daley, and he had survived the 1950 disaster by winning the county clerk's office and thus saving its patronage for the Democrats. In 1953, Gill stepped down and Daley laid claim to the chairmanship for himself. Two other factions challenged him, but when the leader of the opposition was killed in an automobile accident, Daley succeeded to the post of chairman of the Democratic Party of Cook County. A new era in the history of the city (and the party) was about to begin.

Richard Joseph Daley was born in a traditional Chicago "two-flat" apartment on May 15, 1902, in the area of the city known as Bridgeport and sometimes as "Back of the Yards" because of the adjacent stockyards and packing houses. He was baptized at the nearby Nativity of Our Lord Roman Catholic Church, where he was to attend mass every day of his adult life when he was in Chicago. At De LaSalle, the Catholic high school serving the neighborhood, he augmented the traditional subjects with classes in bookkeeping and typing. After graduation, he worked for a short time in the stockyards; his spare time was divided between work as a precinct captain in the Eleventh Ward Democratic organization and membership in the Hamburg Athletic Association, which elected him president when he was just twenty-two years old. Soon his typing skills and capacity for work earned him a position as paid secretary of the Eleventh Ward Democratic organization, where he came under the sponsorship of Joseph McDonough, a Democratic powerhouse. In the evening, he attended DePaul University, where after eleven years of part-time study he was to earn his law degree.

In 1930, McDonough was elected county treasurer and took young Daley downtown with him to do the hard work while McDonough played to the galleries. The year 1936 was an eventful one for the thirty-four-year-old Daley. First, he married his childhood sweetheart Eleanor Guilfoyle, and together they started plans to build a home at 3536 South Lowe Street, where he was to spend the rest of his life. Political opportunity beckoned when an elderly Republican state representative died after the ballots had been printed, and Daley was able to organize a write-in campaign and win the post for himself. Elected nominally as a Republican, he nonetheless chose to sit with the Democrats when he arrived in Springfield. Two years later, the state senator whose district included the Eleventh Ward also died, and Daley moved up to the senate. There he proved a valuable ally to Mayor Kelly in pushing legislation that enabled the city to take over two bankrupt public transportation companies.

Daley was a man with his eye on higher office and working hard to get there. His only defeat came in 1946, when he lost a contest for sheriff. But he still had enough influence to throw out the Democratic ward committeeman in the Eleventh Ward and take the post himself; he was now in a position to wield power within the highest circles of the party. After the 1948 election, in which the Eleventh Ward delivered the first of the tremendous Democratic pluralities that were to become traditional, Arvey recommended young Daley to the newly elected governor Adlai E. Stevenson as state revenue director. But in 1950, death opened another door for Daley when County Clerk Michael J. Flynn died. Daley was chosen to serve out the term and survived the Dan Gilbert debacle to win reelection in his own right. He was now not only a party leader but had his own power base in the patronage jobs under the jurisdiction of the county clerk.

After Daley assumed the chairmanship of the county central committee in 1953, it was clear that he had higher aspirations than county clerk. In the campaign of 1954, the issue of whether he would or would not run for mayor was constantly raised and just as regularly evaded by the candidate. But after the election, he was not long in making his next move.

As county chairman, Daley designated a slate-making committee to interview the candidates and decide whom the party would endorse for mayor. Although he ostentatiously removed himself from the slate-making process, he nonetheless kept a seat in the corner of the room to keep an eye on proceedings. When the charade was over, the slatemakers—to the surprise of no one with the possible exception of Mayor Martin H. Kennelly himself—decided Dick Daley would be their candidate for mayor. Kennelly, his substantial ego bruised, decided to make a fight for the nomination; after all, he had fought against the organization in previous battles at the side of Governor Henry Horner and State's Attorney Thomas J. Courtney. The primary campaign was one of the most expensive and bitter in history; but the ability to marshal the voting strength of the traditional Democratic wards paid off as Daley won with a plurality of more than 100,000 votes.

Daley still had a battle ahead of him. The Republicans, with no strong candidate of their own, nominated an independent Democrat, reformer and crime fighter, Robert E. Merriam, to oppose Daley. Merriam's father, a distinguished political science professor at the University of Chicago, had himself been a reform candidate who was counted out of the mayoralty when he ran against William Hale Thompson in 1919.

As a successor to Paul H. Douglas in the city council from the Fifth Ward, which encompassed the University of Chicago, Robert Merriam had established a reputation as a crime fighter. As chairman of the city council committee investigating the links between crime and politics—dubbed "The Big Nine"—he had turned the spotlight on the wide-open gambling and bribery of public officials that had flourished anew under the benign indifference of Kennelley. Merriam's campaign was geared to the theme that Daley, as the candidate of the Machine, would allow Chicago to become a wide-open city. Daley, a devout family man, was stung by the charge, and his efforts to refute it were to color many of his future actions. In an emotional speech, Daley said, "I would not unleash the forces of evil. It's a lie. I will follow the training my good Irish mother gave me—and Dad. If I am elected, I will embrace mercy, love, charity, and walk humbly with my God."

When the votes were counted, Daley had carried twenty wards and Merriam twenty-one. Merriam received more votes than anyone who ever ran against Daley, but his total of 581,255 was exceeded by the 55 percent of the vote cast for Daley—708,222, a number that Daley used as a license

PADDY BAULER AND CRONY ALDERMAN CHARLES WEBER CELEBRATE: "Chicago ain't ready for reform yet."

plate on his limousine throughout his terms as mayor.

The Democratic organization was jubilant that the "reformer" Merriam had been defeated. Alderman Paddy Bauler, in top hat and holding a mug of beer in his tavern, chortled, "Chicago ain't ready for reform yet." But then he added a cautionary note. "Keane [Alderman Thomas E. Keane, chairman of the city council finance committee] and them fellas—Jake Arvey, Joe Gill—they think they're gonna run things. They're gonna run nuthin'. They ain't found it out yet, but Daley's the dog with the big nuts, now that we got him elected. You wait and see; that's how it is going to be." Alderman Charles Weber, another Machine stalwart, echoed the theme: "This Daley, he is going to be one tough sonofabitch."

Election night was not over before their prophecies began to be fulfilled. It had been Big Ed Kelly's custom on election night to call the ward committeemen and thank them for their support, perhaps invite them down for a drink. Daley made no such calls. Political commentator Len O'Connor noted that in the past the ward committeemen had considered the organization as superior to the man; now, he said, "they had the gut judgment that under Daley it was going to be the other way around."

Immediately upon his inauguration, Daley moved to eradicate the notion of a wide-open city. Dice games were shut down, bookmakers got the word to close their doors and operate from under their hats, the vice squad suddenly found evidence on which to make arrests. In the city council, aldermen who formerly chattered idly or read the newspapers while Kennelly attempted to preside over the council received word to conduct themselves with appropriate decorum. Using his combined powers as county chairman and mayor, Daley inexorably tightened his control by taking away the cherished perquisites by which the aldermen and ward committeemen had maintained their individual baronies. First to go was the right to pass on all contracts over $2,500, then the right to grant zoning variations, and even the right to pass on driveway permits that had been selling at prices from $500 to $20,000 per driveway.

Richard J. Daley was not only mayor; he was boss.

AFTER A BOOKIE RAID. Investigators examine telephones used to accept bets

DOWNTOWN SKYLINE LOOKING TOWARD MONROE STREET HARBOR. Standard Oil Building in center; Marina Towers at lower right

"The Most Exciting City in the United States"

WITH Richard J. Daley as mayor, Chicago took a look at itself and suddenly discovered it was alive and well. Within weeks of his taking office, the new pillars of steel and concrete sprouting against the sky seemed to be making Chicago a different city.

If there was to be a renaissance in Chicago, it would be the architects who would play a leading role. Chicago always had been a city of builders, and the opportunity to give the city's buildings a democratic design and structure had made the city a center of world architecture from the days of the Great Chicago Fire.

For thirty years from 1880 to 1910, the Chicago school of architects essentially designed the engineering and structural systems that have made possible the multistory buildings of today. "Here is where it all began," the editors of *Architectural Forum* magazine were to write. Later, from 1900 until about 1920, the Prairie School flourished under such leaders as Dankmar Adler, Louis Sullivan and their brilliant pupil Frank Lloyd Wright.

The Depression put an end to any construction of significance; but in

1953, the Prudential Insurance Company announced that it would build a forty-one-story skyscraper at the edge of the Loop—the first major office building to be erected in downtown Chicago since the completion in 1933 of the Field Building (now the LaSalle National Bank Building).

Suddenly a dormant Chicago had rediscovered its own vitality. Even at the low point, when it seemed the city was adrift, it had never injured the backbone that was to support its revival—its industrial power. During World War II, Chicago had outstripped all other cities with investments of $1.3 billion in war plants. Another $1.7 billion was poured into plant facilities after the war. Four out of ten workers in the Chicago area were employed in manufacturing.

The *U.S. News and World Report* observed what was happening and reached back to the poems of Carl Sandburg for a comparison. "Chicago, which poet Carl Sandburg called 'a tall, bold slugger set vivid against the little soft cities' is making a comeback," the magazine reported in May of 1955, less than six weeks after Mayor Daley took office. "Chicago is awake after a fretful sleep that lasted a quarter of a century, more or less. Industry, commerce, money and people are flowing into Chicago once more, now that the sprawling American crossroads is back on the upgrade."

Fortune magazine was equally enthusiastic. "Right now the most exciting city in the United States is Chicago, Illinois," it reported. "Chicago has needed the rebuilding in the worst way; it is getting it in a big way."

But it was not a native American architect who was to set the style for this new revival in the most American of American cities; it was an immigrant from Germany, Ludwig Mies van der Rohe, whose imprint was to be most dominant on the new skyline of Chicago.

Born in Aachen Germany, Mies, as he was to be known, had no formal professional education but acquired valuable experience in the Berlin office of Bruno Paul, a noted designer, and Peter Behrens, Germany's outstanding industrial architect, in whose office Walter Gropius and Le Corbusier also worked. In the early 1920s, Mies had developed a series of radically new projects for tall office buildings and houses with daring use of glass and steel, clarity of structure and a widely praised sense of proportion and application of modern materials.

After a term as director of the Bauhaus in Berlin, Mies in 1938 fled Hitler's regime to become head of the department of architecture of the Illinois Institute of Technology (IIT). Here, in the center of Chicago's black ghetto and slums, he created a coherent modern campus, whose centerpiece, Crown Hall, was clear-span steel with glass walls that departed radically from the traditions of academic architecture.

In 1948, in the design of the Promontory Apartments on the lakeshore near the University of Chicago campus, Mies had an opportunity to express his philosophy of boldly allowing the structural strength of a building to be recognized. But his philosophy of "less is more" did not achieve its total expression until the design and construction of the twin apartment buildings at 860–880 Lake Shore Drive.

Ira Bach, in *Chicago's Famous Buildings* describes the 860–880 building in these terms: "These apartments are universally admired for their openness and the frank expression of the steel frame; experts are further intrigued by the refinement of the design, including the subtle distribution of emphasis between the horizontal and vertical. . . . An interesting refinement is found in the fact that the outer two windows in each group of four are slightly narrower than the inner two. This kind of effect is better put down to the creative energy of the artist, at this moment in his career which no explanation can quite capture . . . the variation adds zest and vitality to the design and reminds us that we are in the presence of architecture as art rather than as mere engineering."

The Miesian style, instantly recognizable in these twin towers, was to be repeated in various adaptations in more than forty structures, including the three federal buildings on Dearborn Street, two more twin apartments at 900–910 Lake Shore Drive and in the first three office structures in the Illinois Center development, completed after his death. A bust of the architect today sits in the lobby of the IBM Building on North Wabash Avenue, the last building he designed before his death in 1969.

As dramatic as the buildings created by Mies himself was the seventy-story Lake Point Tower apartment building, which two of his students derived from a project that Mies had proposed for Berlin almost half a century earlier. Designed by John Heinrich and George Schipporeit, who were students of Mies at IIT, the apartment at the time of its completion was both the highest reinforced concrete structure in the world and the tallest apartment building. Set in the isolated splendor of the Outer Drive Bridge, Lake Point Tower used curved forms to replace the traditional plane surfaces. In sunlight or at twilight or sunrise, the curtain walls of bronze-tinted glass set in a framework of dark aluminum create patterns of reflection ranging in color from intense golden sunlight to black shadows of passing clouds.

Other architects were also reaching for the sky, but with designs distinctly different from those of Mies van der Rohe and as individualistic as the city itself.

The first and most spectacular of these were the two round sixty-story Marina City Towers (1965) designed by Bertrand Goldberg. Chicagoans had never seen a round skyscraper before. The "corncobs," as they were affectionately known because of the appearance of the railing on the exterior balconies, soon became a photographic favorite. The buildings were more than architectural innovation; they were also a precursor to a new way of urban living, with apartments, stores, recreational facilities, theaters—and even a marina, from which the towers took their name—located under a single roof.

On North Michigan Avenue, the John Hancock Building (1969) rose starkly black against the gray stone facades of the elegant shops on the Magnificent Mile, as it had been successfully christened by realtor Arthur Rubloff. Bracing high buildings against the wind had always been a challenge; in the Hancock Building, Skidmore engineer Fazlur Khan solved the problem by building huge trusses into the side, in effect turning a series of bridges on their sides and forming them into a building. Like Marina City, it was a multi-use building with shops and offices on the lower floors and apartments on the floors above.

For a short period of time, the Hancock satisfied Chicagoans needs to boast of the world's tallest building. It lost this distinction to the World Trade Center in New York but quickly regained it in 1974 with the completion of Sears Tower. At 100 stories and 1,468 feet, it is the world's

SEARS TOWER. Tallest building in the world

tallest building, exceeding the World Trade Center by 100 feet. The staggered black silhouette of the building designed by architect Bruce Graham is actually the outer frame of nine elongated tubes, each 75 feet square. These tubes are banded together structurally to form a megatube that provides lateral strength to withstand wind loads.

While Sears was constructing its corporate monument, Standard Oil Company (Indiana) was commissioning Edward Durell Stone to design a marble-clad headquarters (1974) for its operations on land acquired from the Illinois Central Railroad at the northern edge of Grant Park. While yielding the battle of heights to Sears, "Big Stan" had some innovations of its own, including a core design that left every floor free of pillars and provided for a maximum of flexibility in office design. Double-cage elevators, moving simultaneously to serve odd and even floors, further enhanced the economics of its interior space.

The Standard Oil Building, standing starkly white against the anodized aluminum Miesian skyline, provoked intense controversy, much of it generated because it had not been designed by a Chicago architect. Today its position overlooking the open spaces of Grant Park gives it an assured identity and acceptance on the horizon of Chicago.

Another marble-clad building to arise was Water Tower Place (1976), adjoining Chicago's most famous landmark. It was a precedent-setting concept that envisaged a vertical shopping center, surmounted by a tower containing both a hotel (the Ritz Carlton) and apartments. Its bland and formless marble exterior was less than universally admired, but its interior took Chicagoans into a world of shimmering chrome and glass reached by two escalators set between greenery and a series of waterfalls that suggested the terraced beauty of Villa d'Este in Italy.

The skills of the new generations of Chicago architects were applied not only to Chicago. They were engaged in projects of comparable size around the world. When Washington, D.C., wanted to build its subway, for example, it called upon Chicago architect Harry Weese to design it.

The construction of these "megabuildings," as the *National Geographic* called them, took place under the benevolent eye of Daley. To be sure that eye was benevolent, every new project was announced in the mayor's office; there was the clear implication that all credit was to be shared with the mayor in the corner office of the fifth floor at City Hall.

Typical of the importance of the mayor's good will was the experience of the architects and contractors in building the handsomely thin and tapered First National Bank Building (1969). As *Fortune* magazine reported it: "Construction was started without building permits, a patently

FIRST NATIONAL BANK PLAZA. Noon entertainment

risky procedure and it continued for months before permits finally were issued by City Hall." The bank's chief executive recalled that "We tried time and time again to get the permits but the building department was so fussy about little details that we decided to go without them." A lesser project might have been shut down for such audacity. But Building Commissioner Joseph Fitzgerald knew his mayor. "He told me to enforce the code," Fitzgerald told a reporter, "but he also expected the least interference possible with all that new construction. If I went to his office and told him I had stopped construction of a major office building like the First National because it didn't have a permit, he would have sent me to a psychiatrist—or fired me."

The city itself joined in the Miesian chorus with the commissioning of the thirty-story Civic Center and adjoining plaza (renamed the Richard J. Daley Center and Plaza following the mayor's death). The building, winner

THE PICASSO STATUE AT THE CIVIC CENTER

of many architectural awards was the combined product of three of the city's leading firms—C. F. Murphy Associates; Loebl, Schlossman and Bennett; and Skidmore Owings and Merrill—but the idiom of its style came clearly from Mies van der Rohe. The architects used a self-weathering Cor-ten steel, which over the years has turned from what Chicagoans first considered ugly rust to a handsome tone of russet.

After the completion of the Civic Center, William Hartmann, one of the architects associated with the project, conceived the idea of a massive sculpture for the plaza that would add substance to its vast open area. He decided Chicago should have the best, which in his mind meant Pablo Picasso. After many trips to Europe and visits with the master, Hartmann brought home the design for his prize. It was to be a 50-foot high, 135-ton sculpture of the same Cor-ten steel as the Civic Center.

But what was it? At the unveiling, Daley put on one of his masterful shows with music by the Chicago Symphony and a poetry reading by Chicago's Pulitzer Prize poet Gwendolyn Brooks. Her poem was appropriate:

> Does man love art? Man
> visits art, but squirms.
> Art hurts.
> Art urges voyages—and it is
> easier to stay at home,
> the nice beer ready

Though Hartmann called it a "singular event in the cultural history of the world," Chicagoans were inclined to nurse their beer and wonder what it was. A woman? An Afghan hound? A bird? Or, as the *Tribune* suggested, a predatory grasshopper?

Picasso, as always, let the art speak for itself. Art scholars, however, were busy tracing the statue's forebears back to a metal cut-out titled *Head of a Woman*, then on exhibition in London. Others found a resemblance in a figure in Picasso's famed *Demoiselles d'Avignon*.

Picasso would probably have preferred the comment of a Chicago policeman who said, "I like it fine, whatever it is." Or as Picasso himself put it, "Everyone wants to understand art. Why not try to understand the song of a bird? Why does one love the night, flowers, everything around one, without trying to understand them." To another viewer, he said, "Chicago selected itself." Even though he had not seen the city, he said, "Chicago is like me, its beauty is in its vitality and its vitality is planted in the earth."

This striving for "cultured urbanity," as one English writer said, put art at a level where it seemed good for the city and consequently good for business, two ideas that most Chicagoans tended to relate. Local sculptor Richard Hunt was commissioned to provide an adornment celebrating *The Great Lakes* for a downtown parking garage. The Picasso was followed by an arching red steel *Flamingo* by Alexander Calder in the plaza of Mies's Federal Center; nearby Marc Chagall created an 85-foot ceramic mosaic on a wall in the plaza of the new First National Bank Building; Standard Oil used a Harry Bertoia sculpture of copper rods that sang in the wind and was appropriately called *Sounding*; the showpiece of the lobby of Sears Tower was a motorized Alexander Calder mobile of swinging, twirling metal called *Universe*; in a government plaza on the near West Side, Chicago's native-born Claes Oldenburg contributed an airy sculpture called *Batcolumn*, and on the University of Chicago campus Henry Moore created a squat, strong sculpture commemorating the place where the energy of the atom was first controlled. The trend continued in 1980 when Hartmann scored another coup with the announcement that Joan Miro had donated a sculpture to be located just opposite the Picasso. It was called simply *Miro's Chicago*, though the director of the Arts Council saw it as the likeness of woman. Like Picasso, Miro declined to put an interpretation on it.

ALEXANDER CALDER'S "UNIVERSE" IN SEARS LOBBY

The building revolution that had begun with the construction of the Prudential Building on Illinois Central (IC) land, now shifted back to its point of origin. For years, the land north of Grant Park had been one of the railroad's great unexploited assets. Now, under the aegis of a holding company, IC Industries, steps were initiated to create a city within a city.

The railroad had acquired the land in 1852, when Chicago, then a sprawling city of 40,000, sought a way to provide its shoreline some protection from Lake Michigan's waves. Since the city lacked money even to pave its streets, it turned to the Illinois Central Railroad, which had been seeking permission to build a downtown terminal. City officials reasoned that if the railroad built tracks along the lakefront, it would also have to build the necessary breakwaters and take other precautions; protection for the lakefront would cost the city nothing (except, as it was to turn out a century later, some of its most valuable real estate). The rail trestle actually came in over the water but, as the years passed, this area and the shoreline to the East were filled in to form Grant Park.

In the 1960s, as building was resumed in the area, Chicagoans perceived another threat to their lakefront. As a result, in 1969, a lakefront ordinance was passed, setting zoning and residency restrictions for all future development in the area. Once the conditions were established, a plan was developed to provide a mixture of commercial and residential buildings in a planned context. A portion of the development is complete, and construction on other phases is underway. When completed, it will provide offices for a work force of 45,000 and housing for 35,000 people. At street level, the buildings are connected only by pedestrian malls while street traffic is routed through the center at three different levels beneath the plazas.

Lecturing in London in 1939, Frank Lloyd Wright had predicted, "Eventually, I think that Chicago will be the most beautiful great city left in the world." Looking around at Chicago's new generation of buildings, the plazas and the public sculpture that surrounded them, sculptor Richard Hunt thirty years later believed Wright's prophecy had been fulfilled. He told Ethel Gofen of *Art Gallery* magazine that Chicago might even be ranked with that other great art city, Florence. "Chicago is more like Florence. New York is more like Rome. There's a certain intensity to the artistic life here, a more human scale." Art dealer Richard Gray echoed Hunt's verdict. Citing the beauty of the lakefront, the open spaces and the physical attributes that made it appropriate for public sculpture, he summed up Chicago as "livable, human and civilized."

MAHALIA JACKSON, DR. MARTIN LUTHER KING, JR. AND MAYOR DALEY in a show of unity

"I Never Believed This Would Happen Here"

As THE silhouette of Chicago's skyline changed, an even more fundamental change was occurring in the city's population. Beginning with the war years, a new wave of immigration had washed into the city. These immigrants came not from foreign shores but from America's Deep South; they did not speak a foreign language, but they were of a different color. It was a difference that was to have a great impact on their assimilation.

During the decade from 1940 to 1950, Chicago had a growing population —up by more than 18 percent in the heart of the city. The ratio of that increase, however, said much about what was happening. In this period the rate of increase in the central city for whites was 9.1 percent; for blacks it was a startling 196.1 percent. Overall, the total white population of the city actually decreased a fraction of a percent while the nonwhite population increased 80 percent.

Obviously, these newcomers required a place to live. As very little new housing was being built, they tended to push into areas where only whites had lived before. Housing tensions were great as whites tended to flee whenever a black family moved into a block; statistically these "move-ins" were occurring at the rate of one every ten days. Panicky white families, fearful of falling real-estate values, sold and fled to the outer perimeters of the city or the suburbs.

The trend continued into the sixties. From 1960 to 1970, Chicago was to lose 505,000 white residents while gaining nearly 300,000 blacks. Nearly one-third of Chicagoans had dark skins. The ghetto, formerly a long narrow strip on the South Side, spread east to the lake and west through Lawndale and the old Jewish settlements in Douglas Park.

Resisting this change were the traditional ethnic conclaves. Poles tended to live in the Northwest and Southwest sides, Jews (some of whom had fled the West Side) in Rogers Park and along the lakeshore, Greeks around Lawrence and Western, the Italians on the near West Side, the Norwegians around Andersonville; there were various other clearly identifiable ethnic neighborhoods. The Irish, who had been running the city's politics since the earliest days, were fairly well dispersed, though the wealthiest might be found in either Beverly or Sauganash.

These Chicagoans, many of them second- or third-generation Americans who may have moved once in the face of the Negro tide, were determined not to move again. Their influence with Daley and the Democratic organization was substantial, as they provided a major component in Daley's majorities.

With the decline of Negro voting on the South Side after the death of Congressman William Dawson in 1970 at the age of eighty-four, the blacks seemed unable to bring their subtantial numbers to bear with any political effectiveness. By shrewdly redistricting Dawson's domain, Daley also made certain that no single black leader with Dawson's power would emerge again.

Dawson had been one of Daley's strongest supporters—but on the condition that it was Dawson and not Daley who ruled the South Side turf. It was Dawson who passed on the police commanders in the black districts; it was Dawson who decided when "policy wheels" and other gambling games for the poor would be allowed to operate. He was also the final arbiter of the jobs at City Hall. On election day, his majorities were substantial and predictable, based not only on getting out the vote, but paying for it openly with everything from two-dollar bills to live chickens. Senile in his later years, he basked in his seniority in Congress, and did little to improve the well-being of his constituents. With his death, a father figure disappeared from the scene, leaving as a heritage only frustration and fear.

On the West Side, tensions were even worse as blacks found themselves ruled by absentee precinct captains and ward committeemen whose influence at City Hall had been built in years past. In the summer of 1965, these tensions came seething to the surface when a hook-and-ladder fire truck without its rear section properly manned came wheeling out of a firehouse, swung onto the sidewalk and killed a black woman passing by.

Negroes surged into the street, venting their anger at the all-white complement of the fire station. Rock-throwing and looting erupted for two days; more than 170 persons were arrested.

Daley, making his judgments on the basis of his traditional upbringing in Bridgeport, seemed insensitive, if not oblivious to the pressures that were building. Political power was the pressure he understood and to which he responded; the blacks did not have it.

Perhaps this fact of political power was what Dr. Martin Luther King, Jr., understood as well as Daley. Having won a series of victories in the South, King announced that in 1966 he would bring his civil rights crusade to Chicago. He chose Chicago, he said, not because its record on civil rights was worst, but because it was typical, adding that in Chicago one man—Mayor Daley—could make the difference. To dramatize the fact his goals were practical, King bought an apartment building on the West Side and rehabilitated it as a symbol of what could be done at minimum cost to make housing more habitable for black people.

Unfortunately for Dr. King and those who shared his beliefs, Daley dealt in power and not in symbols. When King announced the rehabilitation of one building, Daley issued a sheaf of statistics about the number of buildings that had been rehabilitated in the entire city. When King announced a demand, Daley issued a press release blanketing it with figures indicating it had already been accomplished.

On July 10, 1966, the efforts of King and his associates to mobilize Chicago reached their climax with a rally at Soldier Field that attracted more than 40,000 people. After the rally, a core group of perhaps a thousand marched to City Hall, where they posted a list of demands on the City Hall door much in the manner of the theological rebel from whom Dr. King took his name. On Monday, Mayor Daley met with King to discuss the demands; afterward King could report only cordiality and no progress.

But if King's tactics that had proved successful in the South were failing to have an impact, other events were occurring that were to focus attention on the problem.

The summer was to be long, hot and violent. On July 12—just two days after the Soldier Field rally—with the temperature reaching 95 degrees, a group of black youngsters were cooling themselves in water gushing from an open fire hydrant—an American scene as familiar as a Norman Rockwell painting. Two white police officers, who must have seen the same thing in a dozen weather pictures in the newspapers, decided that it was illegal and closed the hydrant. When a black youth opened the hydrant again, he was arrested. The crowds in the street, many of them there to escape the stifling heat of their slum apartments, pushed and shoved to see what

DR. KING LEADS MARCH PROTESTING SCHOOL SEGREGATION

was happening. In the resulting disturbance, seven more blacks were arrested. Soon rumors spread through the neighborhood that the arrested youths had been beaten and that police were turning off fire hydrants in Negro neighborhoods but leaving them on in white areas. Sporadic rock-throwing, window-breaking and fire-bombing lasted for several hours.

After a day of uneasy calm, the rioting broke out again. Police and firemen responding to calls were pinned down by random gunfire. The media speculated that it was the beginning of urban guerrilla warfare in the United States. The rioting continued for several days, and it was not until Governor Otto Kerner called out the Illinois National Guard that order was restored. Most of the business district along the central core of the West Side had been destroyed. There were 533 arrests, of whom 155 were juveniles. Three blacks were killed by stray bullets.

Mayor Daley's reaction, as customary, was to deal with the problem at hand, postponing dealing with the larger issue until absolutely necessary. To this end a program to attach sprinkler heads to fire hydrants was announced, so that minimum water pressure would be required. Hours at swimming pools were expanded. *Daily News* columnist Mike Royko wrote in *Boss*, his biography of Daley, that by the summer of 1967 the hydrant-sprinkler program "had taken on the proportion of Niagara Falls." There were more than two hundred spray pools in operation and the Fire Department was offering splash parties at eighty local schools. As Royko commented wryly, "There shouldn't have been a dry black in Chicago."

Throughout the summer of 1966, King and his lieutenants, aided by local civil rights leaders, led a series of marches into white neighborhoods demanding that housing be opened up to blacks. Though the police were vigorous in protecting the rights of the marchers—with the exception of the occasion when Dick Gregory made the mistake of leading a march into the mayor's own neighborhood of Bridgeport—a number of ugly incidents developed. The situation grew sufficiently tense that it attracted the concern of Chicago's business establishment, which, in turn, communicated that concern to City Hall, where it was received with considerable more attention than a delegation of civil rights leaders.

After a particularly tense Sunday on August 14, 1966, when there were three separate marches, Daley took action to defuse the confrontations. A "summit" meeting was called under the chairmanship of the Episcopal bishop with Ben W. Heineman, chairman of the Chicago and North Western Railway, prominent friend of the mayor and liberal member of the business establishment, acting as moderator. Present were members of the labor, business and political alliance who made the decisions in Chicago, as well as both Mayor Daley and Martin Luther King.

Good will emanated from the meeting—but no decisions. It was announced that a subcommittee would be appointed to try to work out a solution and to report back by the end of the month. Two weeks later, the committee made its report, calling principally for an agreement on open housing. King called it "the first step in a thousand mile journey, but an important step . . . one of the most significant programs ever conceived to make open housing a reality." Unfortunately, he underestimated the difference in Chicago between a committee report and a political program; ten years later, the United States Justice Department and Department of Health, Education and Welfare were still calling Chicago the most segregated city for housing in America.

One of the young men who gathered around King during his Chicago visit was the Reverend Jesse Jackson, a tall, charismatic Baptist preacher who assumed the foremost role in the Chicago activities of King's Southern Christian Leadership Conference (SCLC). Jackson, although unsuccessful in his attempts to position himself as a spokesman for all Chicago blacks, was unsurpassed in finding ways to use the media as a platform. If not the most powerful of black leaders, he was the most articulate and certainly the most often heard. Within a few years, he formed his own organization separate from the SCLC, which he gave the globally ambitious name of People United to Save Humanity (PUSH). Operating out of a converted Jewish temple on the South Side, he used the Saturday morning meetings of Operation PUSH as a means of dramatizing his message that "I am somebody." In what he called a litany of personhood, he admonished his followers: "Have pride in what you are. Excel in what you do! You are somebody!"

A less visible development growing out of the riots and King's visit was the formation of Chicago United, a coalition formed to open a dialogue between the leaders of the white business community and the leaders of the black community. The idea originated with John Gardner, who wanted to form a Chicago chapter of his national Urban Coalition. Mayor Daley, as always, opposed any power base not directly Chicago-controlled. Rather than force the issue, a group of businessmen in 1973 formed Chicago United on the same pattern. It operated by using its connections at City Hall to influence major decisions or to secure actions that it thought could deter racial violence. It also used its leverage to persuade its members to take on assignments of civic responsibility.

Though Daley was successful in preventing King from disrupting the ethnic white base on which Daley's pyramid of power was based, Daley was aware that these new issues could not be dealt with in traditional ways. "We have conditions in Chicago that shouldn't exist anywhere in the United States," he told a reporter for the *Chicago Sun-Times*. Although those conditions were muted by continuing efforts at accommodation in the summer of 1967, nothing could prevent the explosion of anger in the ghettoes of America following the assassination of Dr. Martin Luther King, Jr., on April 4, 1968. Chicago was no exception; again it was on the West Side, where conditions were the most miserable even by ghetto standards, that the worst violence occurred.

After attending mass on Sunday morning, Mayor Daley flew over the riot scene in a Fire Department helicopter in the company of his close friend Fire Commissioner Robert Quinn, who had done everything in his power to maintain an all-white fire department in Chicago. The conversation in the helicopter was reflected in the mayor's comments after he landed. "It was a shocking and tragic picture of the city," the Mayor said. "I never believed this would happen here. I hope it will not happen again."

At a subsequent press conference, Daley's rhetoric was even more emotional. He was not about to permit anyone to damage the city he loved so much. "I have conferred with the superintendent of police this morning and I gave him the following instructions: I said to him very emphatically and definitely that an order be issued by him immediately and under his signature to shoot to kill any arsonist or anyone with a Molotov cocktail in hand because they're potential murderers, and to issue a police order to shoot to maim or cripple anyone looting stores in our city." When

THE CITY BURNS. Riot aftermath of assassination of Dr. Martin Luther King, Jr.

asked about children, Daley replied. "You wouldn't want to shoot them but you could use mace to detain them."

A world-wide cry of protest followed publication of the mayor's remarks, which he promptly denied making, even though they were ineradicably recorded on film. Police Superintendent James Conlisk, a bland career officer, remained silent during the controversy, though his defenders pointed out that he had been following official department policy, which expressly forbade the firing of armed weapons in riot situations. In Chicago, of course, policy was what Daley said it was; but Conlisk deftly avoided implementing Daley's order until Daley himself saw the necessity of disavowing it.

Daley, who thought he had "solved" the problem of the civil rights protests by co-opting the issues raised by Dr. King, found it difficult to comprehend the instinct to destroy as a form of protest. He would have done well to listen to Dr. John P. Spiegel of the Brandeis University Center for the Study of Violence, whose study of the nationwide disorders of the sixties led to these comments:

"The chances for riots are least likely in cities in which there is sincere recognition of ferment, more likely where there is insincere recognition and most likely where there is 'massive denial' that a serious racial problem exists. . . . Chicago lies between massive denial and insincere recognition."

Daley had little time to contemplate such advice. He had promised the president of the United States that the 1968 Democratic convention could be held in Chicago, and there was much to be done.

DEMONSTRATORS ATTACK POLICE CAR

U.S. TROOPS ON MICHIGAN AVENUE. Democratic Convention, 1968

"Nobody Is Going to Take Over This City

> In the year 1968, Richard J. Daley surveyed the city of Chicago and was master of it.
> DAVID HALBERSTAM in *Harper's*

PARTY LOYALTY was the credo by which Mayor Richard J. Daley lived. He had been taught it as a young man, and he had been richly rewarded by following its precepts. What the party asked, he would give; and in 1967 the Democratic party in the person of President Lyndon Baines Johnson had asked him to hold the 1968 Democratic convention in Chicago. Daley did not relish the idea, in part because he did not wish to get caught in the political crossfire between Johnson and Robert F. Kennedy, and in part because he sensed it would provide a focus for the anti-Vietnam War demonstrations that were recurring with increasing frequency.

At the time the convention was scheduled for Chicago, it was anticipated that Johnson would again be the party's nominee. But in March he suddenly withdrew his candidacy in the face of growing opposition to the war and the spreading protest movement. With Johnson's withdrawal, there was some speculation that the convention might be moved to another city less plagued by riots and tension than Chicago had been. Daley was stubborn, however. "You gave it to us and we're going to keep it," he said. Defying the threatened protests, he warned, "As long as I am mayor, there will be law and order in Chicago. Nobody is going to take over this city."

Many observers believe there was another reason for keeping the convention in Chicago, where Daley exercised such a tight control. Although Johnson had formally withdrawn, students of the Johnson style believe he was still hoping for a draft and that Daley had the power to engineer it for him. The occasion was to be ostensibly a birthday party for the president, whose sixtieth birthday occurred on August 27, during the convention week.

As the convention neared, and Johnson forced Hubert Humphrey and the Democratic party into a rigid defense of his Vietnam policy, a coalition of peace groups mounted a national campaign to bring hundreds of thousands of demonstrators to Chicago. The result was to produce a siege mentality in a city already torn by racial tensions; preparations for the convention took on the aspect of a military exercise.

A harbinger of what was to come occurred on Saturday April 27, 1968, when about five thousand peace advocates gathered for a rally and march from Grant Park to the Civic Center. In one of a series of disputes over parade permits, the marchers were denied use of the street and forced to march on the sidewalk. The advance section of the group had just reached Civic Center when, for reasons never made clear, the police ordered the marchers to disperse.

In the confusion that followed, demonstrators were beaten, maced, dragged down the streets and pulled from nearby coffee shops where some of them had taken refuge. Because the media had evaluated the march as "just one more protest gathering" and because of the peculiarity of weekend news deadlines, there was very little news coverage of the event. By the time the harassed marchers took their case to the media, there was no way of accurately reconstructing events, but it was generally assumed the police had broken discipline and attacked the protesters without provocation.

Ten years later, a young policeman on duty at the Civic Center had an opportunity to tell his version of the story to Paul Galloway, a writer for the *Sun-Times*. "The crowd kept building [until] things got out of control. A commander was hit in the head with a stick and went down. The police at the plaza formed lines and moved everybody out and down the different streets. We got to the corner of State and Washington, about twenty or twenty-five of us, when all of a sudden we heard these shouts and screams echoing off the building, 'Kill the pigs. Get the pigs.'

"I don't like to run, but my first reaction was that we should get out of there, find some more policemen and then come back. But a lieutenant was there, a fine man, a bull of a man. I'll never forget his face. He turned red and said, 'No sons-of-bitches are going to chase us out of here. . . . Form a double line, get your clubs at high port and count off.' We formed a double line and started marching into them and they came at us screaming and hollering and attacking us. The people in the front lines tried to get away from us when we met, but the people behind them kept pushing them into us. . . . It was like fighting for your life. It was either run or fight for your life."

The stage for confrontation had been set; in the weeks before the convention, it was to be managed with theatrical skill by the protest groups which had coalesced in their opposition to the Vietnam War. They were basically native American radicals, with no common ideological orientation. They included the Mobilization to End the War in Vietnam (MOBE), whose leaders included David Dellinger and Tom Hayden; the Youth International Party (Yippies), of which Abbie Hoffman and Jerry Rubin were the flamboyant ringmasters; and Students for a Democratic Society (SDS).

The week before the convention, a group of Yippies set up a camp headquarters in Lincoln Park and throughout the week staged a media circus. They claimed to be the forerunner of a hundred thousand protesters due to arrive on the eve of the convention. The Yippies were basically apolitical; their principal goal was to change society by winning acceptance for a counterculture of what they called "liberated life styles." Throughout the week they could be seen practicing karate, judo, and the *washoi*, a form of snake dance used by Japanese students to break police lines. In an imitation of Paris students, the Yippies built barricades of park benches and litter baskets, while Chicago police a hundred yards away watched in curiosity and bewilderment. Other police on three-wheel motorcycles rode through the camps much like motorized blue-clad frontier scouts surveying enemy territory. Trooping down to the Civic Center, the Yippies nominated a pig, Pigasus, for president. Chicago police finally broke up the gathering, but not before the television cameras had sent throughout the world images of a city near anarchy.

At both the White House and City Hall, preparations were being made to deal with the anticipated massive influx of protesters. Security arrangements at the International Amphitheatre, where the convention was to be held, were under the direct control of the White House, a further indication of Johnson's intent to come to Chicago. By the time the convention opened, Chicago resembled an armed camp. The city's 12,000 police were on twelve-hour shifts. The Illinois National Guard was activated and on a stand-by basis, as were 5,000 specially trained federal troops billeted at O'Hare field and Glenview Naval Air Station. So tight was White House control of the situation that, on the Sunday afternoon before the convention opened, even Mayor Daley had not received his allocation of tickets.

Sunday was to be a fateful day. After allowing the Yippies to cavort unmolested in Lincoln Park throughout the week, Mayor Daley ordered Police Superintendent Conlisk to enforce the 11 P.M. curfew for Chicago parks and to clear the area of the demonstrators. The first line of police, wearing gas masks, moved west from Lake Shore Drive, with instructions to toss tear gas into the area where the demonstrators had gathered behind their flimsy barricades. A second line of police then followed to make a sweep of the park.

The protesters fought back with rocks, bricks, bags of filth and anything they could tear loose from the park benches. Police in the second rank, moving past comrades fallen to the ground with bleeding foreheads, chased and clubbed the demonstrators as they ran out of the park toward refuge in nearby Old Town, a haven for hippies and the new life style. Newsmen as well as protesters were beaten. The result of this needless assault on a chilly band of the radical fringe was to make the battle of Lincoln Park a world-wide media event, completely overshadowing the convention itself.

The violence inflicted upon newsmen, particularly those who were cameramen or photographers, worsened an already tense relationship between the city and the media. A strike by telephone technicians had produced an additional aggravation for the television newsmen, already irritated by the need to move their cargo of technical equipment from the Republican convention in Miami to Chicago in less than a week's time. Many suspected that Daley had not made a real attempt to settle the telephone strike in order to minimize any street coverage of convention demonstrations (all equipment required special hookups, as the portable minicam had yet to be developed).

Sporadic violence continued through Monday and Tuesday as the protesters not only taunted police but pelted them with such missiles as human excrement, razor blades inserted in apples and various other kinds of filth. It was the kind of provocation only the most disciplined police force could have withstood; but Chicago's police—and their mayor—were in no mood to impose self-discipline.

The eyes of the world were on Chicago. The image that the mayor had worked so hard to achieve was being destroyed. Television was carrying the confrontation throughout the world, with the TV commentators picturing Daley as a petty dictator; one reporter even attempted to draw a parallel with the previous week's takeover of Czechoslovakia by Soviet troops and tanks.

Wednesday, August 28, was the day that Hubert Horatio Humphrey was to see himself nominated for president of the United States. But he could only watch helplessly from his suite in the Conrad Hilton Hotel as events unfolded outside his window that probably as much as any single factor doomed his hopes of holding America's highest office.

The trouble began at the rally that had been authorized for the afternoon at the Grant Park band shell. A young man climbed the flagpole and lowered the American flag to half-staff; others pulled it completely to the ground and ran up what was later described as a Viet Cong flag, a black flag of anarchy, a red flag of revolution, or just as probable, someone's red

DEMONSTRATORS OUTSIDE CONRAD HILTON HOTEL
Democratic Convention, 1968

underwear. Police moved in to tear it down, whatever it was, and waded into the crowd to arrest the culprits. Met by a barrage of missiles, they fell back and then moved into the crowd again, with batons swinging.

The demonstrators then attempted to organize a march to the Amphitheatre, but retreated under a cloud of tear gas that also wafted across Michigan Avenue into the window of Humphrey's suite, where he was watching the convention on television. As night approached, thousands poured out of Grant Park to join the crowd already gathered in front of the Hilton Hotel. The entire scene was eerily lighted by the huge lights mounted on the massive vans containing TV equipment parked outside the hotel.

The police officer in charge at the scene thought the crowd too large for the police detail to handle and made an emergency call for assistance. The reinforcements formed another police line at Wabash and Balbo, one block to the west, then started east to disperse the crowd in front of the hotel. The demonstrators, caught in a crush between the two police lines, fought back, and a violent street battle ensued.

The TV cameras had been in place since the demonstration early in the afternoon. William Braden of the *Sun-Times* reported "that if it had not been for the intrusion of reality, it might have been a movie set." Chaos prevailed.

A young English journalist attempting to enter the Hilton Hotel was stopped by a policeman who wanted to know his name. "Winston Churchill," replied the young Englishman truthfully. "O.K., wise guy," replied the policeman, "You're under arrest." Demonstrators were either chased or fled, and forced their way into the hotel; several were arrested on an upper floor serving as headquarters for presidential aspirant Senator Eugene McCarthy. People in the crowd were pushed and beaten as they were hauled or dragged to paddy wagons. Police stood with blood streaming down their faces from the assault of rocks and missiles.

In nineteen minutes, it was all over. But the "Battle of Chicago" had given the world a view of Chicago that was to produce a cry of outrage. Not since the massacre of striking workers at the Republic Steel works on Memorial Day in 1937 had the Chicago police been so severely criticized.

Following the convention, the National Commission on the Causes and Prevention of Violence contracted with Daniel Walker, a politically ambitious Chicago attorney, to prepare a report on the disturbances. The report, summing up the findings of its investigative staff, contained a single paragraph that was to become as controversial as the protests themselves: "To read dispassionately the hundreds of statements describing at firsthand the events of Sunday and Monday nights is to become convinced of the presence of what can only be called a 'police riot.' "

The term *police riot* was only applied to the events of Sunday night and Monday in Lincoln Park. But in the public mind, it quickly came to be associated with the actions of the police during the entire week of the convention. The Walker report did not apply the term to the actions in front of the Hilton on Wednesday night, though it did say that "police discipline broke during the melee" and that "the weight of violence was overwhelmingly on the side of the police."

Mayor Daley conceded nothing, however. "I say again," he told an interviewer, "and I am proud of it, that there was no one killed in Chicago and no one shot in Chicago . . . The American public was defrauded by television coverage of the convention. We didn't create the turbulence [in front of the Hilton Hotel]. Everybody knows that television forced it. There wasn't a fair presentation of the news. I had nothing to do with setting up the convention or running the police department. I gave no orders to the police department and I defy anyone to show that I did."

Some years later, the author of this history was to ask Daley in a private conversation at dinner with their wives at The Tavern Club about how much of the responsibility for the actions at the convention was Daley's and how much was Johnson's. The author knew from personal involvement that the order to clear Lincoln Park was Daley's; he also had considerable evidence that the security precautions were Johnson's.

Daley's answer was in the character of the man. "Emmett," he said, "I was raised in the Eleventh Ward and taught party loyalty. Whatever it was, they will never hear it from me." But then he added, in one of the few moments that it might be said he was ever off guard, "But I will tell you that twice I had to tell the president of the United States that he could not come to Chicago—once when he was sitting in Air Force One on the runway with the engines running." This later reference, of course, was to the night of the president's birthday, when Johnson had obviously anticipated coming before the convention for an ovation and, hopefully, a nomination by acclamation.

History has a way of correcting its own errors. Despite the denunciations on television, the pictures of violence and the indignant outpourings of the editorialists, it was apparent when the emotions of the moment had passed that Daley was closer to the heart of America than were the protesters. Ten years later, Daniel Walker, whose name was on the report critical of Daley and who was a perennial political foe of the mayor's, was to add his own qualification. "The problem with the phrase 'police riot,'" he said, "was that it was too colorful—it was kind of picked up and used to characterize everything I said. And, of course, that's not true. It was specifically limited to a few officers and to a few incidents. And maybe I shouldn't have used that phrase. Because it does color everything."

Charles Remberg, a free-lance writer and member of the Walker commission staff who actually wrote the sections on the Grant Park melee, added his own reservations. "I wasn't on the streets when all this happened," he said. "I just had television contact with the actual events and then came back and tried to recapture some of the things that happened.

"One impression really stuck with me in processing the material and in talking to some of the people who had actually been there. I think I became more sympathetic with the police position than I would have if I had just relied on what I had heard about the event at the time. When you consider some of the stuff the cops had to put up with, it became more understandable how things got out of hand. And there was a lot more flavor of deliberate provocation and really degrading sorts of things that were done to these cops on the line than I ever found filtered through TV or the newspapers.

"Objects thrown at police lines included rocks, bottles, bricks, ceramic tiles, chunks of concrete, cherry bombs, balloons filled with paint, beer cans filled with sand, eggs and tomatoes, flaming rags, plastic golf balls and Ping-Pong balls studded with nails, as well as paper bags filled with feces and soda cans filled with urine. One demonstrator offered a policeman a sandwich filled with excrement. Thirteen policemen suffered eye burns from unknown chemicals. Glass ashtrays, wet towels, rolls of toilet paper and plastic bags of urine were dropped from upper windows of the Hilton. Some demonstrators flicked lighted cigarettes at the police and others spit in their faces.

"By the time this filtered through the standards of TV and the newspapers," Remberg said, "these kids were really sanitized. Whereas the errors the cops made—being in the violence area—were not sanitized away. So the whole thing really looked out of whack when you tried to follow it."

These views were from the perspective of a decade later. But so intense were the criticism and the media representation of events at the time, that Mayor Daley called a surprised Walter Cronkite and told him that he would like to go on television with Cronkite and give his version of events. Daley had been avoiding all press interviews, but he knew that Cronkite with his network show had access to the hearts and minds of America, and it was to them that Daley wanted to speak.

In the interview, Daley demonstrated that even such a master interviewer as Cronkite was no match for the master politician. Daley not only evaded the tough questions but startled interviewer and audience alike with the claim that the tight security was the result of intelligence reports that "certain people planned to assassinate the three contenders for the presidency; that certain people planned to assassinate many of the leaders, including myself. So I took the necessary precautions."

Media commentators tended to deprecate this statement as without substance. But Daley's actions after the convention, whether based on fact or paranoia, tended to confirm the fact that he genuinely believed himself to be in danger of physical harm. Jane Byrne, one of his political aides at the time and later to become mayor of Chicago, confirmed this view.

Byrne was furious with the Kennedy people. She felt they owed Daley much (early in the convention Daley had even tried to persuade Edward Kennedy to stand for president) and she felt they had walked away from Daley in his moment of trouble. Before the convention started, Pierre Salinger, President John F. Kennedy's press secretary, had told her he

WAR PROTESTERS RALLY AT STATUE OF GENERAL JOHN A. LOGAN

wasn't coming to Chicago. "If I wanted to give blood," he said, "I would do it in Vietnam, not in Chicago." This confirmed her view that there would have been incitements to violence, even without the tactical mistake at Lincoln Park.

Thursday morning, the day after the episode at the Hilton, she received a call from Kenny O'Donnell, one of the Kennedy inner circle. He wanted her help in getting to see Daley. She refused, adding that it was her view Daley would not see him or any other member of the Kennedy camp. In that case, said O'Donnell, he would like to give her a message to give to the mayor. It was this:

After the fracas at the Hilton and the convention session on Wednesday night, he had stopped by the bar at the Pick-Congress Hotel for a drink. There he had encountered two of the top members of the party, who were furious at what had occurred and told him they were going to "get Daley." O'Donnell wanted Daley to have this information.

Byrne, who hesitated to pass on the bad news, finally did so, thinking she was passing on political information. Daley received it quite differently. As she was to describe it, "His hand jumped, he almost broke the pencil in his hand and said to me, 'Is it to be physical?'" Byrne was flustered; she had anticipated a strong reaction to bad news, but she had no idea the mayor would associate it with assassination. "But they are Democrats, Mister Mayor," she replied weakly.

A further confirmation of his actual fear for his physical safety came in the changes he ordered in the security arrangements in the area of the mayor's office at City Hall. A steel sliding door replaced a pair of glass doors, the number of his bodyguards was increased and security precautions were doubled.

The convention left Daley both wounded and exhausted, his own pride and his pride in his beloved Chicago both visibly damaged by the events of the convention week. Many political obituaries were prematurely written. But for eight more years he was to serve the city as its mayor, elected by greater majorities than ever.

The government, of course, could not let the rioters' flouting of authority go unchallenged. Eight demonstrators were charged with violating the federal antiriot act, which made it a crime to cross state lines with the intention of inciting, promoting, encouraging or participating in a riot. Those indicted were David Dellinger, Tom Hayden, Rennie Davis, Jerry Rubin, Abbie Hoffman, Lee Weiner, John Froines and the black militant Bobby Seale. They were put on trial in the United States District Courtroom of Julius J. Hoffman and promptly converted their street guerrilla warfare into guerrilla theater in the courtroom. Seale's defiance in the courtroom so angered the judge that he had Seale bound and gagged and eventually separated from the rest of the trial.

The "Chicago Seven," as the remaining defendants came to be known, were treated more like folk heroes in Chicago than potential criminals on trial. The trial itself dragged on for 103 days, with the judge in constant confrontations with the defendants and their lawyers. When it was over, the jury—which most observers had cynically predicted would quickly come in with a guilty verdict—deliberated for five days before reaching decisions. They found none of the five guilty of conspiracy and only five of the seven guilty of crossing state lines as individuals with intent to violate the federal antiriot law. Two of the seven—Lee Weiner and John Froines—were cleared of all charges.

Judge Hoffman, whose conduct of the trial was to be severely criticized by an appeals court, promptly imposed contempt sentences to compensate for the jury's leniency. These, too, were appealed and, ultimately, dismissed. Despite the expense, the notoriety and the comic aspects of this particular exercise of the American judicial system, none of the defendants was ever to spend a day in prison for the events that shook Chicago in the summer of 1968.

Two views probably serve as well as any to put the events of the week in perspective. Sociologist Peter Berger was to look back and say: "The terribly exaggerated expectation of change in 1968 has not come true. . . . In Chicago, in 1968, all of us thought the roof was coming down. And when the smoke blew away, the roof was still there. The basic institutional structure of the country remained intact, and in that sense the system showed great resilience. The system has adapted, or from the radical point of view, co-opted many of these impulses."

Remarkably, another equally balanced view came from Tom Hayden, one of the Chicago Seven tried for conspiracy and a leader of the demonstrators involved in the confrontation. Hayden saw it some years later as the playing out of a Greek tragedy. "Chicago," he said, "was the inevitable playing out of a conflict which had become extreme. There were no rules; no law prevailed. The behavior of the demonstrators was the flip side of the attitude of the government and the police. . . . The lesson is that some chain reactions are uncontrollable, once they're unleashed."

CHICAGO-STYLE TELEVISION. (From left: Kukla, Fran & Ollie; Studs Place with Studs Terkel; Dave Garroway; Clint Youle; and Walt of Walt's Workshop. Not shown—Dorsey Connors)

Life Styles in Nude and Black

THROUGHOUT Chicago's history, there is precedent for believing that, when a new art form emerges, Chicago will evolve a "school" to refine and develop it. Such was the case with architecture after the Fire. Later, writers such as Sherwood Anderson, Upton Sinclair and poet Carl Sandburg fulfilled the prophecy of an 1867 visitor who wrote of the prairie-born man who "some day would make his own books as well as his own laws." And in journalism, Ben Hecht and Charles MacArthur gave form and style to a raucous era in American journalism. When daytime serials on radio became America's favorite diversion, it was Irma Phillips and "Ma Perkins" in Chicago who were its epicenter.

Then when television added a new dimension to the capacity of the American people to see and to be entertained, TV entertainment was nurtured and cradled in Chicago. Technically, it was fostered by Captain William C. Eddy, who had been hired to head Chicago's first TV station, WBKB, as early as 1939. Eddy held more than 100 TV, radio and electronic patents. But probably the station will best be remembered as the

THE NEW CHICAGO 384

home of "Kukla, Fran and Ollie" and the Kuklapolitan players, the puppets whose gentle humor and exchanges with actress Fran Allison were skillfully written and executed by their creator Burr Tillstrom.

Soon a form of television evolved that was sufficiently distinct to be known as the Chicago school. It flourished for the most part at the Midwest television studios of the National Broadcasting Company under the creative leadership of station manager Jules Herbuveaux. With the philosophy that "You can't make a $10 idea out of a $2 idea, but you can take a $10 idea and bring it down to a budget without hurting it too much," he put a wide variety of shows on the air.

Dave Garroway's "Garroway at Large" introduced a low-key style to television; it was so successful that he was lured to New York, where the approach was promptly hyped and smothered. "Studs Place" gave Studs Terkel the easy interview form he was later to use in producing a number of best-selling books based on tape recordings of Americans talking just as they might have at "Studs Place." Lincoln Park Zoo director Marlin Perkins launched a lifetime television career on Herbuveaux's "Zoo Parade." Frances Horwich's children's show "Ding Dong School" was an instantaneous success and set the pattern for such derivations as "Captain Kangaroo." Don Herbert became "Mr. Wizard," Dorsey Conners used wire coat hangers to influence a generation of homemakers, Clifton Utley and his wife Frayn did literate news commentary (while raising a son, Garrick, who was to be one of the network's star reporters) and Tom Duggan introduced the element of controversy (both verbal and physical) into sports coverage; he would have found Howard Cosell a bit bland.

Joel Sternberg, in writing of this period, commented: "It was a short-lived school as Chicago schools go [it lasted only into 1953 by most reckonings] and maybe it was born, as some things, out of the challenges of too little of everything—too little money, small studios, and even smaller names—but it was a genius period." This was the period when Fred Allen, the famous radio comedian, came to Chicago at his own expense to appear on "Garroway at Large" and see how it worked. Allen then announced that they "ought to tear down Radio City, New York, rebuild it in Chicago, and call it Television Town." Unfortunately, the advertising agencies that paid the bills for television were in New York City; the actors and actresses needed to supply the insatiable demands of this new medium for entertainment material were in New York and Los Angeles. The development of the coaxial cable made television a national medium, and Chicago again found itself the Second City to the temples of entertainment on the coasts.

If Chicago was the "Second City," as New Yorker writer A. J. Liebling had derisively labeled it, it was not without a sense of humor. To Paul Sills, a young graduate of the University of Chicago, it seemed quite an appropriate name for the cabaret theater he wanted to found in which young actors and actresses could use improvisational theater to poke fun at the foibles of mankind. Although the University of Chicago had no drama department, Sills found himself there in the 1950s in the company of Edward Asner, Mike Nichols and Elaine May. They created theater wherever they could; after graduation they established themselves first as the Playwright Theater and then as the Compass Players, with Sills as director. In both instances they were shut down by the Fire Department because of the rickety nature of their surroundings.

Sills was a native Chicagoan who had grown up learning about the theater at the side of his mother Viola Spolin, who was introduced to "recreational training" at the old Hull House. With her son in tow, Spolin traveled to various settlement houses, working on children's shows and adult classes with innovative nonverbal, nonauthoritarian theater games. This early predilection was to reach its full expression in Second City, the cabaret theater Sills founded in 1959 in a former Chinese laundry on Wells Street. There the players of the earlier companies were joined by Shelly Berman, Barbara Harris, Howard Alk, Bernard Sahlins and others who were to become among the luminaries of the American theater.

A SECOND CITY CAST. The setting remains the same

Since the founding of Second City, very little has changed in its format, even though it is now an international institution. There are still five men, two women, a piano player, a group of wooden chairs on a bare stage and what critic Richard Christiansen has called "the inspiration of improvisation." Christiansen went on to comment, "Few realized that the improvisational technique of those early revues would go on to become standard training for American actors."

Although Second City companies were founded elsewhere, Sills remained a Chicagoan. "I have lived and worked in New York, and I've worked in Los Angeles, which is out of the question for me as a place to live," he told Christiansen, "and I still come back to Chicago. It's a place where you can live the whole life of a city. It's my home."

Encouraged by Sills's experience, other small theaters sprung into being, some to flourish and some to disappear. At St. Nicholas Theater, a young artistic director, David Mamet, studied his craft and sought fresh approaches to the American theater. In 1976, he was rewarded when his *Sexual Perversity in Chicago* won the *Village Voice* Obie and in 1977 when his play *American Buffalo* won both the *Village Voice* Award and the New York Drama Critics Award.

Sills was not the only young Chicagoan with new ideas about entertainment. At a kitchen table on the South Side, an aspiring cartoonist labored over the layouts for a new magazine that would reach an audience television could not touch. The mass circulation magazines such as *Life* and *Look*, with their heavy dependence on pictures, were clearly on their way out, as they could not compete with the sense of immediacy that television gave to the news. But, reasoned Hugh Hefner, the incipient publisher, neither television nor the mass magazines could offer nudity; with nudity as his showcase, he would launch a magazine to offer America not only entertainment but the concept of a new life style. He would call it *Playboy*.

The magazine had a modest start in 1953. Its first issue carried no address or date—a device to keep it on the newsstands as long as possible or until a second edition could be produced, not at the moment of birth a certain event. But, success was meteoric, and *Playboy* became the cult authority for a generation seeking sexual freedom.

"We want to make it clear from the very start," Hefner wrote in an early issue, "that we aren't a family magazine. If you're somebody's sister, wife or mother-in-law and picked us up by mistake, please pass us along to the man in your life and get back to the *Ladies' Home Companion*."

Time magazine called "Hef"—as he wanted to be known—"a prophet of pop hedonism." Driven by the exigencies of being a prophet, Hef laboriously typed out reams of his view of life, which he elevated to the status of the *Playboy* "philosophy," while alternately relighting his pipe and

INSIDE THE PLAYBOY MANSION

downing flagons of Pepsi-Cola (his own life style did not include alcoholic beverages, possibly because they might interfere with the level of sexual activity demanded by the *Playboy* code). Eventually, the articulation of this philosophy was to extend over three years, twenty-five issues of the magazine and more than a quarter of a million words.

Playboy Clubs soon followed, where members could be served by "Bunnies" in skintight costumes adorned with white cotton tails and bunny ears and containing mysterious supports creating an illusion of bosoms larger than life-size. The costumes required the Bunnies to serve drinks somewhat in the manner of an acrobat doing a back flip, and their posture was carefully policed; even their ears had to be bent in a certain way, otherwise said a "Bunny adviser," "You'll look like you have just had a fright." Bunnies were told, "Your Bunny tail is your proudest possession. You must make sure it is always white and fluffy."

Hefner, once he could afford it, lived in the *Playboy* style. He bought an elegant residence on the near North Side of Chicago and converted it into a playground for pleasure; it was famous enough to be known only as "the Mansion" and attracted celebrities from civil rights leaders and editorial-page columnists to Hollywood starlets. A swimming pool was built in the basement, adjoined, of course, by a "love grotto."

In the Mansion, Hefner created a world of his own making. Eternal night, the time of sybaritic pleasures, reigned supreme. With the shades always drawn, he conducted most of his business in dressing gown and pajamas from the center of an eight-foot circular bed, which he could rotate mechanically so as to give himself the illusion of moving about the room.

One of the best descriptions of the Mansion was that of the European journalist Oriana Fallaci. She wrote: "He stays in it as a pharaoh in his grave, and so he doesn't notice that the night has ended, the day has begun, a winter passed, and a spring and a summer. Last time he emerged from the grave was last winter, they say, but he did not like what he saw and returned with great relief three days later. The sky was again extinguished beyond the electronic gate." Eventually, however, even the Mansion could not shut out Chicago's weather, and Hefner exiled himself to a second Mansion in California, where hedonism could be practiced in the sunshine. The magazine, however, continued to maintain its offices in Chicago.

Another South Sider had a different kind of magazine in mind as Hefner was launching *Playboy*. John Johnson had been editing a house magazine for the black-owned Supreme Life Insurance Company and in that position had been preparing a digest of news about black people. He reasoned that there should be a wider audience for such news than just com-

WORLD HEAVYWEIGHT CHAMPION MUHAMMAD ALI. "I am the greatest!"

COACH GEORGE HALAS AND HIS STAR QUARTERBACK, SID LUCKMAN.
Two from football's hall of fame

pany employees and borrowed $20,000 to start a small magazine called *Negro Digest*. Its success was modest, but it permitted Johnson to think of a magazine in which black people might read about themselves as whites could in their magazines, which at the time contained few black faces.

The theme of the magazine was not to be black protest but black achievement. An achiever himself, Johnson was sure there were many more stories like his own that not only could be told but could be a model for self-improvement for many blacks. At the suggestion of his wife Eunice, Johnson called the new magazine *Ebony*, and it was to become the most widely read black magazine in America. Success was not easy, as many dealers were reluctant to take on what they termed "a colored magazine." Johnson overcame this by giving his friends money to buy the magazine at the newsstands and create a demand for it; on occasion the same magazine might be returned to the news dealer and sold several times. But the quality of the magazine was high and its acceptance rapid; its editor, Lerone Bennett, Jr., emerged as the leading American author in the field of black culture and history.

But of the black achievers of American society, none could compare in fame with Muhammad Ali, heavyweight champion of the world and self-proclaimed "The Greatest." Born Cassius Clay, he changed his name after joining the World Community of Al Islam in the West, or, as it was more popularly known, the Black Muslims, and taking up residence in a mansion on the South Side of Chicago. He was the first heavyweight boxer to gain the world championship three times, winning and defending his title in places as widely disparate as Zaire, Las Vegas and the Philippines. His personality, his politics (he refused to serve in the Vietnam War on religious grounds), and the doggerel he composed to celebrate his exploits or annoy his challengers, as well as his boxing skills, made him a world celebrity.

But if Muhammad Ali was "the greatest," the same could not be said of Chicago's sports teams. Although a few superstars emerged, the teams themselves seemed to be noted more for their eccentricities than for any flirtation with greatness. Nowhere was this drama of losing played out in such a long-running soap opera as within the confines of "beautiful Wrigley Field—Home of the Chicago Cubs."

The last National League pennant won by the Cubs was recorded in 1945 at the end of World War II when its collection of draft rejects and over-age players was just a bit better than those of the other teams in the league. So were the players of the Detroit Tigers, whom the Cubs met in the World Series of that year. "I don't think either one of them can win it," commented Chicago sports writer Warren Brown. He was wrong; the Cubs managed to make Detroit a winner by losing the seventh and final game of the series.

Cub owner Philip K. Wrigley, who had inherited the team from his father, William Wrigley, was a patient man and an unconventional one. He tried every means possible of improving the team, including hiring eight coaches and no manager, later an athletic director, and at one time a hypnotist. Chagrined, he took out newspaper advertisements to confess failure and accept the blame. One advertisement read:

> "The Cub management wants you to know we appreciate the wonderful support you are giving the ball club. . . . We also know that this year's rebuilding job has been a flop."

It was an advertisement which could have been etched in stone—or at least reprinted every year.

It was during these various experiments with the alchemy of producing a winner that Branch Rickey and the Dodgers broke the color line which had barred blacks from major league baseball by hiring Jackie Robinson. The Cubs bowed to the trend, despite some apprehension about the reaction of their almost totally white North Side constituency. In 1953, Wid Matthews, the director of player personnel signed second baseman Gene Baker. A few days later Matthews told Wrigley he had hired another "Negro player" from the Kansas City Monarchs.

"Who?" Wrigley asked.

"Fellow named Ernie Banks," Matthews replied.

"Gee whiz," Wrigley answered. "We are bringing up one Negro player. Why go out and get another one?"

"Well," Matthews replied, "we had to have a roommate for the one we've got." (It was true. For many years in professional baseball, football and basketball, blacks were only assigned blacks as roommates.)

The nearest the Cubs came to glory was in 1969. On September 2nd, under the lash of Leo Durocher (famous for his statement that "Nice guys finish last."), the Cubs led their division by five games. However, in a late season swoon that their fans have come to regard as traditional, the Cubs lost 11 out of 12 games and yielded the pennant to the Mets.

Over the years, however, the player from the Kansas City Monarchs was not only the star of the team but its heart as well. Ernie Banks became "Mr. Cub," playing his way into the record books and the Hall of Fame without ever having shared the thrill of being with a winning team.

Finally, in the spring of 1980, the sorry condition of the Cubs led to a defection that to Chicago sports fans ranked in emotional drama with those of Mikhail Baryshnikov and Rudolf Nureyev. Columnist Mike Royko, whose annual essays on the agony of being a Cub fan signalled the opening of the baseball season, surrendered and defected to the White Sox.

As Royko put it, "Thus ended more than 40 years of loyal servitude to the Cubs—years that had joyous moments (homers by Pafko, Sauer, Banks, Williams or Moryn; fielding gems by Hack, Kessinger, Jeffcoat, Hubbs or Waitkus) and moments of gloom (the mad flailing bats of Serena, Terwilliger, Ramazzotti and Chiti; the ground balls caroming off the foreheads of Merullo, Smalley, Madrid or Miksis). "But that didn't matter. To the contrary, I always believed that being a Cub fan built strong character. It taught a person that if you try hard enough and long enough, you'll still lose. And that's the story of life."

Citing the pitiful cries of woe from Cub players whose salaries were considerably more impressive than their batting averages, Royko stood before the famous Sox Park scoreboard, placed his hand upon Bill Veeck's wooden leg and solemnly took an oath to be a White Sox fan. The following year, however, Royko confessed that being a Cub fan was an "addiction" and switched his loyalty back to the Cubs.

Then, in the waning spring of 1981 after the most dismal start in history for the Cubs, William Wrigley, the third generation of the family to own the Cubs, gave up as well. For a sum approximating $20 million, he sold the Cubs to another venerable Chicago institution, The Tribune Company, publisher of *The Chicago Tribune.*

It was not the first time around in Chicago for the Sox's Veeck, whose wooden leg was the result of a wound suffered while serving as a Marine in the South Pacific. Veeck, who had known other adversities, including at one time owning the lowly St. Louis Browns baseball club, was not a favorite of baseball's establishment. But if he did not have the funds to buy the best ballplayers or give the fans a good ball game, he could at least give them a good show.

He was a knowledgeable baseball man. In 1958 he had purchased the Chicago White Sox and the following year under manager Al Lopez, the team scratched, slid and singled its way to an American League championship. It was the first Sox pennant since the notorious Black Sox scandal of 1919.

The White Sox clinched the pennant on the night of September 22nd, 1959 in a game at Cleveland. They won by surviving a typically crucial situation with men on base in the bottom of the ninth inning. With the final out, Chicagoans started to celebrate. Six days earlier the City Council had passed a resolution at the instigation of Mayor Daley, an ardent Sox fan, stating: "Be it commanded that bells ring, whistles blow, bands play and general joy be unconfined when the coveted pennant is won by the heroes of 35th Street."

No one mentioned sirens, but Fire Commissioner Robert Quinn, a close friend of Daley's who often accompanied the mayor to Sox games and who was also the head of the Chicago Civil Defense organization, saw no reason why they should not be included in the "general joy." At precisely 10:30 p.m., 47 minutes after the end of the game, Chicago's air raid sirens sounded in unison. Much to the Commissioner's surprise, there were people in Chicago who did not know the White Sox were fighting for a pennant. They did recognize an air raid siren, however, and reacted with various kinds of alarm. One family packed its car with canned goods and headed for Milwaukee. But most tried to call City Hall to find out what was going on.

Veeck's health and financial pressures continued to plague him; in 1961 he was forced to sell the team. But in 1975, he returned as head of a group of Chicagoans and took over for a second time. The years were not happy ones; attendance continued to slide and Veeck was forced to sell his best ballplayers in order to finance the club. Finally, in 1980 after a customary battle with the baseball commissioner, he and his co-owners sold the team to a group of local investors. Bill Veeck was gone from the Chicago baseball scene; but he had made Sox Park an exciting place to watch a baseball game.

Fans of the Chicago Bears were also forced to live for the most part on memories. George Halas, who was called simply "Coach" by most of those who knew him, directed the Bears to their last National Football League title in 1963 when his team defeated the New York Giants 14 to 10 in a championship game played in sub-zero weather at Wrigley Field. Although generally given credit for inventing the game of professional football, Halas was unable to find successors to his own coaching heritage with the talent or formations to duplicate the 73–0 win over the Washington Redskins in 1940 which had been engineered by Halas, coach Clark Shaughnessey, the T-formation expert, and quarterback Sid Luckman.

There were other problems. Wrigley Field was built for baseball and Halas desperately wanted a football stadium of his own. He watched enviously as the American Football Conference merged with the National Conference and one city after another built Superdomes, Astrodomes and Silverdomes. He had only a badly outdated Soldier Field. Finally, after years of negotiation, it was agreed that Soldier Field would be updated to put it on at least a comparable level with other modern stadiums.

But if the Bears were not winners, they had their superstars. In 1965, they drafted both Gale Sayers and Dick Butkus, who despite injuries that shortened their careers, were enthusiastic choices for Football's Hall of Fame. A few years later, Walter Payton—"Mr. Sweetness"—joined the rush to glory in the league's record books.

But the star of the Bears, who earned such nicknames as the "Monster of the Midway" for their rough style of play, remained Halas himself. Until he retired in 1968, Halas would follow the ball up and down the field, teeth clinched, hands thrust deep in his overcoat pocket or pulling on his fedora, meanwhile bellowing at his players, badgering the officials and blatantly coaching from the sidelines beyond the prescribed limits. Trying to lend moral assistance to a Bear field goal attempt, he once booted a 240-pound guard right off the bench. Another time he curtly ordered a rookie, "Taylor, we've run out of time outs. Go in and get hurt."

Halas always kept his sense of humor. When he stepped down from professional coaching as the recognized founder of professional football, he gave this explanation: "I suppose I began to realize it was time to quit when, in one of our final games of the season, I started rushing after a referee who was pacing off a penalty and it suddenly dawned on me that I was not gaining on him." Even in football's Hall of Fame in Canton, Ohio, the bust of Halas is side-by-side with a mural picturing him arguing with an official.

Sports fans looked for heroes and found few. In 1960–61, the Black Hawks won the Stanley Cup, symbolic of a world championship in hockey, for the first time since 1938. A "Golden Jet" named Bobby Hull captured Chicago's imagination and in three seasons set scoring records of more than 50 goals.

Other teams came on the scene as sports widened its appeal. The Chicago Bulls became Chicago's entry in the National Basketball Association. The Sting tried both to interest and educate Chicagoans in the excitement of soccer. And the Hustle brought women's professional basketball to Chicago.

It was perhaps symbolic in 1980 that the great Muhammad Ali, slowing down at the age of 37, was not able to reclaim his title from Ernie Holmes. Now there were no champions in Chicago. But there was always "next year."

MIKE ROYKO SWEARS LOYALTY TO WHITE SOX ON BILL VEECK'S WOODEN LEG

SIR GEORG SOLTI CONDUCTS
THE CHICAGO SYMPHONY
ORCHESTRA

"I Hate Mediocrity"

THEODORE THOMAS, it may be recalled, commented that one of his reasons for founding a symphony orchestra in Chicago was that he "understood the excitement and nervous strain that everyone, more or less, suffered from who lived there." What he could not have anticipated was that some of that nervous strain and excitement would one day apply to Chicago's musical community.

Through the years, the Chicago Symphony Orchestra had been one of Chicago's more stable institutions. In half a century, it had only two musical directors, Theodore Thomas and Frederick Stock. But with the death of Stock in 1942, the orchestra suddenly found itself searching for a new musical identity. Over the next ten years, it was to have three different directors, Desire Defauw, Artur Rodzinski and Rafael Kubelik. Each departed unhappily, Defauw and Kubelik retreating in a barrage of criticism from Claudia Cassidy, the acerbic music and drama critic of the *Chicago Tribune*; Rodzinski also departed unhappily, even with Miss Cassidy's support, because of a dispute over the relationship of the orchestra to a possible opera season.

Stability returned in 1953 with the arrival of Fritz Reiner. The new maestro ran the orchestra in the Toscanini tradition, autocratic and tyrannical, and his tongue was even sharper than his musical beat. He was a perfectionist, and, as one player recalls, "always had a list of people to fire." During the next ten years the reputation of the orchestra grew rapidly. Under the direction of Margaret Hillis, a Chicago Symphony chorus was organized. The Hungarian-born Reiner was accustomed to the German sonorities in which many members of the orchestra had been trained, and he was able to give the orchestra a richer and more substantial tone as well as a strong musical identity—offset, in part, by a sense of personal insecurity on the part of the musicians. When a European tour was canceled because of Reiner's health, the musicians staged a locker-room revolt to show their displeasure.

Reiner was succeeded in 1963 by Jean Martinon, a one-time French resistance fighter and prize-winning composer. Martinon was an innovator. With the skills of the Chicago orchestra at his command, he sought to introduce a strong contemporary flavor to the orchestra's programming. "The Chicago Orchestra is the best I have ever had as a musical director," he said, "and because of that fact, I repeated only four pieces in the five years I was there."

His relations with the orchestra were not as firm as his admiration for it, however. Discipline declined, disputes with the players arose, and Claudia Cassidy used her podium to demand a change. In 1968, his contract was not renewed. "There was a little game of destruction and too many people played it," he said laconically before returning to France.

Martinon's successor was Sir Georg Solti, who had turned down an offer of the post prior to the hiring of Martinon. Solti, who had been musical director of the Royal Opera House, Covent Garden, accepted on the condition that the orchestra travel both nationally and internationally; he said he wanted to make the orchestra's gifts clear to the nation and to the world. Solti was no stranger to the orchestra or Chicago; he had first conducted the Chicago Symphony at the Ravinia Festival in 1954 and had made his debut as a guest conductor in Orchestra Hall in 1965.

Solti and the orchestra seemed destined for each other. "Something extraordinary happened in Chicago," Solti told writer William Barry Furlong. "I made no changes. We didn't have to adjust to each other. Our ways of making music were the same. Wine became champagne; we sparkle together. It's like Siegfried and Brunnhilde. The girl was beautiful and Siegfried turned out not to be impotent."

Solti was not long in achieving the recognition he desired. A smashing concert at Carnegie Hall in New York (at which he broke his own rules by playing an encore to a foot-stamping, shouting crowd of admirers) was followed in 1971 by a triumphant tour of Europe. Vienna was typical of the acclaim. "The applause was in direct proportion to the occasion," wrote the critic in *Die Presse*. "The Chicago Symphony acquitted itself, under Solti, as probably the best ensemble possessed by America at the present time." The critic in Stockholm wrote, "In his movement and manner, Solti greatly resembles a well-trained professional boxer. . . . His authority is total and he radiates it enormously, and first and last one is struck by his tremendous force." Other tours to Europe followed in 1974 and 1978; in 1977 the orchestra repeated its triumphs in Japan.

What was this sound that Solti drew from the Chicago Symphony that struck such responsive chords in listeners? "The Chicago Symphony has a very particular sound which I would call the 'German' sound," Solti said. "It is a heavy German sound combined with American virtuosity. The sound which no other American orchestra has, which maybe you can compare with Vienna or Berlin. Having more virtuosity than a European orchestra—a combination of a solid European base with American virtuosity. It is like IBM machines would be made in Germany. A very fortunate combination."

Before Chicago could boast of its Picasso, its Chagall, its Miro and its Calders, it suffered some civic embarrassment because it had no opera company it could call its own. Playing second city to New York and the Metropolitan Opera was perhaps to be forgiven, but there was no real rationalization for Chicago's failure to match the success of San Francisco and its widely heralded operatic season.

Since the demise of the Chicago Opera Company, the city had been forced to rely upon traveling companies of both the Met and the New York City Opera Company. These itinerant troupes of singers sometimes found being on the road a little more than they could bear.

Such was the case in 1953, when the New York City Opera Company was presenting a performance of *Carmen*. Joseph Rosenstock was the conductor, and David Poleri was the tenor singing the role of Don Jose, the jealous lover who brings the opera to a passionate conclusion by stabbing Carmen. In Chicago, however, Poleri found his passions more aroused by Rosentock's unfamiliar tempo (musician union regulations required most of the orchestra to be locally recruited) than by the frustration of his spurned love. To the astonishment of the opera aficionados, Poleri suddenly stalked off the stage in the final act, leaving Carmen alive and well. Gloria Lane, the Carmen on the occasion, was forced into the ignoble pretension of a fake suicide.

It was the kind of opera that Chicago newspapers, in the best tradition of the play *The Front Page*, found fascinating. The company manager, however, was not flustered. "You can attribute Poleri's show of temper to the fact that he's a tenor," the manager said. "You're always asking for trouble when you've got a tenor in the company."

Chicago thought it deserved something better than the opera of improvisation. It remained for a young woman who was a graduate of the city's Girls' Latin School and who had studied voice in New York and Italy to succeed to the mantle of Harold McCormick, Ganna Walska, and Mary Garden. She was Carol Fox, who originally aspired to an operatic career as a singer and actress but abandoned it with a self-appraisal as remarkable for its candor as her later achievements. "I hate mediocrity," she said bluntly in evaluating her qualities as a singer.

Mediocre as a singer she may have been; but when she turned her attention from singing opera to producing opera, her qualities as an impresario proved extraordinary. Along with her former vocal coach Nicola Rescigno and businessman Lawrence Kelly, she established in 1954 the Lyric Theatre, which began modestly with a pair of performances of *Don Giovanni*. Having proved to herself that opera in Chicago was possible, she immediately embarked on a trip to Europe, where she engaged the services of the dramatic soprano Maria Callas (who had been snubbed by the Metropolitan) and the distinguished conductor Tullio Serafin. Once again, Chicago had an opera company.

Carol Fox was not an executive destined for a role as consul in a triumvirate, however. Within two years, she and her two partners were engaged in a struggle for the control of the Lyric that was only settled after the intervention of Mayor Daley, his close friend, United States District Judge Abraham Lincoln Marovitz, and *Chicago Tribune* critic Claudia Cassidy. When the final note of this backstage drama was sounded, Carol Fox was firmly in control and Messrs. Rescigno and Kelly had departed to direct an opera theater in Dallas. Asked about the reason for the manner in which the dispute was resolved, Carol Fox, replied, "I was stronger than they were," a statement few were to dispute for the duration of her reign.

Now totally in charge, Fox changed the name of the company to the more ambitious Lyric Opera of Chicago and, as such, it was to flourish for more than a quarter of a century. In addition to Maria Callas, who made her American debut in Bellini's *Norma*, the Lyric over the years introduced for the first time to American audiences a list of superstars who included Walter Berry, Anita Cerquet, Renata Scotto, Alfredo Kraus, Elenea Suliotis and Nicolai Ghiaurov. Others, including Joan Sutherland, Beverly Sills, and Marilyn Horne, sang in Chicago long before making their debut at the Metropolitan. In another coup, Fox succeeded in signing Callas and her arch-rival Renata Tebaldi, for the same season.

There were times when the opera was as stormy offstage as behind the

"NOT SO PRIM A DONNA" The *Chicago Sun-Times* caption writer chose this description of diva Maria Callas in a dramatic backstage performance with a bewildered process-server

footlights. At one of Maria Callas's appearances, a process server attempted to serve her with some papers in connection with a contract dispute with a former manager. The diva's Greek temper was never more dramatically displayed; with cameras snapping the entire scene, the process server fled for his life.

Chicago responded to this new civic adornment by filling the Opera House for every performance; the business community cheerfully funded the deficits without which grand opera would not be quite so grand. On its silver anniversary in 1979, Lyric celebrated its own success with a gala concert featuring four of the world's great tenors—Luciano Pavarotti, Carlo Cossutta, Alfredo Kraus and Jon Vickers. They were joined by such superstars as Mirella Freni, Nicolai Ghiaurov, Sherrill Milnes, Margaret Price and Leontyne Price.

In the audience was Princess Margaret of Great Britain, who happened to be in Chicago as part of an American tour in which she was raising funds for the Royal Opera Covent Garden Development Appeal. Chicagoans, who were accustomed to digging deep in their pockets for the Lyric, were not enchanted with this competition, but on the other hand rather liked this royal recognition of their young opera company.

It was not for her attendance at the Lyric Opera gala that Princess Margaret's visit to Chicago was to be remembered, however. At a party given by local heiress Abra (Rockefeller) Prentice Anderson, Margaret found herself chatting with Mayor Jane Byrne about the mayor's recent trip to Great Britain as an official representative of President Carter at the funeral of Lord Louis Mountbatten, killed by a bomb planted by the Irish Republican Army. "The Irish," said the princess to the mayor, whose forebears came from County Mayo, "they are pigs." When the mayor's eyes flashed with anger, the princess attempted to recover. "Oh," she exclaimed, "I forgot you were Irish."

The episode was reported shortly thereafter by Irv Kupcinet, whose column of the goings, comings and sayings of Chicagoans had earned him

LYRIC OPERA'S CAROL FOX
WITH PRINCESS MARGARET
OF BRITAIN

the title of "Mr. Chicago." His own paper, the *Sun-Times*, went even further and compared Kup to the poet Homer chronicling the events in the life of the Greek semigods. When Kup, whose sources were thought to be both mysterious and infallible, reported this exchange, it assumed the proportions of an international incident. It was the most controversial comment by royalty in Chicago since Her Royal Highness, the Infanta Eulalia of Spain, referred to Mrs. Potter Palmer as "the wife of my innkeeper."

Apologies were demanded on all sides, and vehement denials were issued by the entourage of the princess. The controversy took additional flavor when the "scoundrel" who leaked the conversation to the press turned out to be (by most accounts) the mayor's husband Jay McMullen.

The furor in a teapot recalled the observation of Long John Wentworth, one of Chicago's early mayors, who said, "Chicago is noted for its sensations and that is one of the reasons why I have never liked to leave it. You cannot find any other place that has so many of them. Why travel about when there is so much of interest transpiring at home?"

While the Lyric was flourishing at the Opera House, another group of preservation-minded citizens and devotees of music were struggling to save and restore the once-grand Auditorium Theater, where opera itself had flourished for so many years. Chicago has always been of two minds about its landmarks. It is proud of the architectural heritage they represent; on the other hand, it only seems good business to tear them down and replace them with more modern buildings to make money. After all, reasons a Chicagoan, isn't that why they were put up in the first place?

Such was the debate that had raged for more than a quarter of a century about the classic Auditorium Building designed by Dankmar Adler and Louis Sullivan. Its Auditorium Theater was often acclaimed their masterpiece. It survived the Depression principally because no one had the money to tear down its massive stone walls. During World War II it suffered the ignominy of being turned into a recreation center; its stage, designed for grand opera and ballet, was converted to a bowling alley.

Following the war, President Edward J. Sparling was able to acquire the building as a home for his infant Roosevelt University. As the university grew and became more securely established, Sparling eyed the theater as a possible source of income for the university and sought a means of restoring it to its former grandeur. He was fortunate in persuading Mrs. John V. (Bea) Spachner to take on what appeared to be an impossible task; as the Opera House was empty most of the time, there seemed little justification for a second, comparable facility. But with co-chairman attorney Harold W. Norman, Mrs. Spachner battled on for seven years. Along the way she enlisted the support of architect Harry Weese, a vigorous defender of landmarks, who volunteered his services for the restoration.

On October 3, 1967, more than three-quarters of a century after its first grand opening, the Auditorium was rededicated to the arts in a fully restored condition. On the stage was the New York City Ballet performing *A Midsummer Night's Dream;* in the audience were the governor, mayor and every civic leader of consequence in the city.

There were new aspirations in art as well as in music. The Art Institute, increasingly crowded and with its resident school clamoring for more recognition, announced a $45 million expansion program that provided funds for the construction of an angular concrete wing along Columbus Drive designed by Walter Netsch. Fortuitously, the construction came at a time when it was possible to save the trading floor of the old Chicago Stock Exchange (in the process of being demolished for a Miesian office building) and reconstruct it within the Art Institute.

Another group of Chicagoans were more interested in experimentation than restoration. Finding the Art Institute more comfortable with its inherited collection of Impressionists than with the new art of America, they organized in 1967 a Museum of Contemporary Art under the leadership of such outstanding Chicago collectors as Joseph R. Shapiro, the first president, and Edwin Bergman. Art critic Harold Haydon gave the venture a Chicago flavor by commenting, "They believed that competition is the breath of life for culture as well as business."

Nicknamed "the little museum that could," it opened its doors in a modernized brick structure that had originally been built as a bakery around the turn of the century; later it had been used as offices by Playboy Enterprises in less affluent days. The heart of the museum was its series of temporary exhibitions, which included light and sound as well as the traditional artistic materials. The building itself became part of art history when Christo, in 1969, did his first major "wrapping" in the United States by covering the entire structure with canvas held in place with two miles of rope. After only ten years, the museum was able to double itself in size (pausing long enough in the remodeling to declare part of the demolition of the old building a "work of art.") "We must have filled a deeply felt need in the community," founder Shapiro commented on the opening of the enlarged museum. "It was a need for the new, presented with youthful ebullience, verve and imagination."

Chicago was to prove less hospitable to its authors than to its artists and sculptors. Only Saul Bellow, sheltered at the University of Chicago, and Gwendolyn Brooks, writing her poetry out of the black experience on the South Side, seemed at home in the city. Nelson Algren, making

SAUL BELLOW RECEIVES THE NOBEL PRIZE FOR LITERATURE as
University of Chicago professor Milton Friedman waits for his Nobel Prize in Economics

scornful comparisons of his Division Street gamblers, prostitutes and hustlers with Bellow's re-creation of Chicago's West Side Jewish experience, moved on to Paterson, New Jersey, to write of a boxer whose chief fame was that of a loser with the law. But before he left, Algren gave the city books such as *The Neon Wilderness, City on the Make* and *The Man with the Golden Arm*, which would leave an indelible imprint.

It was not easier for Algren when Saul Bellow, against whose talent Algren clearly matched himself, received three National Book Awards—a record still unmatched—for *The Adventures of Augie March, Herzog* and *Mr. Sammler's Planet*. Then, after a series of other international honors, Bellow in 1966 received the Nobel Prize in literature, the forty-first winner of the Nobel Prize to have been associated with the University of Chicago.

Other honors also came to Chicago authors. Gwendolyn Brooks's book of poems *A Street in Bronzeville* was a poignant portrait of what it meant to be black and live in Chicago. In 1950, she was awarded the Pulitzer Prize in poetry for her black poetic ballad *Annie Allen*. Leon Forrest, an associate professor of African-American studies at Northwestern University, was another author who used the novel as his means of translating the black experience in America.

On the North Side, William Brashler, whose *The Bingo Long Travelling All-Stars and Motor Kings*, recreated the harrowing but humorous saga of the Negro baseball leagues, assiduously pursued new ventures, while immersing himself in his city as a precinct captain for the ward's Democratic organization. Harry Mark Petrakis, writing from a rural setting near the Indiana dunes, re-created the sounds, sights, smells and food of Chicago's Greek-American community. James Park Sloan taught at the University of Illinois Chicago campus and sought Chicago settings for fiction with universal appeal. At the University of Chicago, Richard Stern followed scholarship and a study of James Joyce's *Ulysses* with a series of novels.

While these heirs of the Chicago literary tradition practiced their traditional disciplines, Studs Terkel used his tape recorder to produce oral history—and best sellers. His *Hard Times*, *Working* and *The American Dream* earned the kind of identification with the reader for which every author yearns. It also placed Studs, who had identified himself with every lost and underdog cause for almost half a century, in the uncomfortable position of being a rich radical. Still, with the same red-checked shirt, Hush Puppies and unlit cigar, his image endures. But it was an irony that Chicago's most recognizably indigenous author had based his success not on the printed word, but on the tape recorder. Perhaps it was a final victory for the electronic revolution that started in Chicago's broadcast studios.

MAYOR RICHARD J. DALEY

"The City That Works"

FOR MORE than twenty years, longer than any other man, Richard Joseph Daley ran the city of Chicago. Visiting reporters looking at his total domination of the city called him the "last of the old-time bosses"; he called himself the "first of the new breed of leaders" where "good politics was good government."

There was no doubt that Daley's management of the city was the quintessence of good politics. To the traditional alliance of the business community with City Hall, he added an alliance with labor. It was a government of consensus, but the consensus was what Mayor Daley said it was; as political reporter John Dreiske once observed, "Daley is the only man I know who can hold a committee meeting in his head."

The importance of access to the man who made these decisions elevated *clout*, a word with a special meaning in Chicago, to the level of a civic virtue. Clout belonged to those business leaders who invested in Daley's Chicago and served on Daley's blue-ribbon committees; clout belonged to labor leaders who were willing to settle a labor dispute without a strike after marathon negotiations (and usually a healthy settlement) in the mayor's conference room; and clout belonged to political leaders (often to become judges) who delivered the vote and, as political scientist Milton Rakove observed, "made no waves."

Daley's firm control of the city through these various alliances made Chicago a conspicuous exception among the troubled cities of America. "The experts are all saying our cities have become ungovernable," Daley told a *Newsweek* reporter, adding in one of his rare public uses of profanity, "What the hell do the experts know?" Newsweek yielded the point, commenting that "it is a demonstrable fact that Chicago is that most wondrous of exceptions—a major American city that actually works." Starting his fifth term as the mayor, Daley could point out that the city had an expanding tax base, hadn't had a budget deficit in sixteen years, enjoyed the highest possible rating for its municipal bonds and was able to hold the line on real estate taxes.

Daley was proud of his city and was at his best when entertaining distinguished visitors. In 1959, with the opening of the St. Lawrence Seaway, those visitors included England's Queen Elizabeth and Prince Philip, who dropped anchor off Chicago's lakefront after traveling down the newly opened seaway on the royal yacht *Britannia*.

THE SMILING QUEEN AND THE BEAMING MAYOR. A night to remember

Daley was determined the city would look its best when the humble lad from Bridgeport entertained the English queen. Streets she would travel were literally scrubbed. A special landing dock was erected and the lake dredged where the royal yacht would be anchored. Along the route the queen would travel on Lake Shore Drive, all concrete gutters were replaced, and every traffic light received a fresh coat of paint. At the Drake Hotel, the Sapphire Suite was specially prepared for the royal party with new Irish linen and hand towels identical to the linen used in Buckingham Palace and the White House. A special rose-scented soap was provided for the queen's bath.

Receptions and parades gave Daley special pleasure. Queen Elizabeth was followed by the queen of Denmark, the king of Sweden, the king of Jordan, the prime ministers of Ireland, Israel and seemingly most of the free nations of the world. In 1974, the emperor of Japan received the royal Daley treatment. The mayor, who had walked side by side with Queen Elizabeth when he escorted her into dinner, was required by protocol to walk two steps behind the emperor as they made their entrance to the civic dinner in the emperor's honor. Chicagoans found it a remarkable sight.

Daley enlarged the city's celebration of St. Patrick's Day into a national institution; clad in a green suit, wearing a green derby and carrying a thorn

MAYOR RICHARD J. DALEY IN GREEN HAT AND CARRYING A THORN CANE leads the Democratic faithful in the St. Patrick's Day parade

cane, he personally led the tens of thousands of Irish down State Street. Each year the Chicago River would be dyed green to mark the occasion.

Daley was not an articulate or gregarious man, but he had a flair for showmanship that reached its pinnacle in the enthusiastic welcomes he arranged for America's astronauts. On twelve different occasions, as these new American heroes returned to earth, Daley would invite them to Chicago for a parade and a civic luncheon. Conscious that young people generally were critical of his old-fashioned form of government and ideas, Daley hoped that an identification with the astronauts would show that he was in tune with new America. The astronauts reciprocated by carrying an unauthorized number of Chicago flags to outer space to give to Daley on

CHICAGO—AND CITY HALL—WELCOME THE ASTRONAUTS

their return. When the Americans teamed up with the Russian cosmonauts on a space mission, Daley entertained the Russians as well.

Though he could walk with kings and queens, Daley at home remained very much in the character of the Bridgeport man. Evenings at home were for the family. Few politicians were invited to the Daley bungalow. Dinner was a family affair, which his wife and only confidant Eleanor ("Sis") Daley cooked herself, occasionally baking bread to put on the table. An outing might involve taking his children to a White Sox baseball game or a Black Hawk hockey game at the Stadium. To Daley it was important that his house did not become his office. Few but his family saw him at home.

Daley seemed to operate through some sort of native-born political instinct that enabled him to act without any real explanation for what he did. When he did try to explain, he often fell afoul of the English language. Among the most famous malapropisms were the following:

"We must reach higher and higher platitudes of achievement."

"Gentlemen, get the thing straight, once and for all: the policeman isn't there to create disorder, the policeman is there to preserve disorder."

"It's amazing what they will be able to do once they get the atom harassed."

"That isn't true enough to answer."

"They have vilified me, they have crucified me; yes, they have even criticized me."

"I resent the insinuendos."

"O'Hara Field" (for O'Hare, which he never did learn to pronounce.)

Though Daley's syntax may have been addled, his mind was equal to any situation. Novelist Saul Bellow said of Daley, "He was like Chicago itself in many ways . . . tough, even crude at times. Yet he had a hidden sophistication and genuine talent and intelligence. I think a lot of Chicagoans are like that, living up to the lowbrow image when they're really not lowbrows at all."

Daley's prominence on the national scene derived not only from his position as mayor but from his role as a key political figure in the Democratic Party. Presidents Truman and Kennedy both believed they owed their election to the huge Democratic majorities turned out by Daley. He hated it when reporters called the Democratic organization a "machine" ("Organization, not machine," he told a reporter angrily. "Get that straight—organization.") Whether organization or machine, it functioned for many years as efficiently as a machine, with Daley sitting behind a big desk at Democratic headquarters on election night waiting for the ward committeemen to deliver in person the tallies from the wards (which had better be what Daley expected or some jobs at City Hall might go to another ward organization).

After the 1968 convention, however, Daley's power was never quite the same. Many key county offices were lost as voting power shifted to the suburbs. In 1972, his own Democratic party refused to seat his delegation from Illinois because it had been chosen in the way Daley always chose it, rather than in conformity to the new rules. And in 1976, he failed to come out for Jimmy Carter until the issue was resolved, thereby losing his chance to become a "kingmaker" again as he had once been for the Kennedys.

Other troubles beset him. Conceded to be personally honest himself, his administration was to become mired in a series of events that were to bring shame to his city and send a number of his closest associates to prison. The first major scandal to jolt his administration came in 1960, when a small-time burglar blew the whistle on eight Chicago policemen from the Summerdale district who were actually part of a burglary ring, even hauling loot away in police cars. Over a two-year period it had added up to about $100,000, mostly in TV sets and other electrical appliances. (This led to a popular Chicago joke: A motorist is stopped for speeding and given a ticket. "Thank heavens," he says, "I was afraid it was a stick-up.")

Using a technique he was to employ in other comparable crises, Daley called in blue-ribbon consultants and on their recommendation hired a professor of criminology from the University of California named Orlando W. Wilson, to head the police department. Wilson was given a free hand, a greatly increased budget and told to "professionalize the force."

Wilson, who had great administrative skills, modernized the force, improved its reporting procedures and projected the image of reform that Daley desired. But, although there was a more sophisticated structure for the department, Chicagoans noticed that the "clout" captains in the Loop and South Side black districts where the organization had its power base remained firmly in place, untouched by the computers and aura of professionalism that appeared on the surface.

Daley's most serious difficulties began with the election in 1968 of Richard Milhous Nixon as president and the appointment of a Republican district attorney for northern Illinois. James Thompson, who was named the federal attorney, surrounded himself with a team of bright young lawyers headed by Joel Pflaum (later a federal judge), Samuel Skinner, Daniel K. Webb (who was himself to be named U.S. Attorney in 1981) and Tyrone Fahner (later appointed Illinois attorney general). Daley felt he was being persecuted because Illinois had been one of the key states that gave the election to John F. Kennedy when Nixon ran against him in 1960. Thompson denied this and insisted he was merely out to end the official corruption.

When Thompson resigned from the U.S. Attorney's office in 1976 to run successfully for governor of Illinois, he had compiled a conviction record that included some of the proudest names in the Democratic party of Illinois. Among them were former Governor Otto Kerner, a federal judge on the U.S. Court of Appeals who was convicted of conspiracy, tax evasion and perjury in connection with a racetrack scandal; party wheelhorse and County Clerk Edward J. Barrett, convicted of soliciting a $18,700 bribe in connection with the purchase of voting machines; Daley's own protégé, Bridgeport neighbor and patronage boss Matthew Danaher, indicted for conspiracy in connection with a $400,000 real estate scheme (he died before being brought to trial); and Alderman Thomas E. Keane, next to Daley the most powerful man in Chicago, convicted of conspiracy and mail fraud in connection with a million-dollar real estate scheme that needed his vote. Lesser officials who were convicted included Daley's own press aide, three aldermen who were convicted of soliciting bribes, and the chief of traffic and eighteen detectives in the police department involved in a vice-protection ring.

Despite the political defeats and the embarrassment of court decisions, Daley's hold on the city and his power remained undiminished. But on May 6, 1974, nine days before his seventy-second birthday, Daley suffered a small stroke caused by the blockage of the carotid artery that supplies blood and oxygen to the brain. After consulting with his good friend and ally, Dr. Eric Oldberg, a distinguished neurosurgeon whom Daley had named to head the Board of Health, Daley agreed to an operation by Dr. Hushang Javid to remove the blockage. Still worried about his personal safety, as he had been since the 1968 convention, Daley insisted the operation be performed one day ahead of the announced schedule as he feared there would be an attempt to assassinate him, possibly by interrupting the power supply during the operation.

According to Dr. Oldberg, whom Len O'Connor quotes in his book *Requiem*, one artery was so badly blocked it was inoperable, although the doctors did not inform Daley of the fact. After the operation was over, Daley retired to his home at Grand Beach, Michigan, for three months, working to regain his speech and motor capabilities. Later he was to brag to political associates on several occasions about how he had outfoxed his enemies. Daley said he wanted his own security and "everybody checked out. . . . The police will stand guard over the power while the operation is going on." Later Daley recalled "Nobody tried anything, and I thank the good Lord I am all right. What do the doctors know about these things? The doctors don't know anything."

It was Labor Day before Daley returned to City Hall. To outward appearances the mayor had resumed his old routine. Appearances were deceptive, however. Mayor Daley would never regain the full use of his powers, but because he represented the image of stability, his inner circle sought to protect him from the kinds of pressures that might cause a recurrence of the stroke. This small group consisted of Thomas Donovan, the unofficial deputy mayor; Edward Bedore, the budget chief; Michael Daley, the mayor's son; and Jane Byrne, who had been named commissioner of consumer affairs and later co-chairman of the Cook County Democratic Central Committee. Each day Michael Daley would check his father's calendar both at City Hall and at Democratic headquarters. Then a decision would be made as to whether the mayor had the vitality on that particular day to carry out the schedule. The mayor had good days and bad days; on the bad days, his hand was so feeble that Michael would have to guide it when Daley was signing checks for party headquarters. Still, he was determined to carry on. "This may give out on me," he told Jane Byrne one day, pointing to his heart, "But this brain won't," he said pointing to his head. Ill though he was, he was determined to run for another term. "Hell," he told Commissioner Byrne, "the doctors won't assure me I will live even if I don't run. And, since it's my decision, I'm going to die as mayor of Chicago."

In April of 1975, Chicago's voters returned him to office for the sixth time with more than 70 percent of the vote. But on December 20, 1976, he had a sense that the heart he had worried about might be failing him. At 1:35 P.M. he walked into the office of his physician Dr. Thomas Coogan on North Michigan Avenue, stopping to shake hands with the other patients in the waiting room. But within half an hour he was dead. The inconceivable had happened. There was to be a Chicago without Daley. At the wake in the church where Daley was baptized, tens of thousands of Chicagoans lined up in bitterly cold weather to pay tribute to him; for his funeral, all of the mighty people he had once honored with parades, luncheons and receptions—including the president of the United States—returned to pay him homage.

The city's grief was great, but neither death nor politics takes a holiday in Chicago. A new consensus quickly developed, in part to block the elevation of a black man, Wilson Frost, president pro-tem of the city council, to the post of mayor. An alliance consisting of the Daley family, Tom Donovan (who had the patronage book that was the mayor's power base), and the most powerful ward committeemen agreed to split Daley's two power bases so that no one could again be so powerful. George Dunne, president of the Cook County board (which controlled 10,000 jobs) was named chairman of the county central committee, and Alderman Michael A. Bilandic, a Bridgeport son from the mayor's Eleventh Ward, was named mayor. Frost and the black community were appeased by giving Frost the position of chairman of the powerful city council finance committee.

The eulogies to Daley were many and the analyses of his long rule and what it meant to the city even more numerous. But most Chicagoans probably found it best summed in the words of cab driver, who said, "He's the guy who got t'ings did."

THE SNOWS CAME, 1978–1979.
A total of 87 inches

34

"The Ultimate American City"

THE COALITION that Daley had forged and that made Chicago "the city that works" moved easily into a new alliance with Bilandic. Acknowledging his heritage, Bilandic wrote that "an alliance between business, labor and government has created a partnership for success for everyone." But Bilandic seemed more interested in the office of mayor than in its power. His most visible impact on the city was the creation of Chicago Fest, a week-long entertainment festival at Navy Pier, which Big Bill Thompson had constructed "to sell Chicago to Chicagoans."

Bilandic's preoccupation with the ceremonial allowed real power to devolve onto Thomas Donovan, his top aide who had also been Daley's patronage aide. Donovan and his political allies were not long in taking steps to assure that Jane Byrne would no longer have the access to the power and authority she enjoyed under Daley. She was quickly deposed as co-chairman of the central committee and many of her perquisites as a city department head were withdrawn. At the memorial service for Daley in the city council chambers, she was assigned to a folding chair in the back row while the other department heads sat in the front row with the business leaders of the city. The one thing she did have was her power as commissioner of consumer affairs, which included the authority to regulate the taxicab industry. An open break came in November of 1978, when she accused the new mayor of "greasing" an unauthorized increase in fares for the taxicab companies. Stung by the accusations, Bilandic fired her.

Her Irish temper aroused, Jane Byrne announced that she would run against Bilandic in the Democratic primary, even though Chicagoans were not inclined to give her much of a chance. But then the snows came.

On New Year's Eve, 15 inches of snow fell. Two weeks later, another 20 inches fell. Day after day it snowed, until a total of 82.3 inches had fallen and the city found itself paralyzed in a snowbank. The trains did not run. The public buses did not run. Worse, Bilandic and Donovan told Chicagoans that the problems were solved and that the city was functioning normally. Chicagoans huddled in the cold at bus stops and elevated stations knew better. The only person who seemed to share their rage and listen to their problems was a woman wading indomitably through the crusted snow that lined the edges of the streets; her name was Jane Byrne.

The Democratic organization did not really believe it could be beaten in a primary. As the primary was to be held on a cold day in February, certainly no one could get out the vote as efficiently as its precinct captains. But the weatherman had one more card to play for Jane Byrne. Primary election day dawned bright and clear; when the sun set on what the politicians called "Jane Byrne weather," she had beaten Bilandic and the organization by the narrow margin of 17,000 votes out of 809,000 that were cast. When the votes were counted at the general election in April, Jane Byrne had been elected mayor of Chicago by an overwhelming margin.

Jane Byrne had grown up on the Northwest Side of Chicago in an area of upper-middle-class homes called Sauganash. After graduating from Barat College, a Catholic institution in Lake Forest, she married William Byrne, a young pilot in the Marine Corps. But on May 31, 1959, his plane had crashed in a fog-shrouded approach at Glenview Naval Air station, leaving Jane Byrne a widow with a two-year-old daughter to raise.

Searching for a commitment to bring some meaning to her life, she heard the voice of John F. Kennedy on the radio and decided to enlist in his campaign. She worked hard at Kennedy headquarters; among her rewards was a seat in President Kennedy's box at the Army-Air Force game in November of 1961. It was the weekend of the Cuban missile crisis, and Kennedy was called back to Washington; but Daley, who wanted to know every detail of events around him, wondered who the blonde woman with the little daughter was. Three weeks later, fate threw Daley and Byrne together again at a dinner honoring Monsignor Francis Dolan of Queen of All Saints Basilica, where her family attended church. Her father was master of ceremonies, and she was standing in the receiving line when

Daley arrived. "Why do I keep seeing you?" he asked. "What do you do?"

Encouraged by Monsignor Dolan, who had known the mayor in his Bridgeport days, Daley invited Byrne down to City Hall. There he encouraged her to maintain her interest in politics, suggesting she start as a precinct captain in Sauganash, working for Daniel Ward, later an Illinois Supreme Court justice. Daley made it plain that working for the Kennedys was not the same as working for the party and the organization. "There are many ahead of you," he said. "They have worked the route. They have come up through the ranks."

Later, Daley found a place for her in the city's antipoverty program, where most of the employees in this federally funded program were hostile to Daley and where it was plain she was not wanted because of the mayor's sponsorship. Several times she asked for another assignment, but each time Daley sent her back because that was where "the party needs you." Each time she went back, often arguing with the mayor, but finding that his trust in her had given her access to his office. Then, unexpectedly, on February 4, 1968, he called her into his office and announced he was naming her commissioner of consumer affairs. Eleven years later, by defeating the supposedly invincible political machine molded by her mentor, she was mayor of Chicago.

With her election, a tumultuous era in Chicago politics began. Struggling to establish control over the same politicians whom she defeated, she

THE SNOW QUEEN. Mayor Jane Byrne takes over from Mayor Michael A. Bilandic

struck at the heart of Daley's own Eleventh Ward organization, firing with abandon those whom she believed opposed her (later many of these discharges were reversed by the courts). In a bitterly fought primary, she went so far as to publicly express support for a Republican state's attorney in order to keep the office from the mayor's son, State Senator Richard M. Daley, whom she feared might be her mayoral opponent in 1983. Daley won by a narrow margin, but the once proud Democratic organization was in shambles.

Mayor Byrne had other problems. As she turned to an examination of Chicago's finances, she found that "the city that works" was almost bankrupt. The city had undisclosed debts of $78 million and the Board of Education—on which Daley had imposed settlements it could not afford in order to avoid teachers' strikes—was using money designated for interest on bonds to pay current expenses. Daley, it was revealed, and Bilandic as well, had been shifting funds in order to avoid the political risks of raising real estate taxes or cutting back city services. Through the sixties, federal revenue sharing and licensing revenues imposed under Chicago's "Home Rule" authority had been sufficient to fill the gap between rising expenditures and an eroding tax base. The seventies brought a shortfall in revenues, which Daley made up by using bond proceeds designated for capital projects to pay current bills.

At Byrne's urging, the city council had no alternative but to raise taxes. The legislature came to the rescue of the Board of Education, but only with the unusual caveat that the entire board resign because of its fiscal ineptness. The crisis was temporarily surmounted, but the revelations seriously damaged the image of Daley as a "master administrator."

The city was in for another shock. When preliminary figures were released on the 1980 census, it appeared that Chicago had lost its place as Second City to Los Angeles. Only after a court-ordered adjustment in the census figures was Chicago able to hold its edge, with 2,979,570 residents compared to 2,950,100 in Los Angeles. There was scant comfort in the figures, for they showed Chicago had lost about 897,000 residents since the 1970 census and had fallen below the 3,000,000 mark for the first time in sixty years.

If there were fewer Chicagoans, they were nonetheless as determined as their forefathers to continue building a great city. Chicago had once counted 3,000 ships a year docked at its lakeside and riverbank; as the age of airplane and truck flourished, more than 50 million passengers a year passed through its O'Hare Field terminal, busiest in the world. A new city of office buildings and hotels rose from the marshy lands around the airport. The traffic over the city's expressways made it the trucking center of America, providing direct trucking connections to 54,000 different communities. Chicago's waterways remained important arteries of traffic as they were a century ago. Since the opening of the St. Lawrence Seaway, Chicago ports handled more waterborne traffic than the Panama Canal. Although several of the railroad passenger stations and several of the freight yards were abandoned, one-third of America intercity rail traffic still originated in, passed through or terminated in the rail yards in Chicago.

The stockyards were closed, but the city remained the center of America's agri-business. If it no longer slaughtered pigs or steers, it still had much to say about the cost of the grain they ate or the price they brought. Chicago's Board of Trade did one-half of all the nation's commodity trading. The Chicago Mercantile Exchange, expanding beyond its traditional trading in eggs and butter, became the international center of trading in commodity futures. Its subsidiary, the International Monetary Market, traded more than $14 billion a year in foreign currencies. The Midwest Stock Exchange was the second largest in the nation.

The city's industrial and commercial base remained as diverse as its peoples. It was the shipping hub of the enormous steel-producing, oil-refining

O'HARE AIRPORT. More than 50 million passengers a year

industrial complex that stretched along the south shore of Lake Michigan into Indiana and beyond. A third of the nation's capital goods were shipped from the area, which outranked Pittsburgh in steel production and dwarfed West Germany's powerful Ruhr Valley in industrial output. The *National Geographic* in 1978 still called Chicago "one of the earth's great industrial colossuses."

Commercially, the city continued to reach out, from trunk highways built over trails worn bare by the first fur trappers (and immortalized in diagonal streets such as Archer, Ogden and Milwaukee avenues) to expressways that confirmed the vision of Samuel Insull, who built his electric railways and power lines toward the northwest, where Chicago has grown.

The man who dominated and presided over this growth was Mayor Richard J. Daley. Among the businessmen with whom he dealt there were no titans such as William B. Ogden, Philip D. Armour, Marshall Field or George Pullman, but there was a new generation of corporate managers still willing to commit the resources of their companies to the city's goals.

Still, the city, was hospitable to the individualist, the giant, who could build his own marketplace. The great retailing giants, the great packers were gone; but in their places came other men with their own view of how to make a fortune; among them was Ray Kroc, a man who not only made a fortune but changed the eating habits of America.

In 1954, Ray Kroc was a fifty-two-year-old diabetic suffering from incipient arthritis. What he had going for him was his enthusiasm. Kroc was selling multimixers for milk shakes when he met two Californians named McDonald, who he decided had a different way of selling hamburgers and a unique way of making French fries. Seeing the possibilities of economically providing fast food and fast service, Kroc negotiated the right to franchise this process. Out of this idea came a fortune greater than that of the commercial titans of the past. In 1980, there were more than 6,500 McDonald's locations in the United States and countries around the world. The yellow arches of McDonald's were as famous as the script of Coca-Cola. In its irreverent recognition of commercial success, Chicago even gained a new educational institution; it was called Hamburger University, and its graduates were awarded a Bachelor of Hamburgerology with a minor in French fries!

Chicagoans liked the idea that Ray Kroc and his Hamburger University were as world-famous as the University of Chicago with its forty-two winners of the Nobel Prize who had been associated with the university as teachers, students or researchers.

It remained a city of contrasts that continued to fascinate visitors as it had for more than a century. A. J. Liebling had scornfully referred to the city with its line of skyscrapers along the lakefront as "a theatre back-

THE LAKEFRONT AT NIGHT

drop with a city painted on it." But an English writer was a more perceptive visitor. Standing near the Adler Planetarium one crisp spring morning, he recorded his impressions: "Consider the view. . . . A bit of green parkland fills the foreground, plonked about by tennis balls, splashed with tulips and cherry blossoms; then a moving strip of traffic, steaming relentlessly along the expressway; then beyond the sunken railroad tracks, the tightly packed pace of Lake Shore Drive, which reminds me of Prince's Street in Edinburgh," wrote James Morris in *Places*.

"Above and behind all of this rises the skyline of downtown Chicago, and there it all comes true. It is one of the grandest of all silhouettes. It is all a glorious jumble of styles and conceptions—here a cylinder, there a pyramid, Gothic bobbles and Victorian scrolls, bumps, domes, cubes, towers like the lattice masts of old battleships, gables and even a steeple— a tremendous congeries of buildings without balance or symmetry, which properly suggests a metropolis thrown together in an enormous hurry by a race of unappeasable giants."

Time magazine, looking at Chicago during the period Daley was mayor, saw these unappeasable giants as male—ironic, in view of the fact that power was soon to shift to the city's first woman mayor. "If a city has sex," the magazine's correspondent observed, "Chicago is surely male—its smell of sweat, its feel of muscle and its unceasing masculine drive for power. 'There are no ladies in Chicago,' an old saying went, 'Only widows, wives and girls.' "

The correspondent was inclined to agree with Paddy Bauler that Chicago was not ready for reform. The city's solid vitality, he reported, "happily continues to beat out the jazzy cacaphony that gives Chicago its rowdy rhythm and its imperishable lustiness. Chicago can no more do without its bawdy peep shows or its cackling Paddy Baulers than without its Fields, Swifts, and its Dick Daleys. In its own broad-shouldered way, in its anatomy and in the art of its clout, in its indestructible zest for life, Chicago is a man among cities."

Andrew Neil, writing in the *Economist* in 1980, called Chicago "the ultimate American city," based as it is on "the sturdy individualism of the Midwest, the ethnic diversity of the European immigrants, the preju-

LOOKING NORTH ALONG THE LAKEFRONT. Water Tower Place and the John Hancock Center are at left center

dices of middle America and the problems of the blacks and Hispanics."

James Morris echoed his impressions of the grandness of scale. "The uniquely Chicago phenomena are less stirring than stunning," he wrote. They bowl you over by scale or momentum. . . . Almost nothing about it is small. Its area is vast. Its energy is tireless. Its problems are tremendous problems—Race, Poverty, Violence. [But] Its solutions are grand solutions—immense slum clearances, huge new roads, gigantic universities."

Most Chicagoans would agree with Morris's view that "Chicago is, in a newly significant sense, the All-American capital. It remains . . . the last great stronghold of American values . . . where time is a little less compressed." And though, as a visitor from England, Morris might term it "provincial," he found provincial cities the quintessence of America. And, he said, "Of all these cities, Chicago is boss."

Mayor Daley would not have liked the term; but he would have approved the idea.

Index

Abbey, Henry, 170
"Abraham Lincoln Walks at Midnight" (Lindsay), 277
Academy of Music, 165
Adams, Cyrus, 244
Adams, Henry, 238
Adams, John Quincy, 22
Adams, Maude, 231
Adams Street, 32, 50, 95, 100, 116
Addams, Jane, 246–249
Ade, George, 205
Adler, Dankmar, 174, 187, 355, 402
Adler, Max, 345
Adler Planetarium, 345, 421
Adventures of Augie March (Bellow), 404
Agri-business, 419. *See also* Grain business; Meat packing industry
Air travel, 337–338, 418, *ill.* 419
Albany *Journal*, 16
Aldermen, 257–258. *See also* City Council
Alexandra, Queen of England, 131
Algren, Nelson, 403–404
Ali, Muhammad (Cassius Clay), *ill.* 389, 391, 395
Alk, Howard, 386
Allen, Fred, 385
Allen, Lizzie, 147
Allen Law, 260
Allerton, Samuel W., 183, *ill.* 193, 222
Allison, Fran, 385
Altgeld, John Peter, 129–130, 232, 242–244, 260, 262
Always Room at the Top (Walska), 311–312
Ambrose and Jackson (restaurant), 142
America (literary magazine), 207
American Baptist Education Society, 198
American Buffalo (Mamet), 387
American Dream, The (Terkel), 405
American Railway Union, 241–242
American Theater Guild, 209
Anarchist movement, 149, 153–162
Anderson, Abra (Rockefeller) Prentice, 401
Anderson, Margaret, 277–279, 280, 281
Anderson, Gilbert, 273
Anderson, Sherwood, 278, 279–280, 281, 283, 384
Andersonville, 366
Anglo-Saxo-Yankees, 18–25. *See also* Yankees
Annie Allen (Brooks), 405
Anthony, Susan B., 236
Anti-slavery movement, 49–51, 54, 61, 64
Antoine, Prince, 229–230
Apartment houses, 302, 356–357, 359, 363
Aquarium, 343–344, 345
Arbeiter Zeitung (newspaper), 149, 156, 157, 159–161
Archer Road, 61, 420
Archey Road, 203
Architectural Forum magazine, 355
Architecture, 15, 25, 187–189, 355–361, 363–364; at "A Century of Progress" fair, 336; Adler and Sullivan, 174–175, 187, 355, 402; Burnham and Root, 187–188; "Chicago cottage," 13; Chicago school (1890s), 187–189, 336, 355, 384; Chicago Style (1870s), 115; hollow-tile fireproof construction, 113–114, 187; Miesian, 356–357, 359, 360, 361, 362; 1960s to 1970s, 357–360 and *ill.*, 361 and *ill.*, 363–364; post-1871 fire, 113–115, 118, 128, 132–133; Prairie School, 355; pre-1871 flimsy construction, 96; skyscrapers, *ill.* 185, 187–189, *ill.* 355, 356, 357–358 and *ill.*, 359–361; at World's Columbian Exposition, 221, *ill.* 223, *ill.* 226, 232–233, 275, 336, 345; Wright, 208, 355
Arena, The (brothel), 147
Arkansaw Traveler, The (Read), 205
Armory, 32, *ill.* 78, 83, 263–264

Armory Court, 82, 83
Armour, Allison, 230
Armour, Joseph, 186
Armour, Ogden, 194
Armour, Philip D., 19, 114, 141, 183, 184, 186–187, 194, 238, 247, 317, 420
Armour Institute of Technology, 187
Armour Mission, 186
Arms and the Man (Shaw), 325
Armstrong, Louis, 283
Arnold, Edward, 274
Arnold, Isaac, 46, 55, 64, 65, 105
Art Institute of Chicago, 118, 127, 200, 201, 217, 339–341, 343; collection of, 129, 200–201, 403; expansion, 403
Art Gallery magazine, 364
Art patronage, 129, 191, 200–201, 302–303, 307–310, 339–341, 344, 362, 400; combined with business, 89–92, 173–175, 326–328; municipal, 361–362
Artie (Ade), 205
Artists colony, 208
Arts Council, 362
Arvey, Jacob M., *ill.* 347, 348–350, 351, 353
Asbury, Herbert, 145
Ashland Avenue, 73, 132
Asner, Edward, 386
Assembly Association, 182, 302
Assembly Balls, 182; Bachelors', 37
Astor, John Jacob, 20, 118
Astor, Mrs. William, 222
Astronauts, Chicago reception of, 409 and *ill.*, 410
"Athens marble," 25
Atlantic Monthly, 37, 204, 206
Attic Club, 207
Auditorium, 131, 174 and *ill.*, 175–177, 187, 197, 218, 246, 326; Chicago Opera Company at, 302, 306–309; preservation of, 402–403

Auditorium Hotel, 175, 189–190, 232
Aurora, 190
Automobiles, early, 189
Avery, Sewell, 345
Aviation. *See* Air travel
Ayer, Harriet Hubbard, 121–122

Bach, Ira, 357
Bachelors' Assembly Balls, 37
"Back of the Yards," 350
Bad Lands district, 136
Baker, Gene, 392
Balls, 119–120; Assembly, 37, 182; Charity, 45–47, 131–132, 182; early years, 6–7, 37, 41, 42; First Ward, *ill.*, 251, 263–266, *ill.* 267; invitation, *ill.* 37
Baltimore & Ohio Railroad, 149
Banking, 21
Banks, Ernie, 392
Banyon, Augustus, 94
Baptist Theological Seminary, 198
Baptists, 198–199
Barrett, Edward J., 412
Barrett, Lawrence, 121
Barrymore, Ethel, 321
Baseball, 391–394, 405
Basketball, 395
Batcolumn (Oldenburg), 362
Bateham's Lumber Mill, 98
Bathhouse John. *See* Coughlin, John "The Bath"
"The Battle Cry of Freedom" (song), 62
"Battle of Chicago" (1968), 378
Bauhaus, 356
Bauler, Paddy, 353 and *ill.*, 422
Baum, Frank, 207
Beaubien, Mark, 6, 182; tavern, *ill.* 3
Bedore, Edward, 413
Beebe, William, 337
Beer controversy and riot (1855), 52–53
Beery, Wallace, 273
Behrens, Peter, 356
Beiderbecke, Bix, 283, 299
Belasco, David, 214–216
Bellew, Kyrle, 212–214

Bellinger, Richard, 106–107
Bellow, Saul, 403–404 and *ill.*, 410
Beman, S. S., 233, 239, 303
Bengal Tigress, 32
Bennett, James O'Donnell, 328
Bennett, Lerone, Jr., 391
Berger, Peter, 383
Bergman, Edwin, 403
Berman, Shelly, 386
Bernhardt, Jeanne, 167
Bernhardt, Sarah, 166–170, 172, 173, 215–217 and *ill.*, 218
Berry, Walter, 399
Bertoia, Harry, 362
Better Government Association, 294
Betting pools, 139–140
Beveridge, Julia, 186
Beverly, 366
Bicycles, 189–190 and *ill.*, 191 and *ill.*
"The Big Nine," 352
"Big Stan" building, 359
Bigelow Hotel, 100
Bilandic, Michael A., 413, 415–416, *ill.* 417, 418
Bingo Long Travelling All-Stars and Motor Kings, The (Brashler), 405
Bird, Margaret. *See* Insull, Margaret Bird
"Bishop's Palace," 25
Black Crook, The (musical), 88, 92, 264
Black Hole district, 136
Black Road riots of 1886, 155–157
Blackhawk, Indian Chief, 3–4
Blacks, 288–289, 365–372, 413–414, 423; civil rights rallies, 367, *ill.* 368, 369; discrimination against, 288–289, 365, 367–369, 392; magazines for, 389–390; in major league baseball, 391–392; police treatment of, 288–289, 367–368, 369, 370–371; population increase, 288, 365; protest riots of 1919, 289; protest riots of 1965, 366–367; protest riots of 1966, 367–368;

INDEX 426

riots after King assassination, 370–371 and *ill.*; South Side ghetto, 288, 348, 356, 366, 403, 411; spread of ghetto, 366; voting, 366; West Side, 366, 368, 370; writers, 403, 405
Blackstone, T. B., 121
Blackstone Hotel, 313
Blair, Chauncey, 19
Blair, Mrs. Edward Tyler, *ill.* 181
Blair, Lyman, 19
Blair, William, 19, 25
Bloom, Ike, 252, 290
Bloomer, Amelia, 127
Blue Island Avenue riots of 1886, 155–157
Board of Education, 418
Board of Police Commissioners, 34–35, 139
Board of Public Works, 114
Board of Trade, 62, 66, 74, 81, 90, 139, 153–154, 192, 194, 200–201, 274, 419; building, *ill.* 148, 153; trading (1891), *ill.* 158
Bodenheim, Maxwell ("Bogie"), 281
Bohrod, Aaron, 293
Bombings: anarchist, 153, 160–162; gangland, 298
Bon Ton Directory, 115
Bonfield, John, 154, 159
Boodle (graft), 259–261. *See also* Corruption, political
Bookmaking, 139–140, 141, 348, 353–354; raid, *ill.* 354
Boone, Dr. Levi D., 52–53
Booth, Edwin, 88–89, 121
Booth, John Wilkes, 71, 88
Bootleg industry, 290, 292–293, 297; speakeasies, 298–299
Borden, Mary, 347
Borglum, Gutzon, 340
Borowski, Felix, 302
Boss (Royko), 368
Boston Oyster House, 142
Boulevard system, South Side, 128, 343
Bourget, Paul, 188
Bournique, Eugene A., 120

Bournique's Dancing Academy, 120, *ill.* 196
Bowen, Louise de Koven, 247–250
Bowler, James P., 291
Boxing, 140–141, 171, 391
Boyle, Billy, 204
Boyle, John S., *ill.* 347
Boyle's English Chophouse, 204
Braden, William, 378
Brady, James Buchanan ("Diamond Jim"), 236
Braeside, Margaret Anderson's camp at, *ill.* 277, 278
Brashler, William, 405
"Bread Riot" of 1872, 149
Bremer, Frederika, 15
Brennan, John, 244
Brennan, Ray, 350
Brenner, Nathan T., 258, 259
Breton, Jules, 340
Brewster, Edward, 318, 331
Brewster, Mrs. Walter, 182
Bridge tenders, 24–25, 53
Bridgeport, 61; Daley home, 350, 367, 369, 410
Bridges, 18, *ill.* 23, 24–25, 53, *ill.* 163
Briggs House, 9, *ill.* 82
Brink, Washington P., 19
Brisbane, Arthur, 122
Briston, Rev. Frank, 202
British Blondes, 92–93
Brooks, Gwendolyn, 361, 403, 405
Brooks, Virginia, 267
Bross, William "Deacon," 38, 44, 51, 106
Brothels, 28–32, 76, 135, 136, 143–147, 237, 251–256, 268–269, 290, 292, 297
Brown, John, 65
Brown, Warren, 391
Browne, Charles Francis, 207
Browne, Francis Fisher, 208, 209
Browne, Maurice, 209
Brownson, Dr. Orestes A., 22
Bruno, Paul, 356
Bryan, William Jennings, 192, 262
Bryan Hall, 61

Bryant, William Cullen, 22
Buchanan, James, 67
Buckingham, Kate, 340
Buckingham Fountain, 340
Buffalo Bill. *See* Cody, Col. William F.
Buildings, 355–356, 418, 421; apartment houses, 302, 356–357, 359, 363; first, other than log cabins, 6; flimsy construction before 1871 fire, 96; of frontier Chicago, 14–15; hollow-tile fireproof construction, 113–114, 187; lakefront, public, 343–346; multi-use, 357–358, 359; number in 1871, 96; raising of, with street raising, 12–13 and *ill.*; skyscrapers, *ill.* 185, 187–189, *ill.* 355, 356, 357–358 and *ill.*, 359–361. *See also* Architecture; Houses
Bull, Ole, 88
Buntline, Ned, 166
Burgstaller, Alois, 130
Burlington Railroad, 151, 152, 155
Burnham, Daniel H., 187–188, 221; Chicago Plan of, 288, 301–302, 345–346
Burnham, Daniel H., Jr., 336
Burnham and Root, 187–188
Burnside, General Ambrose E., 64, 65
Burrough's Place, 33
Burton, W. P., 109
Bus lines, 189
Bushman, Francis X., 274
Business community, 36, 47, 419; arts patronage of, 89–92, 173–175, 200–201, 302–303, 308–310, 326–328, 344, 362, 400; and blacks, 369, 370; Chicago Boosters Club, 288; civic responsibilities recognized, 344–345, 370, 420; Daley's alliance with, 406, 420; after 1871 fire, 114, 121; expositions sponsored, 164, 336, 346;

427 INDEX

Business community (cont.) millionaires, 183–187, 302–305, 317, 328, 345; reaction to Haymarket episode, 162; as "unofficial city government," 192, 336, 406
Business district: 1871 fire damage, 98–99, 104, 106, ill. 107; freight delivery subway, 258–259; Long John's sign raid (1857), 33 and ill., 34; the Loop, 260; riot damages of 1966, 368; State Street, ill. 35, 96, 124, 346
Busse, Fred, 265, 266, 268, 302
Butkus, Dick, 394
Butler, Charles, 18
Bygone Days in Chicago (Cook), 82
Byrne, Jane, 381–382, 401, 413, 415–417 and ill., 418
Byrne, William, 416

Cabell, James Branch, 280
Cable cars, 189, ill. 210, 259. See also Streetcars
Cabot, Charles, 250
Calder, Alexander, 362, 400; *Universe*, 362, ill. 363
Caldwell, Archibald "Billy," 5–6
California (brothel), 252
Callas, Maria, 399–400 and ill.
Calumet Avenue, 114
Calumet Club, 122
Camp Douglas, 65–66 and ill., 67, 68
Campanini, Cleofonte, 290, 308–309, 313
Campbell, Major Colin, 195
Canal Street, 4, 95, 150
Canby, Henry Seidel, 208
Capone, Al, ill. 285, 292, 293–300
Capone, Frank, 295
"Captain Kangaroo" (TV show), 385
Carleton, Will, 113
Carlyle, Thomas, 9
Carmen (Bizet), 398
Carpenter, Philo, 20
Cars, early, 189

Carson Pirie Scott & Co., 193
Carter, Jimmy, 401, 411
Carter, Leslie, 210–212, 214, 216
Carter, Mrs. Leslie (Caroline Louise Dudley), 209, 210–216
Cartter, David Kellogg, 57
Caruso, Enrico, 290
Casey, Pat, 29
Cassidy, Claudia, 396, 397, 399
Castleneau, Francis, 5
Catherwood, Mary Hartwell, 203
Caton, John Dean, 5, 20
Cavalieri, Lina, 309
Caxton Club, 208
Census of 1980, 418
Centennial celebration, 335
Central Church, 240
Central Music Hall, 172, 202, 256
"A Century of Progress" fair (1933), ill. 335, 336–339, 345, 346; visitor statistics, 339
Cermak, Anton, 348
Cerquet, Anita, 399
Chagall, Marc, 362, 400
Chalmers, Mrs. William J., 132
Chamber of Commerce, ill. 19, 210
Chapin, Francis, 340
Chapin, Gardner S., ill. 135, 141–142
Chapin and Gore's restaurant, 103, 135, 141–142, 171; wall decorations in, ill. 140, 142, ill. 171, ill. 220
Charity Balls, 45–47, 131–132, 182
Chatfield-Taylor, Hobart, 123, 195, 206, 207–208, 227, 230
Chatfield-Taylor, Mrs. Hobart (Rose Farwell), 195, 207–208
Chicago, Aurora & Elgin Railway Co., 320
Chicago, North Shore & Milwaukee Railway, 320
Chicago, South Shore & South Bend Railroad, 320
Chicago American, 85

Chicago and Alton Railroad, 152
Chicago and Milwaukee Railroad, 39
Chicago and Northwestern Railway, 103, 133, 244, 369
Chicago Artists Equity, 339
Chicago Avenue, 343
Chicago Bears, 394
Chicago Black Hawks, 394
Chicago Boosters Club, 288
Chicago Bulls, 395
Chicago Civic Center. See Civic Center
Chicago Club, 105–106, 121, 122, 131, 166, 197
Chicago Conspiracy, 66–69
"Chicago cottage," 13
Chicago Council on Foreign Relations, 349
Chicago Cubs, 391–393; players named, 392
Chicago Daily Globe, 209
Chicago Daily News, 159, 167–168, 170, 173, 182, 205, 235, 275, 280, 281, 325, 368; "Sharps and Flats" column, 203
Chicago Democrat, 26, 43
Chicago Driving Park, 76, 78–79
Chicago Edison Company, 233, 318
Chicago Erring Women's Refuge for Reform, 36
Chicago Evening Post, 280, 281
Chicago Fest, 415
Chicago Fire (1871), 95–101 and ill., 102 and ill. 103–106; casualties and damage statistics, 107; destruction of business district, 98–99, 104, 106, ill. 107
Chicago Gazette, 142
Chicago Golden Jets, 394
Chicago Herald, 258
Chicago Herald-Examiner, 131
Chicago Historical Society, 45
Chicago Hussars, 192
Chicago Journal, 29, 86, 195, 208, 224, 314
Chicago Latin School, 204

INDEX   428

Chicago Life, 142
Chicago Literary Club, 117, 208
Chicago Literary Times, 281
Chicago Magazine of Fashion, Music and Home Reading, 20, 41–42, 108
Chicago Mercantile Exchange, 419
Chicago Methodist Temple, 296
Chicago Morning News, 202, 211
Chicago Musical College, 142, 165
Chicago Opera Company, 302, 305–313, 398
Chicago Plan, Burnham, 288, 301–302, 345–346
Chicago Plan Commission, 302, 326
Chicago Poems (Sandburg), 275–276, 283, 356
Chicago Post, 189
Chicago Record, 205, 229, 236
Chicago Record-Herald, 182, 262, 265, 302
Chicago Republican, 91
Chicago River, 11, 17, 62, 409, 418; bridges, 18, ill. 23, 24; tunnels, 18
Chicago Rock Island and Pacific Railroad, 163, 255
Chicago school of architecture, 187–189, 336, 355, 384
Chicago school of television, 385
Chicago school of writing, 274–283, 384
"Chicago Seven," the, 382–383
Chicago Sharpshooters Association, ill. 63
Chicago Sporting Life, 142, 145
Chicago Stock Exchange, 403
Chicago Street Gazette, 142, 144, ill. 146, 147
Chicago Sun-Times, 346, 350, 370, 374, 378, 400, 402
Chicago Symphony Orchestra, 164, 196–198, 287, 361, 396 and ill., 397–398; chorus, 397; international acclaim, 397–398
Chicago Theater, 299
Chicago Times, 20, 32, 63–64, 65, 75, 77, 93, 172, 202, 211, 222, 224, 227, 231, 328, 331; first full-page ad, 141
Chicago Tribune, 32, 35–36, 38, 45, 57, 79, 85, 91, 92, 106, 108, 136, 171, 175, 189, 206, 216–217, 264–265, 309, 328, 393; critics and reviews, 168, 197, 202, 203, 280, 362, 396, 399; "fireproof" building (1871), 96, 104; "In the Wake of the News" column, 280; and lakefront buildings, 342, 343, 346; pro-Republican in 1860 election campaign, 49, 51, 55–56; society news reporting, 81, 127, 131, 176, 183, 211–213, 232, 236, 314; stance during Civil War, 64–65, 70, 72
Chicago United, 370
Chicago University, 198
Chicago White Sox, 392, 393–394
Chicago's Famous Buildings (Bach), 357
Childs, S. D., 150
Chippewa Indians, 4
Christiansen, Richard, 387
Christo (artist), 403
Church of the Holy Family, ill. 54
Churches, 15, 38
Churchill, Winston, 378
Cicero, Illinois, 307; Capone in, 295–296
Cimini, Pietro, 313
Cincinnati, 108, 150
Cincinnati Commercial, 57
Citizens' Law and Order League, 138, 252
City Council, 63–64, 152, 257–259, 260, 288, 322, 352, 353, 354, 393, 413–414, 418
City on the Make (Algren), 404
Civic Center, 326, 360–361 and ill., 374, 375
Civic Federation, 241, 244, 246, 250, 259, 266–267
Civic Opera House, 326–327 and ill., 328, 400, 402
Civil rights movement, 367, 369, 371; demonstrations, 289, 367, ill. 368, 369; disorders, 289, 366–368, 370–371 and ill., 372
Civil War, 31, 49, 58, 59–70, 74, 133; Chicago Conspiracy, 66–69; newspaper controversy, 63–65; PW camp, 65–66 and ill., 68; troop statistics, Chicago, 70
Clark Street, 9, 32, ill. 43, 53, 104, 106, 113, 140, 144
Clarkson, Ralph, 207
Clay, Cassius. See Ali, Muhammad
Clay, Henry, 132
Clayton, Mrs. Evelyn, 195
Cleaverville, 40
Cleveland, Grover, 226, 242–244
Cliff Dwellers, The (Fuller), 206, ill. 207
Cliff Dwellers (Attic Club), 207
"Clout" in Cook County politics, 406, 411, 422
Clubs, 105–106, 117–118, 121, 122, 182, 193, 282; bicycling, 189–190; literary, 117, 205–208
Cobb, Henry Ives, 221
Cobb, Silas B., 183
Cochran, Alexander Smith, 311–313, 314
Cody, Colonel William F. ("Buffalo Bill"), 88, 142, 165–166
Cohan, George M., 290
Cole, George E., 267
Coliseum, 264–265
Collins, Charles, ill. 282
Collins, Morgan, 296
Colosimo, Big Jim, 289–291, 300

Colosimo, Victoria de Moresco, 290, 291
Colosimo's Café, 290–291, 292
Columbia Theater, 236
Columbian Exposition. See World's Columbian Exposition
Columbus Drive, 403
Colvin, Harvey Doolittle, 138, 139–140
Comiskey, Charles, ill. 140
Commercial Club, 114, 162, 174, 301
Committee of One Hundred, 138
Committee of Seventy, 138
Committee of Twenty-five, 138
Commodity trading, 74, 419. See also Board of Trade
Commonwealth Edison Co., 325, 329, 332
Compass Players, 386
Concert saloons, 137, ill. 138
Concerts, 87, 89, 94, 163, 164–165, 196–198, 396–398, 400–401
Condit, Carl, 188
Condon, Eddie, 266, 299
Congo, The (Lindsay), 277
Congress Street, 100, 106
Conley, Mother, 32
Conley's Patch, 32, 99, 102
Conlisk, James, 371, 376
Connelly, Frank, 82–83
Connelly, Jimmy, 262
Conners, Dorsey, 385
Constable, William K., 212, 214
Contracts, municipal, 348, 355
Coogan, Dr. Thomas, 413
Cook, Frederic Francis, 31, 82
Cook County, 331, 349–350, 351–354, 413; Daley as Democratic Chairman, 350, 352, 354
Coombs, Jane, 88
Copperheads, 67, 68
Coquelin, Constant, 216–217
Corbett, James J., 235
"Corncobs" towers, 357–358
Corrigan, Michael J., 308

Corruption, political, 74, 137, 139, 257–266, 287, 289, 291, 295–298, 347–348, 350, 352; Daley and, 354, 411–412
Cosell, Howard, 385
Cosgriff, Mollie ("Irish Mollie"), ill. 73, 76–77, 79, 144
Cossutta, Carlo, 400
Cottage Grove Avenue, 65, 122
Coué, Emile, 309
Coughlin, John "The Bath," 261 and ill., 262–266, ill. 267, 290, 291
Counselman, Jennie Otis, 121
Courthouse, 12, 15, ill. 39, 45, ill. 51, 72, 98; fire of 1871, 100, 113
Courthouse Square, ill. 39, ill. 41, 53, 61, 62
Courtney, Thomas J., 349, 352
Couzins, Phoebe, 228–229
Covici, Pascal, 281, ill. 282
Cowley, Malcolm, 278
Crane, Hart, 278
Crane, Richard T., 164
Crerar, John, 121
Crerar Library, 201
Crime and criminals, 27–28, 36, 74, 136, 142, 289–300; politicians' relationship with, 136, 139–140, 289, 291, 295, 296–298, 350, 352; rarety in early years, 73
Cronkite, Walter, 380
Crosby, Albert, 92, 94
Crosby, Bing, 299
Crosby, Uranus H., 89–93, 174, 326
Crosby Art Association, 90
Crosby's Opera House, 45–47, 89 and ill., 92–93 and ill., 94, 95; fire of 1871, ill. 102, 163; lottery, 90–92
Cross, Henry H., 193
Crown Hall, IIT, 356
Cudahy, John, 184
Cudahy, Michael, 184
Cullon, Shelby M., 221
Culver, Allan, 108
Currey, Margaret, 281

Curzon, Lord George, 194–195
Cyrano de Bergerac (Rostand), 216–218

Daley, Eleanor Guilfoyle ("Sis"), 351, 410
Daley, Michael, 413
Daley, Richard J., 350, ill. 365, 399, ills. 406–408, 410–413, 415, 423; background and career, 350–352; Byrne and, 416–417; Cronkite interview, 380; and events of 1968 Democratic National Convention, 372, 373–374, 376, 379–382; his fear for his life, 380–382, 412; his malapropisms quoted, 410; as mayor, 346, 353–354, 356, 359–360, 366–376, 382, 393, 406–407 and ill., 408–412, 418, 420; power bases of, 366, 371, 406, 411, 413; and problems of blacks, 366–371; his riot order to shoot, 370–371
Daley, Richard M., 418
Daley (Richard J.) Center and Plaza, 360. See also Civic Center
Dalton, Captain, 140–141
Dana, Charles A., 221
Danaher, Matthew, 412
Dandy First Regiment, 204
Darrow, Clarence, 244, 275, 282, 289
Dato, Edward, 315
Daughters of the American Revolution, 249
David, Joseph B., 338, 339
Davis, Philip, ill. 282
Davis, Rennie, 382–383
Davis, Theo R., 115
Dawes, Rufus C., 335, 336
Dawson, William, 366
Dead Man's Alley district, 136
Dean, Mrs. M. J., 143
"Dear Midnight of Love" (song), 262
Dearborn Park, 25, 69
Dearborn Street, 9, ill. 47, 100, 140, 254, 357

INDEX 430

Debs, Eugene, 241–242, 244
Deering, William, 183
Defauw, Desire, 396
De Koven, Mrs. Reginald, 175–176
De Koven family, 247. *See also* Bowen, Louise de Koven
De Koven Street, 97
De LaSalle High School, 351
Dell, Floyd, 206, 281
Dellinger, David, 375, 382–383
Demidoff Collection, 201
Democratic National Amphitheater, *ill.* 67
Democratic National Conventions held in Chicago: of 1864, 67–68; of 1896, 192; of 1968, 372, 373–374, 375–378, 411
Democratic National Convention of 1972, 411
Democratic Party, 50, 55, 57, 192, 262, 349, 373–374, 410–412; in city politics and government, 63–64, 142, 192, 193, 222, 238, 257–258, 261–266, 285–288, 289, 323, 348–354, 366, 406, 410–418; during Civil War, 61, 62–64, 67; Daley power bases and machine, 366, 371, 406, 410–411, 413–418; primary (Chicago) of 1979, 416; reform movement, 348–349, 352–354
Demonstrations and riots: black (1919), 289; black (1965 and 1966), 366–368; black, after King assassination (1968), 370–371 and *ill.*; "Bread Riot" (1872), 149; civil rights rallies, 367, *ill.* 368, 369; Civil War, 64, 65; Lager Beer riots (1855), 52–53; Market Hall riot (1854), 51–52; during 1968 Democratic Conven-
tion, *ill.* 373, 375–380, *ill.* 381, 383; of temperance crusaders, 138; worker (1877), 150–152, *ill.* 153, *ill.* 156; worker (1886), 155–160 and *ill.*
d'Engor, Baron Arcadie, 310
Denslow, Arthur W. W., 207
DePaul University, 351
Depression, 329–332, 335, 355, 402
Derby Day, *ill.* 119, 122 and *ill.*, *ill.* 132, 236
Desplaines River, 11
Desplaines Street, 157, 159, 161
Detroit Tigers, 391
Dever, William E., 267, 295, 335
Dexter, Wirt, 64, 176, 203
Dexter (horse), 76–77 and *ill.*
Dial, The (magazine), 201–202, 208, 275, 277
Dill Pickle Club, 282
"Ding Dong School" (TV show), 385
Dippel, Andreas, 308
Dirksen, Everett McKinley, 350
District of Lake Michigan, 286–287
Division Street, 404
Dixon, Joseph, 152
Doane, J. W., 114, 118, 145
Doane, Mrs. J. W., 118
Dolan, Monsignor Francis, 416–417
Dole, James, 24–25
Donovan, Thomas, 413, 415–416
Douglas, Paul H., 349, 352
Douglas, Stephen A., 50–52, 54–55, 57, 61, 63, 142, 198, 239; monument to, *ill.* 60, 72, 245
Douglas Park, 366
D'Oyly Carte, Richard, 170
Drake, John B., *ill.* 46, 47, 100–101, 108–109, 171
Drake Hotel, 315, 316, 408
Dreiser, Theodore, 209, 274, 275, 279, 280
Dreiske, John, 406

Dressmakers' and Milliners' Guide, 42
Drew, John, 321
Drew, Mrs. John, 88
Drexel Boulevard, 142
Driveway permits, 354
Drummond, Henry, 65
Duggan, Tom, 385
Dunne, Finley Peter, 205
Dunne, George, 413
Dupré, Minnie, 321
Durocher, Leo, 392
Dyer, Dr. C. V., 50
Dyer, Thomas, 27
Dyhrenfurth, Julius, 87

Eagle Exchange, 6
Eaton, Cyrus, 329
Ebony magazine, 390–391
Economist, 422
Eddy, Captain William C., 384
Eden, W. S., 126
Edison, Thomas A., 233, 318, 320
Edison (Thomas A.) Company, London, 318, 325
Edith Rockefeller McCormick Trust, 315–316
Edithton, 315–316
Edward VII, King, 131; visit to Chicago, when Prince of Wales, 42–45
Eighteenth Amendment, 139, 289
Eight-hour day, strikes for, 155
Eisenhower, Dwight D., 349
Elections, 259, 267; black vote, 366; chain voting, 262; frauds, 266, 295, 296, 348. *See also* Mayoral elections
Electricity, 118, 318–320, 322
Elevated railways, 260, *ill.* 293, 319, 322
Eleventh Ward, 351, 379, 413, 418
Elgin, 190
Eliot, T. S., 276, 278
Elizabeth, Queen, 407 and *ill.*, 408
Ellis, Havelock, 139
Ellsworth, Col. Elmer, 59–60

Emancipation Proclamation, 69, 70; reaction to, 62–63
Emerson, Ralph Waldo, 9, 22
Engle, George, 160–162
Entre Nous Club, 182
Episcopalian Cathedral of SS. Peter and Paul, 266
Erie Canal, 12, 17
Essanay Studios, 273
"Eternal Monopoly" bills, 260
Ethnic diversity, 148, 192, 422
Ethnic neighborhoods, 366
Eulalia, Infanta, 229–230 and *ill.*, 231–232, 402
Evans, Dr. John, 38, 39
Evanston, 39
Everleigh, Ada, 147, 252–256, 265, 268
Everleigh, Minna, 147, 252–256, 265, 268–269
Everleigh Club, 252–256, 268–269; music room of, *ill.* 255
Executions, public, 73, 161–162
Exposition Hall. See McCormick Place
Expositions, 164, *ill.* 165, 220, 335–336, 346. See also "Century of Progress" fair; World's Columbian Exposition

Fables in Slang (Ade), 205
Factory legislation, 248, 249
Fahner, Tyrone, 411
Fairbank, N. K., 121, 131, 166, 215, 287
Fairbank, Mrs. N. K., 166, 215
Fallaci, Oriana, 389
Farragut, Admiral David G., 72
Farwell, Arthur Burrage, 252, 265, 306
Farwell, Charles B., 195
Farwell, John V., 151, 195
Farwell, Rose. See Chatfield-Taylor, Mrs. Hobart
Fashion styles, 22, 41–42, 117, 175–176

"Father, Dear Father, Come Home with Me Now" (song), 62
Fay, Amy, 169
Federal Center, 362
Feminist movement, 127, 129, 236, 247, 250
Ferber, Edna, 280
Ferdinand, Archduke of Austria, 232
Ferris, George, 234, 338
Field, Ethel, 119
Field, Eugene, 173, 203–204, 208, 209, 234
Field, Marshall, 19, 71, 114, 118–119, 121, 124, 176, 182, 192, 194, 195, 238, 246, 247, 260, 317–318, 344, 420; assets of, 145, 183; philanthropy of, 199, 343
Field, Mrs. Marshall, 118, 119–120, 175
Field, Marshall, Jr., 119
Field, Marshall IV, 346
Field, Palmer & Leiter, 342
Field, Stanley, 328
Field Building, 356
Field Museum of Natural History, 343, *ill.* 344, 345
Fielden, Samuel, 154, 159–162
Fields, Vina, 252
Fifth Avenue, 32, 102
Fifth Ward, 349, 352
Fifty-seventh Street, 281
Film industry, 273–274
Finances, municipal, 329, 335, 407, 418
Financier, The (Dreiser), 274
Fine Arts Building, 207, 208–209, 345
Finn, Mickey, 137
Fire Department, 17, *ill.* 28, 29–30, 44, 95, 97–100, 103, 366–368, 386; all-white, 367, 370
Fires, 29, 96; of 1871, 95–196 (see also Chicago Fire); 1871 casualties and damage statistics, 107; Iroquois Theater (1903), 218–219; riot aftermath of King assassination, *ill.* 371

First Church of Christ, Scientist, 233
First Congregational Church, 107
First National Bank, 246
First National Bank Building, 359–360 and *ill.*, 362
First Regiment Band, 182
First Ward Democrats, 261–262, 267; Ball, *ill.* 251, 263–266, *ill.* 267
Fischer, Adolph, 160–162
Fischetti, Charles, 295
Fish Fans Club, 298
Fishbein, Dr. Morris, *ill.* 282
Fisher's Beer Garden, 189
Fitzgerald, Joseph, 360
Flamingo (Calder), 362
Florence, Chicago compared to, 364
Flynn, John T., 320, 331
Flynn, Michael J., 351
Flynt, Josiah, 139
Foerster, Norman, 208
Fontanne, Lynn, 325
Foods, 176, 225; menu for Thanksgiving Game Dinner, 47–48
Football, 394
Ford, Henry, 328
Forrest, Edwin, 88
Forrest, Joseph K. C., 182
Forrest, Leon, 405
Fort Dearborn, 3, *ill.* 7, 8, 11, 20, 203, 247; massacre site, 5, 6, *ill.* 16, 32; torn down, 12
Fort Sheridan, 162, 242, 244
Fortnightly Club, 117, 182, 208, 249
Fortune magazine, 356, 359
Four Deuces (saloon/brothel), 292, 299
Fowler, Nettie, 22, 133
Fox, Carol, 399, *ill.* 401
Foy, Eddie, 218
Fraenkel, Dr. Joseph, 310–311
Franchises: frauds, 259; McDonald's, 420; transit, 260, 320
Frank, Dutch, 29
Franklin Street, 32, 98
Franks, Robert, 289
Free-silver movement, 192, 262

INDEX 432

Freeman, Bud, 283
Freiberg's Dance Hall, 252
French Elm, 252
Freni, Mirella, 400
Friday Club, 324
Friedman, Milton, *ill.* 404
Frink & Walker stagecoach company, 8, *ill.* 14
Frohman, Charles, 215
Froines, John, 382–383
Front Page, The (Hecht), 398
Frost, Robert, 276
Frost, Wilson, 413–414
Fugitive Slave Law, 50
Fuller, Henry Blake, 186, 206, 207, 217
Fuller, Margaret, 15, 22
Fullerton Avenue, 106
Furlong, William Barry, 397

Gage, Lyman, 241, 246, 266
Galena and Chicago Union Railroad, 18, 21
Galli-Curci, Amelita, 290, 308
Galligher, William, 29
Galloway, Paul, 374
Galsworthy, John, 247, 277–278
Gambler's Alley, 204
Gambling and gamblers, 28, 31, 32–33, 74–75 and *ill.*, 76–83, 136, 138, 139–140, 142, 144, 222, 237, 251, 254, 257, 266, 286, 287, 291–292, 348, 350, 352–354, 366, 404; raids, 33, 83, 266, 269, *ill.* 354
Game Dinner, Thanksgiving, 47–48
Gander, Gussie, 224
Gangland bombings, statistics on, 298
Gangland killings, statistics on, 295
Gangsters, 289–300; wars between, 291, 292–296, 299
Garbage collection, 247
Garden, Mary, *ill.* 302, 305–307, 308, 309–310, 326, 327, 328, 330, 399
Garden City, 22, 96, 136, 302

Gardner, John, 370
Garland, Hamlin, 206, 207
Garnier, Charles, 133
Garroway, Dave, *ill.* 384
"Garroway at Large" (TV show), 385
Gary, Joseph E., 161
Gas lighting, 9
Gaston, Lucy Page, 268, 308
Gasworks, *ill.* 78, 79, 322
Gates, Frederick, 198
Gates, John W. "Bet-a-Million," 142
General Electric Co., 318
General Managers' Association of Railroads, 242
General William Booth Enters into Heaven (Lindsay), 277
Genna, Angelo, 292–293, 294
Genna, Anthony, 292, 294
Genna, Mike, 292, 294
Genna brothers, 292–294
George V, King of England, 296
George, Henry, 246
German community, 52–53, 62, 130, 149, 192, 285; in World War I, 287
German language, use of, 148–149
Germania Orchestra, 87
Gest, Morris, 291
Ghiaurov, Nicolai, 399, 400
Gibbons, Floyd, 314
Gilbert, Daniel, 349–350, 351
Gilbert, J. B., 212, 214
Gilford, Roswell, 9
Gill, Joseph, 349, 350, 353
Gilmore, Edward, 212, 214
Gilmore, P. G., 45, 47, 163
Given, Rev. Hugh F., 257
Glenview Naval Air Station, 376
Goble, Leroy T., *ill.* 282
Godey's Lady's Book, 42
Gofen, Ethel, 364
Gold Coast, 282, 292
Gold rush of 1849, 8
Goldberg, Bertrand, 357
Goldman, Emma, 279
Goll, Bruno, 98
Good Samaritan Society, 236
Goodman, Benny, 283
Goodrich, Grant, 38, 84

Goodspeed, Thomas W., 198–199
Goraud, Col. George E., 318
Gordon, Archie, 93
Gore, James, 141–142
Gould, Jay, 117
Government, municipal, 27–29, 31–36, 52, 137–140, 152, 245, 247, 256–262, 266–269, 286–289, 295–297, 348–350; Daley tenure, 353–354, 359–360, 366–371, 406–407, 411–412; finances, 329, 335, 407, 418; post-Daley problems, 418; response to civil rights movement, 367–371. *See also* City Council; Mayors; Police
Graceland Cemetery, 245–246
Graft, 137, 259–261, 287, 348. *See also* Corruption, political
Graham, Bruce, 359
Graham, Charles, 163, 200, 248
Grain business, 32, 74, 183, 194, 419; grain elevators, 45
Grand Boulevard, 244
Grand Pacific Hotel, 47, 100, 152, 171
Grant, Frederick Dent, 120, 126
Grant, Mrs. Frederick Dent (Ida Honore), 126
Grant, Mrs. George Roswell, 117
Grant, Ulysses S., 70, 72, 92, 108, 126, *ill.* 127
Grant Park, 307, 339, 342, 343, 345, 359, 363; anti-Vietnam War demonstrations in, 374, 377–378, 380
Graustark (McCutcheon), 206
Gray, Mark, 88–89
Gray, Richard, 364
Great Lakes, 17, 32, 74
Great Lakes, The (Hunt), 362
Great Northwestern Sanitary Fair of 1865, 69, and *ill.,* 70

Greek community, 366, 405
Greeley, Horace, 16–17
Green Mills Gardens, 299
Gregory, Dick, 369
Gregory, D. S., 211, 244
Grenfell, Colonel G. St. Leger, 68
Gropius, Walter, 356
Gross, Samuel Eberly, 216–218
Guinan, Texas, 339
Gunsaulus, Rev. Dr. Frank, 186, 204
Gunther, John, *ill.* 282, 298
Guzik, Jacob "Jack," 297

Hackett, Francis, 280, 281
Haines, John C., 34
Hairtrigger Block, 76, 77
Halberstam, David, 373
Halas, George, *ill.* 390, 394
Hallam, Rev. Isaac W., 3
Halstead, Murat, 56–57
Halsted Street, 36, 157, 165, 266, 306, 343; riot of 1877, 152, *ill.* 156
Hamburg Athletic Association, 351
Hamburger University, 420
Hamilton, Dr. Alice, 248, 249
Hammerstein, Oscar, 302, 305, 306, 326
Hammond, Percy, 280, 305
Hamsun, Knut, 203
Hancock Building, John Hancock Center, 358, *ill.* 422
Hand, Johnny, 119, 182, 231
Hangings, public, 73, 161–162
Hanna, Mark, 241
Hansen, Harry, 281, *ill.* 282
Hard Times (Terkel), 405
Harding, Fred, 62
Hardy, Jack, 339
Harmon, Johnny, 137
Harper, Lou, 30, 144
Harper, William Rainey, 198–200, 317
Harper's magazine, 181, 250, 257, 298, 347, 373
Harris, Barbara, 386
Harrison, Benjamin, 176–177, 221
Harrison, Carter H., 122, *ill.* 127, 132 and *ill.*,

ill. 220; assassination of, 237; as mayor, 135–136, 220, 222–223, 230, 237, 268; and worker riots, 156, 159
Harrison, Mrs. Carter H., 122–123, 175
Harrison, Carter II, 123, 285–286; as mayor, 257–258, 260–261, 268
Harte, Bret, 113
Hartmann, William, 361, 362
Hastings, Madame, 147
Haven, Dwight, *ill.* 282
Haverly, Colonel Jack H., 139
Hawkins, George, 222
Hawthorne Smoke and Inn, Cicero, 296
Hayden, Sophia G., 227
Hayden, Tom, 375, 382–383
Haydon, Harold, 403
Haymarket Riot (1886), 157–162, 222, 246
Heacock, Russell E., 20
Healy, George P. A., 10, 22, 89; portraits by, *ills.* 116, 124, 181; self-portrait, *ill.* 113
Heap, Jane, 278, 279
Heartbreak House (Shaw), 325
Heath, Monroe, 151
Heathcote, Thomas, 241
Hecht, Ben, 280, 281, *ill.* 282, 384
Hecht, Peter, *ill.* 282
Hefner, Hugh, 387–388
Heineman, Ben W., 369
Heinrich, John, 357
Hell's Half Acre district, 136
Hemingway, Ernest, 278
Henderson, Mr. (manager of British Blondes), 93–94
Henrici, Philip, 9
Henry, Prince of Prussia, 254–255
Herbert, Don, 385
Herbuveaux, Jules, 385
Herrick, Robert, 274
Herzog (Bellow), 404
Higgins, Van H., 64
Highland Park, 190
Higinbotham, Alice, 227

Higinbotham, Harlow, 192, 221, 226, 229, 232, 238, 246
Hildreth, James H., 100
Hill, John, 28
Hill, Mary, 28
Hillis, Margaret, 397
Hilton Hotel, demonstrations of 1968 at, 377 and *ill.*, 378–380, 382
Hinch, Uriah, 50
Hinky Dink. *See* Kenna, Michael
Hispanics, 423
Historic preservation, 402–403
Hockey, 394–395
Hoffman, Abbie, 375, 382–383
Hoffman, Charles Fenno, 7
Hoffman, Julius J., 382–383
Hogan, Nick, 140
Holbrook, Stewart, 17
Holmes, Ernie, 395
Holmes, Mrs. Ira, *ill.* 116
Holt, George, 83
Holy Name Cathedral, 292, 296
Home decoration, early Chicago, 23, 117, 128, 132, 133
Home Insurance Building, 188
Honore, Bertha. *See* Palmer, Mrs. Potter
Honore, Ida. *See* Grant, Mrs. Frederick Dent
Hooley's Theatre, 215
Hopkins, John P., 242, 244
Hopper, Edna Wallace, 321
Horan, Al, 349
Horne, Marilyn, 399
Horner, Henry, 349, 352
Horse racing, 76, 78–79, 122 and *ill.*, 236
Horses, 122–123
Horwich, Frances, 385
Hostelries, early Chicago, 10
Hotchkiss, Jed, 38
Hotel de Goodrich, 144
Hotels, 100–101, 109, 125, 175; early Chicago, 6, 8–10
Hough House, *ill.* 31
House of All Nations, 252
House of David, 266
House of Mirrors, 147
Houses, 15; of Anglo-Saxo-Yankees, 22–24, 25;

INDEX   434

"Chicago cottage," 13; lower class, lack of plumbing, 247; number destroyed in 1871 fire, 107; relocation of upper class after 1871 fire, 114–115; third floor ballrooms, 225; unsafe pre-1871 construction, 96; upper class, 22–25, 114–115, 118–119, 128, 132–133, 225. See also Buildings

Housing, post–World War II, 363–364, 365, 367; open, 348, 369; segregation, 365, 369; shortage, 365

Howard, Mrs. William B., 175

Hoyne, Thomas, *ill.* 127

Hubbard, Gurdon Saltonstall, 20

Hull, Bobby, 395

Hull, Charles J., 36, 246

Hull, Paul, 159

Hull House, 246–247, 250, 386

Humphrey, Hubert H., 374, 377–378

Hunt, Richard, 362, 364

Hunt, Richard Morris, 118, 221

Hunting, 14

Hurd, Harvey, 39

Huron Street, 24, 133

Hustle, the (team), 395

Hutchinson, Charles L., 201

Huxley, Aldous, 278

Hydrant-sprinkler controversy, 367–369

Hyman, "Cap," 79–82

IBM Building, 357
Ibsen, Henrik, 203
IC Industries, 363
Ickes, Harold, 268
If Christ Came to Chicago (Stead), 257
Igoe, Michael L., 291
Illinois: at 1972 Democratic Convention, 411; State Legislature, 34, 270, 296, 418
Illinois and Michigan Canal, 17, 18, 25, 45, 74, 337
Illinois Center, 357

Illinois Central Railroad, 60–61, 72, 232, 258, 359, 363
Illinois Crime Survey, 295
Illinois Institute of Technology (IIT), 187, 356, 357
Illinois National Guard, 368, 376
Illinois River, 17
Illinois State Council of Defense, 321–322
Illinois Theater, 325
Illinois Trust and Savings Bank, 238
Immigrants, 148–149, 247, 290, 422
Incorporation of Chicago, centennial of, 335
Indians, 3–6, 11; treaty of 1933, and annuity payments, 4
Industry, 20, 21, 32, 164, 356, 419–420. See also McCormick reaper works; Meat packing industry; Railroads; Steel industry; Utility companies
Ingersoll, Robert, 236
Insull, Margaret Bird (Gladys Wallis), 321, 323–324 and *ill.*, 325, 330, 331
Insull, Martin, 323, 328–329, 331
Insull, Samuel, 233, 316, *ill.* 317, 318–330 and *ill.*, 331–332, 335, 420
Insull, Samuel, Jr., 321, 324, 328, 329, 331
International Amphitheatre, 375, 378
International Harvester Company, 250, 313, 316. See also McCormick reaper works
International Monetary Market, 419
International Workers of the World (Wobblies), 282
International Working People's Party, 153
Inter-Ocean (newspaper), 171, 261
Interstate Industrial Exposition, 164, *ill.* 165, 336

Irish community, 50, 52, 53, 61, 259, 366, 408–409
"Irish Mollie." See Cosgriff, Mollie
Iroquois Theater fire, 218–219
Italian community, 130, 259, 290, 366

Jack, Waterford. See Warren, Frances
Jackson, Rev. Jesse, 369
Jackson, Mahalia, *ill.* 365
Jackson Avenue, 73, 98, 100
Jackson Park, 189, 234; Pavilion, *ill.* 200
Jackson Park Hospital, 294
James, Henry, 206
Jamieson, Egbert, 213
Jarecki, Edmund K., 295
Javid, Dr. Hushang, 412
Jazz, 283, 299
Jefferson, Joseph, 84–85, 88, 141
Jelke, Frazier, 194
Jenney, William Le Baron, 188
Jennison, Colonel Charles, 65
Jewett, Mrs. John W., 176
Jewish neighborhoods, 366, 404
Joffre, Marshal Joseph, 288
Johnson, Andrew, 72
Johnson, Eunice, 390
Johnson, George H., 113, 187
Johnson, Herbert, 312–313
Johnson, John, 389–390
Johnson, Lyndon B., 373–374, 375, 379
Joliet, Louis, 18
Jones, Fernando, 45
Jones, Mrs. Fernando, 175
Jones, Jack, 282
Jones, Jenkin Lloyd, 209
Jones, Nathaniel, 303
Jones, Roy, 256
Journalism, literary, 203–206, 208, 209, 274–283, 384
Joyce, James, 280, 405
Jucklins, The (Read), 205
Judd, Norman B., 55–56, 57
Judicial appointments, 406
Jump, E., 171
Jung, Dr. Carl, 307

435 INDEX

Jungle, The (Sinclair), 274
Justice (Galsworthy), 247
Juvenile Protection Association, 249

Kahn, Otto H., 310
Kansas City Monarchs, 392
Kansas-Nebraska Act, 51
Kaulback, Frederic August von, 306
Keane, Edmund, 88
Keane, Thomas E., 353, 412
Kefauver, Estes, 350
Kelley, Florence, 248, 249
Kelly, Edward J. ("Big Ed"), 338–339, 348–349, 351, 353
Kelly, Lawrence, 399
Kelly-Nash machine, 291, 348, 349
Kendall Building, 113
Kenna, Michael "Hinky Dink," 261–264 and ill., 265–266, 267 and ill. 290
Kennedy, Edward, 381–382
Kennedy, John F., 381, 410, 411, 416
Kennedy, Robert F., 373
Kennelly, Martin H., 349, 352, 354
Kerfoot, S. H., 24
Kerfoot, W. D., 108, 109
Kerner, Otto, 368, 412
Khan, Fazlur, 358
Kilfoil, Jimmy, 32
Kimball, William Wallace, 19, 89
Kimball Music Hall, 236
King, Martin Luther, Jr., ill. 365, 367, ill. 368, 369–370; riots after his assassination, 370–371 and ill.
Kinsley, H. M., 89, 116–117, 119, 125
Kinsley's Restaurant, 89, 116, 119, ill. 120, 142, 221
Kinzie, John, 6, 183
Kinzie, Mrs. John, 9, 203
Kipling, Rudyard, 187, 188
Kirkland, Joseph, 203
Knights of Labor, 155
Knights of the Golden Circle, 67
Know-Nothing Party, 52, 53
Kohlsaat, Christian C., 218

Kraus, Alfredo, 399, 400
Krenn, Edwin, 314–316
Kroc, Ray, 420
Kubelik, Rafael, 396
"Kukla, Fran and Ollie" (TV show), ill. 384, 385
Kuklapolitan players, 385
Kupcinet, Irv, 401–402

Labor: Daley's alliance with, 406; reforms, 248–250; statistics, 356; unemployment, 148–149, 152
Labor movement, 149–162, 193, 241–244. See also Strikes
Laemmle, Carl, 274
LaFramboise, Josette, 3
Lager Beer Riots, 52–53
Lake Calumet, 239
Lake Forest, 38, 113, 307
Lake Forest College, 195
Lake front development, 114, 128, 342–343, 363–364, ills. 421–422; parks, 128, 342–343, 363; parks only rule (1837), 114, 343; public buildings, 343–346; zoning ordinance of 1969, 363
Lake House, ill. 7, 8–9
Lake Michigan, 8, 12, 13, 38, 39, 72, 258, 315, 363, 420; "A Century of Progress" fair site, 336, 342, 346; port, 16, 32, 337, 418–419; Streeter's lake front claim, 136, 286–287; waterworks, 96, 103. See also Lake front development
Lake Point Tower, 357
Lake Shore Drive, ill. 195, 302, 303–304, 376, 408, 421; apartment buildings, 302, 356–357
Lake Street, 9 and ill., ill. 35, ill. 47; fires, 29, 96, 104; raising of, above mud level, 12, ill. 13; rebuilding after 1871 fire, ill. 115
Lame Jimmy, 145, 263
Lamont, Daniel S., 242

Landmark preservation, 402–403
Lane, Gloria, 398
Langner, Lawrence, 209
Lannigan, Jim, 283
Lardner, Ring, 280
LaSalle National Bank Building, 356
LaSalle Street, ill. 39, ill. 41, 55, 149; fire of 1871, 99, 100, 103; rebuilding of, ill. 115
LaSalle Theater, 292
Lathrop, Julia, 248
Law and Order League, 138, 252
Lawndale, 366
Lawrence Street, 366
"Lay Me Down and Save the Flag" (song), 62
Leather-badge force, 34–35
Le Corbusier, 356
Lee, A. H., 91–92
Lee, Doris, 340
Legislative districting, 366
Leiter, Joseph, 194
Leiter, Levi, 194
Leiter, Mrs. Levi, 194
Leiter, Marguerite (Daisy), 195
Leiter, Mary, 194
Leiter, Nancy, 195
Leland Hotel, 144
Lenska, Augusta, 330
Leonard family, the, 236
Leopold, Nathan, 289
Leslie, Amy, 235
Leslie's Illustrated Weekly, 73
Lespinasse, Dr. Victor D., 313
Letters of a Merchant Prince (Lorimer), 203
Levee district, 136, 244, 251–256, 261–269, 289–290; in 1898, ill. 253
Lewis, J. Hamilton, 282
Lewis, Joe E., 299
Lewis, Lloyd, 281, ill. 282
Lewis, Sinclair, 278
Lewis, Wyndham, 278
Lewis Institute, 187
Libraries, ill. 198, 201, 240
Library, The (brothel), 252
Liebling, A. J., 347, 349, 385, 420
Lincoln, Abraham, 17, 54–58, 60, 61, 64–65, 67, 68, 70–72, 277, 297;

INDEX 436

funeral procession in Chicago, *ill.* 71, 72
Lincoln, Robert Todd, 120–121
Lincoln Gardens, 283
Lincoln Park, 105, *ill.* 127, 128, 189, *ill.* 248; 1968 Yippie-police battle in, 375–376, 379, 382; Zoo, 385
Lindsay, Vachel, 276–277
Lingg, Louis, 160–162
Liszt, Franz, 169
Literary clubs, 117, 205–208
Literary magazines, 201–202, 204, 208, 275–280, 281
Literature, American, 209, 276, 283, 404–405. *See also* Writers
"Little Boy Blue" (Field), 208
Little Cheyenne district, 136
Little Egypt, 234, 338
Little Giant Fire Co., 97–98
Little Review, The (magazine), 277–279, 280, 281, 283
Little Room club, 206–207
Little Theater, 209
Loeb, Richard, 289
Loebl, Schlossman and Bennett, 361
Logan, Mrs. Frank G., 339–341
Logan, General John A., *ill.* 132, 136; statue, *ill.* 381
Logan Prize, 339–340
Lohr, Lenox R., 339
Lombardo, Antonio, 296; funeral of, *ill.* 297
London *Daily Mail*, 251
London *Times*, 15
Lone Star saloon, 137
"Long John" fire engine, *ill.* 28, 29
Loop, the, 260, 292, 356, 411
Looting: in 1871 fire, 102–103, 108; in black protest riots, 367, 370–371
Lopez, Al, 393
Lorimer, George Horace, 203
Lorimer, William, 323

Los Angeles, 385, 387, 418
Louis Philippe, King of France, 22
Love for Three Oranges, The (Prokofiev), 310
Lovett, Robert Morse, 281
Lowden, Frank O., 289, 321
Lowell, James Russell, 202–203
Lucas, Scott, 350
Luckman, Sid, *ill.* 390, 394
Lumbard, Frank, 62
Lumbard, Jules, 62
Lumber mills, 20, 32, 105
Lunt, Alfred, 325
Lunt, Orrington, 38, 39
Lyons, Lord, 44
Lyric Opera of Chicago, 399–402
Lyric Theatre, 399

McAllister, Ward, 222–225
MacArthur, Alfred, *ill.* 282
MacArthur, Charles, 384
McCall's magazine, 250
McCarthy, Eugene, 378
McCarthy, Justin, 202
McClellan, General George C., 68
McClurg, General Alexander C., 204, 208
McClurg, Ogden, 204, 302
McClurg's bookstore, 203–204, *ill.* 205, 208, 269, 281
McComas, E. W., 44
McCormick, Chauncey, 340–341
McCormick, Cyrus H., 21–22, 23, 24, 38, 63, 133, 142, 183, 317; mansion of, 132–133
McCormick, Cyrus, Jr., 246, 250
McCormick, Edith Rockefeller, 302–305, *ill.* 306, 307, 311, 314–316
McCormick, Fowler, 311
McCormick, Hall, 123
McCormick, Harold, 302–305, 307, 309–311, *ill.* 312, 313–314, 316, 326, 399
McCormick, John Rockefeller, 305
McCormick, Leander Hamilton, 23, 133

McCormick, Mrs. Leander, 23
McCormick, Nettie Fowler (Mrs. Cyrus H.), 22, 133
McCormick, Robert Hall, 133
McCormick, Robert Rutherford, 267, 342 and *ill.*, 346
McCormick, Robert Sanderson, 133
McCormick, William Sanderson, 133
McCormick Place, 346 and *ill.*
McCormick reaper works, 21, 23 and *ill.*, 62, 151, 239, 250; strike and riots of 1886, 155–157, *ill.* 160
McCormickville, 133
McCulloch, John, 121
McCutcheon, George Barr, 206
McCutcheon, John, 206, 251, 261, 264, 267
McDonald, Mike, 138, 139–141, 289, 300
McDonald's franchises, 420
McDonough, Joseph, 351
Macfadden, Bernard, 235
McFeely, Otto, 222
McGee, William F., 281, *ill.* 282
McGrath, J. J., 246
McGurn, "Machine Gun" Jack, 299
Mackay, Clarence, 302
McKeever, William, 78
McKim, Charles, 221
McKinley, William (U.S. President), 192, 193
McKinley, William (utility owner), 323
McLean, James E., 107
McMasters, Eileen, 82
MacMonnies, Frederick William, 232
McMullen, Jay, 402
McPartland, Dick, 283
McPartland, Jimmy, 283
MacRae, David, 74
MacVeagh, Mr. and Mrs. Franklin, 172
McVicker, James H., 62, 88
McVicker, Mary, 88
McVicker's Theater, 71, *ill.* 87, 88, 104, 166–167, 214

Madison Street, 88, 137, 296, 326; scene of jobless and anarchists' riots, 150, 151, 152, 154
Maeterlinck, Maurice, 203, 324
Mafia, 290, 291
Magazines, 20, 41–42, 387–390; literary, 201–202, 204, 208, 275–280, 281
Mahler, Frau Gustav, 310
Mahzar, Fahreda, 234
Mail-order houses, 342, 345, 420
Mamet, David, 387
Manhattan Opera, 302, 305
Man with the Golden Arm, The (Algren), 404
Mann, Fred, 298
Mansfield, Richard, 218
Maratta, H. G., 253
"Marching Through Georgia" (song), 62
Maretzek, Mr., 92
Margaret, Princess, 401 and ill., 402
Margherita, Queen of Italy, 130, 227
Marie, Queen of Rumania, 315
Marina City Towers, ill. 355, 357–358
Marinuzzi, Gino, 313
Market Hall, ill. 49, 51
Market Hall riot (1854), 51–52
Market (Wacker) Street, 55; scene of jobless and anarchists' riots, 150, 151
Markham, Pauline, 93
Marovitz, Abraham Lincoln, 399
Marshall Field & Co., 114, 119, 151, 344
Martinon, Jean, 397
Mary Garden's Story (Garden), 310
Masefield, John, 276, 282
Mason, Roswell B., 100, 108
Mason, Dr. William (pianist), 22
Mason, Senator William, 261
Masonic Temple, ill. 185, 188

Masters, Edgar Lee, 275, 276, 322
Matthews, Wid, 392
May, Elaine, 386
Mayer, Mrs. David, 305
Mayoral elections: of 1855 (Know-Nothing Party's Boone), 52; of 1893 (Carter Harrison I), 222; of 1915 (Big Bill Thompson), 285–286; of 1919 (Thompson), 288, 352; of 1927 (Thompson), 296; of 1947 (Kennelly), 349, 351; of 1955 (Daley), 352–353; of 1975 (Daley), 413; of 1979 (Byrne), 416
Mayors of Chicago, 139–140, 406; first, 18; first native-born, 257; New Englanders preponderant, 18. See also Bilandic, Michael A.; Boone, Dr. Levi D.; Busse, Fred; Byrne, Jane; Colvin, Harvey Doolittle; Daley, Richard J.; Dever, William E.; Dyer, Thomas; Haines, John C.; Harrison, Carter H.; Harrison, Carter, II; Heath, Monroe; Hopkins, John P.; Kelly, Edward J.; Kennelly, Martin H.; Medill, Joseph; Morris, Buckner S.; Ogden, William B.; Thompson, William Hale; Wentworth, John
Meat packing industry, 20, 121, 183–185, 193, 320, 420; Armour, 19, 183, 184; Swift, 121, 184–185. See also Stockyards
Medill, Joseph, 46, 49, 55–58, 69, 70, 108, 247; as mayor, 137, 139, 267
Medill, Katherine, 108, 133
Meeker, Arthur, 182, 302
Meeker, Mrs. Arthur, 182
Melba, Nellie, 218
Mellon, Andrew, 298–299

Memoirs of an American Citizen, The (Herrick), 274
Mencken, H. L., 282–283
Mendel, Edward, 13
Mercantile Exchange, 419
Merchant Prince of Cornville, The (Gross), 216
Merchants Club, 301
Merlo, Mike, 293–294
Merriam, Charles E., 268, 352
Merriam, Robert E., 352–353
Methodists, 38–39
Metropole Hotel, 297
Metropolitan Life Insurance Company, 327
Metropolitan Opera, New York, 175, 302, 308, 398, 399
Mezzrow, Mezz, 299
Michigan Avenue, 13, 25, 44, 46, ill. 67, ill. 80, 104, 114, 123, 176, 189–190, 197, 258; brothels, 147, 268; Capone HQ, 297; 1837 non-building ordinance violated, 342–343; 1884 Convention parade, ill. 168; events of 1968 Democratic Convention, ill. 373, 378; "Magnificent Mile," 358; Millionaires' Row, 114–115; Terrace Row, ill. 24, 25, 106
Michigan Avenue Hotel, 100–101, 109
Michigan Central Railroad, 43
"Mickey Finn," origin of, 137
Middle West Utilities, 323, 328, 331
Midway Plaisance, 232, ill. 233, 234–236; of 1933 fair, ill. 335, 338–339
Midwest Stock Exchange, 419
Mies van der Rohe, Ludwig, 356–357, 361, 362
Migration: to Chicago, 17–18; Negro, to Chicago, 288, 365; westward through Chicago, 8

INDEX 438

Miles, General Nelson A., 131, 142, 242
Militia, 60–61
Millay, Edna St. Vincent, 276
Millionaire streetwalker, the. See Warren, Frances
Millionaires, 183–187, 302–305, 317, 328, 345
Millionaires' Row, 114–115
Mills, Luther Laflin, 160
Milnes, Sherrill, 400
Milwaukee Avenue, 420
Minor, Katharine, 228
Miro, Joan, 362, 400
Miro's Chicago (Miro), 362
Mississippi River, 17, 18, 74, 75
Mr. Dooley (fictional character), 205
Mr. Pim Passes By (Milne), 325
Mr. Sammler's Planet (Bellow), 404
"Mr. Wizard" (TV show), 385
Mix, Tom, 274
Mobilization to End the War in Vietnam (MOBE), 375
Modern art, 339–340
Modjeska, Mme. Helena, 173
Monadnock Building, 188
Monk and Knight (Gunsaulus), 204
Monroe, Harriet, 177, 206, 275–276
Monroe Street, 30, 140, 141, 203; harbor, ill. 355
Montgomery Ward & Co., 183, ill. 184, 342, 344
Moody, Harriet, 282
Moody, William Vaughn, 206, 282
Moody and Sankey Tabernacle, 151
Moore, Colleen, 273–274
Moore, Henry, 362
Moore, Marianne, 278
Moore, Nathaniel Ford, 255–256
Moran, Bugs, 294, 299
Morell, Parker, 236
Moresco, Victoria de, 290, 291
Morgan Park, 348
Morin, Henri, 309

Morris, Buckner S., 68–69
Morris, Mrs. Buckner S., 68–69
Morris, James, 421, 423
Morris, Nelson, 183, 201
Morris, William, 117
Morton, Samuel J. "Nails," 292
Mountbatten, Lord Louis, 401
Movie industry, 273–274
Mud problem: in early Chicago, 10–12; tall buildings, 187
Mueller, Adolph, 53
Mulligan, Colonel James, 61–62
Munger, Royal, 325, 331
Municipal Voters League, 267, 285
Munsey's Magazine, 191
Muratore, Lucien, 309
Murphy (C.F.) Associates, 361
Museum of Contemporary Art, 403
Museum of Science and Industry, 345
Museums, 85–86 and ill., 343–344 and ill., 345, 403. See also Art Institute of Chicago
Music, 87, 164–165, 196–198, 283, 396–403. See also Concerts; Opera
Mussolini, Benito, 298
My Thirty Years War (Anderson), 280
Myers, Albert E., 66

Nash, Patrick, 291, 348
Natatorium, ill. 188
Nation, Carrie, 267
Nation, The, 283
National Book Awards, 404
National Broadcasting Company (NBC), 385
National Commission on the Causes and Prevention of Violence, 378
National Convention held in Chicago, first, 55–57. See also Democratic National Conventions; Republican National Conventions
National Geographic magazine, 359, 420
Navy Pier, 415

Neebe, Oscar, 160
Negri, Pola, 316
Negro Digest magazine, 390
Negro migration to Chicago, 288, 365. See also Blacks
Neil, Andrew, 422
Nelson, Captain Jack, 79–81
Neon Wilderness, The (Algren), 404
Netsch, Walter, 403
New Deal, 331
New England Magazine, 202
New Orleans, 17, 74, 283
New Year's Day receptions, 40, 139; calling card, ill. 44; Palmer reception, 131
New York City, 108, 175, 189, 207, 221, 222–223, 280–281, 294, 358, 364, 385, 387, 397, 398
New York City Ballet, 403
New York City Opera Company, 398
New York Drama Critics Award, 387
New York Herald, 27, 65
New York Press, 201
New York Sun, 221
New York Tribune, 16
New York World, 64, 65, 223, 224, 275
New Yorker magazine, 347, 385
Newberry Library, 201
Newcastle, Duke of, 45
Newspapers, 20, 57–58, 63–65; advertising, 141; of vice district, 142–144, ill. 146
Newsweek magazine, 407
Nicholas Engalitcheff, Prince, 195
Nichols, Mike, 386
Nicholson, J. U., ill. 282
Niles, William, 286
Nineteenth Century Club, 117
Nineteenth Ward, 259, 295
Ninth Ward, 258
Nixon, Richard M., 411
Nobel Prize winners, 404 and ill., 420
Noble, Betty, 316
Norman, Harold, 402

439 INDEX

Norris, Frank, 274
North Presbyterian Church, 38
North Side, 8, 13, 18, 96, 392, 405; church congregations, 38; film studios, 273–274; fire of 1871, 103, 104–105, 106; gangs, 292, 296; lake front claim of Streeter, 136, 286–287; "Nord Seite," 53; The Sands, 28–30; society, 22–25, 38, 128, 132–133; Yankee homes, 22–25
"Northern Marseillaise," 62
Northwestern University, 38–39, 139, 405
Norwegian community, 366
Numbers racket, 348

Oak Street, 104
O'Banion, Dion, 292–294, 296, 299
Obie Award, 387
O'Brien, Mike, 28
O'Brien, Mike, Jr., 28
O'Brien's art gallery, 169
O'Connor, Len, 348, 353, 412
O'Donnell, Charles, 306, 307
O'Donnell, Kenny, 382
Ogden, Mahlon D., 46, 106
Ogden, William Butler, 18–19, 21, 22, 28–29, 38, 44, 64, 142, 204, 247, 317, 320, 329, 420; as mayor, 18
Ogden Avenue, 420
Oglesby, Richard, 162
O'Hare Airport, 376, 410, 418, *ill.* 419; passenger statistics, 418
Old Market Hall, *ill.* 49
Old Town, 376
Oldberg, Dr. Eric, 412
Oldenburg, Claes, 362
O'Leary, Big Jim, 266, 291
O'Leary, Mrs. Patrick, 98, 266
Oliver, King, 283
Olmsted, Frederick Law, 221
Olney, Richard, 242–244
Omonundro, "Texas Jack," 166
Ontario Street, 133, 302

Open housing, 348, 369
Opera, 86–87, 89–90, 92, 165, 173–175, 302, 304–313, 327–328, 396, 399–402; "blaze of glory" season, 309–310, 326
Opera houses, 400; combined with office buildings, 89–92, 173–175, 326–328. *See also* Auditorium; Civic Opera House; Crosby's Opera House
Opium dens, 252, 266
Oral history, 385, 405
Orchestra Hall, 207, 397
O'Regan, Rev. Dr., 25
Oriental Village, 338–339
Ottawa Indians, 4
Outer Drive Bridge, 357

Paderewski, Ignace, 229
Paine, Thomas, 276
Palm Garden, 137
Palmer, Courtlandt, 117
Palmer, Honore, 126, 130, 131
Palmer, John, 108, 242
Palmer, Potter, 19, 123, 124–126, 128–129, *ill.* 132, 133, 164, 166, 287, 317; assets of, 145, 183; mansion of, 128–129, *ill.* 230
Palmer, Mrs. Potter (Bertha Honore), 125, 126–132, 133, 134, 182, 303, 304, 402; Civic Federation VP, 241, 246, 250; portraits of, *ills.* 124, 134; role at Columbian Exposition, 227–232, 250
Palmer House, 104, 124, 125–126, 130, 166, 231; roof garden, *ill.* 129
Parades, *ill.* 168, 192, 408 and *ill.*, 409
Park Row, 25, *ill.* 80, 343
Park Theater, 252
Parks, 114, 128, 342–346. *See also* Grant Park; Jackson Park; Lincoln Park; Washington Park
Parmelee, Franklin, 14
Parmelee Omnibus and Stage Co., 14, 98–99

Parsons, Albert, 154, 159–162
Parsons, Mrs. Albert, 160
Parsons, General W. H., 159
Patterson, Rev. Dr. Robert, 38
Patti, Adelina, 88, 177
Pavarotti, Luciano, 400
Pavilion, Jackson Park, *ill.* 200
Payne, William Morton, 201–202, 208, 275
Payton, Walter, 394
Pease, Louis, 141
Peck, Ferdinand Wythe, 173–175, 176, 326
People United to Save Humanity (PUSH), 369–370
People's Gas Light & Coke Company, 322, 325
Peoria Street, 137
Peregrine Pickle (columnist), 45
Perkins, "Ma," 384
Perkins, Marlin, 385
Petrakis, Harry Mark, 405
Pflaum, Joel, 411
Philadelphia, 150, 299
Philadelphia *Evening Bulletin*, 127
Philanthropy, 186–187, 198–201, 340, 343–345. *See also* Art patronage
Philip, Prince, Duke of Edinburgh, 407
Phillips, Irma, 384
Picard, Auguste, 337
Picasso, Pablo, 361–362, 400; Civic Center statue by, *ill.* 361
Pick-Congress Hotel, 382
"Picknicking," 42
Pierce, James F., 211
Pine Street, 133
Pinedo, Francesco de, 298
Pink House (Chapin), 340
Pinkerton, Allan, 36, 50
Pinkerton's agency, 141, 161; poster, *ill.* 95
Pirate Ship (night club), 339
Pit, The (Norris), 274
Pittsburgh, 149–150, 420
Places (Morris), 421
Planetarium, 345, 421
Plant, Roger, 30–31
Playboy Clubs, 388

INDEX 440

Playboy Enterprises, 403
Playboy magazine, 387–388
Playboy Mansion, *ill.* 388, 389
Players Club, New York, 207
Playwright Theater, 386
Plymouth Congregational Church, 186
Poetry magazine, 275–276, 283
Polacco, Giorgio, 309
Poleri, David, 398–399
Police, 34–36, 52, 136, 139; and anarchists' and workers' riots (1870s–1880s), 149, 151–152, 154–155, 156, 157–161; vs. Capone, 295, 296; collusion, 266, 292, 295, 300, 348, 350, 411, 412; confrontations with blacks, 288–289, 367–368; and Daley's order to shoot at rioters, 370–371; after 1871 fire, 107–108; leather-badge force, 34–35; liquor raids, 293; modernization under Wilson, 411; and 1968 Democratic Convention demonstrators, *ill.* 372, 374–380, 383; Republican Steel strike massacre (1937), 378; sign raid of 1857, 33 and *ill.*, 34; and Streeter claim to District of Lake Michigan, 287; vice raids, 31, 32–33, *ill.* 78, 83, 147, 266, 268–269, 354 and *ill.*; women officers, 249
Police board, 34–35, 139
Police "riot," 378–379
"Police wheels," 366
Polish community, 152, 192, 366
Politics, 49–58, 192, 222, 257–267, 274–275, 286–288, 289, 323, 347–354; bosses, 139–140, 259–261, 348, 354, 406, 410–411, 413; graft, see Corruption, political; patronage, 247, 348–349,

350, 351, 354, 366, 406, 410, 413; perquisites, 354. *See also* Democratic Party; Know-Nothing Party; Republican Party
Poliuto (columnist), 190
Polk, James K., 16
Polk Street, 36
Population: of 1852, 363; of 1890s, 197, 220; of 1910s, 286; 1940s increase and white-black shift, 365; 1960s white-black shift, 366; 1970 vs. 1980 census, 418; black, 288, 365–366; ethnic conclaves, 366; German percentage, 52; Irish percentage, 50; Jewish, 366
Port of Chicago, 16, 32, 337, 418–419
Porter, Rev. Jeremiah, 4
Post, George B., 221, 233
Post Office, U.S. troops at (1894), *ill.* 245
Postal Telegraph Company, 302
Pottawatomie Indians, 4, 5–6
Pound, Ezra, 276
Poverty, 148–149, 152, 241, 246, 247–248
Powers, John ("Johnny de Pow"), 259, 295
Prairie Avenue, 114, 117–120, 142, 240, 245–246, 317
Prairie School of architecture, 355
"Prairies," 15
Prentice, Alta Rockefeller, 303
Prentice, Ezra Parmelee, 303
Presbyterians, 38, 113
Press Club, 205
Preston, Keith, 280, 281, *ill.* 282
Price, Leontyne, 400
Price, Margaret, 400
Professionals, first in Chicago, 20
Prohibition, 289, 290
Promontory Apartments, 356–357
Property tax, 137, 145, 407, 418

Prostitution, 27, 28, 30–32, 36, 76, *ill.* 78, 81, 135, 136, 142–147, 222, 237, 251–256, 267–269, 292, 348, 404
Prudential Insurance Company, 356, 363
Public Service Company of Northern Illinois, 319
Publishing, 203–208, 274–283, 387–390
Pulitzer Prize, 405
Pullman, Florence, 239
Pullman, George M., 12, 17, 46, 71, 114, 117, 121, 230, 239–246, 247, 317, 322, 420; assets of, 145, 246; death, burial, and will of, 245–246; in strike of 1894, 241–245
Pullman, Mrs. George M., 118, 120, 134
Pullman cars, 71
Pullman City, 155, 238–245, 246, 322
Pullman Company, 239, 240–244, 249–250
Pullman Land Association, 239
Pullman Strike of 1894, 241–244, 246, 247
Puritan traditions, 18, 20, 49, 236, 307; decline, 115, 195
PUSH (People United to Save Humanity), 369–370
PWA (Public Works Administration), 340

Quinn, Robert, 370, 393
Quirk, Daniel W., 95–96, 103

Racial discrimination, 288–289, 365, 367–369, 392
Radio daytime serials, 384
Ragen, James M., Sr., 300
Railroad Fair (1948–49), 346
Railroad riots of 1877, 149–152, *ill.* 153, *ill.* 156
Railroads, 18–19, 21, 116–117, 239, 337, 419; electrification of, 320; and Pullman strike, 242–244; suburban, 320, 322, 420

441 INDEX

Rainbo Gardens, 298
Raisa, Rose, 309, 328
Ralph, Julian, 250
Rand, Sally, ill. 335, 338–339
Rand McNally guide, 251
Randolph Street, 4, 9, 12, 25, 34, ill. 39, ill. 51, 53, 64, 69, 86, 104, 157, 343; first skyscraper, 188; gambling dens, 75 and ill., 76, 78, 83, 140; Hairtrigger Block, 76, 77
Rascoe, Burton, 280
Ravinia Festival (1954), 397
Ravoke, Milton, 406
Ray, Charles, 57
Read, Opie, 205
Real estate values and speculation, early Chicago, 18, 19, 73–74, 85, 187
Rector, Charles, 142
Red Cloud, Indian, 226
Reform and reform movements, 285, 298, 302, 347–348; anti-vice, 36, 137, 138–139, 265, 266, 267–269, 286; Democratic Party, 348–349, 352–354; literary journalists, 274–275, 276; police department under Daley/Wilson, 411; political, 138–139, 256–257, 267; social, 36, 246–250
Rehan, Ada, 88
Reibnitz, Baroness de, 232
Reiner, Fritz, 396–397
Relief and Aid Society, 149
Remberg, Charles, 380
Rendezvous, 299
Report of Fashions, 42
Republic Steel Corp. strike (1937), 378
Republican national conventions held in Chicago, 262; of 1860, 55–56 and ill., 57; of 1868, 92, ill. 93; of 1884, ill. 168
Republican Party, 54–58, 64, 65, 67, 192, 203, 249, 323; in city politics and government, 27, 35–36, 222, 257, 285–286; founding of, 49, 50, 55; 25th anniversary of Great Fire parade, 192–193
Requiem (O'Connor), 412
Rescigno, Nicola, 399
Restaurants, early Chicago, 89, 116, ill. 120, 141–142
Reszke, Jean de, 218
Reuben Street, 132
Reutan, The, 286
Rice, John B., 86–87
Rice, Wallace, 206
Rice's Theater, 86–87, 88
Richmond House, 44, 56
Rickey, Branch, 391
Riley, Bill, 78
Riots. See Demonstrations and riots
Rise of the Skyscraper, The (Condit), 188
Ritz Carlton Hotel, 359
River and Harbor Convention of 1847, 16
Riverside, 114, 221
Robinson, Jackie, 392
Rock Island Depot, 163
Rockefeller, Edith. See McCormick, Edith Rockefeller
Rockefeller, John D., 198–200, 303, 304, 328
Rodzinski, Artur, 396
Roebuck, Alvah C., 345
Roger's Barracks, 30–31
Rogers Park, 366
Roosevelt, Franklin D., 331
Roosevelt, Theodore, 247, 249, 262
Roosevelt University, 402
Root, George F., 62, 89, 113, 165
Root, John Wellborn, 187–188, 275
Rosenfield, Samuel, 157
Rosenstock, Joseph, 398
Rosenwald, Julius, 345
Rosenwald, William, 345
Rosenwald Foundation, 345
Rostand, Edmond, 216, 218
Rousiers, Paul de, 240
Royal Opera Covent Garden, 397, 401
Royko, Mike, 368–369, 392, ill. 395
Rubin, Jerry, 375, 382–383
Rubloff, Arthur, 358
Rucker, Henry L., 53
Rumsey, Julian, 24
Runaway Road, The (play), 325
Runnells, John S., 177
Rush Street, 8, 23, 133; bridge, ill. 23, 24
Russell, Lillian, 236
Ryan, Paddy, 140–141, 171
Ryerson, Joseph T., 21
Ryerson, Martin A., 200–201

Saddle and Cycle Club, 189
Sahl, Mort, 348
Sahlins, Bernard, 386
St. Gaudens, Augustus, 221, 232
St. James Episcopal Church, 3, 38, 52
St. Lawrence Seaway, 407, 419
St. Louis, 17, 108, 150, 221, 239
St. Louis Democrat, 36
St. Luke's hospital, 65, 210, 325
St. Nicholas Theater, 387
St. Patrick's Day, 408–409; parade, ill. 408
St. Paul's Roman Catholic Church, 98
St. Valentine's Day Massacre, 299
Saints and Sinners Corner, 204, ill. 205, 281
Salinger, Pierre, 381
Salome (Strauss), 131, 305–307
Saloons, 28, 136–138, 142, 251, 252, 287, 292; Sunday closing law, 53, 137–138, 286, 287
Sandburg, Carl, ill. 273, 275–276, 277, 279, 281, 283, 356, 384
Sandow (strong man), 235
Sands, The, 28–30, 104
Sanitary Commission, 69
Sanitation, 247
Sanity in Art (Logan), 340
Santayana, George, 203
Sargent, Frederick, 319
Sarrett, Lew, 281
Satan's Mile district, 136
Saturday Evening Herald, 181
Sauganash (Archibald Caldwell), Indian leader, 5–6
Sauganash (area), 366, 416–417

Sauganash Hotel, 5, 84 and *ill.*, 182
Sau-Ko-Noek, Indian chief, 4
Sayers, Gale, 394
Saylor, Clara E., 113
Scammon, Jonathan Young, 20, 21, 46
Schipporeit, George, 357
Schlesinger, Sebastian, 232
Schlesinger & Mayer, 305
Schlogl's restaurant, 281–282 and *ill.*
Schmedtgen, William H., 140, 220
Schnaubelt, Rudolph, 162
Schneider, Richard, *ill.* 282
School for Scandal, The (Sheridan), 324 and *ill.*, 325
Schwab, Michael, 160–162
Schwartz, Charles, 123
Scotto, Renata, 399
Scribner's Magazine, 135
Scripps, John L., 57–58
Scudder, Mary Arnold, 4, 105
Sculpture, public, 361 and *ill.*, 362, 364
SDS (Students for a Democratic Society), 375
Seale, Bobby, 382
Sears, Richard W., 345
Sears, Roebuck and Company, 345
Sears Tower, 358 and *ill.* 359; Calder's *Universe*, 362, *ill.* 363
Second City, 386–387; cast, *ill.* 386
"Second City" soubriquet, 192, 385, 418
Second Presbyterian Church, 38, 113, 257
Sell, Henry Blackman, 280
Selwyn Theater, 325
Senate (gambling den), 82–83
Serafin, Tullio, 399
Settlement houses, 246
Seward, William H., 55, 56
Sexual Perversity in Chicago (Mamet), 387
Seymour, Ralph Fletcher, 208
Shafter, Walter, 252
Shanks, J. T., 68
Shanty patches, 28–29, 32

Shapiro, Joseph R., 403
Shaughnessey, Clark, 394
Shaw, George Bernard, 209, 318, 325
Shaw, Vic, 256
Shay's Dry Goods Store, 102
Shedd, John G., 344
Shedd Aquarium, 343–344, 345
Sheridan, General Philip, 100, 108, 121, *ill.* 132, 141
Sherman, General William T., 70, 108, 204
Sherman House, 9, 14, *ill.* 51, 53, 71
Ship, The (gambling house), 292
Shipping, 17, 18, 20, 32, 418, 419; canals, 17, 18, 74, 337; Chicago River, 11–12, 17, *ill.* 23, 24, 418; Lake Michigan, 8, 16, 337, 418; St. Lawrence Seaway, 419
Shober, Charles, 67
Sidewalks: early different levels of, 13; around 1850, 10–12; of 1890s, 189; Wentworth's sign raid, 33 and *ill.*, 34
Sign raid of 1857, 33 and *ill.*, 34
Sills, Beverly, 399
Sills, Paul, 385–387
Silver Dollar saloon, 262
Silver Fountain saloon, 29
Sinclair, Upton, 274, 278, 384
Sister Carrie (Dreiser), 209, 275
Skating, 12, 42
Skidmore Owings and Merrill, 358, 361
Skinner, Samuel, 411
Sky Ride, 1933 fair, 337–338
Skyscrapers, *ill.* 185, 187–189, *ill.* 355, 356, 357–358 and *ill.*, 359–361
Slavery issue, 49–51, 54, 61
Sleighing, 42
Sloan, James Park, 405
Slot machines, 287, 348
Smith, Byron, 318

Smith, Frank, 323
Smith, Gypsy, 268
Smith, Henry (promoter), 166–167
Smith, Henry Justin (writer), 281, *ill.* 282
Smith, Perry H., 133, 151
Snow of 1978–79, *ill.* 415, 416
Soccer, 395
Socialists, 149, 152–153; journalism, 276; railroad riots of 1877, 149–152
Society and society life, 37–48, 115–123, 127–134, 181–187, 224–225; at Auditorium, *ill.* 174, 175–176; Chicago's new woman, 250; etiquette, 40, 115–116; events, reporting of, 126–127; millionaires, 183–187, 302–305, 317; and the opera, *ill.* 174, 175, 327; relocation of homes after 1871 fire, 114–115; second generation problems, 194, 246; shunning of actresses, 166, 169, 172, 236
Society for Sanity in Art, 340
Society for the Promotion of Social Purity, 36
Society of Midland Authors, 208
Soldier Field, 394; civil rights rally at, 367
Soldier's Fair of 1863, 69
Solti, Sir Georg, *ill.* 396, 397–398
Song of the Lark (Breton), 340–341
Songs, Chicago: patriotic, Civil War era, 62; post-1871 fire, 113
Sonnets and Other Verses (Santayana), 203
Sons of Liberty, 67, 68
Sons of the Illinois, 68
Sothern, E. A., 88
"Sound money" supporters, 192–193
Sounding (Bertoia), 362
Sousa, John Philip, 231
Sousa, May de, 262
South Park Board, 189, 339

South Side (or Division), 12; black ghetto, 288, 348, 366, 403, 411; boulevard system, 128; church congregations, 38; Columbian Exhibition site, 221, 232, 301; fire of 1871, 98–103, 106; society, 38, 122, 132
Southern Christian Leadership Conference (SCLC), 369
Southerners, 21, 23, 40, 66, 74–75, 132–133, 251
Sox Park, 394
Spachner, Mrs. John V. (Bea), 402
Spanier, Muggsy, 283
Sparling, Edward J., 402
Speakeasies, 298–299
Speculation, 73–74
Spiegel, Dr. John P., 371
Spies, August, 154, 157, 159–162
Spolin, Viola, 386
Spoon River Anthology (Masters), 275
Spoor, George, 273
Sporting and Club House Directory, 142–143 and ill., 145
"Sporting" set, 74–83, 135–147, 257
Sports, 140–141, 391–395
Squire of Dames, The (play), 321
Stacy, Jess, 283
Stafford, Annie, 79–81
Stafford, Countess of, 130
Stafford, Earl of (Thomas Wentworth), 27
Stagg, Amos Alonzo, 199
Standard Oil Building, ill. 355, 359, 362
Stanley Cup, 394
Stanton, Edwin M., 70
Starr, Ellen Gates, 247
Starrett, Vincent, 281, ill. 282
State Street, 12, 34, 35 and ill., ill. 49, 89, 104, 140, 150, 296, 299, 346, 374; emerges as main business street, 19, 96, 124; fire of 1871, 104, 125; St. Patrick's Day parade, ill. 408, 409; skyscrapers, 188

Stead, William T., 256–257
Steel industry, 20, 250, 419–420
Steelworkers' strike (1937), 378
Steevens, G. W., 191–192
Steffens, Lincoln, 267
Stein, Gertrude, 278
Stern, Richard, 405
Sternberg, Joel, 385
Stevens, Ashton, 252, ill. 282
Stevenson, Adlai, 231
Stevenson, Mrs. Adlai, 228
Stevenson, Adlai E., ill. 347, 349, 351
Steward, LeRoy T., 306, 307
Stewart, A. T., 125
Sting, the (team), 395
Stock, Frederick, 197, 198, 287, 396
Stock market, 325; crash of 1929, 316, 328, 336, 345
Stockyards, ill. 30, 121, 169, 183, 193, 201, 244, 320, 350, 419; strike of 1886, 155
Stone, Edward Durell, 359
Stone, Mrs. Horatio O., 132, 172, 175
Stone, Lewis, 273
Stone, Melville E., 205
Stone & Kimball, 203
Stony Island, 281
Store, The (gambling house), 140
Storey, Wilbur F., 63–64, 65, 92–94, 141, 142
Storey, Mrs. Wilbur F., 93–94
Stories of the Streets and the Town (Ade), 205
Stratton, William G., 346
Strauss, Richard, 131
Strawn, Silas, 329
Street in Bronzeville, A (Brooks), 405
Streetcars, 189, ill. 210, 259, 260, 319–320; strikes, 154, 289
Streeter, George Wellington, 136, 286–287
Streeter, Maria, 287
Streets: around 1850, 10–12, 18; of 1890s, 189; boulevard system, 128; franchise graft, 258,

259; layout and naming, 74, 288, 420; paving graft, 266; raising of, above mud level, 12–13 and ill.; traffic, early, 10–11, 14
Streets of Cairo (1893 Midway), 234, 338
Streets of Paris (1933 Midway), 338–339
Strikes: coal miners (1894), 243; McCormick reaper works (1886), 155–157; Pullman (1894), 241–244, 246, 247; railroad workers (1877, 1886), 150–152, 154, 155; Republic steelworkers (1937), 378; streetcar workers, 154, 289; telephone technicians (1968), 376
Stuart, General Jeb, 166
Studebaker Theater, 325
Students for a Democratic Society (SDS), 375
"Studs Place" (TV show), ill. 384, 385
Sturges, Solomon, 62
Sturges Rifles regiment, 62
Suburban railroads, 320, 322, 420
Suburbs, 365, 411
Subway, 322; freight, 258–259
Suffolk, Earl of (Henry Molyneux Page Howard), 195
Suliotis, Elenea, 399
Sullivan, John L., 140–141, 171–172
Sullivan, Louis, 174, 187, 221, 336, 355, 402
Sullivan, Peg Leg, 97–98
Sullivan, Roger, 323
Summerdale, 411
Summerfield, Justice, 136
Summit, Wentworth home at, 25, 27, 36
Sumner, Dean Walter, 266, 268
Sunnyside, Lake View, 80–82
Supreme Life Insurance Company, 389
Sutherland, Joan, 399
Sutherland, W. J., 216
Swanson, Gloria, 273
Swedish community, 192

INDEX 444

Sweet, General J. B., 64
Sweitzer, Robert, 285
Swift, Ann, 185
Swift, Gustavus, 121, 184–186, 201, 317
Swift, Howard, 234
Swift, Noble, 186
Swift & Company, 186
Swing, Rev. David, 240

Taft, Lorado, 206, 207, 221
Taft, William Howard, 249
Tagge, Robert, 346
Tagore, Rabindranath, 282
"Tally-ho" parties, 122, ill. 132
Tarbell, Ida, 70
Taxation, property, 137, 145, 407, 418
Tebaldi, Renata, 399
Tecumseh, Indian chief, 6
Telephone technicians' strike (1968), 376
Television, 384 and ill.; Chicago school, 385; coverage of 1968 "Battle of Chicago," 376, 378–380
Temperance movement, 20, 39, 137, 138–139
Terkel, Studs, ill. 384, 385, 405
Terrace Row, ill. 24, 25, 106
Teschmaker, Frank, 283
Tetrazzini, Luisa, 290
Teyte, Maggie, 308
Thanksgiving (Lee), 340
Thanksgiving Day Game Dinner, 47–48
Theater, 209, 216–219, 236, 240, 321, 324–325; beginnings in Chicago, 84–85, 86–87 and ill., 88–89; Bernhardt, 166–169, 216–217; German-language, 149; Modjeska, 173; Second City and St. Nicholas Theater, 386–387
Theater Guild, 325
Thomas, Theodore, 94, 164–165, 173, 196–198, 208, 229, 274, 396
Thompson, Jacob, 66–67
Thompson, James, 411
Thompson, Rev. John, 296

Thompson, Lydia, 92–93, 142
Thompson, Slason, 207
Thompson, William Hale ("Big Bill"), 285–286 and ill., 352; as mayor, 286–289, 290, 295, 296–298, 335, 415
Three Deuces (speakeasy), 299
Tietjens, Eunice, 278, 281
Tillstrom, Burr, 385
Time magazine, 387, 422
Titan, The (Dreiser), 274
Tooker Street, 282
Torrio, John, 290, 291–294, 300
Trade, 15, 419, 420; Chicago at crossroads of, 8, 17, 32, 74, 337; with Indians, before 1835, 4; mail-order, 342, 345, 420
Traffic violation bribes, 348
"Tramp, Tramp, Tramp" (song), 62
Transportation, 337, 351; air travel, 337–338, 418, ill. 419; Building at "A Century of Progress," 337; buses, 189; carriages, 10, ill. 118–119, 122–123; Chicago as center of, 8, 17, 32, 74, 337, 418–419; electrification, 319–320; elevated railways, 260, ill. 293, 319, 322; expressways, 418, 420; franchises, 260, 320; horseback, 14, 41; "horseless" carriages, 189; Indian era, 11–12; stagecoaches, 8, 14 and ill.; street, early, 10–11, 14; street, 1890s, 189–190; streetcars, 154, 189, ill. 210, 259, 260, 319–320; subway, 258–259, 322; "Tally-ho" coaches, 122, ill. 132; trucking, 418; water, 8, 17, 18, 32, 74, 337, 418, 419; westward migration, 8. See also Railroads; Shipping
Tree, Lambert, 105, 155
Tremont House, 9 and ill., 12, 37, 46, 47 and ill.,

54, 55–56, 62, 79, 286; fires, 9, 100, 109; Michigan Ave. Hotel renamed as, 109; music hall, 87–88
Tribune Company, The, 393. See also Chicago Tribune
"Tricks and Traps of Chicago," visitors' guide, 13
Trowbridge, W. E. S., 14
Truman, Harry S, 349, 410
Trumbull, Lyman, 64, 65
Trussel, George, 76–78, 79
Tunnels, river, 18
Turner, Frederick Jackson, 208
Turner's Hall riot of 1877, 152, ill. 153
Twelfth Street, 25
Twentieth Century Club, 117–118
Twenty-first Ward, 269
Twenty-fourth Ward, 348
Twenty-second Street, 343

Ulysses (Joyce), 280, 405
Under the Willow, 30–31
Underground Railroad, 49–50
Unemployment of 1870s, 148–149, 152
Union League Club, 202–203
Union National Bank, 100
Union Pacific Railroad, 116–117
Union stockyards, ill. 30
Unione Siciliane, 290, 293, 294, 296
Universe (Calder), 362, ill. 363
University of Chicago, 198–200, 201, 256, 274, 281, 345, 362, 386, 403, 405; Nobel Prize winners, 404 and ill., 420
University of Illinois, 405
Upton, George, 197
Urban Coalition, 370
U.S. Customs House, 107
U.S. Department of Health, Education, and Welfare, 369
U.S. Department of Justice, 369
U.S. News and World Report, 356

U.S. Senate, 323
U.S. Steel Corporation, 250
Utility companies, 318–319, 322–323, 331–332; and graft, 258, 259
Utley, Clifton, 385
Utley, Frayn, 385
Utley, Garrick, 385

Valicia, 119
Van Buren Street, 35, 106
Vanderbilt, William H., 117, 118
Van Volkenburg, Ellen, 209
Varnell, Harry, 140, 237, 266
Veblen, Thorstein, 281
Veeck, Bill, 392, 393–394, ill. 395
Veragua, Duke of, 225–227, 229
Vice, 27–33, 36, 74–83, 135–137, 251–257, 266, 267–269, 295, 354; districts, 136, 142; police protection ring, 412. See also Gambling; Prostitution
Vice Commission, 266, 268, 302
Vickers, John, 400
Victoria Hotel, 290
Vienna Die Presse, 398
Vietnam War, 374, 391; protest demonstrations, 373 and ill., 374–375, 377 and ill., 378–380, ill. 381, 383
Villa Turicum, 307
Village Voice, 387
Vincennes Avenue, 126
Vogelsang's restaurant, 259

Wabash Avenue, 14, 38, 44, 46, 69, 104, 114, 203, 290, 292, 357, 378
Walker, Daniel, 378–380
Wallace, Edna, 321
Wallis, Gladys. See Insull, Margaret Bird
Walsh, Charles, 68–69
Walska, Ganna, 310–312 and ill., 313–314, 316, 399
Walt's Workshop (TV show), ill. 384

Ward, A. Montgomery, 183, 342–343
Ward, Daniel, 417
Warren, Frances (Waterford Jack), 147, 206
Washburn, Charles, 254
Washington, George, 297
Washington, D.C., 221, 359
Washington Park, 189, 234; Derby Day, 122 and ill., 236
Washington Square Players, 209
Washington Street, 18, 25, 38, 69, 89, 104, 281, 374; Kerfoot realty after 1871 fire, ill. 109
Washington Home, 36, 247
"Watchdog of the Lakefront," 343
Water Crib, ill. 97, 99–100
Water Street, ill. 43; North, 8; South, 14
Water Tank Library, ill. 198
Water Tower Place, 359, ill. 422
Waterford Jack. See Warren, Frances
Waterworks, 96, ill. 99, 103, 173
Watkins, Thomas, 3
Watson, Carrie, 144–145, 147, 263
Waubun (Kinzie), 203
Wayman, John E., 269
WBKB TV, 384–385
Weather, 41, 42, 197, 208, 221, 239, 274; snow of 1978–79, ill. 415, 416
Webb, Daniel K., 411
Weber, Charles, 353 and ill.
Webster, Daniel, 22
Webster, Freddy, 28
Webster, Henry Kitchell, 206
Weed, Thurlow, 16
Weese, Harry, 359, 402–403
Weiner, Lee, 382–383
Weiskopf's Saloon, 157
Weiss, Hymie, 294, 296, 299
Welfare, public, 245, 248–249
Wells, Captain William, 32
Wells Street, 30, 31–32, 102; Second City theater on, 386

Wendell, Barrett, 208
Wenner, Baroness Violet Beatrice von, 316
Wentsel, Henry, 166
Wentworth, John ("Long John"), 25, 26 and ill., 27, 38, 141, 247, 317, 402; as congressman, 26, 27; as mayor, 26, 27–29, 31–36, 42–45
Wesley Memorial Hospital, 313
West Side (or Division), 18, 274, 348, 362; black population, 366, 368, 370; bootleggers, 292, 296; ethnic conclaves, 366; fire of 1871, 95–96, 97–98, 104, 106; Jewish neighborhoods, 366, 404; McCormick reaper works, 239; 1966 riot damages, 368; 1968 riots, 370; society, 132; southern community, 40, 132
West Side Street Railway Co., 154
Western Springs, 190
Western Avenue, 366
Weston, Edward Payson, 92
Westward migration, 8
Wettling, George, 283
Wheaton, 190
Wheeler, Eleanor, 204
Whiskey Row, 137
Whistler, James McNeill, 120
White, Carolina, 308
White-slave trade, 147, 297
Whitechapel Club, 205–206
Whitefield, Edwin, 23, 24, 51
Whiteley, Alexander, 235
Whittier, John Greenleaf, 113
Wide-Awakes, 57
Wigwam (convention hall), 55, ill. 56, 57
Wild West Show, Buffalo Bill, 142, 165
Wilde, Oscar, 131, 170–171 and ill., 172–173
Willard, Frances E., 139
Willett, A. T., 105
Wilson, Orlando W., 411

Wilson, Woodrow, 208
Windsor, Helen, 321, 324
"Windy City," origin of term, 221
Winesburg, Ohio (Anderson), 279–280
Winnebago Indians, 6
Winter, Dale, 290–291
With Edge Tools (Chatfield-Taylor), 207
Wizard of Oz, The (Denslow and Baum), 207
Woman Beautiful, The (magazine), 128
Women: feminist movement, 127, 129, 236, 247, 250; homes of refuge for, 36, 246–247; professional basketball, 395; Sarah Bernhardt's remarks on, 169–170; scarcity in early Chicago, 3, 22, 37; as servants, 6; social reform movement, 246–250; of society, 37, 40, 41–42, 115–121, 125–134, 175–176, 194–195, 250; Woman's Building at Columbian Exposition, 227–229
Women's Christian Temperance Union (WCTU), 136, 139

Wood, Colonel Joseph H., 85
Woodford, Stewart L., 240
Wood's Museum, 71, 85, *ill.* 86, 337
Work, Henry C., 62
Working (Terkel), 405
Working class, 148–149. See also Labor
Workingmen's Party of the U.S., 151–152
World Trade Center, New York City, 358–359
World's Columbian Exposition, 199, 220–222, *ill.* 223, 226 and *ill.*, 227–237, 238, 250, 256, 275, 281, 301, 303, 336–337, 340, 345; Midway Plaisance, *ill.* 233, 234–236; Woman's Building, 227–229
World War I, 285, 287–288, 321
World War II, 356, 365, 402
Wren, Sir Christopher, 113
Wright, Frank Lloyd, 208, 278, 355, 364
Wright, Frankie, 252
Wright, John, 47, 89
Wrigley, Philip K., 391–392
Wrigley, William, 391
Wrigley, William (grandson), 393

Wrigley Field, 391, 394
Writers, 203–209, 403–405; Chicago school, 273–283, 384
Wust, T., 135
Wyatt, Edith, 206

Yankees: migration to Chicago, 17–18, 22, 26; role in early Chicago, 18–25, 46, 74, 84, 85, 118, 121, 195, 250
Yates, Richard, 60
Yerkes, Charles T., 145, 259–261, 274, 322
Youle, Clint, *ill.* 384
Youth International Party (Yippies), 375, 376

Zeisler, Fannie Bloomfield, 206
Ziegfeld, Dr. Florenz, 142, 165
Ziegfeld, Florenz, Jr., 165, 235, 291
Zoning, lakefront (1969), 363
Zoning variances, 354
"Zoo Parade" (TV show), 385
Zorn, Anders L., 134
Zouave Cadets, 59 and *ill.*, 60
Zukor, Adolph, 274

EMMETT DEDMON, formerly vice-president and editorial director of the *Chicago Sun-Times* and *Chicago Daily News*, is a senior consultant to Hill and Knowlton, Inc. While with the newspapers, he served as a director of both the Associated Press Managing Editors Association and the American Society of Newspaper Editors.

A graduate of the University of Chicago with a degree in economics, Dedmon is a trustee of the university, national chairman of the alumni fund, and member of the Visiting Committee to the Center for Far Eastern Studies. He is a director of the Japan American Society of Chicago, and a founding member of the Tri-Lateral Commission.

He is a trustee of the Chicago Historical Society, and is active in many business and community organizations in Chicago. He is official historian of the Chicago Club.

During World War II, Dedmon served five years in the Air Force, rising to the rank of captain. In 1943, the bomber in which he was flying was shot down, and he was held for two years as a prisoner-of-war in Germany.

He is the author of six books and has contributed articles to *The Economist, Saturday Review* and *Reader's Digest.*